Other titles in Sports and Entertainment

# Tarnished Rings

Sports and Entertainmen'

Steven A. Riess, *Series Editor*

# Tarnished Rings

*The International Olympic Committee and the Salt Lake City Bid Scandal*

Stephen Wenn

Robert Barney

Scott Martyn

SYRACUSE UNIVERSITY PRESS

For a listing of books published and distributed by Syracuse University Press, visit our Web site
at SyracuseUniversityPress.syr.edu.

ISBN: 978-0-8156-3290-0

**Library of Congress Cataloging-in-Publication Data**
Wenn, Stephen R., 1964–
   Tarnished rings : the International Olympic Committee and the Salt Lake City bid scandal /
Stephen Wenn, Robert Barney, Scott Martyn.
      p. cm.
   Includes bibliographical references and index.
   ISBN 978-0-8156-3290-0 (cloth : alk. paper) 1. Olympics—Corrupt practices.   2. International
Olympic Committee.   3. Salt Lake City Bid Committee for the Olympic Winter Games, 2002.
I. Barney, Robert Knight, 1932–   II. Martyn, Scott G., 1966–   III. Title.
   GV721.6.W46 2011
   796.4809792'258—dc23                                              2011042264

Manufactured in the United States of America

To Blanche Geraldine Thompson Barney (1907–2011)
*Mother of Robert, David, and Peter*

*A lady who lived on amongst us until late August 2011, a lady whose lifetime (well into her one hundredth and fourth year) encompassed forty-four modern Olympic festivals (missing only Athens—1896, Paris—1900, and St. Louis—1904), and a lady who, like many Olympic athletes, exuded a presence that inspired those she touched. Honor to her name.*

**Stephen Wenn** is Professor and Former Chair of Kinesiology and Physical Education at Wilfrid Laurier University in Waterloo, Ontario, Canada. He, along with lead author Robert Barney, and Scott Martyn, published an award-winning analysis of the transformation of the International Olympic Committee into a revenue-generating juggernaut in the latter half of the twentieth century, titled *Selling the Five Rings: The International Olympic Committee and the Rise of Olympic Commercialism* in 2002 (rev. ed., 2004). He is also coeditor with Gerald Schaus of *Onward to the Olympics: Historical Perspectives on the Olympic Games* (2007) and has served as President of the North American Society for Sport History (2007–9). He and his wife, Martha, and their children, Tim and Lily, live in Baden, Ontario.

**Robert Barney**, a native New Englander, is Professor Emeritus of Kinesiology and the Founding Director of the International Centre for Olympic Studies at the University of Western Ontario in London, Ontario, Canada. He recently published an anthology of articles that first appeared in *Olympika: The International Journal of Olympic Studies* titled *Rethinking the Olympics: Cultural Histories of the Modern Games* (2010). He has devoted a good measure of his professional life to exploring and encouraging historical research of the modern Olympic Games and received the Olympic Order in 1997. Robert, known to his peers simply as Bob or B², and his wife, Ashleigh, live in London, Ontario.

**Scott Martyn** is Associate Professor of Human Kinetics at the University of Windsor in Windsor, Ontario, Canada. His PhD dissertation, titled "The Struggle for Financial Autonomy: The IOC and the Historical Emergence of Corporate Sponsorship, 1896–2000," shed much light on the IOC's embrace of the corporate sponsor community in the twentieth century. He has given many hours to past work on the executive councils of the North American Society for Sport History, the International Centre for Olympic Studies, and the International Society for Comparative Physical Education and Sport. Scott, his wife, Rebecca, and their son, William, live in Windsor, Ontario.

# Contents

# Illustrations

# Acknowledgments

All authors understand that while their names appear on the cover, the process involved in moving a book from an idea to a reality requires many hands. We are indebted to Steven Riess, the editor of the Sports and Entertainment series at Syracuse University Press, as well as Annelise Finegan, the press's former acquisitions editor, and her successor, Jennika Baines, for their support and encouragement. We also appreciated Annette Wenda's careful copyediting of our manuscript. We have benefited from interaction with professional colleagues who have taken an interest in our work, including Doug Booth, Dick Crepeau, Mark Dyreson, John Findling, Larry Gerlach, Allen Guttmann, Tommy Hunt, Bruce Kidd, Karl Lennartz, John Lucas, Gordon MacDonald, Alan Metcalfe, Roland Renson, Toby Rider, Jan Todd, Kevin Wamsley, and Stephan Wassong. Ron Smith, a wonderful colleague, and even better friend, kindly reviewed a number of draft chapters and offered constructive criticism, as did Tim Elcombe and Bill McTeer, two of Stephen Wenn's fellow professors at Wilfrid Laurier University. Martha Wenn, Jeff Wenn, and Paul and Roberta Wenn volunteered their efforts as proofreaders as the manuscript took shape.

We firmly believe that one of the strengths of this book lies in the sources that inform the narrative. Central in this regard is the correspondence and archival holdings of Richard Pound, a former IOC vice president, who led the IOC's internal investigation of allegations concerning IOC member conduct in relation to Salt Lake City's bid for the 2002 Olympic Winter Games. Without Pound's consent to the use of his files, we would have presented a much-diminished manuscript devoid of an insider's view of developing events. His records permitted us to deal extensively with the IOC's effort to maintain communication with, and invite counsel from, executives with major Olympic corporate sponsors during the crisis. A visit to the IOC Archives in Lausanne yielded a number of important documents, and our research efforts in Switzerland were ably facilitated by Patricia Eckert and Ruth Beck Perrenoud. Former IOC marketing director Michael Payne agreed to sit for an extended interview that assisted us in understanding the day-to-day atmosphere in Lausanne. David D'Alessandro, John Hancock's former president and CEO and a key actor in the Olympic corporate sponsor community in the 1990s, offered details with respect to his company's business strategies at the time. His comments provided important context in terms of understanding his decision to accept many media interview requests during the crisis, as well as his tendency for offering, at times, harsh criticism of the IOC's reform efforts. Our knowledge of preparations for the Welch-Johnson trial was enhanced through Robert Barney's helpful dialogue with defense counsel Bill Taylor, Blair Brown, and Armit Mehta with Zuckerman Spaeder (Washington, DC), and Max Wheeler with Snow, Christensen, and Martineau (Salt Lake City). Many journalists whose duties included the "Olympic beat" in the late 1990s devoted a good deal of column space and hours to coverage of the events we have described, and we tip our hat to the collective efforts of Alan Abrahamson, James Christie, Linda Fantin, Mike Gorrell, Philip Hersh, Glenda Korporaal, Jere Longman, Jacquelin Magnay, Matthew Moore, Lisa Riley Roche, Larry Siddons, Glenn Stanaway, Randy Starkman, Stephen Wilson, and their media colleagues. Their work figured prominently in our research. Brooke Thomas (Getty Images) and Ghyslaine Leroy (Corbis) provided excellent counsel and service regarding the acquisition of photo rights from their respective companies.

We are grateful for the financial assistance afforded by a standard research grant from the Social Sciences and Humanities Research Council (Canada) and a book preparation grant awarded by the Research Office at Wilfrid Laurier University that provided important funds for travel and photo permissions. Without this support, the challenge of producing this book would have been significantly magnified. Deb MacLatchy and Paul Jessop, Wilfrid Laurier University's vice president academic and provost and dean of the Faculty of Science, respectively, and Jim Weese, dean of the University of Western

Ontario's Faculty of Health Sciences, provided the funds necessary for the acquisition of the rights for the book's cover photo. The International Centre for Olympic Studies at the University of Western Ontario served as the hub of operations for the production of this book, contributing both a meeting place and a wealth of resources.

And, last, to our readers, we express appreciation for your interest in our book. It is our hope that we have conveyed the ebb and flow of events in those crucial months for the IOC in 1998 and 1999 when its survival was anything but secure and that our analysis provides a deeper understanding of the festering crisis that enveloped President Juan Antonio Samaranch and other members of the IOC leadership team, as well as their efforts to effect a recovery of the tarnished Olympic brand.

•  •  •  •

Chapter 4 is a much expanded version of "Two Days Lausanne Stood Still: The 108th Extraordinary IOC Session," by Stephen Wenn which first appeared in *Pathways, Critiques and Discourse in Olympic Research: Proceedings of the Ninth International Symposium for Olympic Research*, edited by Robert K. Barney, Michael K. Heine, Kevin B. Wamsley, and Gordon H. MacDonald (London: University of Western Ontario, 2008). Reprinted here with permission.

Part of Chapter 7 first appeared in *Selling the Five Rings: The International Olympic Committee and the Rise of Olympic Commercialism*, by Robert Barney, Stephen Wenn, and Scott Martyn. Rev. ed. (Salt Lake City: Univ. of Utah Press, 2004). Reprinted here with permission.

Chapter 8 contains material that first appeared in "IOC/USOC Relations and the 2009 IOC Session in Copenhagen," by Stephen Wenn, which can be found in *Rethinking Matters Olympic: Investigations into the Socio-Cultural Study of Modern Olympics: Proceedings of the Tenth International Symposium for Olympic Studies* (London: University of Western Ontario, 2011). Reprinted here with permission.

Chapter 8 contains material that first appeared in "The Olympic Movement and the Road Ahead: Status Quo or Will the IOC Tackle the Big Issues?" by Stephen Wenn, in *Intellectual Muscle, Globe and Mail* and VANOC Podcast Series, October 2009. Reprinted here with permission.

# Introduction

On a late November evening in 1998, we journeyed to Montreal to put the finishing touches on the research for our first collaborative effort, *Selling the Five Rings: The International Olympic Committee and the Rise of Olympic Commercialism*. The next morning we convened with International Olympic Committee vice president and chairman of the IOC Marketing Commission Richard Pound, who granted us access to IOC Session and Executive Board minutes from his personal archives. Following a brief but chilly walk from our hotel to Pound's Stikeman Elliott law office, our future research agenda took shape even though we did not recognize immediately this reality. Upon our arrival and following an exchange of greetings, we delved into the documents. Within minutes, Pound's fax machine signaled the arrival of a message. Peering out over his reading glasses, Pound read the text and informed us that he had serious concerns about its content. None of us, including Pound, understood the nature of the precipice that the IOC stood before at that moment. The fax provided information on a Salt Lake media report alleging that the Salt Lake City bid committee assisted Sonia Essomba, the daughter of a deceased IOC member (René Essomba, Cameroon, who died in August 1998), with tuition payments to attend American University in Washington, DC, for a period of time in advance of the 1995 vote on the host city for the 2002 Olympic Winter Games.[1]

Over the course of the next four months, a media crisis gripped the IOC that threatened both its operational autonomy and its financial foundation. Intense media scrutiny and a series of investigations launched by the IOC, the United States Olympic Committee (USOC), the respective organizing committees in Sydney (SOCOG) and Salt Lake City (SLOC), the House Commerce Subcommittee on Oversight and Investigations, as well as the US Department of Justice unearthed disquieting details. Thomas Welch and David Johnson, the president and vice president, respectively, of the Salt Lake City bid committee (who also held the same executive positions with SLOC), authorized the use of a slush fund to curry favor with a number of IOC members through an orchestrated gift-giving program. This decision and the willingness of a number of IOC members to "cash in" on Salt Lake City's largesse tarnished the Olympic brand and imperiled the IOC's position as the guardian of the Olympic Movement. In the end, twenty of the implicated twenty-four IOC members received some form of censure, and of this number, six were expelled and four resigned.[2] Three were exonerated. Essomba, who surely would have faced expulsion (or submitted his resignation), had died. IOC president Juan Antonio Samaranch's successor, Jacques Rogge, who served as a member of the IOC Executive Board in the late 1990s, referred to the scandal as "a profound crisis that nearly destroyed the IOC."[3]

We sat transfixed by events in Lausanne in the early months of 1999, as did most Olympic observers, with emotions ranging from disappointment to disgust. Allegations rolled forth on a steady basis: Amsterdam (1992) plied some IOC members with prostitutes, jewelry, and VCRs; Nagano (1998) spent Can$33,000 on average for sixty-two IOC member visits; Quebec City (2002) bid officials reported approaches from a number of Olympic "agents" who pledged assistance with the city's presentation and enhanced access to some IOC members for a fee between $20,000 and $50,000; and Atlanta (1996) conceded it gave some visiting IOC members golf clubs valued at $475 (the gift-value limit at the time was $200), sent a few others to Disney World, and on occasion provided IOC members with an additional first-class airline ticket (beyond the two tickets permitted for a member and his or her spouse) in advance of their visit to Atlanta.[4] We can attest that the thresholds of our respective offices have never been more populated by faculty colleagues seeking our opinions on Olympic matters than they were in early 1999.

When we were not fielding questions from these office guests or working with our students, we continued our work on *Selling the Five Rings*. In this book we examined the IOC's transformation from an organization that demonstrated neither a desire nor the knowledge base necessary to

1. Juan Antonio Samaranch (*left*) congratulates Deedee Corradini, mayor of Salt Lake City (*second from right*), following her city's triumph in the contest to host the 2002 Olympic Winter Games at the IOC's 1995 Budapest Session. USOC president LeRoy Walker is seated between Samaranch and Corradini, while the USOC's deputy secretary-general, John Krimsky, looks on happily from the right. *Source:* Tom Smart/Getty Images News/Getty Images.

generate commercial revenue in the 1950s to one possessing the drive and the sophisticated understanding of negotiating practice necessary to capitalize on commercial revenue sources, largely as a result of the vision of former IOC president (and the late) Juan Antonio Samaranch. Piloted by Samaranch, the IOC sought to maximize television rights revenue while diversifying and expanding its revenue base through the establishment of a major corporate sponsorship program, The Olympic Program (TOP, now The Olympic Partners).

Published in 2002, *Selling the Five Rings* represented the culmination of six years of research dedicated to exploring this story from the perspective of the IOC leadership looking out to the corporate world. Our primary sources were largely IOC-generated, which encouraged us to look at debates over commercialism as they unfolded within IOC boardrooms and to chart the IOC's negotiations with television networks and corporate sponsors from its side of the negotiating table. In 1999, while there was much writing left to bring that project to fruition, we were planning a future research initiative. It was understood that a companion manuscript, tentatively titled "Buying the Five Rings: Television Networks, Corporate Sponsors, and Olympic Commercialism," investigating the parallel history from the other side of the negotiating table, represented a worthy (and necessary) future project. However, the Salt Lake City crisis proved too much of a magnet for us. Intrigued by the window through which we could further assess Samaranch's leadership, which had been one of our central missions in *Selling the Five Rings*, and the manner in which the scandal reflected the high-stakes nature of the Olympic bid process that evolved during his presidency, we determined that "Buying the Five Rings" could wait.

The Salt Lake City crisis rocked the international sport community for a second time within a six-month period when it exploded in November 1998. "Le Tour de Farce Comes to Sorry End" read a headline in the *Irish Times* on August 1. "Tour de France, Bloodied by Drug Scandals, Limps into Paris," echoed the *International Herald Tribune* on August 3. On July 8, three days prior to the opening of the Tour de France, Willy Voet, a Belgian masseur working for the Festina cycling team, attempted to transport in excess of four hundred doping products, including the red-blood-cell booster EPO (erythropoietin), across the France-Belgium border. Bruno Roussel and Erik

Ryckaert, Festina's team chief and doctor, respectively, were subsequently questioned, and Roussel confessed to Festina's doping program. Tour officials banned Festina from the competition, six other teams subsequently withdrew, and as yellow-jersey leader Marco Pantani (who would fail a blood test at the 1999 Giro d'Italia) and the peloton cruised down the Champs-Élysées at the close of the race, the competitors numbered fewer than 100 of the 189 who started the race in Dublin on July 11.[5] Sadly, Javier Mauleon, a member of one of the teams (ONCE of Spain) that withdrew from the tour, confirmed merely what many long suspected: "You can't ride 35,000 km a year solely on spaghetti. You have to take things."[6] The doping scandal proved a national embarrassment for France, which anticipated another summer spectacle to add to the celebratory atmosphere engendered by its recent 3–0 triumph over the vaunted Brazilians in the FIFA World Cup soccer final in Paris.

However, the 1998 Tour de France, concluded Richard Pound, was the "seminal event" in terms of the genesis of the World Anti-Doping Agency (WADA).[7] The IOC employed this black eye for international sport as a rallying point for pursuing the consensus necessary among national governments and international sport organizations to launch a comprehensive fight against doping. In August 1998, the IOC offered to host the World Conference on Doping in Sport (WCDS) as a means of bringing these agents together in a common cause.[8] It was on course to score a major coup in the fight against the use of banned performance-enhancing drugs. John Kingdon, in his classic work on agenda setting and processes involved in policy formulation, *Agendas, Alternatives, and Public Policies*, classified incidents such as the 1998 Tour de France in the context of the fight against doping in sports as a "focusing event." Often, observed Kingdon, a workable and necessary solution to a problem is known, but it is not translated into policy until an event occurs that pushes policy makers to take action. Stakeholders understood the need for random, unannounced drug testing on a year-round basis by an independent agency, reported Victor Lachance, the former CEO of the Canadian Centre for Ethics in Sport, but "what was missing was the political will and resources to implement [it]." The 1998 Tour de France had a galvanizing effect, as it brought the IOC, government authorities, and the International Sport Federations to the table in February 1999, resulting in an agreement to establish an international anti-doping agency in advance of the 2000 Sydney

Olympics.[9] However, the media's continuing fascination with events tied to the Salt Lake City scandal that burst forth after the IOC announced plans for the WCDS, and the IOC's grave predicament, obscured the IOC's success in laying the foundation for WADA in February 1999. Would the IOC also be able to use this second crisis in Salt Lake City to effect positive change for the Olympic Movement? This is one of the questions we seek to answer in this book. Samaranch, members of the IOC Executive Board, including Pound, and key staff members such as director-general François Carrard and marketing director Michael Payne, scrambled to right the IOC ship that was buffeted on a daily basis by an exercised world media in the wake of the original KTVX Channel 4 (Salt Lake City) story concerning Sonia Essomba. The IOC retained Hill & Knowlton, an internationally recognized public relations firm, to assist in managing its media messaging. Samaranch delegated to Richard Pound the responsibility to lead the organization's internal investigation of implicated IOC members' conduct.[10] Pound's Ad Hoc Commission labored throughout the holiday season to achieve the desired swift resolution to the issue. The commission's recommendation for the expulsion of a number of members and sanctions of varying degrees for a number of others was duly approved by the Executive Board in late January 1999.[11]

Four IOC members resigned (Bashir Attarabulsi, Pirjo Häggman, David Sibandze, and Charles Mukora), while the IOC jettisoned another six delegates (Jean-Claude Ganga, Seiuli Paul Wallwork, Agustin Arroyo, Zein El Abdin Ahmed Abdel Gadir, Lamine Keita, and Sergio Santander Fantini) at its 108th Extraordinary Session in March 1999 as a result of evidence concerning their willingness to accept gifts or financial benefits from Salt Lake City far in excess of what was permitted by IOC guidelines. Juan Antonio Samaranch's reticence to confront rumors of similar transgressions by past bid committee leaders and a number of IOC members jeopardized both his presidency and his legacy. In the most egregious case of discreditable conduct, Congo's Jean-Claude Ganga accepted gifts and benefits totaling more than $250,000 in value.[12]

The six members targeted for expulsion protested their innocence before their colleagues at the March Session, but the IOC members accepted Samaranch's call for their expulsion articulated clearly in his opening address. Samaranch also proposed to the Session his plans for an IOC ethics commission tasked to establish a code of conduct for members and deal with any future cases involving their conduct. Last, he proposed striking the IOC 2000 Commission, which would execute an environmental scan to make recommendations for reform measures to the *Olympic Charter* concerning the IOC's policies and procedures.[13]

The 108th Extraordinary IOC Session marked a turning point in the crisis, as the expulsion of the implicated members and the proposed missions of the IOC Ethics and 2000 Commissions bought the organization enough time to pursue a reform agenda that the IOC leadership, its corporate sponsors and television partners, and its media critics concurred was necessary (even though they differed on the depth, breadth, and preferred pace of the reform process required).[14] In December 1999, the IOC Session passed fifty reform measures addressing matters ranging from the method of appointing IOC members and the institution of term limits on new members to the elimination of IOC member visits to bid cities (Samaranch suspended bid city visits in the early days of the crisis).[15]

Samaranch, who previously declined efforts by US politicians to grill him on Capitol Hill regarding the IOC's well-publicized failings, finally relented. With the reform proposals approved, he appeared in Washington before the House Commerce Subcommittee on Oversight and Investigations. It was a necessary step, as the IOC needed to shore up corporate support for the Olympic Movement within the United States and blunt a congressional subcommittee that had an interest in reducing the IOC's influence in the United States while enhancing the authority of the USOC.[16] While Samaranch handled himself well, Joe Barton (R-TX) upbraided him and called for his immediate resignation. He also absorbed stinging words from Chairman Fred Upton (R-MI): "The record is riddled with evidence of over a decade's worth of blatant abuse which was ignored by those who consistently, arrogantly, unbelievably turned a blind eye to the ugly truth. . . . I fear that these reforms will be cosmetic and purely mask the aristocratic aura that has formed around the organization. . . . But I'm afraid that the enforcement program around the reforms enacted this weekend . . . will show that what the IOC passed will simply be window-dressing and business will go on as usual."[17]

With the US media engrossed with the ticking time bomb that was Y2K and the prospect of Hillary Clinton's run for a seat in the US Senate,

Samaranch's appearance slipped largely under the radar screen. His favorable performance in Washington, combined with Nike's swift decision only days earlier to fill the void when Reebok withdrew as a sponsor of the Sydney Organizing Committee because of a perceived breach of contract, provided a heartening lift for Lausanne officials.[18] The Olympic brand's resilience was clear. When John Hancock's president and CEO, David D'Alessandro, a TOP sponsor and the most strident critic of the IOC's response to the crisis, announced in February 2000 that his company would extend its relationship with the TOP program, IOC officials breathed a little easier and envisioned an end to the crisis.[19] The threatened stampede of Olympic sponsors who would direct their sponsorship dollars elsewhere did not materialize.

Though closure was achieved by IOC officials who worked mightily in 1999 to safeguard the Olympic brand, federal law authorities in the United States did not share this opinion. Tom Welch and David Johnson soon faced a fifteen-count indictment involving bribery, racketeering, fraud, and conspiracy related to alleged acts committed while leading Salt Lake City's bid effort. It is at this time that our collective connection with the Salt Lake City bid scandal was revisited.

Zuckerman Spaeder, the Washington, DC, law firm retained by Welch, launched its search for an expert witness for the defense team who possessed knowledge concerning the history of Olympic bid processes. Welch's legal team selected this book's coauthor Robert Barney. Trial preparations extended through 2000 into 2001. During this time Barney traveled to Salt Lake City and Washington, when summoned by lawyers Bill Taylor (Zuckerman Spaeder) and Max Wheeler, Johnson's lead lawyer based in Salt Lake City. However, US District Court judge David Sam dismissed four of the charges in July 2001. He also concluded that while the government might pursue the other charges, no proceedings would commence until the close of the Salt Lake City Olympic Winter Games. In November Sam trumped his own decision and dismissed the remaining charges. But the case against Welch and Johnson did not disappear, as within the week federal prosecutors announced their intention to appeal Sam's decision. In April 2003, the Tenth US Circuit Court of Appeals overturned Sam's earlier dismissal of the indictment, and Welch and Johnson faced the prospect of a trial. Once again the trial was placed on Judge Sam's docket, and proceedings duly commenced in late October 2003. The prosecution presented its case throughout November and rested in December. Taylor and Wheeler called for, and received from Judge Sam, an immediate dismissal of all charges against their clients for lack of evidence.[20]

Throughout this period of legal thrust and parry in Utah, we monitored trial developments. Once Judge Sam's gavel sounded the close of the trial, we concluded our work on the revised edition of *Selling the Five Rings* and pressed forward with other research initiatives. Two of us (Stephen Wenn and Scott Martyn) examined the events that precipitated the Welch-Johnson trial. We directed our research energies toward mining contemporary media coverage of the scandal, locating pertinent files in Lausanne, as well as reviewing critical documents in Richard Pound's archives pertaining to the IOC's dialogue with its corporate sponsors during the crisis. We published two research articles focusing on the interaction between Richard Pound and major Olympic sponsors, titled "Storm Watch: Richard Pound, TOP Sponsors, and the Salt Lake City Scandal" and "'Tough Love': Richard Pound, David D'Alessandro, and the Salt Lake City Olympics Bid Scandal." However, we understood that when we combined our knowledge base with our "senior" colleague's experience with the trial preparations, collectively we could embark upon a more substantial undertaking.

For an event that has had such a profound effect on the future direction of the IOC, the Salt Lake City crisis has attracted a modest amount of scholarly attention. Doug Booth provided a stern critique of the IOC leadership in "Gifts of Corruption? Ambiguities of Obligation in the Olympic Movement," arguing that Juan Antonio Samaranch was central to the evolution of a bidding environment rife with the possibility for corrupt practices. This line of criticism echoed the conclusion reached in relation to earlier bid competitions by Vyv Simson and Andrew Jennings in *Dishonored Games: Corruption, Money and Greed at the Olympics*. Barbara Kellerman provides a scathing assessment of Samaranch's presidential leadership, with a measure of her focus falling on the Olympic bid process and Salt Lake City crisis, in *Bad Leadership: What It Is, How It Happens, Why It Matters*. Bill Mallon surveyed the major events in the crisis and provided a useful summary of the changes effected to the *Olympic Charter* in December 1999 in "The Olympic Bribery Scandal."[21] Mary Charalmbous Papamiltiades examined the susceptibility of the IOC to a crisis concerning its oversight of the bid process in the context of existing crisis management literature in "IOC: Factors That Fostered the Development of the Most Publicized Crisis in Its History—the Salt Lake Scandal." In *Inside the Olympics* and *Olympic Turnaround*, insiders Richard Pound and Michael Payne, respectively, shed light on events in Salt Lake City; however, their accounts represent only portions of these larger works centered on issues such as judging, doping, politics, corporate sponsorship, television, and Samaranch's mission to bring financial wealth and stability to the organization through a more sophisticated and focused approach of generating revenue from the sale of television rights and corporate sponsorship opportunities. The University of Toronto staged a conference titled *Olympic Reform: A Ten Year Review* in May 2009; however, the vast majority of papers, as one might imagine based on the conference's central theme, dealt with the IOC's status ten years removed from the scandal and steered away from focusing on its survival efforts in 1999.[22] Mitt Romney, the former governor of Massachusetts and the individual selected to clean up the mess at the local Salt Lake City level, recounted (with the assistance of Timothy Robinson) his efforts and thinking at the time with a focus on steps taken to maintain the focus and morale of Salt Lake City organizers in *Turnaround: Crisis, Leadership, and the Olympic Games*.

## Our Mission

In this book we hope to provide readers with the context for the Salt Lake City scandal by assessing the presidency of Juan Antonio Samaranch and the evolution of a bidding environment that invited the actions of Welch, Johnson, and a number of IOC members. Our central purpose is to explore the genesis of the scandal and to chart the IOC's efforts to bring stability to its operations in a trying environment while subjected to intense media scrutiny. This analysis will be underpinned by the use of IOC archival material and a comprehensive review of contemporary media reports. The IOC was clearly not properly outfitted to deal with a media crisis, but its leadership did not wilt in the face of this challenge. What cannot be ignored in assessing its ability to survive this threat was the willingness of its major corporate sponsors to hold firm (while, with the exception of David D'Alessandro, forcefully but privately demanding substantial reform) and not abandon their Olympic sponsor relationships. Therefore, the interplay between IOC officials and corporate sponsors during the crisis garners significant attention. Clearly, our focus falls on the IOC's response to the crisis. We will leave the analysis of the response of local officials in Salt Lake City to other researchers.

At its heart this is the story of an organization that found itself caught in the throes of a crisis facilitated by its own shortcomings in failing to confront the festering problems with the bidding process. Richard Pound conceded that a crisis such as the one that emerged in Salt Lake City percolated for years. It was a "simmering" rather than "sudden" crisis if we employ the labels of those who make crisis management their business.[23] For a period of four months its leaders battled desperately to withstand withering media criticism while simultaneously waging a campaign to recover the Olympic brand. For Juan Antonio Samaranch, the personal stakes were even higher—his survival and his presidential legacy. This critical juncture in the presidency of an individual who brought sweeping change to the Olympic Movement in the 1980s and 1990s merits investigation for those persons interested in the IOC, the Olympic Movement, and the broader concepts of leadership and crisis management.

Readers may recall that in the late 1990s, corporate America, too, was also sitting on a simmering crisis in light of a stock market bubble driven, in part, by investors' interest in a series of initial public offerings for Internet service companies, referred to more commonly as dot-com operations (such as VA Linux, Red Hat, eToys, Amazon.com, and Internet Capital). In 1999 more than 250 dot-com companies were subject to IPOs and recorded an astounding 84 percent average increase in their value in their opening twenty-four hours on the market. However, the US markets had been trending upward for a number of years, with traders enjoying double-digit percentage increases in the Dow Jones Industrial Average in each year from 1994 through 1999. A yearly average of $1.6 trillion in corporate mergers in 1998 through 2000 also reflected the buoyant mood on Wall Street.[24]

These happy days were brought to an end by the combined effect of interest rate increases imposed by former Federal Reserve chairman Alan Greenspan, the period of indecision resulting from presidential election results in Florida in November 2000, and the tragedy of September 11, 2001. With the ensuing decline in the market, soon US television and radio news channels and newspapers were dominated by stories concerning the collapse of the likes of Enron, WorldCom, Global Crossing, Tyco International, and many other corporate giants that swaggered their way through the 1990s before controversies over accounting practices or executive malfeasance brought them down. The US Congress formulated the Sarbanes-Oxley Corporate Reform Act of 2002 to establish more stringent oversight measures concerning accounting practices within corporate America. Aspects of this federal reform initiative have been shown in the fullness of time to present new challenges for America's major corporations.[25] How do the IOC's reforms launched as a result of the Salt Lake City scandal measure up some twelve years after their inception? This question sets out an additional area of interest as we move forward.

An air of arrogance wafting through America's corporate boardrooms in the 1990s that facilitated this spate of business scandals similarly can be highlighted as a source of the IOC's predicament with respect to Salt Lake City. In the IOC's case, arrogance was likely mixed with an equal measure of complacency. The Olympic brand possessed significant appeal to multinational corporations, multiple cities jockeyed for the right to host Summer and Winter Olympic festivals for the foreseeable future, and a parade of International Sport Federation (ISF) officials visited Lausanne seeking new or expanded places for their respective sports on the Olympic event program. Successful games in Albertville (1992), Barcelona (1992), and Lillehammer (1994) also contributed to breeding an absence of necessary oversight within the host-city bidding process.

Meanwhile, Samaranch and Pound secured the Olympic Movement's long-term financial status as a result of their deft negotiation of multifestival Olympic television rights packages between 1995 and 1997. The National Broadcasting Company's president of sports, Dick Ebersol, desired to firmly establish NBC as America's Olympic television network. Samaranch and Pound pounced and subsequently used the contract as a template for discussions with the world's other television networks.[26] Like the US stock market in the 1990s, the IOC and Olympic Movement were in ascendance, easily able to brush off the disappointment of the commercial excesses of the 1996 Atlanta Olympics.

Juan Antonio Samaranch's passing in 2010 will prompt a wave of analysis of his two decades-long presidency within the historical community and, for a briefer period, the popular media. His vision changed the IOC's financial foundation and philosophy concerning revenue generation. This transformation represents a significant aspect of his presidential legacy. With the increasing unwillingness of federal governments to put unlimited resources into the coffers of local organizing committees, it was a necessary step when he arrived in Lausanne in 1980. Moreover, the dollars raised by the approach to television rights negotiations he championed (and his right-hand man, Richard Pound, executed) and the development of the TOP program enriched Organizing Committees of the Olympic Games (OCOGs), National Olympic Committees (NOCs), and ISFs.

This book explores an aspect of the fallout of this success. When major world cities with aspirations of hosting the Olympic world realized that these commercial revenue streams would greatly assist them in achieving their goal, they pursued the Games with vigor. The competitiveness of the bidding environment escalated, and inducements to IOC members for their votes became a tool for some bid committees.[27] Samaranch, whose finger remained on the pulse of the IOC throughout his presidency, heard rumors of these activities. In the 1990s, on this score, his judgment failed him. He did not seek out the culprits. The result of this failure to act was the Salt Lake City bid scandal, yet another facet of his presidential legacy. Aligning our thoughts with Kingdon's notion on the inertia some organizations must overcome as a precursor to the implementation of new policies, this "focusing event" pushed the IOC to overhaul both its guidelines on the Olympic host-city bid process and its formal structures for the twenty-first century.

# Abbreviations

| | |
|---|---|
| ABC | Australian Broadcasting Corporation; American Broadcasting Company |
| AOC | Australian Olympic Committee |
| ASA | Amateur Sports Act |
| BOCOG | Beijing Olympics Organizing Committee |
| CBS | Columbia Broadcasting System |
| EBU | European Broadcasting Union |
| FBI | Federal Bureau of Investigation |
| IOC | International Olympic Committee |
| IOCA | International Olympic Committee Archives |
| ISF | International Sport Federation |
| NBC | National Broadcasting Company |
| NOC | National Olympic Committee |
| OCOG | Organizing Committee of the Olympic Games |
| PFMRP | Personal Files of Michael R. Payne |
| PFRWP | Personal Files of Richard W. Pound |
| SLOC | Salt Lake City Olympics Organizing Committee |
| SOCOG | Sydney Olympics Organizing Committee |
| TOP | The Olympic Partners (formerly The Olympic Program) |
| USOC | United States Olympic Committee |
| VANOC | Vancouver Olympics Organizing Committee |
| WADA | World Anti-Doping Agency |
| WCDS | World Conference on Doping in Sport |

Tarnished Rings

# 1

# The Man from Barcelona

> Cemeteries are full of people who thought they were indispens-
> able. I will leave. And another president will come.
> —Juan Antonio Samaranch, IOC president (1980–2001),
> July 2001

## The Challenge

Labeled a "revolutionary" by his biographer, Juan Antonio Samaranch was
elected as the seventh president of the IOC at a particularly challenging time
in the history of the Olympic Movement.[1] The political problems and trau-
mas his immediate predecessor, Lord Killanin, encountered during his eight
years (1972–80) as IOC president, stole from the Irish peer much of the time
he "would have preferred to have spent updating the Movement."[2] Although
a potential "collapse" of the Olympic Movement, suggested by Killanin's own
predecessor, Avery Brundage (1952–72), an American business magnate and
former Olympian, never materialized, issues such as international politics
and terrorism left an indelible mark on the celebrations surrounding the quadrennial festival in the 1970s.[3]

Beset by the trials of world geopolitics, little representation in some
regions of the world, fractious relations with its Olympic partners, the
National Olympic Committees, and International Sport Federations, and
minimal financial resources, the IOC posed a daunting leadership challenge
for any individual. Richard Pound, an IOC vice president and chairman of
the Marketing Commission during the Salt Lake City crisis, reflected: "In

1980, the Olympic Movement was under sustained attack from political powers and was, indeed, a virtual hostage to world tensions. It was disunited, well short of universal and had no financial resources to give it the autonomy and independence it needed to resist political pressures."[4] Michael Payne, the IOC's former marketing director, echoed that sentiment: "Everybody was writing the Olympic obituary."[5] "Depressed" and concerned about his ability to "cope with all the demands of the job" and the significant problems that he knew existed, Samaranch even considered how he might withdraw from his newly elected position.[6] Despite these misgivings, he pushed forward and, with the exception of Pierre de Coubertin, concludes University of Chicago cultural anthropologist and Olympic expert John MacAloon, emerged as "the most significant leader in modern Olympic history."[7]

Time and time again, Samaranch demonstrated a unique ability to move people and groups toward supporting his goals and agenda. Samaranch, offered the Los Angeles Times's Alan Abrahamson, proved "one of the smartest and shrewdest practitioners of backroom politics and personal diplomacy ever to grace the world stage."[8] His plans were ambitious, and not without controversy, in terms of both their goals and his methods of achieving them. "For sure," argues Olympic historian John Lucas, throughout his presidency "one finds warts and areas to be praised. But that is the nature of humanity and that is the nature of the world we live in. It is an imperfect world of warts and unhealed wounds and also gentility and greatness."[9]

## Samaranch's Background

Born in Barcelona, Spain, on July 17, 1920, Juan Antonio Samaranch was the third son, in a family of six children (two girls and four boys), of Francisco Samaranch Castro, owner of a prosperous upholstery business, and Juana Torelló Malhevy, head of the Barcelona maternity hospital. Their home, situated in the San Gervasio quarter, a sophisticated upper-middle-class district of Barcelona, was located near the original headquarters and courts of the Real Club de Tenis Barcelona 1899.[10] Although his father was a billiards and pelota (or jai alai) enthusiast, the Samaranch family often frequented the private tennis club or soccer matches between RCD Español and FC Barcelona. As a young student of Barcelona's German College, where a significant focus was on gymnastics and athletics, Samaranch developed a strong sense of camaraderie with his Spanish colleagues. Having established friendships that were often cemented by soccer allegiances during his early education, he graduated with a degree in commerce from the Higher Institute of Business Studies prior to the outbreak of the Spanish Civil War.[11]

In 1940, having passed a state examination qualifying him to be a *perito mercantil*, or accountant, Samaranch worked briefly in the family textile business. During this period he further developed his interest in sport, initially competing as a featherweight boxer under the name of "Kid Samaranch" in the Catalan Amateur Boxing Championships and then as a player-promoter of *hockey sobre patinas* (roller hockey).[12] Intrigued by the potential in the sport of roller hockey, he successfully lobbied the Royal Spanish Athletic Club to establish, and permit him to coach, a roller hockey team in 1943. That same year, under the pen name of "Stick," he wrote a series of articles on roller hockey as a correspondent for *La Prensa*, a Barcelona newspaper.[13] Two years later, he directed an effort by the Spanish Roller Hockey Federation to persuade General José Moscardó, leader of the National Council for Sport, to facilitate an application for its admittance to the International Federation of Roller Hockey.[14] The following year, Samaranch emerged on the world sporting scene when he attended the IFRH's international congress in Montreux, Switzerland, where Spain's application was accepted.[15] In 1950, having established the Spanish national team, he joined the IFRH's Executive Council.

In 1951 Samaranch bankrolled the world roller hockey championships staged in his hometown of Barcelona by dipping into his share of the profits from the family business. Disappointment resulting from a fourth-place finish at the 1950 world championships in Milan, Italy, was not to be repeated. The Spanish team toppled the perennial powerhouse from Portugal to win its first world roller hockey title.[16] Samaranch's initiative, combined with the team's success, further elevated his profile within Spain's sport system. That same year, the Spanish Skate Hockey Federation was created, and Samaranch was elected its first president. Soon thereafter, as a journalist, Samaranch attended the 1952 Helsinki Olympics, where he drew much inspiration from watching Emil Zátopek follow up his gold medal performances in the 5,000-meter and 10,000-meter events, with a victory in the marathon. In Helsinki, too, he gained a personal understanding that "the Olympic Games are different from all other sports in the world." At the time of his retirement as

IOC president in 2001, Samaranch mused that it might very well have been a life-changing moment.[17]

Emboldened by his rapid rise in the sphere of sport governance, and not lacking personal ambition, Samaranch wrote to the regional political authorities in 1951, asking to be selected as a candidate for the Barcelona city council elections.[18] Although initially rejected by the regional party, he continued to burnish his reputation within Spain's sport community. Elected vice president of the IFRH in 1954, Samaranch shortly thereafter achieved his earlier political aspirations to be a Barcelona city councilman representing Spain's only political party, the Movimiento, of the authoritarian national government of Generalissimo Francisco Franco.[19] In 1955 he became a member of the Diputació de Barcelona (Barcelona Provincial Council) and was elevated to the position of "provincial deputy responsible for sport."[20] His most significant achievement to date, and one that clearly placed him on the stage of world sport, was his appointment as secretary-general for the Second Mediterranean Games, awarded four years earlier to Barcelona at the time of the First Mediterranean Games in Alexandria, Egypt.[21] Having joined the Provincial Council only a few months before the scheduled opening of the games on July 16, 1955, Samaranch was tasked with the formation of the organizing committee, scheduling the required work, and establishing the press, protocol, accommodation, and transport committees.[22]

## Samaranch Enters the Olympic World

When he was named to Spain's National Olympic Committee in 1954, Samaranch's career in Olympic administration was launched. His path to the SOC presidency (1967–71) wound its way through Cortina d'Ampezzo (1956), Rome (1960), and Tokyo (1964), where he served as his country's *chef de mission*. Samaranch cultivated a relationship with IOC president Avery Brundage through a series of flattering letters and telegrams, an approach that yielded his appointment to the IOC in 1966. Within two years, Brundage appointed him to the role of chief of protocol. Samaranch aspired to a position on the IOC Executive Board and dedicated himself to building a reputation within the organization as a disciplined, meticulous, efficient, and influential individual, resulting in his appointment to various commissions.

Samaranch used these early years, argues Richard Pound, to "bring himself close to the center of IOC power; to be seen with those in power; to build alliances with those in a position to help him in his ambition; to not make waves; to not be out in front of issues, but to stay behind; and to offend no one."[23] He succeeded in becoming a member of the Executive Board in 1970 and secured a four-year term as vice president in 1974.

Samaranch's continued involvement in Barcelona and Catalan business and political affairs paralleled his rise in the halls of sport decision making.[24] Leaving city council in 1961, he retained his position as Barcelona's provincial deputy until 1967, when he became the delegate for physical education and sport in Spain's parliament.[25] Though Samaranch sold the family business, which he had operated since his father's death in 1957,[26] and although his involvement in sport commanded an ever-increasing amount of his time, he served on the board of directors for several real estate firms and banks in an effort to maintain his visibility in Barcelona's business circles. Little more than five years following his departure from the Provincial Council, he was appointed president of the Diputació de Barcelona. Enjoying the initial benefits that resulted from his close ties to the Franco regime, he held this important position until his resignation in 1977.[27]

Following the death of Generalissimo Francisco Franco on November 20, 1975, Spain experienced a dramatic transformation. Despite the lack of significant democratic roots, the transition of the Spanish political system triggered by Franco's passing, from authoritarianism to democratic rule, was characterized by its restraint.[28] In 1976 Spain's parliament voted itself out of existence by passing a package of political reforms that legalized political parties, trade unions, and other private associations. These reforms also included scheduled elections for the following year. In June 1977, Adolfo Suárez and his Center-Right Party emerged victorious from Spain's first free elections in four decades. Following the election, Suárez began the arduous task of liquidating the remaining institutions of Franco's authoritarian regime. In December 1978, the Spanish people ratified a new constitution, thereby completing Spain's transition to democratic rule.

In the midst of these steps toward "democratic consolidation," Samaranch's ties with the Franco regime caught up with him and weakened his political standing in Barcelona.[29] When provided with an opportunity to resign the presidency of the Diputació de Barcelona, Samaranch seamlessly shifted his career path and accepted Spain's ambassadorship to the Soviet Union and Mongolia (1977–80), a post that emerged following the resumption of diplomatic relations between the two countries. His work in helping the 1980 Moscow Organizing Committee, combined with his efforts to minimize the effects of the US-led boycott of the Games, convinced the USSR to lend support to Samaranch's future aspirations within the IOC.[30] With his support network in Eastern Europe established, he returned to the IOC Executive Board in 1979, prior to making his run at the presidency of the IOC.

Samaranch's harshest critics label him a committed fascist operative who leapfrogged his way forward in Catalan society and Spain's political circles owing to his fervent support of Francisco Franco and subsequently imposed the trappings of fascism on his leadership style as IOC president.[31] Despite this view, and although we would not cast him as nonideological, as he was drawn to Franco's policies at a young age, we see him as more of a chameleon, a pragmatic and shrewd opportunist, in his quest for authority and positions of influence and power rather than a zealous adherent of fascism.

On July 16, 1980, at the Eighty-Third IOC Session in the famous Hall of Columns of Moscow's Central House of Trade Unions, Samaranch was elected IOC president, defeating Willi Daume (Federal Republic of Germany), James Worrall (Canada), Lance Cross (New Zealand), and Marc Hodler (Switzerland) on the first ballot.[32] His campaign had unfolded over the course of a few years and was marked by much travel and engagement with sport leaders and sport organizations. His power base in terms of voting support rested largely in Asia, Africa, and Eastern Europe, and he could also count on the Latin vote. So meticulous were Samaranch's preparations, a hallmark of the man, and so susceptible was the IOC to rigid voting blocs that his personal vote count was only one less than he had anticipated. Samaranch also rode the wave of change in sport boardrooms at the time as power shifted away from the Anglo-Saxon community, as evidenced by the arrivals of João Havelange (Fédération Internationale de Football Association), Mario Vázquez Raña (Association of National Olympic Committees), Primo Nebiolo (International Amateur Athletics Federation), and Javier Ostos Mora (Fédération Internationale de Natation).[33]

2. Juan Antonio Samaranch (*right*) receives congratulations from outgoing IOC president Lord Killanin (*center*) following his election as IOC president on July 16, 1980. Tunisia's Mohamed Mzali, an IOC vice president, appears to Killanin's left. *Source:* Bettmann/Corbis.

## Samaranch's Agenda

Samaranch's term of office did not officially begin until after the Moscow Olympics; thus, he deferred laying out his vision for the Olympic Movement until the ceremonial handing over of the symbolic key to the Château de Vidy. Given the seemingly insurmountable difficulties facing the IOC, many viewed his task as "mission impossible."[34] In the weeks that followed, Samaranch identified the priorities that underscored his leadership agenda: pursue an enhanced measure of financial autonomy for the organization, tackle the threat of boycotts by engaging heads of state in discussions concerning the Olympic Movement, and repair the IOC's relations with the ISFs and NOCs that had suffered under Avery Brundage's rule, relations that only minimally improved under Killanin.

Financial autonomy sat at the head of the queue in terms of priorities for the new president. In his first letter to the IOC membership following his election, Samaranch wrote that "the financing of the IOC is a matter of some urgency."[35] Aware of the fact that revenues generated from the sale of television rights would not be sufficient, and concerned about the Olympic Movement's universal dependence on these revenues, he turned to Horst Dassler, Adidas's president, for assistance.[36]

With Dassler Samaranch explored the possibility of establishing a global marketing strategy for the Olympic Movement. In 1982 he established a working group responsible for finding new sources of financing, which soon became an IOC commission. Dassler's vision and Samaranch's energy and direction, when combined with the IOC's efforts to secure the legal protection of the Olympic symbol on a national and international basis, eventually provided the inspiration for the establishment of TOP, a worldwide sponsorship program.[37] It has proven a solid, fruitful source of revenue for the IOC since its initial cycle mounted in connection with the 1988 Olympic festivals in Calgary and Seoul.

In 1983, in an effort to maximize television rights fees, and thereby further his and the organization's financial goals, Samaranch handed authority over television negotiations (in all regions except Europe) to Canadian Richard Pound, a fast-rising, industrious IOC member of some five years' standing. This move undercut the power base of the IOC's longtime director, Monique Berlioux, and foreshadowed her departure from the organization two years later after it became clear to Lausanne officials, and Samaranch himself, that they could not coexist. Samaranch, a micromanager and the first IOC president to reside full-time in Lausanne since Coubertin, could not countenance the sphere of decision making that Berlioux carved out under absentee presidents Killanin and Brundage.[38]

In addition to revenue derived from television rights and the TOP program, Samaranch oversaw the IOC's pursuit of well-targeted commercial programs, including licensing, numismatics, and philatelic initiatives. Establishing a firm financial foundation for the entire Olympic Movement remained a primary focus throughout his presidency.

Deane Neubauer, a senior research fellow at the Globalization Research Center at the University of Hawaii, situated the IOC's transformation into a corporate entity and the steeply increasing trajectory of its learning curve concerning revenue generation coincident with the Samaranch presidency within the overarching story of globalization and its influence on sport in the latter half of the twentieth century. Globalization is a central pillar of any attempt to detail the history of the world's economy in the past forty years, and the 1980s and 1990s were critical decades in terms of the expansion of corporate and individual wealth "resulting from neoliberal reforms that dramatically reduced taxes on corporate and individual incomes." The financial success of the 1984 Los Angeles Olympic Games, and the budgetary plan devised by Peter Ueberroth that rested squarely on the availability of vast sums of private capital, noted Neubauer, paralleled the "explosion of capital out of the older industrial nations and into the developing world." Globalization, concludes Neubauer, was the necessary precursor for the appearance of vast sums of corporate money that fueled the genesis of the TOP program and burgeoning Olympic television revenues.[39]

With this tableau complete, Neubauer invited a debate on the Samaranch legacy as it pertained to the financial foundation of today's Olympic Movement. "He [Samaranch] arrived at the takeoff stage of corporate globalism and can be given credit either for steering the Olympic ship along a bountiful course in this flood tide," wrote Neubauer, "or simply having been fortunate to garner a benefit that came with the massive increase in global wealth during his tenure."[40] Reality rests more with the first of these two postulations.

There is little doubt that Samaranch benefited from the "enormous expansion of global corporate wealth" that coincided with his presidency.[41] However, it was Samaranch who orchestrated the alteration of an organizational mindset fostered by former IOC president Avery Brundage that eschewed embracing commercial revenue. Mere baby steps were taken in exploring the means of enhancing commercial revenue streams under Samaranch's predecessor,

Lord Killanin.[42] Samaranch understood the marketing cachet of the Olympic rings and their attractiveness to multinational corporations who were seeking a platform for marketing their own goods and services to consumers within an ever-broadening worldwide television audience. With a push from Horst Dassler, he tapped into the international corporate wellspring in the 1980s and 1990s with the development of the TOP program only after having convinced his colleagues that the IOC's limited financial resources and its degree of dependence on television revenue impeded its mission. Financial autonomy, argued Samaranch, empowered the IOC to withstand external political forces that plagued the Olympic Movement in the 1970s. This financial path, underscored by the TOP program and the unleashing of Richard Pound to pursue maximum television rights fees (with the exception of the European market), when combined with Samaranch's repudiation of amateurism and welcoming of professional athletes into Olympic competitive venues (as a means of enhancing the marketability of the Games to US television networks and prospective US-based multinational corporate sponsors), set a bold, new course for the IOC and the Olympic Movement.[43] Samaranch unlocked and cast aside the philosophical shackles that governed the IOC's approach to revenue generation prior to his move to Lausanne in 1980.

As a second major priority, Samaranch grappled with the problematic and devastating potential of politically motivated boycotts. To accomplish this task, he utilized his extensive diplomatic skills and network of established contacts to depoliticize the Olympic agenda.[44] Although powerless to get the Soviet Union and the other boycotting nations to attend the Los Angeles Games in 1984, he worked tirelessly to create a dialogue between the IOC and world leaders, thereby avoiding future problems by dint of anticipating them and plotting strategies for their solution before they emerged. Believing that dialogue and negotiations are best done face-to-face, Samaranch reportedly traveled approximately 1,860,000 miles during the first twelve years of his presidency on his quest to enhance the IOC's relationship with the world's political leaders.[45] During personal meetings with each head of state and their various representatives, he explained the role of the Olympic Movement and the damage caused by boycotts on the Games and the "potential of the Olympics as a tool for peace."[46] By the close of his tenure, Samaranch had visited more than 190 countries.[47]

Samaranch's third priority in his recovery strategy targeted improving the working relationship among members of the Olympic Tripartite. He argued that the entire Olympic Movement faced a crisis, and it was only by working together that it would survive. Michael Payne suggests that in Samaranch's "simple plea lay the insight that the Olympic brand is bigger than any one person or group." The late Robert Helmick, a past president of the United States Olympic Committee and former member of the IOC, labeled Samaranch a unifier, one who found a "different balance between the three arms of the movement."[48] By strengthening the unity of the Olympic Movement, Samaranch sought "to make it the leading social force of the 20th century."[49]

In the 1980s and 1990s, Samaranch and the IOC set about achieving his priorities of unity, control of the Olympic agenda, and the Olympic Movement's financial autonomy. Although controversial, Samaranch's decision to open the Olympic Games to professional athletes spurred the popularity of the event and its potential to generate revenue, especially in the financially lucrative US market. The launch of the TOP program in 1985 and the resulting achievement of the IOC's financial autonomy and independence under his presidential stewardship were noteworthy.[50] He strengthened ties between the various members of the Olympic Tripartite. Still, Samaranch's "greatest single accomplishment," stated John MacAloon, "has been a kind of political maturity, an ability to deal with political elites, heads of state, industrial elites. That was something the movement never really had." Samaranch achieved a remarkable "transformation in prestige and fortunes, in every sense, of the Olympic Games," concluded David Miller.[51]

In 1989, at the age of sixty-nine, Samaranch was unanimously reelected as president after nominations closed with no other candidates at the Ninety-Fifth IOC Session in San Juan, Puerto Rico. He ensured staying in this position until 2001 by convincing IOC members in 1995 to raise the age limit to eighty years of age for all members. Rather than employing a secret ballot, Samaranch called for a show of hands. With few people wanting to be seen opposing Samaranch's will, a sea of hands appeared in support of the initiative. Richard Pound was one of few IOC members, and the only member of the Executive Board, to oppose Samaranch's plan. Samaranch's vindictiveness played out in Atlanta in 1996 when he convinced the aging Ashwini Kumar to challenge Pound in an election for an IOC vice presidential post. Pound, who received assurance from Kumar earlier in the year that he would not be running, was caught off-guard but stared down his boss when he informed Samaranch that a loss to Kumar would result in his resignation as head of the IOC's marketing and television negotiations portfolios. Samaranch retreated, fearing a backlash from the IOC's corporate sponsors and television partners, and pointed Pound in the direction of a few members to explain his decision to resign from these responsibilities in the event of a loss. Clearly, Samaranch knew the vote count. Pound escaped with a two-vote margin of victory.[52] Hardworking, full of passion and energy, and fully committed to the Olympic Movement, Samaranch favored the use of the velvet-fist approach, namely, diplomacy. Clearly, this episode demonstrates he was also capable of acts of cold calculation.

Samaranch thrived in the position of IOC president, taking on numerous challenges and setting a pace of work that often left his staff slack-jawed. He deftly maneuvered the IOC away from suffering a compromised Olympic festival in Seoul as a result of political tensions in the Korean peninsula and witnessed athletes from the two Koreas enter Stadium Australia together in Sydney in 2000. He dealt effectively with the China-Taiwan conundrum, the breakup of Yugoslavia, and the changes in Eastern Europe following the fall of the Berlin Wall. He increased the number of opportunities for women on the Olympic program, welcomed enhanced input from athletes by striking the Athletes' Commission, tossed the hypocrisy of amateurism on the scrap heap and welcomed professional athletes into Olympic precincts, and toiled to extend the reach of the Olympic Movement to the world's developing nations. There is much to applaud. However, for his critics, the focus falls on his halfhearted fight against doping,[53] his inability (or lack of desire) to raise the profile of women in the upper ranks of the world's sport bureaucracy, the commodification[54] of the Olympic Games resulting from his embrace of corporate sponsorship, gigantism,[55] and, of course, his unwillingness to rein in members of the IOC who sought personal benefit from the Olympic bid process that gave birth to the Salt Lake City bid scandal.

But what will be written about Samaranch's presidency in ten, twenty, or even thirty years? "My guess," wrote Richard Pound, "is that history will be kinder to Samaranch at a distance than it has been to date. Certain issues will fade into their proper perspective—the scandals toward the end of his term in office; his particular manipulative style; some of the dubious people he promoted to prominence; and the combination of duplicity and blandness that seems to be required of certain leaders—and a longer view of his accomplishments will emerge." Pound is likely right. However, Samaranch's legion of critics will continue to have their say. "Samaranch is your classic second-rate gray suited bureaucrat," comments Andrew Jennings. "[He] worked to advance himself first through the Franco regime in Spain, and then when that dictatorship collapsed in the mid-70s, he transferred his burrowing to the IOC and emerged five years later as their president . . . [where] he fleeced sport of its moral and monetary value and institutionalized doping as an adjunct to victory." On the eve of the 112th IOC Session in Moscow and Samaranch's departure from presidential office, the *Russia Journal,* an English-language newspaper based in Moscow, reported, "It all seems so appropriate. One of the most corrupt organizations in the world coming to one of the world's most corrupt cities to choose a successor to its leader, a former fascist official, who personally chose the location because he was anointed in the former Communist capital exactly 21 years ago."[56] For a man who succeeded in unifying the Olympic Movement, he remains a polarizing figure for those individuals whose business it is to observe and report on it.

Samaranch seemed content to let his presidential record speak for itself and saw no need to defend his performance. It is surprising that a man who accumulated a wealth of experiences while leading the Olympic Movement for two decades did not push for the wider dissemination of his memoirs published in Spanish at the end of his presidency.[57] In an interview with the *Los Angeles Times* in 2001, he stated in reference to his presidency, "I think the balance is not bad." As a final act, and with little concern for the repercussions, he nominated his son, Juan Antonio Samaranch Jr., who lacked any meaningful credentials, as an IOC member. Despite warnings from his IOC colleagues that such action would tarnish his reputation and the good that had come out of the Salt Lake City crisis, Samaranch was defiant. "I don't care," he stated, and "Juanito" was elected a member of the IOC, thereby extending his father's legacy.[58]

Juan Antonio Samaranch joined the pantheon of sport luminaries such as Joe Louis, Willie Mays, Muhammad Ali, and even one of the IOC's past presidents, Avery Brundage, all very accomplished, who plied their trade for too long. For Samaranch the time to bid adieu was 1992, when the Olympic flame was extinguished in Barcelona, his hometown.[59] During the first twelve years of his presidency, Samaranch was the chief architect of a needed remodeling of the Olympic Movement. It was more relevant, popular, and solvent than in 1980 when he moved to Lausanne. However, in the latter nine years of his presidential tenure, he failed to demonstrate the resolve to combat the scourge of doping in sport and the simmering crisis enveloping the host-city bid process. His image and legacy suffered.[60] Still, Samaranch, with much assistance from key IOC members and officials, ultimately guided the IOC through the morass of 1999. This fact, too, merits consideration in the final analysis.

Samaranch left office in 2001, in the wake of the successful 2000 Sydney Olympics, with a measure of his reputation restored, despite his blatant act of nepotism in advancing his son's status in the Olympic hierarchy. Active and engaged in Olympic affairs (he traveled to Vancouver for the Olympic Winter Games in February 2010) until the end of his life in April 2010, Samaranch delivered an emotional, heartfelt, but ultimately unsuccessful appeal to IOC members in October 2009 at the 121st Session to deliver the 2016 Olympics to Madrid. "I know that I am near the end of my time. I am, as you know, 89 years old. May I ask you to consider granting my country the honor and also the duty to organize the Games and Paralympics in 2016. Thank you," stated a frail Samaranch, who then slowly retreated from the podium.[61] IOC members ultimately decided to extend the Olympic brand, a brand whose strength and marketability owe much to Samaranch's vision, energy, and commitment, to South America by electing Rio de Janeiro the host city of the 2016 Olympics.

Historians will debate Samaranch's legacy. There will be praise and criticism.[62] None, however, will challenge the assertion that he committed himself deeply to the Olympic Movement. Still, even the partial restoration of one's image first requires its collapse. We now turn our attention to what Samaranch labeled one of the two most regrettable occurrences of his presidential tenure—the Salt Lake City scandal.[63]

# 2

# A Gathering Storm

**KTVX Channel 4 Breaks the Story**

It was the proverbial pebble tossed upon a calm, shimmering lake with its ripples extending seemingly endlessly. The disturbance in the Olympic world emanating from Salt Lake City in late November 1998 soon rolled over Lausanne, Sydney, Nagano, and other international centers such as Amsterdam, Anchorage, and Toronto that chased the five rings during Juan Antonio Samaranch's presidency. When the waters calmed once again some thirteen months later, Olympic officials might very well have argued that the pebble more resembled a boulder.

Reporter Chris Vanocur's KTVX Channel 4 (Salt Lake City) story, based on a leaked Salt Lake City Organizing Committee document that referenced US college tuition assistance to Sonia Essomba, daughter of the recently deceased IOC member René Essomba (Cameroon), appeared at the outset to be a local issue.[1] SLOC spokesperson Frank Zang characterized the financial support for a small number of international students, including Essomba, as a "humanitarian effort." He reminded those individuals who wished to impugn the actions of bid committee officials that Salt Lake City's sweeping majority first-ballot win at the IOC's Session in Budapest in 1995 confirmed that the financial grants to Essomba and a number of other international students had little to do with the result.[2] SLOC president Frank Joklik similarly denied anything untoward about the payments to American University in Washington, DC, on Essomba's behalf. Joklik referred to charges that Salt Lake City's bid had been fueled, in part, by bribes as "a sort of defamation which is regrettable

. . . destructive and distracting." Tom Welch, the Salt Lake City impresario who orchestrated the city's successful bid in 1995 but resigned as SLOC president in 1997 as a result of spousal abuse allegations, claimed that this type of humanitarian assistance, in Salt Lake's case, a National Olympic Committee Assistance Program, was commonplace in the Olympic family.[3] SLOC board chairman Robert Garff echoed Welch's thoughts in media interviews.[4]

While newspaper reporters in Salt Lake City and those reporters servicing the Associated Press were exercised by Vanocur's report,[5] within the IOC's headquarters in Lausanne, Switzerland, Olympic officials' reaction was muted. Michael Payne, the IOC's former marketing director, with much of his attention at the time focused on finalizing contractual arrangements with Sema Group, the information technology company replacing IBM in The Olympic Partners corporate sponsorship program, observed that his Lausanne colleagues did not sense the immediate need for alarm bells. It had the earmarks of a local issue, asserted Payne, one that SLOC officials would be best positioned to contain.[6]

When Richard Pound, an IOC vice president and chairman of its Marketing Commission, viewed a fax report on the KTVX story at his law office in Montreal's CIBC Tower, he sensed trouble and considered that "this did not bode well for the Olympic Movement."[7] When queried by Lisa Riley Roche of the *Deseret Morning News* (Salt Lake City), Pound stated, "I don't like the public perception." While he, too, desired more information on the Salt Lake City bid committee's activities, in prescient yet understated fashion, Pound concluded, "It's potentially embarrassing to us all."[8]

## Samaranch's Early Response

Salt Lake City reporters doggedly pursued the story, pressing SLOC officials for more information. Their determination, in part, stemmed from frustration with Frank Joklik's dismissive attitude and his repeated effort to characterize the payments as humanitarian aid.[9] Within days Samaranch's "finely honed instinct for danger and self-preservation" prompted him to assign investigative responsibilities to the IOC's Juridical Commission under the leadership of Senegal's Kéba Mbaye.[10]

On the eve of IOC Executive Board meetings scheduled for Lausanne in December, Samaranch caucused with Frank Joklik and a number of

SLOC executives. Joklik, who requested the meeting,[11] presented a progress report on Salt Lake City preparations and shared with Samaranch information that SLOC's chief financial officer, Gordon Crabtree,[12] culled from bid committee files concerning payments benefiting a number of IOC members. Samaranch's meeting with Joklik spelled out a need for an expanded inquiry beyond merely assigning the issue to the Juridical Commission, the administrative body that normally managed IOC legal issues. He deduced that assigning investigative duties to Pound and a number of Executive Board members (Thomas Bach, Kéba Mbaye, Jacques Rogge, and later Pál Schmitt) was the best course of action.

Samaranch's selection of Pound to chair the Ad Hoc Commission was purposeful. Though Samaranch provided the vision in the 1980s and 1990s concerning the IOC's transformation into a revenue-generating powerhouse by embracing corporate sponsorship through its TOP program and maximizing television rights fees, it was Pound, with vital support from Michael Payne and the IOC Marketing Department, who acted on this blueprint and secured the IOC's financial foundation. Pound spearheaded a series of fruitful negotiations with corporate sponsors and television executives eager to establish an affiliation with the Olympic Movement. He proved himself to be a good soldier and a credible face for the IOC in the media. Well spoken, polished, and yet no-nonsense in his approach to his dealings, he was the ideal selection. Samaranch understood the need to demonstrate to the television executives and corporate sponsor CEOs the IOC's commitment to determining the facts. They respected Pound, and his selection sent them the appropriate signal.[13]

Samaranch never forgave Pound for voting against a change in the age limit for IOC members in 1995 that permitted him to serve as IOC president through the 2000 Sydney Olympics;[14] however, he never doubted his commitment to the IOC and the Olympic Movement. Tapped by many pundits as one of the favorites to succeed Samaranch, who was scheduled to retire in 2001, Pound's appointment to lead the IOC inquiry did little to further those aspirations. The role of chief prosecutor was guaranteed to breed suspicion and a few enemies, a fact that Samaranch, according to a number of Olympic insiders who saw a more Machiavellian purpose in the appointment, recognized. Observers saw it as a first step on Samaranch's part to scuttle the Canadian's presidential aspirations.[15] However, at this time, Samaranch needed to appoint the individual best qualified to see the IOC through the investigation and was not concerned with his own eventual exit scenario. Pound's North American base was a bonus that better facilitated an on-site investigation in Salt Lake City. Although known for his ability to operate and maneuver effectively in the more dimly lit rooms of Olympic decision making, when it was time for him to step aside in 2001, Samaranch eschewed such shadowy plots by openly campaigning for one of Pound's rivals, and his eventual successor, Jacques Rogge.[16]

Samaranch established the Ad Hoc Commission when the Executive Board convened on December 11. Pound immediately reviewed SLOC's accounting records and concluded that the "evidence looked very damning at first glance." At a midday press briefing, one that Samaranch had asked him to chair, Pound reviewed the actions taken by the Executive Board, including the establishment of the Ad Hoc Commission, the receipt of a substantial number of files from SLOC, a pledge of complete cooperation from Salt Lake City officials in its investigation, and the firm decision not to withdraw the Games from Salt Lake City.[17]

## Marc Hodler: IOC Whistle-Blower

Members of the world's media dispatched to cover the otherwise mundane Executive Board meetings in Lausanne soon had their story. Executive Board member Marc Hodler, who labeled the Salt Lake City expenditures "not legitimate" and a "bribe" in earlier interviews with National Public Radio's Howard Berkes and the *Salt Lake Tribune*'s Mike Gorrell,[18] held a series of media scrums over the course of the Executive Board meetings during which he made a number of eyebrow-raising assertions. Wrote Stephen Wilson of the Associated Press: "Once Hodler started talking, what was a relatively routine IOC executive board meeting . . . turned into one of the most tumultuous three days in the organization's history."[19] Four agents, including an unnamed IOC member, charged Hodler, approached bid committees with promises of IOC members' votes in exchange for payments ranging from a half-million to one million dollars. Nagano's and Atlanta's recent wins had been tainted, he observed, and he further speculated for the now somewhat transfixed gaggle of reporters that between 5 percent and 7 percent of the

IOC's 115 members sought inducements in exchange for their votes.[20] "To my knowledge," he intoned, "there has always been a certain part of the vote given to corruption."[21] In another bombshell pronouncement, Hodler stated that the Agnelli family (owners of Fiat) distributed cars in support of Sestriere's successful campaign to host the 1997 World Skiing Championships and that a "foremost Swiss politician" informed him that Ferrari sport cars (built by a Fiat subsidiary) might be used by Turin to defeat Sion in the contest for the 2006 Olympic Winter Games.

Hodler's public comments left IOC officials, including Samaranch, Pound, Payne, and the IOC's director-general, François Carrard, aghast. A number of people in attendance wondered if Hodler had perhaps suffered "a stroke or some other mentally imbalancing medical episode."[22] Their collective frustration only climbed when Hodler later conceded to the Ad Hoc Commission that his charges were based on hearsay and that he could not proffer any definitive evidence.[23] Hodler adopted this public approach, he claimed, to prevent the issues from being "swept under the carpet," which had been his sense of the mind-set of a number of Executive Board members during an evening dinner meeting before its first session.[24]

Although perhaps startling in terms of its timing, Hodler's conduct should not have completely blindsided his colleagues. In the December days of his tenure as an IOC member, the eighty-year-old Hodler seized an opportunity to expose the seamy underbelly of Olympic commerce that had long vexed him. One of Samaranch's rivals in the 1980 presidential election, he unsuccessfully lobbied the Executive Board in 1986 to confront the rumors concerning bid committees' largesse and the willingness of some IOC members to accept gifts or benefits beyond that which would be considered reasonable.[25] In 1991 the unsuccessful Toronto '96 bid committee, known as TOOC, filed a detailed report with the IOC concerning the activities of unnamed IOC members and the pressures placed upon the bid committee to supply them with financial favors.[26] Samaranch and the Executive Board were again willing to look past the allegations. We need names, Samaranch responded, and with Toronto unwilling to provide those names given the city's hope to pursue the Games in a future bid competition, he once again neglected to take decisive action to curtail the IOC's burgeoning gift-giving culture.[27]

The Executive Board tasked Marc Hodler with drafting rules to govern IOC member interaction with bid committee officials during bid city visits. The result of this effort, the Hodler Rules, precluded IOC members from accepting gifts in excess of $150 in value;[28] however, importantly, no mechanisms were developed to monitor either IOC member conduct or bid committee compliance. The simmering crisis touched off by this crucial oversight exploded in Salt Lake City. "The Salt Lake City disaster," conceded Pound in his 2004 book, *Inside the Olympics*, was "in the works for years."[29]

With respect to Hodler's activities and events concerning the Olympic bid process in the 1980s and 1990s, the IOC hierarchy exhibited four classic defense mechanisms employed by individuals or groups to avoid dealing with a festering crisis: denial, disavowal, fixation, and intellectualization.[30] In dismissing Hodler's concerns in 1986, Samaranch initially denied the existence of a potential problem for the organization. Disavowal refers to acknowledging the possibility of a threat to an organization but minimizing its gravity.[31] When the Executive Board delegated to Hodler the duty to devise the Hodler Rules following the receipt of the report from TOOC in 1991, Samaranch and his colleagues recognized the threat. However, they did not fully engage themselves in tackling the issue. They did not establish an oversight body to monitor the actions of IOC members and bid committee officials, one that would seek to ensure that the parties (IOC members and bid committees) abided by the Hodler Rules. Such a body might not have prevented the most ingenious methods of exchange between bid committees and IOC members, but its mere presence and work would have demonstrated concern, ameliorated some of the worst criticism foisted on Samaranch and the organization by the media in 1999 (both of which were excoriated for their lax attitude), and signaled the unacceptable nature of these activities to the IOC members who required such a message. Samaranch also displayed fixation, or "the rigid commitment to a particular course of action or attitude in dealing with a threatening situation" when another course of action was advisable.[32] He failed to address the frequent rumors that surfaced concerning the ineffectiveness of the Hodler Rules. His steadfast demand for bid officials to name names rather than launching his own investigation of the rumors left the organization susceptible to a crisis such as the one that emerged in Salt Lake City. John Lucas, an Olympic historian, believes that definitive action from Samaranch would have stopped in their tracks those IOC members who transgressed the rules. "If Samaranch snapped his fingers, this wouldn't have happened," he observed.[33]

Samaranch set as a primary goal of his presidency the expansion and reach of the Olympic Movement across continents and cultures. In doing so, he welcomed into the Olympic family some members whose influence and gravitas in their respective regions assisted in this mission, but they lacked the sense of personal ethics one would desire. "In seeking universality," noted Richard Pound, "[Samaranch] had to make choices. He got some people in that were not as acquainted with the ethical values that you wish."[34] Samaranch's indifference concerning the rumors of discreditable conduct by some of the IOC members revealed that such activities, if contained, were acceptable if the Olympic Movement's influence and authority were secured and enhanced. A hesitancy to address the issue given the differing views of gift giving in cultures other than the ones associated with the Anglo-Saxon world, confirms Payne, existed. It was not a simple matter.[35] John Hancock's president and CEO, David D'Alessandro, a TOP sponsor and strident critic of Samaranch's handling of the crisis in the early months of 1999, pointed to Samaranch's past as a functionary in Francisco Franco's Spanish dictatorship, which "tolerated a good deal of corruption." South African IOC member Sam Ramsamy went so far as to speculate that Samaranch's apathy regarding the failure of the Hodler Rules stemmed from his desire to "not rock the boat" and to protect his past efforts to position himself for a Nobel Peace Prize.[36] Whatever the explanation, in failing to aggressively confront the members whose names surfaced over the years in the context of past bid processes, Samaranch displayed the fourth highlighted defense mechanism—intellectualization, specifically, "the elaborate rationalization of an action or thought."[37]

Samaranch's desire "to take the boycott agenda out of the Olympic lexicon" in light of the political problems enveloping the Olympic Movement in the 1970s and 1980s drove some of his decisions concerning the recruitment of IOC members.[38] The invitation to IOC membership issued to the Republic of the Congo's Jean-Claude Ganga, who soon emerged as one of the higher-profile members under investigation in connection with the Salt Lake City bid, is instructive. Samaranch viewed him as a resource for expanding the IOC's influence in Africa given his role as a leader of the 1976 Montreal boycott by more than twenty African nations and especially following his appointment to the IOC in 1986, when he completed a ten-year term as president of the Association of National Olympic Committees of Africa (1989–99). Samaranch's selection of Ganga to serve on an IOC delegation charged with the responsibility of ushering South Africa's return to the Olympic family prior to the 1992 Olympics surprised few observers.[39] "Did he personally like dealing with Ganga? I don't think so," offered Michael Payne. Ganga's place "inside the [IOC] tent," he observed, served a purpose, "and to the extent that Ganga, you know, lost an airline ticket now and then, wasn't the end of the world."[40] By the mid-1990s, Ganga looked for more than the value of an occasional first-class airline ticket from prospective host cities, as he was soon tied to gifts and benefits totaling $250,000 from Salt Lake City bidders.

### The IOC's Investigation Moves Forward

While retreating from the IOC Executive Board meetings, Richard Pound braced himself for the task ahead. Salt Lake City, stated Pound, offered the IOC the possibility of examining "hard evidence" of this type of corruption that had been long whispered about in Olympic circles. "There's a body of what I understand to be written evidence of cancelled cheques and things like that," he noted.[41] Pound sought to expedite the investigation, largely because of his belief that the IOC could not possibly move forward successfully with the World Conference on Doping in Sport that it was sponsoring in early February without having concluded its investigation.[42] "We want [the investigation] on the front burner and turned up high," commented Pound, "I told [SLOC] I want everything in the files before Christmas."[43] With Pound, SLOC's Board of Ethics, members of the world's media, the USOC, and the US Justice Department all rummaging through files and interviewing key actors before the end of December, and an unrepentant Tom Welch consenting to numerous media interviews, it was not surprising that a cascade of new allegations emerged in the public arena.

An additional series of disclosures cemented the IOC's fate at the center of the media crisis. Salt Lake City Hall officials granted Sibo Sibandze, son of David Sibandze, an IOC member from Swaziland, a one-year internship in October 1993.[44] Tom Welch, who freely chatted with reporters, confirmed that "visiting IOC members had been given gifts such as shotguns, skis and free lift tickets, airplane flyovers of Utah's arresting canyons, tickets to the opera and Utah Jazz basketball games and had been taken on hunting trips for pheasant" in an effort to secure support for the Salt Lake City bid. Intermountain Health Care, the state's largest health care provider, revealed that it supplied medical treatments (knee surgery, hepatitis treatment, and cosmetic surgery) at a cost of $27,675 to three individuals with "Olympic connections" (later shown to be Jean-Claude Ganga and two of his relatives) prior to Salt Lake City's triumph at the 1995 Budapest Session. "It is a process of wining and dining and building relationships," offered a far-from-contrite Welch. "I don't know any other way [we] could have done it."[45]

Meanwhile, the *Toronto Star* revealed that the Salt Lake bid committee retained Mahmoud El Farnawani, a Toronto businessman and self-styled Olympic agent, one of the four individuals identified by Marc Hodler, as a means of enlisting the support of Bashir Attarabulsi, an IOC member from Libya. Attarabulsi's son, Suhel, like Sonia Essomba, received tuition assistance to attend a US college (Brigham Young University), but Welch declined to elaborate on any role El Farnawani played in brokering such an arrangement.[46] Christer Persson, head of Ostersund's bid for the 2002 Olympic Winter Games, bristled at the series of revelations and called for Salt Lake City to compensate Ostersund (Sweden), Quebec City (Canada), and Sion (Switzerland), its rival bid cities, fourteen million dollars. "When Ben Johnson fooled others in Seoul, he lost his gold medal. This time, when we were cheated by a competitor, they will keep the gold medal due to practical reasons," groused Persson.[47] It was also too much for the *Toronto Star*, whose editorial writers recoiled at Welch's claim that the gift-giving program had been constructed "in the Olympic spirit because these people were their friends." In decrying the use of bribery by Salt Lake bidders and the corrupt actions of a number of IOC members, the newspaper reminded its readers that "these guys like to refer to themselves as the 'Olympic family.' If they're a family, they're the Corleones."[48] The stinging rebuke was but a harbinger of the media's vitriol for the IOC.

However, the media reaction provided only one source of stress for IOC leaders. With great concern, indeed alarm, it was realized that the fallout of the scandal jeopardized the Olympic Movement's relationship with the major sponsors who bankrolled much of the IOC's operation and provided vast sums of money to the Olympic organizing committees. Samaranch, Pound, and Payne phoned sponsor CEOs to express the IOC's "absolute resolve to address the problems as quickly and decisively as possible."[49] Payne outlined the IOC's initial response for sponsors in a letter written during the Executive Board meetings and soon thereafter embarked on missions to the United States and Japan to meet face-to-face with Olympic sponsors. When Pound convened the meeting of the IOC Marketing Commission in Munich on December 15, he promised an aggressive organizational response "so as to avoid any residual impact on the Olympic Games and the Movement as a whole." In a follow-up letter to the Coca-Cola Company chairman, Douglas Ivester, Pound stated that the IOC would not accept "impropriety among its membership."[50]

His new role prompted mixed feelings for Pound. He understood that the paper trail in Salt Lake City permitted the IOC to delve into an issue previously wrapped in "rumors and innuendo." Leading the IOC inquiry "is not an activity that I would have chosen as part of my Olympic responsibilities," Pound informed Ivester, "but it does provide a unique opportunity to confront a problem which troubles the overwhelming majority of the IOC membership."[51] Consultation with the sponsors confirmed the priority placed on these relationships, as well as the analysis of Dennis Howard, a business professor and sports marketing expert at the University of Oregon, who noted, "A very big part of the damage control is to maintain corporate allegiance."[52] Through mid-January 1999, Olympic sponsors withheld public comment, but privately "made it clear to the IOC that if the crisis was allowed to drag on and the IOC were not seen to have addressed the issues at hand, the consequences would be fatal for their Olympic partnerships."[53]

Over the course of the ensuing calendar year, Pound logged 149,700 air miles in service to the IOC, many of them related to managing the fallout from the Salt Lake City revelations.[54] This travel commenced with visits to Salt Lake City, New York, and Lausanne in late December and early January as part of his investigative duties. He also secured the assistance of Jim Asperger, a lawyer with O'Melveny and Myers and a former prosecuting attorney with the US Justice Department, to help him in steering the Ad Hoc Commission's investigation through the minefields of US law. A small working group composed of Pound, Thomas Bach, and François Carrard pored over the initial corpus of SLOC files in Lausanne in the first week of January, an action that provided much of the foundation for the recommendations forwarded to the Executive Board later in the month.[55] However, breathing room was not to be found, as more stories surfaced that did little to ease the pressure on Pound and his Ad Hoc Commission colleagues.

Though the IOC's travails were related to Salt Lake City, their public airing liberated a number of past Olympic bid committee officials who previously eschewed public comment on the shadier aspects of their bid experiences. Their comments further roiled the Olympic waters and ratcheted up the tension in the environment in which Pound and the Ad Hoc Commission labored. Rick Nerland, executive vice president of the Anchorage bid committees for the 1992 and 1994 Olympic Winter Games, reported that he had been approached by individuals in the 1980s, one from Asia and one from Africa, who informed him that cash could influence IOC member votes.[56] Jean Grenier, a representative of the Quebec City bid for the 2002 Olympic Winter Games, recalled his encounter with an Olympic "agent" while he sought to promote Quebec City at the IOC Session in Monte Carlo in 1993. Four or five agents approached him over the course of Quebec City's candidature, offering to assist the city with its "presentation and [to] provide greater access to IOC members for a fee between $20,000 and $50,000."[57] Graham Stringer, a key player in Manchester's bid for the 1996 and 2000 Olympics, observed that during one bid city visit, an IOC member claimed that a large sum of money (£12,000) had been stolen from his hotel room, and he sought reimbursement from the bid committee, while in other instances some "submitted double claims for first class air fares."[58] Combined with press revelations that members of the Amsterdam 1992 bid committee plied some members of the IOC for their votes with prostitutes, jewelry, and video cassette recorders, and that officials in Nagano spent an average of Can$33,000 on sixty-two visiting IOC members prior to the vote on the 1998 Olympic Winter Games, few envied Pound his newly minted position of authority.[59]

Pound was not alone in shouldering a heavy load on behalf of the IOC in the first few weeks of the crisis. Michael Payne and his colleagues in the Marketing Department put in long days, leaving them exhausted and drawn. "Completely knackered" was Payne's description of his physical condition in January 1999. Exhaustion was as much mental as it was physical, he reported, because Lausanne officials were worried about what stories might yet surface. They seemed to be flowing from the various ongoing investigations without pause. Carrard, Payne, and a number of other IOC staff members met on a daily basis in morning crisis management meetings in Lausanne to address new developments.[60] These discussions soon yielded the conclusion that the IOC was not properly staffed to manage the conflagration. The IOC's communications director, Franklin Servan-Schreiber, and a trainee fielded more than three hundred media inquiries in the first two days of the crisis. Carrard, with input from Payne, retained the services of Hill & Knowlton, an international public relations firm, to assist the IOC's Lausanne staff. Samaranch later registered his displeasure with this decision because of the cost (approximately $1.5 million by June 1999), the fact that he had not been consulted, and his impression that Hill & Knowlton did little to stem the volume of criticism of his leadership in the media. Despite Samaranch's misgivings, Payne believed that Hill & Knowlton's intervention proved "vital" to the IOC's efforts at damage control.[61]

Meanwhile, in early January, the expanding Salt Lake City scandal claimed David Johnson, SLOC's vice president and Tom Welch's right hand during the bidding process. SLOC president Frank Joklik forced Johnson to resign for being the coarchitect of Salt Lake City's gift-giving program. Joklik himself later resigned despite denials that he knew anything about Welch's and Johnson's lobbying practices (a claim contested vigorously by Welch).[62] The entire mess also hastened the decision of Salt Lake City mayor Deedee Corradini, an avowed booster of the city's efforts to host the Olympic Winter Games, not to seek reelection.[63] Ensnared by the US Justice Department and USOC probes, Alfredo LaMont, the USOC official in charge of international relations, also tendered his resignation because of an "undisclosed business relationship" with Tom Welch's bid committee.[64] And for those Utah morning newspaper readers caught up in the exploding allegations, the *Salt Lake Tribune*'s Greg Burton divulged that the Federal Bureau of Investigation

(FBI), on behalf of the US Justice Department, was looking into possible con-
nections between the bid committee and the city's escort services.[65] Burton's
report raised the eyebrows of even the least-pious members of Salt Lake City's
Mormon community.

## Sydney Rocked by Scandal

Sydney, less than twenty-one months from welcoming the Olympic world
Down Under, also became the target of media scrutiny amid news that the
bid committee funneled A\$2 million to the Australian Olympic Committee
(AOC) to establish a training center for twenty-two African athletes at Can-
berra's world-class Australian Institute for Sport as a means of luring votes
from the African continent. Since 1994 the athletes, who hailed from eleven
African countries, had received \$9,000 per year. When those payments were
scheduled to cease in 1999, the AOC targeted the remaining funds to offset
some of the costs incurred from establishing a pre-Sydney Olympics training facility for African athletes.[66] Subsequently, the press learned that Australian Olympic Committee president John Coates gave IOC members Francis
Nyangweso (Uganda) and Charles Mukora (Kenya) an additional \$70,000
on the eve of the vote in 1993 to supplement the previously pledged support.
Coates believed Sydney's grasp on the hosting prize was loosening in the
waning hours before the vote, and his deal with Nyangweso and Mukora was
his midnight roll of the dice to firm up those two votes from the African continent.[67] Given that Sydney defeated Beijing by a vote of forty-five to forty-three
on the final ballot the next day, the optics of Coates's lobbying efforts, in the
current media climate, were extremely negative.

This news released a torrent of media scrutiny of the Sydney Organizing
Committee at a time when its energies needed to be focused on the challenge
of hosting the 2000 Summer Olympics. Mere days earlier, Sydney organizers
issued a public call for the IOC to ensure that those members who breached
IOC rules were "sacked."[68] They implored the IOC to root out corruption and
do everything possible to "rebuild public confidence" in the Sydney Olympics, given developments in Salt Lake City.[69] It was a classic case of needing to
be careful about what one wishes for. The episode added some drama to the
looming Executive Board meeting with Richard Pound's Ad Hoc Commission because Samaranch sensed a second scandal—Sydney's bidding efforts

called into question and the city's Olympic organizers confronted with a crisis. Might the Executive Board pull the Sydney Olympics from New South Wales's capital?[70]

## John Hancock CEO David D'Alessandro Steps Forward

Within the TOP sponsor community, Coca-Cola and the United Parcel Service (UPS) issued statements of support for the IOC and the Olympic Movement and encouraged the IOC to confront the issue of IOC member conduct and the Olympic bid process aggressively.[71] Still, the collective restraint of TOP sponsors in the public forum displayed a commitment to provide the IOC an opportunity to follow through on promises made by Samaranch, Pound, and Payne when the scandal burst forth. In mid-January, however, from his spacious office in the John Hancock Tower on Copley Square in Boston's Back Bay, John Hancock president and CEO David D'Alessandro determined that Olympic leaders required some prodding. D'Alessandro believed that the IOC's early response lacked focus and a needed sense of urgency.[72]

In the first six months of 1999, D'Alessandro roasted the IOC through repeated media interviews and, on occasion, authored op-ed pieces for major newspapers. He emerged as a frequent correspondent with Richard Pound, who attempted over time, not always with success, to temper D'Alessandro's comments.[73] Michael Payne, IOC Executive Board member Kevan Gosper (Australia), and NBC president of sports Dick Ebersol all questioned D'Alessandro's public sniping at the IOC and his perception that the organization was dealing with needed reform measures at a "lethargic pace."[74] Pound later admitted that D'Alessandro's approach, one that often caused a measure of discomfort for him and his colleagues, left the IOC little room to waver in its commitment to meaningful reform, and in so doing provided an important service to the organization.[75] D'Alessandro's decision in early 1999 to challenge the IOC to act with more resolve through frequent media interviews and his use of provocative language were calculated. He sought to maintain pressure on Samaranch and his colleagues and protect his company's investment (in excess of forty million dollars) in the Olympic brand;[76] however, this point was only one of a number of internal issues at John Hancock that influenced his actions.

D'Alessandro was one of the primary architects of John Hancock's sponsor relationship with the IOC in the early 1990s. Within his 150-member
executive group, some individuals supported the decision, while others
expressed opposition. The scandal left those persons originally opposed
to the decision questioning the company's position and even a number of
executives who supported D'Alessandro's acquisition of John Hancock's
TOP sponsor status expressing doubts. Compounding his difficulties were
concerns about the scandal from a very vocal sales force and threats from a
significant number of John Hancock customers that they would "walk away"
from the company. In the insurance business, the ideas of "trust" and "credibility," explained D'Alessandro, are key considerations. You do not have
packaged goods to sell, but you are promising customers that "your money
will be there when you need it." The qualities of the Olympic brand, such
as integrity, truthfulness, and purity of sport, meshed well with John Hancock's marketing mission, stated D'Alessandro. However, the Salt Lake City
scandal and the resulting damage to the IOC's trust and credibility left his
company extremely exposed.[77]

Of particular concern to D'Alessandro some four or five weeks into the
crisis was that the IOC was in "complete denial" with respect to the severity
of the situation. "Scandals hit everybody," he concluded, "but how they [the
IOC] handled it was appalling. . . . Samaranch needed to do everything to
protect the Olympic brand, but failed to recognize the depth of the problem" from the outset. D'Alessandro did not appreciate a phone call from
Michael Payne in which he was advised to "say nothing." He confirmed that
this call was made to other TOP CEOs and that Payne's counsel was not
framed in the form of a threat. Still, he did not think that Payne or any other
IOC official should have dispensed advice on how to manage his company.
"Americans are sometimes guilty of not understanding other cultures, but
in this case," observed D'Alessandro, "the IOC had little understanding of
how the U.S. media and Congress would react" and how dogged they would
be in their grilling of the IOC for its shortcomings. He believed a lack of
understanding on these two fronts contributed to the ultimate severity of
the scandal.[78]

D'Alessandro's motivation also reflected a need to protect two ongoing
corporate initiatives. First, John Hancock chairman Stephen L. Brown and

D'Alessandro pursued the transformation of John Hancock from a mutual company, owned by its policyholders, to one that would be publicly traded. "We had 300 million shares to sell," noted D'Alessandro. Second, in the 1990s, John Hancock sought to expand its business operations into Asian markets such as China, Japan, and Taiwan. In order to achieve its expansion goals, John Hancock required access to governments and capital partners in these regions. The added profile resulting from the company's TOP sponsor status aided this mission. By the late 1990s, D'Alessandro concluded that the Games would soon be awarded to China. The TOP platform afforded John Hancock a means of "leapfrogging the competition" in these Asian markets, especially China, and D'Alessandro viewed it as important and worthy of protection.[79]

Collectively, an agitated sales force, angered customers, dissent within his executive group, as well as John Hancock's impending transition to a publicly traded company and its goals for Asian expansion resulted in "severe" pressure on D'Alessandro in terms of managing the company's interests in the context of the scandal. He was motivated to remain in the TOP sponsor group but clearly needed to do his utmost to ensure that the IOC dealt with its institutional shortcomings to fend off sources of pressure within his own company. He understood that Richard Pound had a clear understanding of the threat posed by the US Congress and media, and why he was advocating swift action, but D'Alessandro concluded that the IOC as an organization, and Samaranch in particular, did not.[80] Internal company issues, as well as his own observations of the IOC's early management of the crisis and Samaranch's disposition, contributed to his decision to maintain pressure on the IOC through frequent interaction with the media.

D'Alessandro's public comments in January were most assuredly colorful but are also classified as constructive. "Boardrooms will shake if this is mishandled," thundered D'Alessandro in an interview with *New York Times* Olympic reporter Jere Longman, one of a number of journalists who capitalized in the ensuing weeks on D'Alessandro's willingness to share his thoughts on the IOC's response to the Salt Lake City scandal. D'Alessandro encouraged the IOC to engage in a thorough examination of past Olympic bids, as the organization had only one chance with the sponsors to "purge itself." "You only get one bite of this apple," he cautioned. D'Alessandro further noted that a second scandal would be anathema for the sponsors. "If they attempt to line

up 12 IOC members and shoot them and think they can go back to Switzerland, they're wrong," he counseled.[81]

Within the week, when John Krimsky Jr., the USOC's deputy secretary-
general and managing director for business affairs, noted some "uneasiness"
within the US sponsor community toward the Salt Lake City Games in light
of recent events, D'Alessandro echoed those thoughts in his inimitable fashion: "The IOC's sponsorships have become radioactive. All corporate Geiger
counters are off the chart. [The IOC has] got to find a way to make sponsorships safe again." As for the likelihood that Samaranch could emerge from
the scandal as the IOC's president, D'Alessandro stated, "I think he survives if
his changes are extraordinary, sweeping, and he shows extraordinary courage
as a leader. And he takes no prisoners and recognizes that all he has built is
in jeopardy."[82] D'Alessandro's blistering criticism of Samaranch and the IOC
emerged following the IOC Executive Board meeting with Richard Pound's
Ad Hoc Commission in late January and stemmed from his unwillingness
to accept what he considered the slow pace of reform in Lausanne and the
IOC's refusal to label John Coates's offer to Charles Mukora and Francis
Nyangweso a bribe.

## All Eyes on Lausanne

For now D'Alessandro, his sponsor colleagues, organizing committee officials
in Salt Lake City and Sydney, and other Olympic observers turned their collective gaze to Lausanne, as the IOC Executive Board prepared to receive
recommendations drafted by Pound's Ad Hoc Commission. While attending
the Sports Summit in New York City en route to Lausanne, Pound delivered
a somber, heartfelt apology to the Salt Lake City community: "Of all the host
cities I've been involved with—and there have been many, including a couple
in my own country—the Salt Lake City community is as respected, ethical,
and honorable a group as I have ever known." He confirmed Samaranch's
commitment to reform that held IOC members "to the highest standards."[83]
He acknowledged that Salt Lake City's expenses in search of IOC member
votes through cash payments and benefits might have exceeded $750,000.[84]
In an interview with the *Toronto Star*'s Randy Starkman, Pound demonstrated that despite the frenetic past few weeks, he had not lost his sense of
humor. In discussing the oft-mentioned issue of rumors of past IOC member

misconduct and the inability or lack of desire on the IOC's part to deal with wayward members, Pound offered, "You heard enough rumours and it's easy to say where there's that much smoke, there must be some fire. . . . That's a very comforting adage, but when you go to someone and say, 'We're hearing this about you,' they'd say, 'There's absolutely nothing to it. Look at my halo. You can hardly see me for the radiance,'" Pound noted. "At that point, you don't have any evidence, you've got to put up or shut up. What you hope is that if someone has maybe been a little indiscreet, that will stop them from doing it in the future," he concluded.[85] Still, when queried by the press why he could possibly have gone ahead with a holiday in Barbados the previous week when the IOC was consumed by scandal, Pound's blunt response reflected the anxiety and stress of the past two months: "I think one week every six years is not too much. I don't do this crap for a living. I promised my family I would go on a holiday and I did."[86]

In advance of the Ad Hoc Commission meetings with the Executive Board in Lausanne on January 24, Samaranch invited written responses from thirteen IOC members who had been identified for possible censure by the Ad Hoc Commission as a result of its review of SLOC's files. Samaranch informed the Associated Press that the list comprised nine individuals accused of serious breaches of conduct, while four were charged with less serious offenses. "We had wonderful years. We had very successful games. And now we are in a storm," Samaranch wistfully noted in his forty-minute interview. A new bid process was required, and the IOC was considering instituting a code of conduct for its members, confirmed the IOC's boss.[87] Media reporting revealed the names of the thirteen members: Jean-Claude Ganga, David Sibandze, Bashir Attarabulsi, Agustin Arroyo (Ecuador), Sergio Santander Fantini (Chile), Anton Geesink (Netherlands), Un Yong Kim (South Korea), Vitaly Smirnov (Russia), Lamine Keita (Mali), Charles Mukora (Kenya), Zein El Abdin Ahmed Abdel Gadir (Sudan), Louis Guirandou-N'Diaye (Ivory Coast), and Pirjo Häggman (Finland).[88] Two of the implicated members, Häggman and Attarabulsi, resigned before Pound presented his report in Lausanne. Häggman's ex-husband, Bjarne, had accepted a job from a Utah-based engineering firm and served as a paid consultant with the bid committee. Attarabulsi's son's tuition payments and living expenses funneled from Salt Lake City's NOC Assistance Program had been well chronicled in the press.[89]

3. A somewhat harried-looking Richard Pound prepares to enter the conference hall to address those persons gathered for the International Sport Summit and Conference in New York City on January 21, 1999. IOC marketing director Michael Payne is pictured to Pound's right. *Source:* Timothy A. Clarey/AFP/Getty Images.

The scene was now set. Members of the Executive Board descending on Lausanne recognized the need for expressions of public support for their embattled president who faced an increasing number of calls for his resignation. "President Samaranch has an enormous amount of experience in managing the IOC through both good and bad times," stated Pound (the bad times denoting the troubled boycott era that served as the backdrop for Samaranch's move to Lausanne in 1980). "Right now, we need that stability more than ever. No one is more determined to correct this situation than he is," he concluded. "If ever we need a good president, an experienced president, we need him now," chimed in Kevan Gosper. Marc Hodler noted that "if [Samaranch] goes, then I would have to go. All the honest people would have to go. It's the honest people who should stay." In expressing her support for Samaranch, Anita DeFrantz, a member of the IOC Executive Board and a former US Olympic rower, asserted that Samaranch "has taken us through several crises and we can get through this one with his leadership." Samaranch himself expressed his resolute determination to lead the IOC through these dark days.[90] They all sought to put on a brave face for the scores of reporters gathered in Lausanne. Still, nothing could alter the gloomy atmosphere as Jacques Rogge turned to scribes and jostling photographers before entering the Château de Vidy for the Ad Hoc Commission's meeting on January 23 where implicated members would have an opportunity to challenge the commission's findings. "This is a sad day," Rogge noted ruefully, "but we will do what we have to do."[91]

# 3

# Survival Mode

### The Ad Hoc Commission Weighs In

On January 24, a phalanx of reporters and photographers greeted IOC Executive Board members when they entered the IOC's Château de Vidy headquarters. Juan Antonio Samaranch and his colleagues understood the need for decisive action and the perilous consequences of a less than resolute approach. A fifteen-hour marathon meeting of the Ad Hoc Commission held the previous day afforded implicated IOC members an opportunity to respond to the commission's findings.[1] These deliberations resulted in recommendations from Richard Pound and his colleagues for the expulsion of seven members (Agustin Arroyo, Zein El Abdin Ahmed Abdel Gadir, Jean-Claude Ganga, Lamine Keita, Charles Mukora, David Sibandze, and Sergio Santander Fantini), a warning for Anton Geesink, and the need for continued examination of three cases (Vitaly Smirnov, Un Yong Kim, and Guirandou N'Diaye).[2]

Samaranch commenced the proceedings at 10:20 a.m. and invited Richard Pound to brief his Executive Board colleagues on the investigative process. The labor, said Pound, was "the most discouraging and depressing work he had ever had to do." His initial examination of SLOC's files provided to the IOC at the time of the Executive Board meeting in December revealed "a major problem." SLOC possessed a file on each IOC member with records of financial activity, and some of those files contained "suspicious-looking" entries detailing payments to the member, dependents, or third parties. Further examination of the records by Ad Hoc Commission members over the ensuing weeks, along with the hearings of the previous day, provided the foundation for the recommendations. They would have benefited from more time to conduct their work, Pound conceded; however, no one understood the true nature and scope of the investigative demands when they commenced their efforts. He compared their role to the function assumed by a "fire brigade." The Ad Hoc Commission "put many of the fires out quickly and . . . banked down others," stated Pound.[3]

Samaranch and the Executive Board decided to "temporarily exclude" the seven members in anticipation of a vote on their possible expulsion by the full IOC Session in March; however, their fate represented only one element of the discussion. Kéba Mbaye, Kevan Gosper, and François Carrard were tasked with establishing terms of reference for the Ethics Commission that would oversee issues pertaining to IOC member conduct in the future. In the meantime, the Ad Hoc Commission was left to pursue existing and new cases. Carrard and Jacques Rogge were dispatched to Sydney to deal with the fallout from the recent revelations concerning John Coates's decision in 1993 to offer both Charles Mukora and Francis Nyangweso, IOC members from Kenya and Uganda, respectively, thirty-five thousand dollars on the eve of the vote for the 2000 Summer Olympic host city.[4] Sydney's final-ballot triumph by two votes over Beijing only added to the miserable optics of the situation. The Executive Board concurred with the Ad Hoc Commission's recommendation that Samaranch correspond with all bid committees dating back to the 1996 competition in an attempt to solicit additional information that would assist in the IOC's investigation.[5] It was an attempt to get ahead of the story such that the IOC would not be blindsided by an additional slew of unexpected and damaging allegations.

## Searching for, but Not Finding, Light at the End of the Tunnel

Before tackling the press conference at day's end, the Executive Board convened with four representatives of Hill & Knowlton, whose services had been retained soon after the outset of the crisis to steer the IOC's media response. Alan Elias, a veteran of the company's work in relation to the Bhopal, Three Mile Island, and Swissair 111 disasters, observed that "in all his years of experience he had never seen such a media frenzy." The delegation advised the Executive Board that any IOC member assigned responsibility for interface with the media needed to push a "consistent message" and employ "unified language." Executive Board members sifted through an extensive binder of information supplied by Elias and his colleagues geared to shoring up the IOC's image. Despite the presence (and efforts) of Hill & Knowlton officials to give some comfort, a gloomy atmosphere prevailed. Pál Schmitt tried to bolster the resolve of his colleagues before the meeting adjourned when he pledged that "every member of the Executive Board and staff [had worked] day and night to help the President overcome the present crisis affecting the Olympic Movement, and would continue to work under his leadership to re-establish the position which the IOC had enjoyed for more than 100 years."[6]

"This is the beginning, not the end of our work," offered Samaranch to the assembled media horde, and "I am certain," he continued hopefully, "the Olympic Movement will emerge from the crisis stronger than ever."[7] In a move designed to appease the IOC's media critics, and demonstrate an understanding of the severity of the crisis, Samaranch announced that the sus-pension of member visits to 2006 bid cities continued and that an appointed panel of fifteen individuals, a mix of IOC members and sports experts, would select the host city later in the year.[8] Samaranch clearly indicated that Sydney and Salt Lake City, irrespective of questions concerning the actions of John Coates, Tom Welch, and David Johnson during the respective bid processes, retained their host-city privileges for the 2000 Summer Olympics and 2002 Olympic Winter Games.[9] Samaranch also revealed the plans for the Ethics Commission and the broadening of the IOC's investigation to include past bids. He refused to resign, but he indicated that a vote of confidence in his leadership would take place at the IOC Session in March when the member-ship considered the recommendations for the expulsion of Ganga, Arroyo, Gadir, Keita, Fantini, and Mukora (David Sibandze resigned during the course of the Executive Board meeting). Samaranch sought to expedite the work of the March Session by pressing Ganga and the others to avoid drawing out the process: "These members have done great harm to the Olympic ideal. Now their greatest service to the Olympic movement is to accept their fate," intoned Samaranch.[10] Drawn and tired, he expressed his "deepest apology to the athletes, the people of Salt Lake City and Utah, the global Olympic fam-ily and the millions of citizens worldwide who love and respect the games."[11]

Perhaps the most relieved individual on the dais with Samaranch was Australia's Kevan Gosper. The past forty-eight hours had been extremely trying for the IOC Executive Board member and former chairman and CEO of Shell Australia. But he breathed a little easier as Samaranch addressed the media. Two days earlier (Friday, January 22) during a press conference designed to spell out the agenda for the Executive Board's upcoming deliberations, American reporters queried François Carrard on John Coates's first public pronouncements concerning his deal with Charles Mukora and Francis Nyangweso. Gosper sat stunned at the rear of the auditorium, as he had knowledge of neither Coates's actions in 1993 nor his release of this information to the Australian media. Coates revealed later that he learned of China's offer to build a new highway in Mali and believed it dwarfed Sydney's offer of a three-month training opportunity at Australia's renowned Institute of Sport for twenty-two African athletes. Sydney's dream, stated Coates, "was slipping away."[12] This realization prompted his dinner conversation with Mukora and Nyangweso that resulted in the additional funds being offered contingent on a Sydney victory.

Sensing trouble, Gosper tried desperately to contact Coates in Sydney, where it was midnight, but with no success. He spoke to a clearly discomfited Samaranch, who thought a second bid scandal was about to explode, and then spent an uncomfortable evening waiting to speak to Coates, whom he finally reached at midnight (Lausanne time). Gosper also contacted fellow Australian IOC member Phil Coles and Olympics minister Michael Knight. The four power brokers of Australian sport conversed on numerous occasions over the ensuing twenty-four hours, and Coates pledged to fax a full explanation of the situation to Samaranch. This fax duly arrived in the waning hours before the Executive Board meeting on Sunday morning (January 24), and Samaranch and Gosper pored over it for thirty minutes. Samaranch expressed his satisfaction with the explanation, as bid cities were permitted by the IOC to offer such financial support for sport initiatives if they were tied to "official audited programmes." They proceeded to the Executive Board meeting, where Samaranch voiced his support for Sydney and Salt Lake City maintaining their host-city status.[13]

## Scandals, the Media, and Early 1999

For individuals with a penchant for reveling in the misery and missteps of others, there was plenty of high-profile fodder in the months of January and

February 1999. Juan Antonio Samaranch faced repeated calls for his resignation as IOC president, given that the corruption evident in the Olympic bid
process evolved on his watch and that he ignored signals of such activity well
before the conflagration in Salt Lake City. In Washington, DC, US president Bill Clinton and his advisers failed to fend off an impeachment process
on charges of perjury and obstruction of justice owing to conduct related
to his sexual relationship with Monica Lewinsky.[14] Jacques Santer, president
of the European Commission (EC), fought gamely to maintain his position
and safeguard the standing of his EC colleagues, who were flayed for their
inability to account for $5 billion of the previous year's $107 billion budget.[15]
In England events leading to the recent resignation of Prime Minister Tony
Blair's secretary of state for trade and industry, Peter Mandelson, continued
to be dissected. Without disclosing the arrangement to Blair, Mandelson, a
key architect of the "New Labour" movement, accepted a £373,000 interest-
free loan from Geoffrey Robinson, a fellow Labour member of Parliament,
to fund the purchase of a home in London. While Robinson still held the
loan, Mandelson's department launched an investigation of his business
affairs, establishing a conflict of interest for the minister that became part of
the public record.[16] Clinton, Santer, and Mandelson provided company for
Samaranch and his colleagues in the media's crosshairs; however, what distin-
guished the IOC's circumstance was the global nature of the media scrutiny.

Datops and Sportweb analyzed the Salt Lake City crisis by sampling
thirty-five hundred newspaper or press agency sources in six different languages (English, French, German, Italian, Spanish, and Portuguese) through
the use of semiotic technology. In the days leading up to the meeting of the
Ad Hoc Commission and Executive Board, three themes dominated the
press coverage: Samaranch and the IOC had been aware of the excessive
gift culture surrounding the bid process and had done nothing, IOC members did not adhere to the organization's own rules for conduct, and the IOC
was "secretive and arrogant." The meetings at the end of January represented
the high-water mark of press coverage in terms of volume of articles. More
than three hundred articles on the IOC in the American press alone were
collected per day, which represented a sevenfold increase in press attention
on the organization over what had been witnessed at the time of the 1998
Nagano Olympic Winter Games.[17]

From a personal standpoint, the IOC's damage-control efforts on this late-January weekend, ones that yielded negligible results with the media, disappointed Samaranch. Calls for his resignation multiplied, and many observers openly questioned the IOC's ability to champion the fight against doping in sport, one of the main goals of the upcoming World Conference on Doping in Sport. The world's dailies sounded their disgust and frustration with the IOC's overall response, and even if they were not unanimous in their call for Samaranch's resignation, the pressure on the Spaniard mounted. "Chaos still reigns. Samaranch cannot be trusted to carry out the necessary clean-up. He must go," concluded Melbourne's *Herald Sun*. The *Chicago Sun-Times*, *Atlanta Journal Constitution*, and New Zealand's *Waikato Times* echoed these sentiments.[18] Germany's *Bild* stated that "the IOC has been exposed as a pig sty. . . . [T]he only way to save the Games is for a new, strong president to take over and really clean it up."[19] Samaranch's stubbornness and desire to remain in office meant that "a nasty odor still clings to the IOC," according to Holland's *Trouwit*. Norway's *Verdens Gang* joined the chorus of those papers seeking Samaranch's scalp: "The IOC has exposed itself. The organization is rotten. That is something Samaranch can't run away from."[20] England's *Daily Telegraph* and the *Times* and Switzerland's *Tribune de Geneve* and *Basler Zeitung* expressed no confidence in his ability to usher in a reform agenda and urged Samaranch to take the "honorable path" he advocated that Ganga and the others follow.[21] Michael Wilbon of the *Washington Post* highlighted the "shakedown climate" that evolved within the bid city process on Samaranch's watch and confessed surprise at the media's newfound interest in the IOC's gift-giving culture. "I'm at a total loss to explain why the IOC folks are coming under scrutiny only now," wrote Wilbon. "It's not unlike waiting until last week to proclaim that the world isn't flat." Wilbon, too, called for Samaranch's ouster.[22]

Similarly, members of the athlete community delivered a stinging rebuke of Samaranch and the IOC. Canadian Mark Tewksbury, a 1992 Olympic gold medalist in swimming, stormed out of a news conference in Toronto in disgust, leaving his gold medal for anyone who desired it, as for him it no longer had meaning.[23] Tewksbury called for Samaranch's resignation. Graham Bell, a former British downhill skier, likened the IOC membership to a "bunch of crooks." Olympic champion Sebastian Coe, who, along with Paul Deighton, is now ably steering London toward its Olympic host experience in 2012, did not think the IOC would be well served by Samaranch's resignation, but maintained the implicated members should have been "sacked" without being offered the opportunity to resign. He labeled the crisis "the most disfiguring episode in the life of the International Olympic Committee."[24] The tenor of these public comments and the scathing media treatment of the IOC president prompted a response from Samaranch, as well as IOC members.

## Against the Ropes, Samaranch Fights Back

Samaranch issued a counterattack to the media's criticism. IOC members identified the hazards that his resignation amid these turbulent times might entail. "I am pleased with myself, what I have done these 18 years," said Samaranch. He expressed pride in the status of the Olympic Games on the sport calendar and in society. Fending off charges of a luxurious personal lifestyle funded by the IOC's coffers, Samaranch stated, "I am not a rich man. I am a normal man. My style of life is the same for many, many years. I have no yachts. I have no planes."[25] He would not be driven from office by "outside people" and could not accept the thought of resigning.[26] "To resign in this moment when the boat is in a storm, this is not my style," stated Samaranch.[27] Meanwhile, IOC members including Mario Pescante, Gunilla Lindberg, Richard Pound, Marc Hodler, Niels Horst-Sørenson, Rene Fasel, and Denis Oswald provided public expressions of confidence in Samaranch's leadership. Samaranch, they argued, would be critical to the IOC in its effort to emerge from the current crisis.[28] Bruce Kidd, an Olympic historian and former Canadian Olympian, seemed best able to capture Samaranch's thinking and the prevailing view in Lausanne regarding the need for Samaranch to stay. Concluded Kidd, "It provides some measure of stability. The efforts of reform won't be complicated by electioneering for succession. If he resigns now, he resigns in disgrace. . . . [I]f he thinks his historical legacy is in the balance," Samaranch would be highly motivated to take the necessary action to put the IOC on a new and more promising path.[29]

While disappointed and concerned by the nature of the continuing media coverage, Olympic leaders were under no illusion that decisions flowing from the Executive Board meeting would demonstrably alter the dominant media narrative overnight. François Carrard warned his colleagues of the "the difficult ride" awaiting the IOC over the course of the next week prior to the scheduled WCDS.[30] Clearly, Carrard understood the depth of the IOC's troubles. *Time, Newsweek,* and *Sports Illustrated* all published lengthy investigative articles presenting less than flattering portrayals of Samaranch and the IOC's oversight of the bidding process.[31] African IOC members Sam Ramsamy (South Africa) and Kéba Mbaye (Senegal) defended the IOC against charges that it had targeted African IOC members in its investigation.[32] Rome's mayor, Francesco Rutelli, challenged the result of the vote on the site of the 2004 Summer Olympics. The IOC Evaluation Commission ranked Rome ahead of Athens, observed Rutelli, and "the Eternal City" was clearly leading twenty-four hours prior to the vote when IOC members were polled. And then, "who knows what happened?" exclaimed Rutelli. Italian IOC members, he noted, believed a significant number of IOC members from Latin America and Africa switched their preference to Athens just prior to the vote.[33] There too remained the likes of the *Pittsburgh Post-Gazette's* Lori Shontz, who continued hammering away for Samaranch's resignation: "[Samaranch] has made the Olympics such a valuable commodity, and lived such a royal lifestyle while doing it, that he implicitly encouraged the extreme behavior by the Olympic family and the bid cities. Which is exactly why he should resign. Because if he doesn't, this will be another example of the fat cat who presided over the problems abdicating responsibility as the little guys—in this case, IOC members from Third World countries, bid committees and taxpayers—get a raw deal."[34] For IOC officials at the center of the crisis in Lausanne, reviewing the IOC's daily clipping service with one's morning coffee had long lost its appeal.

There was some encouraging news from the sponsor community for Samaranch, Pound, and members of the IOC's Marketing Department in the immediate aftermath of the Executive Board's action. Michael Payne's tour of Japan and North America to hold face-to-face meetings with TOP sponsor CEOs, and Richard Pound's dialogue with these same individuals, paid dividends. The UK magazine *Marketing* contacted eight of the eleven sponsors, including Coca-Cola, IBM, and Visa. All pledged their continued support for the Sydney Games. Even David D'Alessandro, the self-appointed and outspoken watchdog for the Olympic sponsors, gave Samaranch and the Executive Board a passing grade for its recent declarations. "The IOC went further than most people would have expected," stated D'Alessandro, who believed Samaranch deserved an opportunity to push through the reform agenda. Still, D'Alessandro gave the IOC president a short leash. "The moment he is seen as not carrying through with them in the future, he should be removed," he observed.[35]

With money and resources having been directed to their Sydney operations for some time, it would have been a difficult decision for TOP sponsors to walk away from their plans in Australia. What really rested in the balance were their decisions with respect to renewal or continuance of TOP agreements for the 2001–4 quadrennium. Despite the public affirmation for the Sydney Games by the majority of TOP sponsors, sponsor defection (post-Sydney) was a real threat. The IOC might very well have been able to recruit replacement sponsors. For example, one can envision PepsiCo relishing an opportunity to replace Coca-Cola as a TOP sponsor if president and CEO Douglas Ivester and his management team divested Coca-Cola of its TOP sponsorship. However, a large-scale defection of TOP sponsors would have tarnished the IOC's image, compromised the investment in nurturing the Olympic brand during Samaranch's presidency, and likely diminished the sponsorship dollars available to the organizing committees in Salt Lake City and Athens because of a compromised negotiating environment awaiting IOC officials.

Although sponsors, including D'Alessandro, regarded the steps taken by Samaranch and the IOC at its January Executive Board meetings as appropriate, their collective patience diminished greatly in the wake of the negative press enveloping the Olympic enterprise after the WCDS and the release mere days later of the investigative report of the Salt Lake Organizing Committee's Board of Ethics. Managing the sponsors and the media continued to consume the members of the IOC's leadership hierarchy in the weeks leading up to the 108th Extraordinary IOC Session in March.

## The World Conference on Doping in Sport: Intrigue Was in the Air

The WCDS delivered a setback to Samaranch in his campaign to restore credibility to the IOC's image. His effort to install himself as the president of the planned World Anti-Doping Agency was blocked by government officials and further compromised by Prince Alexandre de Merode, the longtime chairman of the IOC's Medical Commission, and Johann Olav Koss, head of the IOC Athletes' Commission. Koss believed the effort to establish the new body's credibility with athletes necessitated leadership other than Samaranch's.[36] Prince de Merode claimed he offered many of the same proposals under discussion in the past ten years, but Samaranch did not support him, and they "had been shot down in flames."[37] Bill Clinton's drug czar, Barry McCaffrey, and Germany's minister of the interior, Otto Schily, dismissed the notion that the IOC should control the agency. Government officials also lectured Samaranch and his colleagues on the need for a complete overhaul of the IOC's operations: "The British Government," declared Tony Banks, the British minister of sport, "expects the IOC to clean up its act."[38] Even IOC Executive Board members Richard Pound and Anita DeFrantz expressed concerns about the prospect of Samaranch at the helm of the agency.[39]

The IOC's lack of moral authority or ethical foundation to lead the fight against doping was a dominant theme in the utterances of a parade of individuals who spoke at the WCDS. "Hardly a single speaker," recalled Pound, "missed the chance to comment on the perfidy and corruption of the IOC and its general unworthiness." A beleaguered Samaranch, commented Tom Humphries of the *Irish Times*, "chaired the proceedings with the wounded solemnity of a condemned man gnawing his final meal." No doubt drawing satisfaction from Samaranch's plight, Andrew Jennings, one of Samaranch's most strident critics and a coauthor of *Dishonored Games: Corruption, Money, and Greed at the Olympics*, commented that "when you develop this belief that you walk slightly above the surface of the globe, there's a long way to fall."[40] For Samaranch, the two-day conference proved largely forgettable, despite the adoption of a six-point resolution by sport officials and government representatives that established a framework for the World Anti-Doping Agency.

Intrigue dominated the subplots in Lausanne during the WCDS. One or more of the members recommended for expulsion lashed out at his or their accusers through a smear campaign. In a series of anonymous faxes described by the *Wall Street Journal* as an exercise in "character assassination," Jacques Rogge, Pál Schmitt, Richard Pound, and François Carrard were targeted.[41] Allegations within the faxes sent to news outlets by an unidentified party from a copy shop in Great Neck, New York, included "affairs between IOC members, shady business contracts, double-dealing and consorting with prostitutes."[42] "Different people fight different ways when they get into a corner," offered IOC member Tay Wilson of New Zealand.[43] "It's like 'I, Claudius,'" commented Robert Storey, president of the International Bobsleigh Federation, who labeled his Lausanne visit a "three-day stopover for innuendo." Some IOC officials believed Barry McCaffrey had another agenda during his stay in Lausanne. They suspected he was in the employ of the Federal Bureau of Investigation, tasked with completing information gathering for US officials. Two IOC members, Alexandre de Merode and Mario Vázquez Raña, openly stated that Samaranch's closest associates were orchestrating his demise. At Le Bar de Relais, a frequent gathering place for conference delegates in Lausanne's Palace Hotel, "the intrigue [was] as thick as the red velvet covering the walls," reported A. Craig Copetas and Roger Thurlow of the *Wall Street Journal*.[44]

In an effort to confront an additional brush fire, a delegation of forty-two IOC members attending the conference convened at a breakfast meeting with members of the Executive Board. Samaranch was purposely absent. The meeting afforded these members a chance to air their complaints about the plan to remove voting privileges from all IOC members for the 2006 Olympic Winter Games host city. Samaranch's absence, concluded one IOC member, was calculated: "The old man knew what kind of anger would be in the air and he wanted no part of it."[45]

Executive Board members listened patiently to the members who resented being tarred with the same brush as those members who faced expulsion and then provided a sobering message to the assembled. Sixty-two IOC members visited Salt Lake City during the bid competition, and all were currently subject to investigation by the FBI, and "if they needed legal or other assistance in coping with the [US] Justice Department inquiry, they should realize that it might be in their own best interests not to rock the IOC boat." A measure of calm was restored and the meeting adjourned.[46] Still, in a media interview, Kevan Gosper signaled that some flexibility in the Executive Board's approach existed.[47] In the weeks ahead, and as a means of maintaining peace within the ranks in advance of the Session in March, Samaranch and the Executive Board accepted a compromise proposal sponsored by

IOC members Mario Pescante (Italy) and James Easton (US). The IOC Session subsequently approved the plan that authorized the establishment of a sixteen-member electoral college that would select the two finalists. All IOC members retained the right to cast a ballot to determine the host city.[48]

## The Sponsors Have Their Say

In January the Olympic Movement's major corporate sponsors adopted a public "wait-and-see approach" concerning the IOC's response to the crisis. Privately, however, they expressed serious concerns to IOC officials, including Juan Antonio Samaranch, Richard Pound, and Michael Payne. They desired a swift resolution to the crisis with substantive reform such that the media's focus would revert to the IOC's central product, the Olympic Games, and the athletes who delivered the memorable sporting performances.[49] David D'Alessandro rejected the approach of his TOP sponsor colleagues by campaigning vociferously in the media for the IOC to take action. In sometimes colorful and provocative language not always appreciated by his TOP sponsor colleagues, not to mention Olympic leaders, D'Alessandro critiqued the IOC's efforts.[50]

The disconnect between IOC officials and TOP sponsor CEOs and marketing executives revolved around the timetable for the reform process. Sponsors desired swift action, while Pound and Payne argued that the process could not be managed according to the corporate model, as the IOC was composed of volunteers located in countries around the globe. The media's clamoring for Samaranch's resignation offered a recipe for disaster, they stated, because the reform agenda would be stalled by a succession battle. However, the fallout from the WCDS and the release of the report of SLOC's Board of Ethics in early February gave sponsors leverage to press their case. SLOC's inquiry put an additional ten IOC members in the media spotlight, including Australia's Phil Coles and Guatemala's Willi Kaltschmitt, for perceived transgressions of existing IOC policies concerning funded travel. Samoa's Seiuli Paul Wallwork was cited for his wife's $30,000 personal loan from Tom Welch. More details emerged on the cases of the five remaining IOC members facing expulsion in March (Charles Mukora resigned following the January meeting of the Executive Board) and Un Yong Kim, who was still under investigation by the Ad Hoc Commission. SLOC's report also

provided a comprehensive list of gifts to IOC members and their correspond-
ing expenses. These gifts included a violin ($524), video games ($1,171), luggage and clothing ($5,189), doorknobs ($673), a trip for three couples to the
1995 Super Bowl (Tom Welch hosted the Coleses and Kaltschmitts), and dogs
($1,010). When TOP sponsors convened with Pound and Payne in New York
on February 11, their message to the IOC was clear, concise, and pointed.

The intent of the summit meeting of the sponsors and IOC officials was
to maintain a channel of communication between the parties. Media reports
indicated Pound and Payne did more listening than talking on this day. The
collection of some two dozen vice presidents and marketing heads informed
Pound and Payne that their TOP company CEOs lacked confidence in
the IOC's commitment to reform. The atmosphere was strained and tense.
"They wanted 'Kumba Ya,' but instead they got 'Fire and Rain,'" observed
one TOP representative. The sponsors urged them to enact necessary reform
measures without delay. The discussions centered on four major issues: possible changes in the IOC's management "at the highest level," even though
none of the sponsors called for Samaranch's resignation; the need to expel
the IOC members implicated in the scandal; new rules for the selection of
host cities beyond the interim measures proposed for the 2006 Olympic Winter Games competition; and enhanced financial transparency driven by the
public release of the IOC's financial reports.[51] For the media's consumption,
IOC officials downplayed the degree of concern expressed by the sponsors
and reiterated Samaranch's desire to advance a reform agenda.[52]

At this time, David D'Alessandro ratcheted up the pressure on Samaranch and his colleagues. In advance of the meeting with Pound and Payne,
he suspended negotiations with the National Broadcasting Company for
advertising time during the network's coverage of the 2000 Sydney Olympics.
He also removed the Olympic rings from John Hancock's stationery. The
first action was intended to place some pressure on the NBC's Dick Ebersol
to press more forcefully for reform. Referring to the IOC as a "cult of roy-
als," D'Alessandro surmised that Samaranch's opportunity to effect necessary
reforms might have passed. "I still think Kenny Rogers said it best: 'Know
when to hold 'em, know when to fold 'em . . .' I think Samaranch is getting
close to the end of his fold 'em stage," chided D'Alessandro. In the aftermath
of the meeting, he unloaded on Samaranch and the IOC in an op-ed piece in

the *New York Times* for what he perceived as foot-dragging in their approach to addressing reform measures. "The lethargic pace of the IOC in rooting out corruption . . . [is] hurting every constituency it serves—the corporate sponsors who write the big checks, the broadcasters who write even bigger checks, and the athletes in places so poor they cannot even afford a team uniform or pair of shoes," wrote D'Alessandro.[53]

The IOC's response to revelations concerning John Coates's midnight deal with Charles Mukora and Francis Nyangweso on the eve of the vote on the site for the 2000 Sydney Olympics triggered D'Alessandro's actions. The IOC's refusal to label Coates's action as "bribery" stupefied him. Disturbed that Samaranch reconfirmed Sydney's IOC host status before a complete investigation of the Sydney bid committee's activities occurred, D'Alessandro blasted away. Clearly, Coates engaged in an act of bribery, stated D'Alessandro, but this fact eluded officials in Lausanne. "The news media may be right when they compare the IOC to royalty," he continued. "The IOC is like a royal family, one in which the cousins have been marrying each other so long it's no wonder that their ideas of what means what are a little daft." He feared that the IOC's internal investigation would not drill down far enough to facilitate the reform steps necessary to assist the IOC in emerging from the scandal. "It seems to be the way the world works: every government that forgets about the people who give it power and, instead, concentrates on keeping its secrets, keeping its perks, maintaining its rituals and preserving its own hide eventually implodes," he wrote. "It happened to Louis XVIth, and it happened to the Soviet Communist Party. Now, it's happening to the International Olympic Committee," D'Alessandro concluded.[54]

D'Alessandro's use of rhetorical flourishes to make his case concerning the IOC's approach did not surprise observers of Boston's corporate elite who knew him well. "Those who cover Boston's business community," wrote the *Boston Globe*'s Joan Vennochi, "know there is nothing shy or restrained about D'Alessandro. From his flashy ties to his flashy quotes, he knows how to make irreverent statements and seize the spotlight."[55] D'Alessandro seized John Hancock, a moribund life insurance company in terms of its brand when he took over its corporate communications program in 1984, and breathed new life into its operations with an advertising campaign framed by the slogan "Real Life, Real Answers" and the need to manage "the financial changes that come with major life changes." He eschewed the standard approach adopted by insurance companies in relation to sport sponsorship initiatives. Golf and tennis were not the hallmarks of his effort to align John Hancock with sport properties. Rather, D'Alessandro targeted the Boston Marathon, a local event draped in history that badly needed an infusion of financial support in the 1980s; the city's beloved and (then) World Series–starved baseball team, the Boston Red Sox; and the Olympic Games.[56]

D'Alessandro's comments tried the patience of IOC officials, who maintained that the pace of reform adopted by corporations engaged in crisis management was not a viable path for the IOC, whose membership resided in countries around the world.[57] He called for the appointment of an independent auditor to conduct an examination of the financial records of past bid

4. John Hancock president and CEO David D'Alessandro enjoys a lighthearted moment in his Boston office in May 1998. *Source:* Boston Globe/Suzanne Kreiter/Landov.

committees, an IOC membership based on the United Nations model, the abolition of bid city visits in the future, full disclosure of all gifts received by IOC members, and the launch of a search for Samaranch's successor (Samaranch was scheduled to step down in 2001). As a skilled marketer, D'Alessandro understood that his profile in the media coverage also provided free advertising for John Hancock. Kevan Gosper bristled at his approach. "I think D'Alessandro's comments are unfortunate," stated Gosper, and "I think it's quite improper for him to debate this through the media. After all, he's a[n] [Olympic] partner."[58]

Michael Payne recalled that Samaranch monitored press reports and handed him press clippings with D'Alessandro's colorful commentary on a number of occasions.[59] Pound confirmed that his boss was sensitive to D'Alessandro's barbs.[60] Payne also recalled "heated discussions" with D'Alessandro on the pace of the IOC's reform process. He hesitated to side with Richard Pound, who believed that D'Alessandro's strident comments, on balance, were helpful in pushing forward the IOC's reform agenda. In assessing D'Alessandro's contribution, Payne commented that "the challenge there is to separate the difference between, I mean, what he genuinely believed in for the movement, what he genuinely wanted to try and do to help," and his "becoming an overnight pop star in the commercial world" in light of his willingness to grant media interviews and the tenor of his comments. He questioned D'Alessandro's ability to discern "when it was helpful to give a good nudge and sound bite and when, you know, it was better served to shut up."[61]

Unwilling to sit idly by and watch its disintegration, D'Alessandro prized the Olympic marketing platform that served John Hancock well since it consummated a deal with the IOC in 1991. The TOP agreement furthered the company's goals for Asian expansion, contributed meaningfully to the company's success in diversifying its consumer revenue base in the 1990s, and provided a boost in international profile not possible with a domestic (USOC) Olympic sponsorship deal.[62] "It's only a matter of time before this splashes over onto the corporate sponsors. You can just hear people saying," stated D'Alessandro, "'What about you big fat-cat sponsors—where's your social responsibility?'" Steve Burgay, who left his position as John Hancock's senior vice president of corporate communications in 2004 to take on the role of Boston University's vice president of marketing and communications, defended D'Alessandro's approach. "It had everything to do with protecting our investment. Our logic was: If the IOC does nothing, eventually the taint will spread beyond the IOC, and leak into consumer perception of *the rings themselves*. If that were to happen, the value of our investment would be diminished significantly."[63]

D'Alessandro faced internal pressure at John Hancock from disgruntled customers and agitated members of his sales force as a result of the scandal, but media speculation touched on how an extended IOC scandal might ensnare John Hancock and spark discussion of the company's own shortcomings in the past decade at a critical juncture in the company's history as it was moving to become a publicly traded company. John Hancock settled with policyholders (the settlement was for $350 million) who were sold unnecessary policies and paid $1.1 million to address federal and state charges that its lobbyists used illegal inducements such as golf outings in advancing the company's interests in meetings with state officials. Such a public relations problem might diminish the value of the company's stock, leaving it susceptible to an unwanted corporate takeover.[64]

Pound, who expended much energy in attempting to keep D'Alessandro informed through letters, faxes, and personal meetings and convince him to tone down his rhetoric prior to,[65] and in the aftermath of, the March Session, seemed more willing than his colleagues to accept the bouts of heartburn precipitated by D'Alessandro's interaction with the media. "I think he is trying to help us by making sure we don't sort of falter in doing the kinds of things that we're planning on doing," Pound concluded at the time.[66] Later, he confessed that he had been "deathly afraid that the [IOC's] response might get watered down and that the IOC would be perceived as soft on its own shortcomings. That would have been the end of us." D'Alessandro's forceful counsel and criticism and his willingness to renew John Hancock's TOP sponsorship deal in December 1999 when the IOC's reform measures were passed by the Session, stated Pound, confirmed his status as a "great partner."[67]

## Laying the Groundwork for the 108th Extraordinary IOC Session

In the weeks before the 108th Extraordinary IOC Session, D'Alessandro's media commentaries, the views of other Olympic sponsors, and new allegations concerning past bid processes provided the daily fodder of discussion and debate at the daily 8:00 a.m. meetings of the crisis management committee chaired by François Carrard. Present for these meetings were Carrard; Payne; Franklin Servan-Schreiber, the IOC's director of communications; Thierry Sprunger, the IOC's operations director; and Howard Stupp, head of the organization's legal department. These were harrowing days for all involved, as Payne recalled: "It was not an exaggeration to say that you went to the office in the morning and you didn't know if the organization would make it through the day."[68] Grim faces, blank stares, and furrowed brows dominated the halls of the IOC's Château de Vidy headquarters.

While Pound and Payne differed in their assessment of D'Alessandro's helpfulness and overall contribution to the IOC's cause, they shared the same opinion on the demands present in their respective work environments.[69] Day trips to visit sponsors, round-the-clock monitoring of media reports, and fears that additional skeletons would emerge, reported Payne, exacted a mental and physical toll.[70] Pound's telephone message log for this period indicates that calls came to his office from sponsors, television partners, lawyers, and reporters (print, radio, and television). At the same time, he maintained a hectic travel schedule in fulfilling his responsibilities in combating the crisis. It was, in his own words, his "Olympic Year from Hell."[71]

The need for the IOC to act swiftly in its effort to confront the crisis "or risk a rebellion" emanated as one of the overriding messages from the February 11 meeting with the sponsors.[72] Samaranch reached out to some TOP sponsor executives within days of this meeting in a series of phone calls and spoke to all of the CEOs prior to the March Session.[73] His briefing notes for telephone conversations with McDonald's vice chairman, Jim Cantalupo, and senior vice president of international marketing, David Green, and Coca-Cola's Douglas Ivester demonstrate the attention given to these entreaties. In the conversation with the McDonald's executives, Samaranch emphasized the process he effected to deal with the crisis and the leadership roles being played by Pound and Payne. He understood that McDonald's executives were dealing with agitated franchise operators, especially in the United States. Samaranch pledged to champion the necessary reforms and ensure the expulsion of members whose conduct warranted such sanction. His discussion with Ivester followed the same pattern, but he also asked for a public expression of support from Coca-Cola, given the media's propensity to frame their coverage of sponsors' opinion on the basis of John Hancock's statements. Clearly, D'Alessandro was under Samaranch's skin. He understood Coca-Cola's desire to witness rapid treatment of the issues, and he pledged to move with purpose.[74] In an ironic twist, Ivester fell prey to the corporate model of dealing with organizational crises when he failed to move fast enough to address concerns following the consumption of tainted Coke by a number of Belgian schoolchildren who then fell ill in June 1999.[75] Ivester resigned his position later in the year.

The Ad Hoc Commission's work entered a second phase in the weeks leading up to the 108th Extraordinary IOC Session. Richard Pound and his colleagues deliberated through a series of conference calls in February and a meeting in Lausanne at the end of the month on cases outstanding from its previous discussions (including those of Un Yong Kim and Phil Coles) and the new allegations stemming from the report of SLOC's Board of Ethics. These discussions, informed by documentation arriving from Salt Lake City right up to the eve of the Session resulted in three exonerations (Henry Adefope, Ashwini Kumar, and Rampaul Ruhee), six severe warnings (Louis Guirandou-N'Diaye, Willi Kaltschmitt, Shagdarjav Magvan, Anani Matthia, Austin Sealy, and Mohamed Zerguini), one very serious warning (Vitaly Smirnov), severe censures for Kim and Coles, and an additional recommendation for expulsion (Seiuli Paul Wallwork).[76]

The decisions concerning Coles and Kim raised the eyebrows of the IOC's media critics. Questions concerning the perception of a double standard dominated the media's coverage of their cases. In Australia they questioned Coles's survival, especially in light of his dinner with Michael Payne and Richard Pound at Lausanne's Palace Hotel within hours of his defense of his actions at the Ad Hoc Commission meeting in late February. Pound dismissed the concerns: "I mean it's done all the time. In circuit court, you have judges and the criminal bar and the defense bar having dinner all the time and the next day they each go in and do their jobs with no difficulty at all." Although he and Coles had been friends since their shared Olympic experience in Rome, Pound denied any conflict of interest.[77] Later, Pound admitted that Samaranch pleaded with him to spare Kim from expulsion. Kim's own words gave credence to Samaranch's posture: "Mr. Samaranch and I remain

close allies. We have a consensus that if I go down, he will go down."[78] Some
reporters believed Kim threatened to reveal damaging information if he was
expelled. Even though issued a severe censure, Kim's case remained open, as
the Ad Hoc Commission believed more evidence concerning Kim's conduct
existed. However, Samaranch soon orchestrated the shift of responsibility of
further investigation of members' cases from the Ad Hoc Commission to the
IOC's newly minted Ethics Commission (Pound was not a member of the
Ethics Commission).[79] Press coverage of the Kim and Coles decisions led
Pound and his Executive Board colleague Kevan Gosper to deny that the
report of the Ad Hoc Commission was a "whitewash."[80]

While Samaranch and his colleagues could find some solace in a vote
of confidence from General Motors, a major Olympic sponsor (USOC) in
the United States with more than one billion dollars in planned Olympic
spending in the next decade, there were signs that the March Session loomed
as the most important meeting of the IOC in its 105-year history. Samsung
Electronics issued mixed signals concerning its commitment to Olympic
sponsorship. Visa revealed it had developed a "contingency plan" in the event
that it was not satisfied with the results of the Session. David D'Alessandro
hired two consulting firms to explore alternative avenues for John Hancock's
sport sponsorship money. He even raised the specter of legal action against
the IOC.[81] Kodak, Xerox, and Matsushita (Panasonic) placed discussions of
renewal contracts for TOP V (2001–4) on hold while awaiting the results of
the meeting in Lausanne.[82]

Still, IOC officials believed if they could push through the needed
reforms, the sponsors would be reassured and abandon any thoughts of step-
ping aside. John Bennett, Visa's former marketing director, confirmed that
companies would struggle with the decision to walk away from their TOP
sponsor agreements because "there really isn't anything that captures the
imagination" in the way that the Olympics do. Bennett referred to the power
of the Olympics to captivate a viewing (and consumer) audience. He also
noted that sponsors such as Visa, Coca-Cola, and Kodak understood that the
likelihood of their competitors swooping in to take up the abandoned sponsorships was high.[83] For Pound, it was imperative for the IOC to act decisively
to "stop the bleeding." The 108th Extraordinary IOC Session, stated Kevan
Gosper, would launch "a sensible process to rescue our reputation and to

maintain our responsibility for putting on the most important sports event in the world." With respect to the agenda, which included items such as the votes on the expulsion of six IOC members, the development of an ethics commission, and changes to the method of selecting the host city of the 2006 Olympic Winter Games, Gosper remained confident that people would "find substance in what we are going to do. It won't be window dressing."[84] Gosper's words would soon be put to the test, as the IOC lurched forward toward two days in March 1999 when Lausanne stood still.

# 4

# Two Days Lausanne Stood Still

## Setting the Scene: The Stakes

Beaten down by media criticism during the intervening three months, Juan Antonio Samaranch, members of the Executive Board, and the IOC's key staff members prepared for the 108th Extraordinary IOC Session in March 1999. The Session offered those individuals caught in the maelstrom of controversy a glimmer of hope and an important opportunity. In any effort to confront an organizational crisis, state Starbuck, Green, and Hedberg, "the greatest need is for dramatic acts symbolizing the end of disintegration and the beginning of restoration."[1] A strong institutional response, highlighted by the expulsion of the six members recommended for such sanction by Richard Pound's Ad Hoc Commission and the Executive Board, might buy the leadership time to push through needed reforms to the *Olympic Charter*. The tenor of the media coverage might improve. But the opposite was also possible. If IOC members did not endorse the recommendations, the media barrage would inflict further damage to the IOC's reputation, and sponsors would question their continuing financial commitment to the Olympic Movement.

The IOC's corporate partners watched the situation closely. Matthias Kleinert, a senior vice president with Daimler Chrysler AG, a supplier of luxury vehicles to the Olympic Movement since 1964, concluded that the upcoming March Session was "the most important event the IOC has ever had in its history."[2] With the organization's image tarnished, David D'Alessandro, John

56

Hancock's outspoken and colorful CEO, understood that Olympic-brand recovery required the IOC to take decisive action: "They sell truth, integrity, [and] sportsmanlike conduct—the Greek ideals, which is why they have to be cleaner than Caesar's wife."[3] One corporate sponsor speculated on the result of the rank-and-file IOC members circling the wagons around some or all of their colleagues (Agustin Arroyo, Zein El Ahmed Abdel Gadir, Jean-Claude Ganga, Sergio Santander Fantini, Lamine Keita, and Seiuli Paul Wallwork) by defying the recommendations for their expulsion. "I see this as the real wild card," the sponsor intoned. "If this implodes, we might be forced to do some things we don't want to do."[4] James Easton, an American IOC member, understood the stakes involved: "If those who are clearly guilty are not thrown off," warned Easton, "I would have real concerns about the credibility of the IOC after that."[5] A fellow IOC member, Zimbabwe's Tomas Sithole, echoed Easton's call for jettisoning the six implicated members. "The public, sports people and the corporate sector are waiting to see if the IOC is serious about cleaning its house. If they see the IOC is serious," offered Sithole, "they will continue to support us. If not, there is going to be serious trouble."[6]

Sponsors made clear their expectations from this Session. Expulsion of the six members was a necessary starting point, but not an acceptable outcome on its own for the Session. The IOC needed to demonstrate a commitment to confront its problems on a number of levels. IBM spokeswoman Debra Gottheimer best articulated this pointed counsel when she declared, "We're looking for thorough reform at the highest levels, expulsion of members, [and] important changes in the bidding process and controls, specifically financial disclosure consistent with any organization that is responsible for billions of dollars in revenue."[7]

The Session's willingness to support the Ad Hoc Commission and Executive Board, at least with the type of majority votes for expulsion required to send a clear signal to the media regarding the organization's resolve to deal with unethical conduct by its members, concerned the IOC's senior administrators. Members hailing from Europe, North America, and Oceania understood the battering absorbed by the IOC in the media in recent months, but Michael Payne confirmed his and others' thinking that those members in other regions had been insulated from the onslaught.[8] Did these members recognize the gravity of the situation, and would they be willing to banish their colleagues? This sense of unease increased when Richard Pound discerned prior to the Session that very few IOC members read the files prepared by the Ad Hoc Commission with respect to each of the six members, complete with the evidence resulting in the recommendations.[9]

## Juan Antonio Samaranch and Preparations for the 108th Extraordinary IOC Session

Government representatives and Samaranch's media critics present in Lausanne for the World Conference on Doping in Sport in early February panned his effort to emerge as the standard-bearer for the IOC's renewed efforts in tackling doping in sport. Bruised by the world's media, and rebuffed in his attempt to install himself as the head of the fledgling World Anti-Doping Agency,[10] Samaranch kept a low public profile during February. When he emerged briefly in early March, his frustration showed in an interview with a series of Spanish newspapers. Samaranch opined that criticism of the IOC "had been exaggerated and it [had] done disproportionate damage."[11] Pound, immersed in damage-control measures with the media and consultations with sponsors, wished his boss pursue silence rather than public utterances. Reporters claimed that Samaranch minimized the depth of the IOC's difficulties. Still, Pound understood Samaranch's comment: "There's probably a little human nature in all of this, and we've been taking it [criticism] for a couple of months. You feel like you're on the ropes and sometimes," Pound remarked, "you throw out a jab just to let people know you're alive." Samaranch, stated Pound, was committed to confronting the crisis and its underlying causes.[12]

Within days Samaranch conceded in a media interview that he should have pursued changes in the IOC's Olympic site-selection process earlier in his presidential tenure. "I'm guilty of one mistake: underestimating everything that was going on around all the bid cities—the money, the interests of all types, the temptations, the weaknesses. I should have realized earlier that the system for selecting host cities had to be changed. . . . I should have achieved a simpler mechanism, one that's easier to control."[13] For Samaranch, a man not given to admitting mistakes in a public forum, it was a humbling disclosure.

Behind the scenes, Samaranch was active. He worked the phones, pleading with IOC members to support the recommendations for expulsion of the six members. In a letter to all IOC members dated March 9, Samaranch noted the need for "concrete" action and some "painful" decisions, while calling for members to contribute "to defining a new policy for the IOC, in a spirit of renewed unity."[14] In phone conversations with Olympic sponsor CEOs, Samaranch remained "upbeat" and assured the corporate partners that the IOC would deal with the immediate issues and prepare the IOC for a corruption-free future.[15] With the Session approaching, not all IOC members shared his optimism. While supportive of Samaranch, Francisco Elizalde of the Philippines confessed that "it's very hard to undo the damage. It will linger. Let's talk reality. Our image is kaput right now."[16]

Nerves were frayed as IOC members converged on Lausanne and pressure on IOC leaders intensified. Samaranch revealed his fears concerning a "palace revolt" and his sense that unnamed IOC members or personnel were attempting to "destabilize" his leadership to force his resignation.[17] One member of the Executive Board confirmed that death threats prompted him to retain the services of a bodyguard.[18] Un Yong Kim, who remained under investigation by the Ad Hoc Commission concerning revelations that his son had obtained a job with a telecommunications firm funded by the Salt Lake City bid committee, lost his composure at an Executive Board meeting on March 16. The Ad Hoc Commission recommended a severe censure for Kim for other transgressions, but its investigation continued with the possibility of a recommendation for expulsion. During a break in the Executive Board's meeting at the Château de Vidy with the Salt Lake City Organizing Committee's newly appointed president, Mitt Romney, Kim confronted IOC director-general François Carrard (a member of the Ad Hoc Commission) on one of the building's terraces. The two exchanged heated words, and Kim struck an aggressive tae kwon do stance. Pound intervened and instructed Kim to "calm down" as Carrard retreated hurriedly from the terrace with the words "I quit!"[19]

The incident startled Mitt Romney, who was attending his first face-to-face meetings with IOC officials. "It was not the diplomatic, quiet decorum that characterized the century-old congregation of international diplomats," concluded Romney in his 2004 book, *Turnaround: Crisis, Leadership, and the Olympic Games*.[20] The embarrassing episode, witnessed by a number of IOC staff members, contributed to Carrard's stumbling performance at a press conference later that day, where reporters grilled him on the IOC's decision to hold its Session behind closed doors when Olympic leaders earlier espoused the need for greater institutional transparency.[21] Samaranch later held a private meeting with Kim, Pound, and Carrard in order to deal with the matter.[22]

At this same series of meetings, the Executive Board established the procedures for hearing from the members recommended for expulsion during the Session. Pound sought ideas on how best to present his commission's evidence, beyond the in-depth files provided to the IOC members, because members of the Ad Hoc Commission wished to avoid the appearance of serving as "prosecutors." Samaranch asked Pound to present his report and recommendations, and in the event that IOC members had queries, he or Pound could field them. They allotted each implicated member (in alphabetical order) twenty minutes to address the information compiled by the Ad

5. IOC Executive Board member Un Yong Kim, shown in September 1999, survived the purge of IOC members in relation to the Salt Lake City crisis despite prevailing opinions that his transgressions were as egregious as those members who were expelled. *Source:* Chung Sung-Jun/ Getty Images Sport/Getty Images.

Hoc Commission. As per standard IOC practice, the vote would be by a show of hands; however, when Anita DeFrantz opined that a secret ballot would be more appropriate, Samaranch noted that if twenty-five IOC members present requested such a voting procedure, a secret ballot would be employed. The votes on all members would unfold at the conclusion of the six twenty-minute speeches. When discussion ensued on the matter of legal representation, Samaranch decreed that a lawyer could sit with the member while he waited to enter the Session hall, but would not be permitted into the IOC Session.[23] A reading of the minutes reveals a president signaling that his hand remained firmly on the tiller.

While not stated in the minutes of the Executive Board, the rationale for staging the Session behind closed doors, a decision that had been a source of Carrard's struggles at the press conference, seems clear. Olympic leaders worried that the six members might elect to embarrass the organization or a number of its members during their opportunity to defend their actions before the Session. Commented one IOC official, "Of course it is a fear. It is impossible to know what they might have, what damage they might try to inflict."[24]

The role of the sponsors in the generation of major planks in the IOC's reform agenda and the push for expulsion of members also provided a topic of discussion for Executive Board members huddled at the Château de Vidy. Pound reiterated that the IOC needed to push through the needed reforms. A less than decisive response from the IOC over the ensuing few days threatened the IOC's sponsor base. "The big risk was the 'herd theory,'" concluded Pound, "which was that the sponsors would get stampeded by public opinion and would get up and take action. This was a very serious threat." Whereas the sponsors offered support publicly, "they had made it known privately that it could be fatal [to their sponsor relationships] if the situation was not cleared up quickly." Kéba Mbaye lamented the prominence of the sponsors in the IOC's deliberations on reform matters and believed they might be "driving" the process with what amounted to "quasi-bribery." Sponsors, responded Pound, "were not telling the IOC what to do, but encouraging them to get it done." Payne echoed these sentiments, while Thomas Bach understood the need for sponsor input. For him, the message was critical, and in that realm, the IOC "had to show the world that the Olympic values and money were not contradictory; in fact, money was the means to realize the values."[25]

Representatives of Hill & Knowlton, the public relations company retained to assist the IOC in managing its interaction with the world's media during the crisis, confirmed the need for decisive measures. Dick Hyde, one of Hill & Knowlton's four executives present, counseled Executive Board members to deliver "a consistent, steady message," specifically one that revealed the "IOC had taken strong and decisive action to root out wrongdoing [and that] reforms [were] enacted to prevent future problems and make things more open and transparent."[26]

## Decision Day: March 17, 1999

By March 1999, Samaranch knew what the price of inaction would be for the IOC. As well, he was all too aware of what the stakes were for his own leadership status. He left no doubt in the minds of his fellow IOC members regarding the gravity of the situation as he opened the 108th Extraordinary Session at Lausanne's Palais de Beaulieu on March 17. "There has never been an occasion," he stated, "on which a President of the IOC has needed to express his opinion, in relation to an issue which so profoundly affects the present and future of the Olympic Movement as much as the current crisis. . . . It is my conviction that unless we act quickly, decisively and unanimously, at this Extraordinary Session, the damage which may be done to the Olympic Movement and to the IOC as a result of the recent disclosures will be very, very serious."[27] Samaranch then delivered a lengthy speech to his rapt audience, which, in part, served as a review of his perceived accomplishments as IOC president. He devised his presidential agenda to address strained relations among members of the Olympic Tripartite, improve the IOC's revenue-generation capacity, enhance the reach of the Olympic Movement by establishing new National Olympic Committees, confront the boycott mentality that gripped powerful political leaders around the world, and preserve the autonomy of the IOC and Olympic Movement by establishing "co-operative relationships" with organizations such as the United Nations. Samaranch touched on a lengthy list of his accomplishments that related to his agenda.[28] With these preparatory comments on the record, Samaranch confronted squarely the issue dominating the day's events, one that brought scores of the world's media to the shores of Lake Geneva.

Samaranch pressed forcefully for decisive action and consensus. "Many of you have been relatively insulated from what has been occurring since the revelations stemming from the Salt Lake Organizing Committee," he stated. The media "fire storm" influenced public opinion concerning the Olympic Movement. "Make no mistake," Samaranch continued, "there has never been a crisis of this magnitude faced by the IOC and the Olympic Movement." He confessed that the organization performed poorly in its monitoring of the host-city bid process. Still, he observed, "no one thought that certain of our members would act in a manner which would eventually bring the IOC into disrepute—in fact, into a crisis which has nearly destroyed the reputation and credibility of all its members and the organization itself." He hammered home his central message: "It is important—vital—that you understand the extent of this crisis."[29]

Samaranch took personal responsibility for the crisis, but also wanted to lead the IOC through this difficult time. In order to emerge from the crisis, "we must root out all forms of inappropriate or unethical behaviour among our membership and expel those members recommended by the Executive Board," implored Samaranch. He also called for the Session's support of the revised procedures for the selection of the host city for the 2006 Olympic Winter Games, which involved the admittedly contentious decision to suspend all IOC member visits to bid cities, as well as the establishment of an electoral college that would whittle the competition down to two finalist cities for the Session's consideration. He urged the Session to support the establishment of an ethics commission and advocated the institution of a study group he referred to as the IOC 2000 Commission, composed of Olympic family members and prominent outside individuals, which would examine all aspects of the IOC's operation with a view to providing recommendations for reform of the *Olympic Charter*.[30]

The IOC 2000 Commission, commented Samaranch, afforded the IOC an opportunity to "move forward on a much stronger footing, in tune with society and its expectations for the leadership of the Olympic Movement." While not wishing to constrain its mandate, he valued such a group's analysis of, commentary on, and recommendations concerning the bid city selection process, the IOC's method of selecting members, the IOC's administrative structure, Olympic revenue distribution, and the Games themselves. "Start-ing today," Samaranch concluded, "our mandate is to heal the wounds inflicted by the inappropriate actions of some of the members of the IOC and by others outside of our organization, and return the prestige to the entire Olympic Movement."[31]

Despite his wish to lead the IOC through the crisis, no doubt to pro-tect what he perceived as his meaningful presidential legacy, Samaranch was unwilling to do so without a formal expression of confidence in his leader-ship from the members. While gratified by the warm and rousing round of applause from members at the conclusion of his remarks, Samaranch called for a secret ballot on a vote of confidence in his leadership and delegated Hungary's Pál Schmitt to oversee the process. Samaranch departed the Ses-sion hall. Syed Shahid Ali (Pakistan), Irena Szewinska (Poland), and Guy Drut (France) duly distributed, and subsequently collected, the ballots. He Zhenliang (China), Kéba Mbaye (Senegal), and Anita DeFrantz (United States) served as scrutineers. Ninety members were eligible to vote, and of the ninety ballots distributed, eighty-nine were returned, yielding a massive vote of confidence (a vote of eighty-six to two, with one ballot spoiled) in the organization's beleaguered president. Upon his return to the hall, Sama-ranch expressed his appreciation for the vote of confidence and pledged "to do his best, with the help of the members, to put the IOC back in the place it deserved in the world of sports."[32]

Following a brief review of the origins of the Ad Hoc Commission, and a summary of its work by Richard Pound, the accused were asked to respond. Agustin Arroyo, former president of Ecuador's National Olympic Commit-tee and an IOC member since 1968, entered the hall. A lawyer, and once his country's ambassador to Great Britain, Arroyo explained his motivation for traveling to Lausanne: "Why am I here? Why did I ask to be heard by the Session? For a very simple reason. Because I've believed in the IOC, I've believed in its principles of justice, fair play. I've been 31 years in the IOC, for years before I was president of my NOC and for about 62 years I have been involved with amateur sport," stated Arroyo. While he conceded that he asked Tom Welch to assist his stepdaughter, Nancy Rignault, to secure employment in Salt Lake City in 1992, he denied knowledge of any support provided to her for living expenses. His stepdaughter, stated Arroyo, worked for the State of Utah for less than three months and then moved to Houston. When his family (his wife, himself, and five other family members) vacationed in Park City, Utah, over Christmas and New Year's a number of years earlier, he tried to pay the accommodations fee, but Tom Welch told him that they "were his guests." Arroyo stated that he paid for the airfares involved. Welch paid $5,000 to fly Arroyo's wife, Racquel, to the 1995 Budapest IOC Session as his "personal guest" and gave him a dog, confirmed Arroyo, but his support of Salt Lake City dated back to its first bid, and Welch's largesse was not an inducement to secure his vote. Arroyo firmly stated that he had neither "betrayed the Olympic Oath nor the Olympic principles." He then departed the Session hall.[33]

Next, a somewhat disheveled General Zein El Abdin Ahmed Abdel Gadir took the floor, apologizing for his appearance owing to the misfortune of having lost his luggage in transit. Gadir, founder of the Sudanese Parachute Regiment and a former minister for youth, sports, and social affairs, understood the need to "restore confidence in the Olympic Movement" through actions at this Session; however, allegations concerning his conduct had "caused irreparable damage" to himself and his family's reputation. He asked for the Session to examine his case "judiciously in the light of principles of justice, equity, and good conscience." Gadir's son, Zuhair, studied in the United States (in 1993) at a time that his own financial resources could not support such an endeavor. When efforts to secure funds from a number of agencies failed, he learned of the "NOC support programme," but denied knowledge of its connection with the Salt Lake City bid.[34]

Gadir's reputation was not particularly good. The Stockholm 2004 bid committee's dossier on him revealed he was "noisy" and "hard." Swedish officials complained to the IOC that Gadir was "constantly drunk" and disturbed other guests during his visit to Stockholm. In Berlin during the run-up to the vote on the site of the 2000 Olympics, Gadir compiled a room service bill of more than $1,800.[35] Rather than addressing additional allegations that he accepted cash transfers of $7,000 to a London bank account for Zema Gadir, a daughter that did not exist,[36] Gadir changed course to address matters concerning the process, no doubt as a means of generating some sympathy. Gadir cited the Ad Hoc Commission report: "The International Olympic Committee stresses that members whose expulsion is proposed are not accused of any crime or offense; they are men and women who certainly have made mistakes, but should not be stigmatized or treated like unworthy human beings." Finally, he offered that the process had been media driven and that the IOC should not convict long-standing members. "Victimisation is a negative act," stated Gadir, "contrary to the principles of justice and shall defeat the purpose for which it was applied."[37] General Gadir then retreated from the Session hall.

Next to appear before the Session was Jean-Claude Ganga of the Republic of the Congo, the highest-profile member to face expulsion. Ganga carved much of his reputation in international sport circles as the leader of the African boycott of the 1976 Montreal Olympics. The world's media found Ganga to be a particularly assailable character in the context of the Salt Lake City crisis. Ganga's profile and spirited defense of his actions explain the fascination with his case. Dubbed the "human vacuum cleaner" by Salt Lake City officials,[38] Ganga stood accused of accepting benefits in excess of $250,000 from Salt Lake City. This sum included medical treatments for himself and two relatives, six trips to Salt Lake City, a trip to Las Vegas for his wife and mother-in-law,[39] cash payments, profits on a land deal approximating $60,000, and assorted gifts, including a refrigerator, fax machine, and exercise machine. When Ganga and his wife, Eugenie, visited Walmart, "the staff of Salt Lake City's bid committee drew in a deep breath." Jason Gull, a member of the bid committee who was delegated responsibility for the Ganga delegation, permitted his credit card to be taken "to the maximum" on multiple occasions to support Eugenie's appetite for home furnishings.[40]

Ganga lobbied hard in the weeks before the Session to retain his standing in the organization, directing much of his ire at Richard Pound, who, charged Ganga, profited from the IOC's long-term contracts with the National Broadcasting Company and targeted African members in his investigations as a means of excluding "Africa from the center of decision making in world sports."[41] Un Yong Kim's sanction and the continuing investigation into the Korean's actions reeked of politics, charged Ganga. Ad Hoc Commission members Pound, Jacques Rogge (Belgium), and Pál Schmitt (Hungary), all of whom expressed interest in succeeding Samaranch in the next presidential election, conspired to eliminate him from the competition. "Mr. Kim did not do anything wrong," said a clearly uninformed Ganga. "They want to kill him because he's a candidate for the (IOC) presidency. . . . They look for lice even if the head is clean-shaven." Pound calmly rebutted his accusations: "As a lawyer, I can tell you: If you have a case with bad facts, you attack the law. If you have a case with bad law, you attack the facts. If you have bad law and bad facts, you attack the prosecutor." Ganga lashed out at the "corruption fever" gripping the IOC's Lausanne headquarters. "If you want angels and saints, go to heaven to organize the Olympic Games. If you organize the Games on this earth, it must be organized with human beings with good sides and bad sides."[42] Swinging wildly at his accusers, Ganga attacked Samaranch, who decided to "sacrifice his friends." "That is dangerous for him," warned Ganga. "It is war now."[43] Even longtime friend LeRoy T. Walker, USOC president at the time Salt Lake City secured host-city privileges for the 2002 Olympic Winter Games, found Ganga's conduct embarrassing. "He changed the handshake from palms together to palms up—what's in it for me," Walker concluded.[44]

Given the wealth of evidence before IOC members, Ganga's audience in Lausanne wondered how he would explain his actions. More than a few must have cringed when he stated that "simple concepts as hospitality and courtesy have been qualified as attempts to bribe, attempts to corrupt, values such as friendship and solidarity have been defined as offences." Names had been disclosed to the press before the IOC members heard from implicated members in order to humiliate them and secure resignations. The IOC engaged in "harassment," concluded Ganga. Money directed to his personal account ($70,000) had been handled in this fashion so as to facilitate its distribution to a number of African NOCs, Ganga claimed, because of problems with the Republic of the Congo's banking system. Documents in his possession, stated Ganga, confirmed the allocation of the money to the designated NOCs. He understood that cash paid to him came from Welch directly, not Salt Lake City's bid committee, as a result of the Utahan's personal visit to Africa and his shock and horror at the lack of sport amenities for African youth. He said Salt Lake City doctors turned aside his efforts to pay the medical bills for his treatment and the artificial knee provided to his mother-in-law. But he was willing to pay his family's medical bill today if Lausanne staff pursued the bill from SLOC. The refrigerator and fax machine were in their room in Salt Lake City but were not transported to Brazzaville. An exercise machine, which he claimed to have reluctantly accepted, was not even delivered to their possession, he stated. He challenged his accusers to find the refrigerator and fax machine in Brazzaville.[45] A bewildered Ganga stated that the Ad Hoc Commission provided no evidence in support of its claims.

Ganga also pursued Gadir's theme that the world's media drove the process and asked to be "judged in a fair manner and not be sentenced simply because the media sees this affair, that international public opinion sees this case and that culprits should be found at all cost." Transparency, asserted Ganga, was not in the best interests of the IOC. "As a diplomat, I would like to say that this is certainly not the first organization which has encountered this type of problem. But the difficulties which arise," he continued, "are usually dealt with behind closed doors. When an organization goes public, goes before the international press and gives all these sordid details and its secrets, this is very bad for the organization."[46] Ganga championed for a "junketeering culture built on lavish trips, expensive gifts, and . . . cash payoffs," wrote the *Boston Globe's* John Powers and Mitchell Zuckoff, but within minutes the Salt Lake City scandal brought his IOC tenure to a close. Ganga, too, departed the Session hall following his remarks.[47]

Next to appear was Mali's Lamine Keita, a twenty-two-year member of the IOC and president of his National Olympic Committee. He made it clear early in the investigative phase of the Ad Hoc Commission's work that he would defend himself against charges he received benefits not less than $97,000, the bulk of which represented tuition support and living expenses for his son at Washington's Howard University through the bid committee's NOC Assistance Program. "I'm a fighter by nature, not someone who resigns," Keita stated in an interview with *Le Matin* in January.[48] He attempted to send documents by fax to all members of the IOC prior to the Session and apologized if some had not received the package. Keita admitted that he queried Salt Lake City bid committee vice president David Johnson on the scholarship program. Johnson informed him that recipients had to be in process with studies in the United States and pledge to return to their home countries to volunteer to work for their National Olympic Committee. Keita stated that his NOC examined the possibility of tapping into this source of support and concluded that "the only person who met the conditions was my son." More than a few IOC members must have shaken their heads and looked skyward. If the Mali NOC determined that his son was the logical choice for the award, "I do not see what my liability is or what my responsibility is." Keita pushed forward the thought that the Salt Lake City bid committee brokered the deal with the Mali NOC, and he had simply been an innocent bystander (despite having been the individual who originally discussed the aid program with Johnson and who himself served as the president of the Mali NOC, the organization that ultimately struck the agreement with Salt Lake City officials). In a contradictory statement, one indicating a truer motive for his involvement with the bid committee—he needed the money—Keita concluded his remarks: "Those who are weak are always more vulnerable and therefore easy targets. Weak economies are vulnerable. If I had sufficient money to pay for my son's studies, I would not be standing before you."[49] Keita then exited the hall.

Seventy-two-year-old Sergio Santander Fantini, a chartered accountant, president of Chile's National Olympic Committee, and an IOC member since 1992, appeared next. He called his appearance before the Session "the most significant and transcendental moment in his life." He disputed the claim that Christian Rodriguez, the secretary-general of the Chilean NOC, served as an intermediary in securing a financial donation from Tom Welch for his ultimately failed mayoralty run in the city of Talca in December 1993. Marcelo Contreras, countered Santander, controlled his campaign, including its fund-raising component. While he (Santander) was abroad, and without his knowledge, Contreras launched a campaign for soliciting funds for the campaign from Santander's colleagues and associates. Santander noted that from this set of contributions emerged a personal one from Tom and Alma Welch. He denied any knowledge that the source, in fact, had been bid committee funds.[50]

Welch's testimony before the SLOC's Board of Ethics in January 1999 that Rodriguez approached him for money before and after the political run, the latter initiative as a means of eliminating campaign debts, was not believable, according to Santander.[51] In his first interview before the Board of Ethics, Welch failed to recall the circumstances of the donation. After a brief period of reflection, and in a second interview in early January 1999, Welch recounted the communication with Rodriguez.[52] But Santander had a letter from Welch written at the time of the contribution (January 3, 1994), stating that the contribution was "a personal one from Alma and myself." "It is impossible to believe that Mr. Welch could have suffered temporary amnesia and only remembered the truth when put under pressure to clarify his lack of administrative control and financial disorder." Santander attempted to shift the blame to Welch without considering (publicly) whether the funds had come from the bid committee or Tom Welch directly. At any rate, accepting them under either circumstance during a bid city competition involving Welch (president of one of the candidate-city bid committees) was clearly improper. Santander denied any wrongdoing, called on his colleagues' support, and retired from the hall after having requested that his remains be buried in "the Olympic park in Athens, where my name is inscribed in marble next to an olive tree I planted with my wife."[53]

The last to appear was Seiuli Paul Wallwork, an IOC member since 1987 and the permanent secretary for Samoa's Ministry of Youth, Sports, and Cultural Affairs. Wallwork's wife, Julia, requested financial support ($30,000) from Tom Welch, a family friend dating back to 1989. She requested the money from Welch in November 1991 at a time when she and Wallwork were experiencing marital difficulties and were not cohabiting.[54] She informed Welch that she sought the money "to help a friend in a serious situation."[55] But, indeed, she herself was the one needing the funds. Wallwork denied any involvement in soliciting the loan,[56] one that Welch extended by tapping into his daughter's trust-fund account.[57] At that time, Wallwork asserted, mere months after Salt Lake City lost the vote at the IOC's Ninety-Seventh Session in Birmingham for the right to host the 1998 Olympic Winter Games, Salt Lake City was not a declared candidate for 2002. Welch provided the funds, not the bid committee, observed Wallwork, testifying to the personal business arrangement between the two. The Wallworks reconciled in 1992, and they repaid Welch in two cash payments in September 1992 and March 1993, according to Wallwork. "I am at a total loss as to what I might have done wrong. . . . As I did not know, nor I was not [sic] involved [in the acquisition of the loan], how can my actions or conduct have jeopardized the interest of the IOC?" queried Wallwork. "I was totally ignorant as to the negotiation, conduct, development and finalization of the loan transaction, right up to its successful conclusion," he stated. "Through no action or conduct of mine, I stand before you like an outcast," he lamented. "Whatever decision is made, my mind is very clear and my heart is at peace that I have told the truth."[58] After wishing members of the IOC well, he departed the hall.

IOC members listened to the impassioned pleas of their colleagues, and then focused on the task of determining their fates. Samaranch outlined that the vote would take place by a show of hands; however, when New Zealand's Tay Wilson advocated a secret ballot, Samaranch duly polled the members, and forty-six members agreed with Wilson. Austria's Philipp von Schoeller said that some of the members "had been lured into situations in a nasty way." He called for reconsideration of the Keita and Wallwork cases. Von Schoeller's request yielded no response either from Samaranch or from Pound, nor did it generate any reaction from members of the IOC. Ballots were duly distributed, and Agustin Arroyo's status was the first addressed. The scrutineers, Kéba Mbaye (Senegal), Marc Hodler (Switzerland), He Zhen-liang (China), and Julio César Maglione (Uruguay), determined that Arroyo had been expelled by a vote of seventy-two to sixteen and passed the result to Samaranch, who informed the Session.[59] With a two-thirds majority (sixty-one votes) required for expulsion, the closeness of the vote concerned IOC leaders, who desired a much stronger signal of the membership's refusal to countenance such activities.[60]

Richard Pound was just one of the IOC members whose eyebrows arched following Samaranch's announcement concerning the result of the Arroyo vote. French members Jean-Claude Killy and Guy Drut quietly approached him during the interval before the commencement of the vote on Zein El Abdin Ahmed Abdel Gadir.[61] They suggested that Pound rebut the claims made by the remaining five members in their defense. The prosecution always has the last word, noted Killy and Drut. In recounting the episode, Pound noted that "we had not followed a simple procedure that is common to such prosecutions. We had let the accused speak last and their emotional, if inaccurate explanations" played on the sympathies of some of the members.[62]

When the Session reconvened, Killy rose to present a question from the floor. He asked whether the Ad Hoc Commission possessed any "supplemental information" following the presentations of the implicated members. Pound stated that "it might be helpful to have some extra comments from the (Ad Hoc) Commission." So, he proceeded to render some. "It was true that the spoken intervention from the members was more compelling than a written document," Pound noted. With respect to the six individuals, they "requested what had been given to them," stated Pound. "This is what differentiated them from other cases where things had been pushed on people." General Gadir, stated Pound, "had been quite candid about needing the money." He noted that Jean-Claude Ganga adopted a similar approach with other bid committees, even though such activities had not been addressed in the Ad Hoc Commission's report. Ganga directed much energy in attacking the process and charged that "insufficient time" had been spent examining his case. "Indeed, had they more time," observed Pound, "they would have probably found more evidence against him." With respect to Lamine Keita, he requested the support, and it was obvious that "Keita's son was not the only person in the whole of Mali" qualified for the educational assistance. The Ad Hoc Commission held that Sergio Santander Fantini was aware of the source of the funds (the Salt Lake bid committee) for his political campaign "and had been sent cheques confirming this" fact. Concerning Seuli Paul Wallwork, the Ad Hoc Commission "was satisfied that he knew of the loan well before he claimed." No proof had been unearthed to confirm repayment of the loan, and "it was not the first time the same behaviour had occurred. It was an obvious breach of regulations for a spouse of an IOC member to make such a request." The subsequent votes on Gadir (eighty-six to four) and Ganga (eighty-eight to two) provide an indication that Killy and Drut's intervention keyed the desired, albeit temporary, effect.[63]

Lamine Keita (seventy-two to sixteen), Sergio Santander Fantini (seventy-six to twelve), and Seuli Paul Wallwork (sixty-seven to nineteen) were also expelled, with voting results resembling the tallies for Arroyo rather than Gadir and Ganga. Wallwork's case posed the most difficulty for his colleagues. Given that only eighty-eight IOC members cast ballots on his case, fifty-nine were required for expulsion.[64] The marathon six-hour meeting yielded the results sought by Samaranch. The IOC drummed out the six members whose expulsion he urged. His leadership had been confirmed in overwhelming fashion in a secret ballot (eighty-six to two), exceeding even the most optimistic expectations of his allies: "We were thinking that about 30–40 members might get organized against him, on a worst case scenario, but obviously the powerplay that we were expecting did not get up," noted one Samaranch confidant.[65] "At the risk of sounding Churchillian," Pound said to assembled reporters, "I think we are at the end of the beginning or nearing the end of the beginning."[66] Those individuals who resided in the vortex of the crisis knew only too well that the expulsions represented a mere start on the path to brand recovery.

The expelled members hustled out through a back entrance to avert the media crush outside the Palais de Beaulieu.[67] But they did not remain silent for long. In media scrums at the Palace Hotel, their comments revealed a common theme—they were scapegoats. Paul Wallwork described himself as the "proverbial sacrificial lamb," while Lamine Keita concluded that "justice was not done. I am a sacrifice."[68] "I do believe the public and press wanted to have heads knocked down," chimed in Arroyo. "Mine happened to be in the way."[69] It was a "purely political act," speculated Santander. "[My expulsion] probably occurred because Chile [is] such a small country."[70] Ganga, seated in a gilded chair in the Palace Hotel's vast lobby, recounted his efforts in the past to tackle "racial discrimination, poverty, and indifference," but accepted his fate with unexpected grace given his trashing of Samaranch, Pound, and other Olympic officials prior to the Extraordinary Session. "I will accept the decision as a sportsman," he said.[71]

Charges lingered in the aftermath of the Session that the IOC sacrificed members, exclusive of Ganga, who carried a low profile while protecting the charismatic Phil Coles and powerful Un Yong Kim by issuing each severe censures. Coles withstood withering attacks in the Australian press with respect to his conduct, which included multiple paid visits to Salt Lake City and a trip to the Super Bowl.[72] Pound's admitted friendship with Coles was raised in the press as a possible explanation for Coles's escape. The Ad Hoc Commission's recommendation on Coles did not satisfy some IOC members. "If you look at Arroyo or Paul Wallwork," offered one member, "they did much less than Coles, yet they were thrown out and Coles survived. He was unbelievably lucky."[73] Coles resigned from SOCOG's board in June, and the IOC barred him from serving on any of its commissions or working groups for two years after additional allegations emerged.[74]

Pound wrote in 2004 that suspicions concerning a double standard, at least with respect to Kim, were justified. Samaranch asked Pound to "protect" Kim without explaining why such action was necessary when information gathered placed Kim's status in jeopardy.[75] Steven Downes bluntly stated that "twenty years of dirt-digging and fastidious filing away of misdemeanours committed by his friends and colleagues finally paid off this week for Dr. Kim

Un Yong," who retained his IOC member status. Kim allegedly possessed "dirt dossiers" on senior IOC officials whose content dated back to the 1970s. Kim, stated Downes, was ready to "fight dirty" if his position was threatened. He arrived in Lausanne with an entourage thought to be composed of "lawyers and bodyguards." One IOC member judged that "if they [the Executive Board] go after Kim, I would not rule out the possibility that he sends his ninjas after Pound."[76] Pound and Kim were rivals to succeed Samaranch as IOC president. Pound wanted Kim out, reported Jacquelin Magnay, but consensus was not reached within the Ad Hoc Commission.[77] Pound refused Samaranch's dictate and vowed to continue his investigation into the South Korean's conduct, only to see the Ad Hoc Commission dissolved at Samaranch's urging and its responsibilities transferred to Kéba Mbaye's Ethics Commission shortly after the Extraordinary Session. Pound was the chair of the former but not a member of the latter body.[78]

For Kim, the IOC's decision in March 1999 was a temporary reprieve. Following his failed run for the IOC presidency in 2001, his business dealings fell under the scrutiny of South Korean authorities. Charged and convicted of embezzling $2.8 million, principally from the World Taekwondo Federation, the "Kukkiwon" (headquarters of the WTF), and the General Assembly of International Sports Federations, Kim was also found guilty of seeking $679,000 in kickbacks from sport officials. The embezzled funds, in part, funded his campaign for Samaranch's job. Kim received a two-and-a-half-year prison term, but the sentence was eventually reduced to two years on appeal based on his contribution to Korean sport and his poor health. Kim spent one year in prison and was granted parole soon after having resigned from the IOC (which had prepared to vote on his expulsion in Singapore in July 2005) in May 2005.[79]

While the world's media focused on events in Lausanne in mid-March 1999, so too did members of the academic community who harbored an interest in Olympic affairs. Olympic boosters and skeptics within this cohort viewed the expulsions through the same lens. John Lucas, Olympic author and professor emeritus at Penn State University, whom Samaranch appointed an "official Olympic lecturer" during his presidential tenure, stated that "many will rightly say there's a double standard, the IOC's going to have to live with that."[80] Professor John MacAloon, a specialist in cultural anthropology at the University of Chicago and an individual who served as a consultant for the IOC on academic and educational issues, noted that the "big fly in the ointment" remained Coles and Kim. The IOC's reluctance to expel them for transgressions that appeared at least as egregious as the actions of the six members would lead people to conclude that "the reform process is unwilling to go after the really strong and threatening actors in the system and has only taken down weak persons."[81] Sport historian Douglas Booth of the University of Otago, a critic of most things Olympic, concluded that the IOC netted members, save for Ganga, with "minnow status."[82] Despite these criticisms, Samaranch and other Olympic officials asserted that the expulsions demonstrated the IOC's resolve to confront corruption within its ranks. It had been the organization's "worst, best day" in its 105-year history, concluded Australia's Kevan Gosper.[83]

While Samaranch and other IOC power brokers breathed a sigh of relief, the next day's agenda was loaded with dynamite, given the need to demonstrate to key stakeholders, most notably the corporate sponsors, the organization's commitment to overhauling the structure and operating policies of the IOC. Would the concept of an ethics commission be greeted with favor by members? Would Samaranch's IOC 2000 Commission concept find support? Would the IOC members rise up to contest Samaranch's decree that eliminated bid city visits for the 2006 Olympic Winter Games? Would the Session pass revised procedures for selecting the host city for the same festival, including a small electoral college that would determine the two finalists? Still, at the close of the first day, in the privacy of his suite at the Palace Hotel, Samaranch could permit himself a few moments to enjoy the eighty-eight roses (eighty-six yellow and two red ones) sent to his room by IOC member Alex Gilady (Israel) to celebrate (and symbolize) the result of the vote of confidence in his leadership.[84] He had survived. The feared palace revolt, real or imaginary, did not topple the battered, but resilient, Spaniard. So far, so good, thought Samaranch. There was room for a little optimism as he turned off the light to find a few hours' sleep before returning to the Palais de Beaulieu for the next day's events.

## Day Two: March 18, 1999

Hoping to capitalize on the momentum gained from support for his leadership and the expulsion of the implicated members, Samaranch opened the following day's proceedings with the proposal for modifying the selection procedure for the 2006 Olympic Winter Games. An electoral college composed of the IOC president, IOC doyen, eight IOC members elected by the IOC Session (at its June 1999 Session, where the winning bid would be determined), the chairman of the Evaluation Commission (Chiharu Igaya, Japan), a representative of the Winter Sports Federations (appointed by the Association of International Winter Federations), a NOC representative (appointed by the Association of National Olympic Committees), and the three athletes elected by the athletes in Nagano (1998), announced Kéba Mbaye, would reduce the competing cities from six to two. The Session would select the winning city from those two bids.[85] A number of members raised a series of minor concerns; however, Guy Drut, Prince Albert of Monaco, and Denis Oswald (Switzerland) expressed strong support for the proposal. Oswald, for one, chafed at what he considered "quibbling over details" by a number of his colleagues. Having been resident in Switzerland, "the epicenter of the earthquake," during the crisis, he recognized the gravity of the situation. "The IOC had lost a great deal of credibility and the institution and its values had been threatened," lectured Oswald. "If members believed in these values they should put them ahead of their personal interests." Samaranch reiterated his support for the proposal before calling for a vote. By a show of hands, the Session passed the proposal with one abstention but no votes against.[86]

Kevan Gosper, who spearheaded the effort to draft terms of reference and composition of the proposed Ethics Commission, along with Mbaye and Carrard, met some resistance when he presented the Executive Board's recommendation that such a body be established. While Norway's Gerhard Heiberg and Canada's Carol Ann Letheren voiced their acceptance of the proposals,[87] which included the proviso that only two of the seven members of the Ethics Commission would hold IOC membership,[88] a number of their colleagues balked. Philipp von Schoeller, Willi Kaltschmitt Luján (Guatemala), Ivan Slavkov (Bulgaria),[89] Lambis Nikolaou (Greece), and Ung Chang (North Korea) expressed concern about the dominance of outside members on the commission, while Ashwini Kumar fretted that the IOC might be establishing a "supra-IOC" body, thereby undercutting its own authority.[90]

Craig Reedie (Great Britain) and Executive Board members Anita DeFrantz and Thomas Bach countered these fears by indicating that the outside members gave the body credibility with the media and public. It would be "an advisory body which served the IOC," stated Bach. Gosper echoed Bach's sentiment and clarified that the chair of the Ethics Commission would be an IOC member appointed by the president.[91] Samaranch, sensing the resistance, but requiring the passage of the concept of an Ethics Commission, intervened.

The majority of the members of the Ethics Commission needed to be from outside, said Samaranch, but the current proposal—a commission whose membership comprised two IOC members, one athlete who had recently competed in the Olympics, and four non-IOC members—could be tweaked. Samaranch offered that a third IOC member could be added at the expense of one non-IOC member, leaving a member balance of four (non-IOC) to three (IOC). Samaranch called for the provisional acceptance of the Ethics Commission, to be confirmed at the June Session following consideration of IOC-member input over the course of the next few months. The dissenting members, whose opposition stemmed, in part, from an absence of their input concerning the generation of the proposal, found this palatable. The vote in favor of the motion was unanimous.[92]

Samaranch then explained carefully the rationale for striking the IOC 2000 Commission. He conceived of a body comprising twenty to twenty-four members, the majority of whom held IOC membership. Their task was clear: generate ideas that would assist the IOC in strengthening its structure and function in the twenty-first century.[93] He noted that the goal of the commission would be to present a preliminary report to the Session in June and a final report to be submitted to the IOC prior to a yet-to-be-called Session in December 1999 or early 2000.

A number of IOC members weighed in on the proposal; however, the discussion was brief. He Zhenliang supported the initiative, noting the importance of hearing from people outside the Olympic Movement while informing his colleagues of a Chinese poet who once noted, "We don't know the real face of the mountain because we are inside it." Ashwini Kumar touched on his perception of two troubling aspects of the Olympic Movement. He regretted the existence of voting blocs in the IOC. While not mentioning Europe by name, he commented that most IOC members came from one of the world's regions and by extension greatly influenced the awarding

of the Games to bid cities. The Games needed to be "more equally distributed among the continents," asserted Kumar. "The Olympic Games," stated
Kumar, "were symbolic of friendship and cooperation between nations and if
the IOC did not strengthen this, all their restructuring would be cosmetic."
While no one could argue with Kumar's central message concerning the
distribution of the Games, the reality in 1999 was that the financial and infrastructural demands on a host city and nation, as well as the size and scope
of logistical operations underpinning a host city's efforts, greatly limited the
cities (and hence nations) that could accept the challenge. Sheikh Al-Sabah
(Kuwait) supported Samaranch's proposal for the IOC 2000 Commission,
noting that the Session's actions over the past two days had been "a bitter pill
to swallow but it was necessary to resolve problems in the world of sport."[94]
The motion passed unanimously.

At any other IOC Session, the IOC members' subsequent decision to support the formulation of an anti-doping agency, a necessary step following the
WCDS held in Lausanne in February 1999, would have dominated newspaper
headlines the next day.[95] In March 1999, however, the expulsions and reform
initiatives overshadowed this decision. Still, the IOC signaled its intent to play
a more significant role in tackling the modern-day scourge of international
sport, and IOC officials had another talking point in their efforts to convince
reporters that the IOC kept its promise to confront its problems.

Juan Antonio Samaranch declared the Session closed following a number
of interventions by IOC members, including Syed Wajid Ali (Pakistan), Hein
Verbruggen (Holland), Ashwini Kumar, Patrick Hickey (Ireland), Sheikh Al-
Sabah, Francis Nyangweso (Uganda), Anita DeFrantz, Thomas Bach, Mario
Vázquez Raña, Kevan Gosper, and Richard Pound.[96] He was succinct in his
analysis of the Session in his comments to the press: "We promised to clean
house. We did it. We promised reforms. We did it. We promised an Olympics
united. It's done."[97] If Samaranch anticipated that events of the past two days
would change the tenor of the media's treatment of the IOC and his stewardship in the short term, he was soon disappointed.

Many reporters were galled that Samaranch, who in their minds had
been disgraced by the scandal, first, survived and, second, was installed as the
chairman of the IOC 2000 Commission, the body that would generate reform
proposals. "It might sound like what the IOC did was momentous—until

you realize what the IOC did not do. . . . Juan Antonio Samaranch escaped unscathed," wrote Christine Brennan of *USA Today*. Tom Knott was similarly unimpressed, but even more strident in his column in the *Washington Times*: "So Samaranch is in charge of making the world safe from corrupt blowhards such as himself. This is just great. This piece of Euro trash impersonating royalty is leading the reform effort while the lies persist." The *Toronto Star* concluded that "the Olympic chalet still has a lot of dirty corners. The IOC didn't so much clean house as dust lightly around the edges. . . . What hope can we have for true reform with the task of restructuring the organization given to the man who led the IOC into the worst scandal in its history?" The IOC's decisions resulted in mere "tinkering with a system that needs root and branch reform," noted the *Sydney Morning Herald* in renewing its call for Samaranch's resignation. In panning the IOC's efforts, Cathy Harasta of the *Dallas Morning News* wrote that "more sham than substance came out of the 48 hours in the puppet master's [Samaranch] palace."[98]

James Easton captured the feelings of many IOC members and staff who considered the decisions made as significant, especially for an organization with "European sensibilities." "Other than having a public hanging out in the square," commented Easton, "we couldn't have done anything to satisfy the critics. I don't know what they expect. It is our organization. We are trying to reform it, and we should be (the ones) doing it."[99] As IOC members retreated to their home countries, all were better informed on the extent of the crisis and surely realized the path to brand recovery would more resemble a marathon than a sprint.

# 5

# Managing the Crisis

## The Road Ahead

The tumult that defined IOC officials' work environment for the past three months lessened in the wake of the 108th Extraordinary IOC Session. Moving forward, however, the crisis management roles served by the organization's senior administrators were no less critical to the IOC's efforts to emerge from the Salt Lake City crisis. IOC leaders who operated under the intense glare of the media's spotlight in January, February, and March, and who, by necessity, managed the crisis on an hour-to-hour basis, turned their collective attention to leveraging the crisis as a "catalyst for reform" for the long-term benefit of the organization.[1]

The decisions to establish the Ethics Commission and the IOC 2000 Commission appeased some but failed to impress high-profile individuals such as John Hancock's David D'Alessandro and Arizona senator and US presidential aspirant John McCain. "Absolutely nothing breathtakingly performance-oriented happened" in Lausanne, railed D'Alessandro. He disagreed with his TOP sponsor colleagues at McDonald's and the United Parcel Service who reported satisfaction with the results of the March Session. McCain, who planned to hold hearings on the IOC's tax-exempt status in the United States before the Senate Commerce Committee that he chaired, was also disenchanted. He observed that leaving the IOC president in charge of selecting members of the IOC 2000 Commission was "worrisome at best." McCain reserved a witness chair for Samaranch but signaled that a frosty reception awaited him in Washington. "I am afraid the IOC leadership is less concerned about reform than preserving the power of an elite few," McCain charged.[2] He also shared D'Alessandro's opinion that Samaranch's actions lacked decisiveness and failed to offer the prospect of "transparency and accountability" to the IOC.[3] Their pointed critiques of the IOC's reform process frustrated Lausanne officials in the weeks ahead.

Central to the process of turning the crisis into an opportunity for positive change was a concerted effort on the part of IOC officials to engage the major corporate sponsors in discussions concerning initiatives to restore public confidence in the Olympic enterprise. Richard Pound and Michael Payne briefed the TOP sponsors at the close of the Session via a conference call and requested an opportunity for a face-to-face meeting in New York at the end of March.[4] Held in New York on March 30, this meeting, stated Pound, unfolded without the "sense of discomfort, unease and suspicion" that pervaded the summit with the TOP sponsors in February.[5] UPS spokeswoman Susan Rosenberg confirmed Pound's characterization of the gathering: "The IOC has been very open and receptive to our input. They want to hear our point of view."[6] Pound and Payne requested TOP executives' input as the IOC 2000 Commission commenced its work in anticipation of filing a preliminary report to the 109th IOC Session, scheduled for Seoul in June.[7]

Within two weeks of the meeting with the sponsors, the IOC announced two initiatives. First, the composition of the newly constituted Ethics Commission, highlighted by the participation of former United Nations secretary-general Javier Pérez de Cuéllar, was revealed.[8] Second, future Olympic sponsorship contracts, confirmed IOC officials, would contain a morals clause. Such a clause afforded the sponsors an opportunity to opt out of their financial commitments if the IOC became embroiled in another scandal owing to an "ethical lapse."[9] Sponsors viewed this possibility, along with the IOC's release of its financial records,[10] with favor. For them, this demonstrated IOC officials' resolve to advance their reform agenda prior to the Session in June. However, in the short term the Phil Coles affair, which entered a second phase in the wake of the March Session, impeded the IOC's efforts to shift the media narrative from scandal to tangible reform and the transition of their own operations from crisis management to brand recovery.

## The Coles Affair

Phil Coles retained his IOC membership and his position on the Sydney Organizing Committee following the March Session despite evidence that he made multiple trips to Salt Lake City and accepted outings to a Super Bowl contest and a National Basketball Association All-Star Game.[11] Richard Pound's Ad Hoc Commission had established a principle on expulsion decisions, that is, whether a member asked for gifts and benefits. If a member had not asked for gifts and benefits but exhibited a lack of discretion in accepting that which had been offered, the penalty was not as harsh.[12] Coles, who did not seek these opportunities,[13] received a severe censure. Defenders of the well-liked and affable Australian included Pound, Jacques Rogge ("Mr. Coles is a man I appreciate"), and Australian Olympic Committee president John Coates ("He's hardly the gravy train type").[14] Still, the revelations sullied Coles's reputation and angered many members of SOCOG who were scrambling to deal with the challenge of soliciting necessary private-sector dollars in a compromised environment. Coles defended his conduct but soon conceded that "I should have been more circumspect in my actions. I've been careless." He resigned his office as the AOC's director of international relations as a means of mollifying those individuals who sought his ouster from SOCOG.[15] However, new charges concerning Coles's activities in relation to Salt Lake City's and Athens's bids exposed him to additional censure.

Coles's former wife, Georgina, confirmed that they received a set of diamond cufflinks and a gold necklace valued at $6,000 from an official with Athens's 1996 bid committee. Coles claimed his ex-wife might have received the items without his knowledge, as their relationship was strained at the time. He recalled nothing except having received a set of silver cuff links whose value he estimated at A$20–$30. Within days, a 1990 photograph of Georgina Coles appeared on the front page of the Sydney Morning Herald that showed her wearing the necklace and, as well, earrings that she indicated had been made from the cuff links.[16] Coles complained that his ex-wife had been drawn into a conspiracy to discredit him, and her actions simply reflected the "bitter and acrimonious" nature of their divorce.[17] Georgina Coles's statements provided an additional blow for her ex-husband, who was on a self-imposed leave from SOCOG owing to health reasons.[18]

Olympics minister and SOCOG president Michael Knight and Australian deputy prime minister Tim Fischer pressured Coles to resign from SOCOG's board, as did NBC's president of sports, Dick Ebersol and Australia's federal (Labor) opposition leader, Kim Beazley.[19] Coles understood that many of his board colleagues shared a desire for his exit. He also believed (correctly) that a faction of those persons undermining his position resided not in his own backyard (Sydney) but in Melbourne. A number of businessmen affiliated with that city's failed effort to secure the 1996 Olympics smelled blood. Melbourne officials learned that Coles, a member of the bid committee, made forty-four phone calls to Atlanta in the eighteen-month run-up to the 1990 vote in Tokyo. They perceived his actions as counter to their city's interests.[20] However, neither Knight nor SOCOG's board possessed the unilateral power to relieve Coles of his duties, given that his position existed by virtue of his IOC membership.[21] Coles did not buckle under the scrutiny and refused to resign from SOCOG's board or, for that matter, the IOC.

Coles's troubles were not limited to the allegations concerning the jewelry. The Australian Broadcasting Corporation revealed that it possessed files and IOC member dossiers compiled by Coles and his partner, Patricia Rosenbrock, that conveyed information about the members' "honesty, affluence, wealth, shopping preferences, sincerity, trustworthiness, and racial prejudices."[22] A source in Utah's capital supplied the documents to ABC. Coles denied Australian media speculation that he exchanged the dossiers for Salt Lake City's largesse and hospitality that had been the subject of the Ad Hoc Commission's initial investigation concerning his conduct. He denied profiting from any transaction with Salt Lake City officials, but he did note a "synergy" or "a sort of sister relationship" between the Sydney and Salt Lake City bid committees.[23] Coles's assertions concerning a collaborative working relationship between Sydney and Salt Lake City bid committee personnel puzzled compatriot Kevan Gosper.[24] Richard Pound dismissed the files as "low-grade psycho-babble" that failed to "amount to much,"[25] but his IOC Executive Board colleagues Pál Schmitt and Jacques Rogge found Coles's conduct discreditable. Schmitt chastised Coles for collecting the information,[26] and Rogge regretted the activity that he likened to "spying."[27]

SLOC officials, occupied with crisis management activities at the local level, suspected ABC's source to be a former member of the Salt Lake City

6. IOC Executive Board member Jacques Rogge (*left*) and director-general François Carrard traveled to Sydney, Australia, in April 1999 to address concerns with respect to the effect of the Salt Lake City crisis on SOCOG's fund-raising efforts. *Source:* Torsten Blackwood/AFP/Getty Images.

bid committee.[28] This wave of negative press coverage was too much for SOCOG's CEO, Sandy Hollway, who abandoned his neutral posture and called for Coles to resign.[29] No doubt discouraged by this recent turn of events, Coles blamed Michael Knight for orchestrating the campaign to force him from SOCOG's board.[30] The optics of the Coles affair were less than favorable for the IOC, which anticipated the March Session serving as a springboard for more sympathetic press coverage of its effort to confront the crisis.

### He's Back . . .

From the comfort of his fifty-ninth-floor office in Boston's John Hancock Tower, David D'Alessandro grew increasingly agitated with the media reports concerning Coles and the IOC's unwillingness to expel him. Once again he inserted himself into the media narrative. "The IOC talks about being

held to a higher standard, but it performs at the lowest possible denomina-
tor. Phil Coles broke all the rules but he gets a pass because he is one of the
boys," charged D'Alessandro.[31] He urged Coles to resign from the IOC to
permit Sydney officials to proceed with preparations unencumbered by the
distraction and harm caused by his situation. Coles "is damaging the [Olym-
pic] movement worldwide as well as Australia's outstanding efforts to stage
what will be extraordinary games," read a John Hancock press release.[32] The
IOC's failure to jettison Coles and Samaranch's decision to expand the size of
the IOC 2000 Commission by pushing the number of sitting IOC members
over forty were "stupid" actions.[33] D'Alessandro feared the prospect of a set
of Samaranch sycophants on the commission that had been conceived as a
smaller body numbering twenty to twenty-four members. He lectured Samaranch on the folly of this plan: "You have now loaded your reform committee
with people who have Olympic DNA, and clearly the offspring of that union
will be as cross-eyed as the other results you have brought so far."[34]

D'Alessandro's comments on Coles and the composition of the IOC
2000 Commission represented merely one of a number of salvos he fired
in Lausanne's direction. He also decried the IOC's decision to increase the
value of a TOP V (2001–4) sponsor agreement from forty million dollars
(TOP IV) to fifty-five million. Any TOP sponsor CEO who signed a TOP V
deal before considering the results of the IOC's reform initiatives, observed
D'Alessandro, "should be fired."[35] In mid-May he released internal company
polling data indicating that 20 percent of Americans had "lost faith" in the
Olympic Games and Olympic sponsors. Only 3 or 4 percent of respondents
were more likely to buy a sponsor's product than one manufactured by a non-
sponsor. The diminished pull of an Olympic sponsorship in the consumer
marketplace concerned him. Only a few short months earlier in the wake of
the 1998 Nagano Olympic Winter Games, 30 percent of respondents indicated that they would strongly consider a company's Olympic-sponsor status
in their purchase decisions. "When you put $40 million into this type of ven-
ture, you don't expect it to go the other way on you. You're spending money
to club yourself over the head," stated D'Alessandro.[36]

Michael Payne stewed about D'Alessandro's proclivity for headline-
grabbing commentaries. He suggested that Pound engage the John Hancock executive in a discussion, as his own attempts to temper D'Alessandro's

comments failed.[37] Pound, having read D'Alessandro's comments on Coles and the IOC 2000 Commission in Philip Hersh's May 5 piece in the *Chicago Tribune,* had already moved to discuss with John Hancock's boss how his media profile and approach compromised the IOC's efforts.

During May Pound provided some of his most critical service to the IOC during the crisis by liaising with D'Alessandro and reducing the toxic fallout of his interaction with media outlets. In a series of missives, Pound challenged D'Alessandro's strident tone and cautioned him that there was no benefit to those individuals within the IOC working for meaningful reform resulting from his media campaign. He was part of the problem for the IOC now, not the solution.

In a May 10 fax, Pound expressed his disappointment with D'Alessandro's use of the term *stupid* (if, in fact, he had been quoted accurately) and explained the motivation behind expanding the IOC 2000 Commission.[38] The change offered them a better opportunity to achieve the two-thirds vote required to usher the structural changes and policy reforms through the Session. The Executive Committee of the IOC 2000 Commission retained control of the process, possessed the responsibility for drafting the reforms, and drew on the thoughts of an equal number of IOC and non-IOC members. He implored D'Alessandro to "trust our judgment in determining the best manner in which to obtain the necessary consensus within our organization." All the sponsors were concerned that measurable reform result from the IOC's effort and that these reforms unroll in a contracted time frame, noted Pound. "But," he added, "they have not second-guessed each step we have taken along that road. Nor have they made statements that denigrate both the efforts which are under way and the value of Olympic sponsorship." "A single negative statement," Pound reminded D'Alessandro, "gets more play than a hundred positive statements." Finally, Pound informed D'Alessandro that his public comments were "*hurting* us [the IOC], the Olympic Movement, the upcoming Olympic Games and the Olympic athletes." He offered to meet him at a time and place of D'Alessandro's choosing to discuss these matters further, given their shared goal of preserving the Olympic brand.[39]

The sun did not set over Boston's corporate skyscrapers before D'Alessandro fired off his reply. He had been quoted accurately with respect to the use of the term *stupid,* and he regretted the damage caused by the appearance of a double standard in judging members' conduct as it related to Phil Coles's case. D'Alessandro cared little that other TOP sponsors remained silent and granted the IOC additional time to demonstrate meaningful reform. Samaranch missed an opportunity to confront the issues, he concluded. While the IOC is "somewhat slow moving and bureaucratic, organizations are only as frozen as their leadership allows," offered D'Alessandro. On a personal note, he wrote, "Dick, I certainly understand the fine line you have to walk these days and appreciate the difficulty of your position. I'm not sure, however, that you and others fully understand the public sentiment concerning the 'IOC Club.'" He learned of the proposed changes to the IOC 2000 Commission in a press report and was disappointed. He wanted to "feel more like a partner besides [just] sending in substantial checks on time."[40] He, too, believed a face-to-face meeting advisable.

On May 19, in response to the call for input issued at the meeting with the sponsors on March 30, D'Alessandro provided Pound with his thoughts on the steps required to emerge from the crisis. He emphasized the unacceptable pace of the IOC's reform process. Almost six months following the IOC's descent into a state of crisis, the only initiative, beyond the expulsion of a few "fringe" members, was the IOC 2000 Commission, an initiative that amounted to nothing more than a "study group that's promising to study the problem." The IOC shunned "decisive action to correct every climactic condition that encouraged corruption."[41]

D'Alessandro remained primarily interested in the concepts of transparency, accountability, and democracy. With an obvious but unstated reference to the likes of Phil Coles and Un Yong Kim, the IOC, he said, could no longer investigate itself, as the public's confidence had been shaken, and "insider-dispensed justice is neither credible nor effective." He did not support the composition of the IOC 2000 Commission and argued that such a body should be composed entirely of "outsiders." Term limits for IOC members, members of the Executive Board, and the president were required. Actions taken in regard to the selection process for the 2006 Olympic Winter Games did not rise beyond the level of a "Band-aid solution." He recommended establishing a streamlined selection committee composed of IOC members, athletes, sponsors, broadcasters, and ISF personnel. In what, for Pound at least, proved the most unpalatable suggestion, D'Alessandro highlighted the model of the United Nations and argued that each Olympic nation should be represented on the IOC.[42]

Pound appreciated D'Alessandro's candor and pledged two days later to address his concerns in like fashion. "I should have thought that the example of the United Nations would have demonstrated precisely why an organization established along these lines is *not* the answer to the problem," stated Pound in challenging D'Alessandro's view of the global institution's operational effectiveness. "The United States is not the same as San Marino (to take an example at random) and the IOC's structure is such that the interests, experience and knowledge of the important countries in sport shape its decisions, not the great majority of countries with no sports traditions or knowledge of international sport issues." He also disagreed with D'Alessandro's characterization of the pace and breadth of the IOC's actions. It expelled six members, four resigned, and ten others absorbed public reprimands. The label "fringe members," stated Pound, applied to the expelled individuals only so far as they did not "reflect the morality and responsibility of the vast majority of the IOC members." The newly established Ethics Commission possessed a majority of non-IOC members, the IOC 2000 Commission's mandate was clear with respect to the need to revitalize the organization, audited financial statements had been released, and the IOC produced an alternative selection process for the 2006 Olympic Winter Games.[43]

On other matters, there was some consensus between the two men. He concurred with D'Alessandro's thoughts concerning term limits, and his proposals that a comprehensive review of the IOC's policy concerning travel funds for members was advisable and that IOC members should be required to disclose any financial benefits accruing from their status. He pledged to work with D'Alessandro, who complained about the absence of a true partnership and working relationship between John Hancock and the IOC's US-based marketing arm, Meridian Management. However, he asserted that the IOC, much like many organizations and professions, could maintain its self-regulating status. Pound preferred a process that permitted the selection of Olympic host sites by a larger group than D'Alessandro suggested, as it offered "greater reliability" and avoided the possibility of a smaller body missing "some important consideration, or [being] swayed by persuasive members." He looked forward to their upcoming face-to-face meeting in New York, but held little back in passing judgment on D'Alessandro's public posturing in recent weeks:

> I must say I have been disappointed with the position that has been presented in the media as that of John Hancock. It has not been supportive of our sincere efforts to solve the problem and has, in fact, been quite harmful. I do not necessarily expect that you would be out there cheering us on through this trying period, but to damage the entire Olympic Movement with repeated statements, publicly doubting the sincerity of our efforts to solve the problem, hurts not only the IOC but also all Olympic athletes (mainly in the United States) and the Games themselves. I can only say that had the tables been reversed, I would not be publicly criticizing John Hancock as it tried to work its way out of the difficulties, whatever they were, that arose.[44]

In reflecting on Pound's words, D'Alessandro pledged to monitor the work of the IOC 2000 Commission without prejudging its deliberations; however, this promise was contingent on "the IOC and its public relations people" withholding attacks on "John Hancock's motives, integrity and financial condition."[45] Then, too, he was likely still vexed by the public criticism Kevan Gosper directed at him prior to the March Session.

Communication between Pound and D'Alessandro extended beyond the exchange of fax messages and scheduled face-to-face meetings to phone conversations. The pace of the reform process was one of the issues that occupied their time on the phone.[46] An agitated D'Alessandro stated that John Hancock required "tangible rather than theoretical reform" measures to satisfy its "board, employees, and American clientele" well before the IOC's year-end Session scheduled for December. He held Samaranch accountable for the IOC's failings in this regard, claiming that the IOC president did not exhibit "bold and decisive leadership" in the wake of the March Session. On Pound's assessment of the efficiency of the United Nations, and the wisdom of applying its structure to the Olympic world, D'Alessandro conceded his point; however, there was need for improvement in the IOC's membership structure. The United Nations might not be the most appropriate framework, concluded D'Alessandro, but "neither is Mr. Samaranch's unilateral selection of individuals from favored nations (Italy at last count had four members while the U.S. had two) or royal gene pools. Neither of these criteria have much to do with expertise in sport, site selection or athletic development. True, good members may emerge from this process from time to time. But let's not confuse luck with the need for a better system."[47]

D'Alessandro sympathized with Pound's position, but the need to press forward with the reform agenda was paramount and explained his pressure tactics in the media. "You have undertaken a difficult task under treacherous conditions with no small amount of personal risk. I applaud your courage. . . . Dick, I recognize that in some quarters, John Hancock is the 'enemy.' No doubt, some of our comments have stung. But your colleagues must understand that our criticism is a very small contributing factor to the problems they face today. The real enemy is public perception, the passage of time and the IOC's reluctance to realistically assess and manage both."[48] He, too, looked forward to their meeting in New York.

During their New York meeting, D'Alessandro shared with Pound his intent to publish an op-ed piece titled "The Games Must Go On." Pound's willingness to maintain a consistent channel of communication with him since the outbreak of the IOC's difficulties paid dividends at this time. When Pound reviewed the draft copy at D'Alessandro's request, he found many sources of discomfort. The disheartening financial prospects for Sydney and Salt Lake City and their existing revenue shortfalls discouraged sponsors from aligning themselves with a tarnished Olympic enterprise, wrote D'Alessandro. Pound argued that Sydney surpassed Atlanta in sponsorship dollars despite a smaller corporate base in Australia. SOCOG raised its original sponsorship goal by one hundred million dollars, reached that goal, and then against IOC advice raised its target again. Sydney knew the extent of this challenge in the summer of 1998, and "the political escape route has now been to blame the IOC for a problem that was SOCOG-created in the first place." Salt Lake City, offered Pound, brought in more sponsorship money than any other Winter Olympics Organizing Committee but elected to stage a Winter Games festival on a budget nearly matching the budget of Atlanta (a much larger enterprise). "One should not confuse an unrealistic wish-list with a shortfall caused by the IOC," countered Pound.[49]

In his multipage reaction, Pound emphasized the document's unhelpful nature. D'Alessandro's claim that the IOC moved at a "glacial" pace in dealing with needed reforms stupefied him. "Come on," Pound wrote in once again reviewing the IOC's initial series of actions in response to the crisis and challenging D'Alessandro's view. D'Alessandro stated that corporations might elect to sponsor athletes directly as opposed to "routing rivers of money to the IOC headquarters in Switzerland," thereby circumventing the IOC's Olympic Solidarity program. Given that the IOC retained but only 10 percent of the TOP sponsorship dollars with the remainder distributed to the OCOGs and NOCs, Pound objected to the phrase "rivers of money," which he labeled "purple" language. In counseling corporate CEOs who contemplated establishing a sponsor relationship with the IOC to withhold launching such initiatives until the IOC revealed its reform measures in their entirety, Pound believed D'Alessandro threatened to "spoil or retard the efforts of Salt Lake." If published in its current form, Pound noted, the article would elicit a response from the IOC. Such a response, he said, would "add heat, but not light, to the difficulties we face."[50]

The final version of the article published by D'Alessandro in the *Salt Lake Tribune* and the *Sydney Morning Herald* was less damaging than the incendiary original draft, clearly reflected Pound's call for tempered language, and ended with John Hancock's pledge to wait for the IOC's promised reforms.[51] Had Pound reined in John Hancock's president and CEO, or had D'Alessandro determined that Pound's promises would carry the day and he should allow him some room to operate unfettered by another round of negative press?

Pound's efforts unraveled temporarily within days when NBC's Dick Ebersol succumbed to "at least 60 days of pent-up rage" and unloaded on D'Alessandro in media interviews. D'Alessandro, stated Ebersol, was a "two-bit bully."[52] In attempting to explain his ongoing media commentary concerning Olympic matters, he claimed that D'Alessandro drew his motivation from "his own desire to be on a soap box." Ebersol advised the IOC to walk away from its deal with John Hancock, refund D'Alessandro's investment, and pursue any of a number of other willing sponsors in the financial services category. Moving forward without advertising dollars from John Hancock did not disturb Ebersol, who had already signed a deal with an unidentified insurance company for its upcoming Sydney telecasts. D'Alessandro's quest to see his name on the front page of newspapers hurt American athletes and the fund-raising prospects for Olympic organizers in Salt Lake City, concluded Ebersol.[53]

Ebersol's public rebuke enraged D'Alessandro. In a brief three-sentence fax to Pound, D'Alessandro wrote, "This is what I mean by attacks. And you expect me to be supportive?! Ebersol is your friend."[54] In the public forum, D'Alessandro called Ebersol's outburst a "desperate and sad commentary" from an individual who was scrambling to burnish the sagging image of the Olympic Games. "If I were Dick Ebersol and had hitched my career to the Olympics, I'd be pretty scared too," offered D'Alessandro, underscoring NBC's $3.5 billion outlay for US Olympic television rights to five Olympic festivals (2000–2008).[55] He believed the personal attack went "far beyond a reasonable businessperson's approach."[56] Their spat played out in the media over the course of the first week of June and, as a media story line, provided unwanted competition for the initial gathering of the IOC 2000 Commission, a more hopeful and positive narrative from the IOC's perspective. The two American corporate giants did not begin to bury the hatchet until they met at the Ryder Cup golf matches held outside Boston in September 1999. Eventually, D'Alessandro and Ebersol established a contractual relationship for advertising on NBC's Sydney telecasts when John Hancock announced its intent to renew its TOP contract in February 2000.[57]

## TOP Sponsors Provide Input

April and May 1999 were important months in the consultation process with TOP sponsors, as the IOC sought meaningful input prior to the launch of the work of the IOC 2000 Commission in June. Accountability, financial transparency, and the need for ethical standards resonated in letters from TOP sponsor executives sent to Richard Pound in his role as chairman of the IOC's Marketing Commission. David D'Alessandro and his fellow TOP sponsors shared similar visions for the depth and breadth of reform required to position the IOC for the twenty-first century; however, they differed on the preferred means of promoting this change. While D'Alessandro provided his assessment of the IOC's response to the crisis and suggestions for reform in the public arena, other TOP sponsors conveyed their thoughts privately to IOC officials.

Rosemary Windsor-Williams, UPS's vice president of Olympic and corporate events, emphasized the need for financial transparency and clear reporting on the ways in which TOP sponsors' dollars were apportioned to various Olympic agencies or initiatives. She urged the IOC to establish term limits for its members and to enhance the geographical representation of its membership. The bid process required standardization as a means of improving the confidence people had in the results, and the IOC, she noted, must tackle the doping issue and the injustices tied to those sports that employed subjective judging.[58]

Nancy J. Wiese, Xerox Corporation's director of worldwide marketing communications, echoed all of these thoughts on behalf of the company's chairman, Paul Allaire, but also challenged the planned increase in the cost of a TOP V sponsorship deal and what theretofore had been sacrosanct—the IOC's clean, advertisement-free venue policy. She also supported David D'Alessandro's proposal that OCOGs and the IOC needed to improve their methods of transferring knowledge on sponsorship matters from one OCOG to the next.[59]

McDonald's Corporation's director of global sports marketing, Jackie S. Woodward, discussed the need for term limits, improved methods of financial disclosure, and stringent ethical standards as well as the need to enhance the voice of active or recently retired Olympic athletes within the IOC. The latter suggestion drew favor from many of the sponsors.[60]

Kodak's chairman and CEO, George Fisher, identified term limits for IOC members as an absolute must for sponsors and relayed his concerns about the underrepresentation of women and athletes on the IOC.[61] The spiraling costs of staging an Olympic festival, and the fallout for sponsors, who were called upon for increasing sums of money, also concerned Kodak.[62] While he pledged his company's patience in waiting for the reforms, Kodak expected results. Kodak aimed for a top-five brand ranking in the world every year, and "we are concerned when external influences, such as the current situation facing the IOC, can potentially collide with the value of our brand."[63]

In a comprehensive and sweeping document, Charles B. Fruit, Coca-Cola's vice president and director of media and marketing assets, provided his thoughts on matters extending from the composition of the IOC's

membership and numerous commissions to the need for financial transparency and improved knowledge transfer between successive OCOGs.
Fruit echoed Kodak's concerns about the rising costs of staging Olympic
festivals and called it "one of the most ominous circumstances facing the
IOC and the Olympic movement." "Unchecked," continued Fruit, "the
escalating costs will create even greater pressures on sponsorship revenues
(both directly and through the escalating costs of advertising on the Games
broadcasts). The ultimate outcome of the escalating costs is a Games that is
more commercial, cluttered with sponsors, and increasingly economically
untenable for all sponsors."[64]

TOP sponsors remained largely silent on Samaranch's future; however,
Michael J. Klingensmith, president of *Sports Illustrated*, broke ranks and
advised that the IOC's recovery would be expedited with new leadership,
as "this horrible crisis has irreparably damaged the credibility of the current
IOC President." Klingensmith noted that his thoughts on the reform process
did not represent an official company response but rather reflected his own
and the thoughts of a few other *SI* executive colleagues. While he stood apart
from his fellow TOP sponsor CEOs on Samaranch's future, Klingensmith
summarized their collective thinking on the need to avoid a second scandal.
"If similar circumstances were to rise again, our continuing association with
the games would be seriously jeopardized. We have weathered intense criticisms from shareholders, employees and our own editors, and would not look
forward to doing so again. Nor can we imagine that other sponsors would be
willing to endure this again. Therefore, addressing the matter of institutional
reform *now* seems to us to be a matter of survival for one of the greatest
institutions of all time: The Olympic Games." Richard Pound responded to
Klingensmith and the other correspondents in detailed point-by-point fashion.[65] Clearly, he understood the sponsors' need for the IOC to "perform" in
the weeks ahead.

The IOC 2000 Commission, replete with world-celebrated individuals
such as former US secretary of state Henry Kissinger, former United Nations
secretary-general Boutros Boutros-Ghali, and former president of Costa Rica
and Nobel Prize recipient Oscar Arias Sánchez, convened in Lausanne on
June 1 and 2 to initiate discussions regarding possible reforms.[66] Armed with

advice from the sponsors and other interested constituencies within the Olympic world, commission members set to their task.

## Meanwhile, in Washington . . .

In the 1980s and 1990s, Washington proved a troublesome environment for the IOC, in no small measure because of the collaborative efforts of the USOC and a number of US lawmakers to reduce the power and influence of the Lausanne-based organization in the American market. The root of the IOC's difficulties lay in Congress's passage of the Amateur Sports Act (ASA) in 1978. Conceived as a means of bringing to an end the internecine disputes among the National Collegiate Athletic Association, Amateur Athletic Union, and the USOC for control of the country's participation in the Olympic Games, it also granted an important financial lever to the USOC. The ASA gave the USOC exclusive US territorial rights for the use of all Olympic terminology and designations, most important the five-ring logo devised by Pierre de Coubertin in 1913.[67]

The USOC did not realize the financial bonanza of this clause until the mid-1980s when it wielded the ASA to secure 15 percent of TOP revenue for permitting access to the major sponsors in the US market for TOP I (1985–88).[68] Preparations for rolling out successive TOP programs on a quadrennial basis aroused USOC threats of nonparticipation in the absence of a percentage increase in its share. By the mid-1990s, the USOC used the terms of the ASA, together with the IOC Marketing Department's (and the sponsors') need for access to the United States, to enhance its share to 20 percent of all TOP revenue.[69]

In 1985 the USOC demanded remuneration for permitting prospective advertisers to employ the Olympic rings in commercials on US Olympic telecasts.[70] This latter initiative resulted in the signing of the Broadcast Marketing Agreement (BMA) in 1986. This IOC-USOC deal provided a payment of $15 million to the USOC for ceding the right to the American Broadcasting Company to feature the five-ring logo in commercials produced by its Calgary and Seoul telecast sponsors who purchased advertising time. The BMA also granted the USOC 10 percent of all future US Olympic television contracts.[71] Over the ensuing years in advance of the Salt Lake City scandal, the

USOC aggressively pursued increases to its share of revenue from the TOP program and US Olympic television deals.

The USOC wielded Congress as a brickbat in an attempt to lessen the IOC's authority in the US market and enhance its own financial treasury in late 1990. Representative Tom McMillen (D-MD) drafted the Olympic Television Broadcast Act in collaboration with the USOC and US network television executives. Three major aspects of the legislative initiative concerned IOC officials. The bill transferred the right to negotiate US Olympic television contracts from the IOC to the USOC. Such a scenario empowered the USOC to increase its 10 percent share of the US television contracts independent of discussion with the IOC. A waiver from the Sherman Anti-Trust Act for US television networks also figured in the bill.[72] Television executives who were concerned with the spiraling cost of acquiring US rights argued that a collaborative bid from all three major networks provided a necessary reduction in their outlay. The IOC correctly envisioned that a hugely reduced sum of money from the US market would result if the waiver was granted, to say nothing of a vastly diminished share for the IOC. Last, a ban on commercials during the network consortium's live coverage of events, argued McMillen, limited the premium paid by US citizens on products sold by Olympic advertisers. From an IOC perspective, overall advertising revenue would plummet as a result of this restriction and further suppress the amount of money offered by the networks.[73]

Why the USOC would wish to be party to the latter two initiatives puzzled Richard Pound, who spearheaded the IOC's effort to head off Mc-Millen's endeavor. Pound successfully discouraged McMillen from moving forward with the legislation in 1991 by explaining the nature of the USOC's current arrangement with the IOC via the BMA, something that no other NOC in the world enjoyed, and by noting that Salt Lake City might suffer a backlash from IOC members in the upcoming vote on the host city of the 1998 Olympic Winter Games.[74]

When Pound resisted the USOC's repeated demands for an increase in its 10 percent share of US television contracts in the 1990s, American Olympic leaders once again conspired with US politicians to pursue this goal. The tipping point for the USOC in electing for this course of action for a second time occurred when the IOC signed two megadeals with NBC (totaling $3.5

billion) within mere months of each other in 1995 for the US television rights to the Sydney and Salt Lake City festivals and the yet-to-be-awarded Games of 2004, 2006, and 2008. Pound, who pursued the deals with Samaranch's blessing, appreciated the financial security offered by this approach and knew that the USOC's share would be limited to 10 percent by virtue of the BMA. He thought $350 million to be a sufficient payout for the USOC.[75]

Angered by Pound's lack of consultation with them on negotiations for the initial NBC contract, USOC officials discussed their share of the contract for the 2004, 2006, and 2008 festivals directly with Samaranch, who desired an amicable resolution. The USOC's executive director, Dick Schultz, moved from the USOC's oft-repeated demand for 20 percent of US Olympic television money to 15 percent in relation to the second IOC-NBC contract. However, he failed to inform Samaranch of his parallel efforts in Washington to shift responsibility for negotiating US television contracts from the IOC to the USOC through clauses buried deep in an unrelated Senate bill. The IOC escaped this undesirable outcome because of the keen eye of an NBC staff person who brought it to the attention of his superiors, who then duly informed the IOC.[76] In the 1980s and 1990s, an unmistakable fissure between the IOC and USOC existed in relation to Olympic revenue and the power and authority of the IOC to conduct business in the United States.

Samaranch deeply resented Schultz's activities behind his back and called for an IOC-USOC summit in October 1996. When representatives of the two organizations convened in Cancún, Mexico, Samaranch issued the threat that the IOC was willing to move forward without the USOC.[77] The IOC, stated Samaranch, was a club. "Being a member was not compulsory," he added, "but members had to abide by its rules." The threat to shut the USOC out of the Games was at best veiled, but in stating it, Samaranch conveyed the depth of his anger. Samaranch and Pound realized that some sort of resolution was required, and the two teams agreed that the USOC's share would increase to 12.75 percent commencing with the 2004 Summer Games.[78] Schultz achieved his goal of enhancing the USOC's allocation from US television revenue, but in pursuing the Washington option sacrificed any hope of gaining the desired 15 percent.

In 1999 the IOC's beleaguered state drew Arizona senator John McCain's attention. McCain, chairman of the US Senate Committee on Commerce,

Science, and Transportation, scheduled hearings on possible financial sanctions against the IOC.[79] He called for the hearings as a means of encouraging the IOC to adopt reform proposals forwarded by George Mitchell. Mitchell, engaged by the USOC to lead an investigation of the organization's failings in regard to Salt Lake City's bid, provided numerous reform suggestions for the IOC and the USOC.[80] McCain placed Samaranch squarely in his crosshairs; however, much to his chagrin, the IOC president declined the invitation to appear before the committee. He preferred to make his appearance in Washington following the acceptance of the reform proposals by the IOC Session. McCain, who criticized Samaranch's status as chairman of the IOC 2000 Commission, noted that his decision reflected a lack of understanding of "the gravity of the situation for the future of the Olympic Movement."[81]

McCain's committee was scheduled to discuss scrapping the IOC's tax-exempt status that permitted US corporations to receive a tax break on their Olympic donations. Michael Payne calmly rebutted the wisdom of such a policy initiative by noting how this decision would disadvantage US companies in relation to their European and Japanese competitors.[82] Senator Ted Stevens (D-AK),[83] the architect of the ASA, stood poised to introduce legislation to permit the USOC to negotiate US Olympic television contracts, while Representatives Henry Waxman (D-CA) and Rick Lazio (R-NY) drafted the International Olympic Committee Reform Act of 1999, a bill that proscribed transfer of any US corporate moneys to the IOC until the recommendations of the Mitchell Commission had been accepted by Lausanne officials.[84]

McCain's comments and the intervention of other US politicians irritated US IOC member James Easton, who saw it as the height of hypocrisy. Easton, who eventually appeared before McCain's commission, along with Anita DeFrantz, unloaded his frustration. "You talk about people in glass houses. Here we have our politicians who live daily with conflicts of interest criticizing us on the way we run our business. I think it's out of line." The actions of McCain and other politicians reflected their search for "political advantage" rather than any desire to aid the Olympic Movement, he concluded.[85] Before facing McCain's committee, Easton took a conciliatory approach in apologizing to McCain for accusing him of "preaching righteousness" and standing on a "soap box." Having educated himself on McCain's activities, he believed him to be "sincere."[86]

7. In April 1999, Senator John McCain (R-AZ), chairman of the Senate Committee on Commerce, Science, and Transportation, held hearings on Olympic matters. Even though invited to appear, Samaranch declined the opportunity in favor of remaining in Lausanne to work toward achieving definitive reform measures. *Source:* Mario Tama/AFP/Getty Images.

George Mitchell blunted the possible disaster for the IOC. Mitchell's report for the USOC outlined the need for sweeping reform of the IOC, including the need for a review committee composed entirely of outsiders, unlike the IOC 2000 Commission, which included IOC members and was chaired by Samaranch. Prior to his testimony in Washington, Mitchell signaled that the IOC's reform agenda was a work in progress. Some good work had been done, said Mitchell, but much work remained. "You've got to give people time to do things," observed the former Senate majority leader.[87] Committee members Ernest Hollings (D-SC) and Richard Bryan (D-NV) called for Samaranch's resignation. When called before the committee, DeFrantz and Easton spent an uncomfortable forty-five minutes under pointed questioning. However, Mitchell's comments aided the IOC's cause. His assessment of the IOC's efforts to date was music to the ears of Pound and Payne, who publicly lobbied for the time necessary to achieve consensus for change within the IOC membership. Still, the IOC's resolve warranted careful monitoring, noted Mitchell. "If the odor of scandal is allowed to hang over the Olympic Movement," he offered in his closing comments to the people gathered in the Senate committee's chambers, "those Games will lose their meaning and, worse, will take on a new meaning—one that speaks of excess, elitism, and money."[88]

McCain, too, accepted the need to grant IOC leaders some breathing room to accomplish their goals, even though he would have preferred a "better feeling and understanding of the IOC's intentions on reform."[89] He expressed his impatience with DeFrantz's inability to field questions concerning the extent of the IOC's financial interests in the American market as well as Easton's and her unwillingness to accept all recommendations forwarded by Mitchell's panel. McCain called the task of marshaling the support for reform within the IOC a "heavy burden," but it was imperative. "Without a rigorous reform process, I fear the Olympic ideal may end up a relic of the past."[90] He asked for monthly reports from the IOC on the progress with its reform agenda; however, the IOC Executive Board denied his request.[91] Still, McCain told the *New York Times*'s George Vecsey that threats were not part of his arsenal, despite the public discourse prior to the committee's hearings. "The biggest mistakes I've made came when I was in a hurry." The hearings, concluded McCain, accomplished their purpose in putting the IOC on notice. "I say we should let the tea sit in the saucer for a while."[92]

### A June Deadline

The next benchmark for IOC officials was the 109th IOC Session scheduled for Seoul, South Korea, in mid-June. While even the likes of McCain and D'Alessandro did not expect to see the full breadth of the reform agenda in June, Samaranch and the Executive Board needed to move the ball closer to the goal posts. The IOC leadership's focus fell on the mandates and early efforts of the Ethics and IOC 2000 Commissions.

Kéba Mbaye, Kevan Gosper, and François Carrard spearheaded the development of the Ethics Commission in the wake of the recommendation for its establishment by Richard Pound's Ad Hoc Commission in January. Their efforts were informed, in part, by discussions within the Executive Board. Pál Schmitt and Chiharu Igaya opposed developing a commission whose mandate extended beyond assisting the IOC to recover from the current scandal. Igaya spoke against a body that would investigate member conduct "like some sort of police force." To address the public's diminished confidence in the IOC, Gosper strongly asserted its need for a standing committee to monitor IOC member conduct in relation to a yet-to-be-established code of ethics. Gosper reminded Igaya and Schmitt that oversight of IOC member conduct represented merely one means of how the Ethics Commission could benefit the organization in the long term. He said that the IOC's interactions with governments, television networks, and corporate sponsors should also adhere to best practices.[93]

The Executive Board also reflected on the Ethics Commission's scope of authority. IOC members, candidate cities, and OCOGs would fall under its purview, and the commission was tasked with promoting best practices by the NOCs and ISFs. NOCs and ISFs possessed their own codes of conduct, and in light of the cross-membership in the Olympic Movement that witnessed many IOC members serving on an ISF or NOC, the IOC needed to set the highest of standards.[94] The Ethics Commission's eight-person structure drew Session approval in March along with a draft of the Code of Ethics.

Within a month of its first meeting on May 3, the Ethics Commission, composed of Mbaye, Gosper, Igaya, Howard Baker, Javier Pérez de Cuéllar, Robert Badinter, Kurt Fürgler, and Charmaine Crooks, completed the necessary revisions to the Code of Ethics. The IOC Session formally approved this code in Seoul as well as the commission's responsibility to meet, at minimum, on a semiannual basis.[95] IOC members, including Franco Carraro, Guy Drut, Bob Hasan, Un Yong Kim, Yong Sung Park, Richard Pound, Henri Sérandour, Ivan Slavkov, and even former USOC financial heavyweight John Krimsky, have been subject to investigation by the Ethics Commission since its inception.[96]

The IOC Session approved the establishment of the IOC 2000 Commission in March; however, its eventual structure did not match the original design of some twenty to twenty-four members. Samaranch had a change of heart within days of IOC members retreating from Lausanne following the

108th Extraordinary IOC Session. He subscribed to the tenets of participative leadership in pushing for an expansion of the number of IOC members to some forty individuals. More IOC members, concluded Samaranch, were necessary to ensure ratification from the Session.[97]

Samaranch's call for an expansion of the size of the commission to more than eighty members in total drew Pound's rebuke. Pound warned Samaranch that this decision exposed him to criticism from the media that he was trying to exert undue control over the reform dialogue.[98] At the IOC Executive Board's May 4 meeting, Samaranch dismissed Pound's concerns when he stated that "the media tended to do nothing but criticize anyway," and he had grown accustomed to their treatment. Although he lost the argument within the Executive Board on the size of the IOC 2000 Commission, Pound convinced his colleagues to place the smaller Executive Commission, with a fifty-fifty IOC member to nonmember ratio, in charge of placing the IOC 2000 Commission's final reform recommendations before the IOC Executive Board.[99] Pound correctly predicted the eventual backlash in the media, driven in part by David D'Alessandro's criticisms.[100]

The Executive Board also considered the danger of the reform process spinning wildly out of control. They determined that all external members of the IOC 2000 Commission required some background on the history of the IOC and its structure in the form of a "briefing book" that could be supplemented by copies of the *Olympic Charter*. This educational initiative empowered the outside members to make a meaningful and informed contribution. Pound asserted that the IOC must ensure that the public's expectations were realistic and that the IOC 2000 Commission's mandate was not "to completely revolutionize the IOC." Gosper echoed Pound's cautionary message: "They had to be careful not to turn the organization upside down. He knew from experience that if one attempted to move too far, too fast, it could be a destabilizing factor. The IOC should move at its own pace and not be driven by other people's timetables, particularly those of politicians or the media."[101]

In an effort to give direction to the reform process, the Executive Board created three working groups within the IOC 2000 Commission chaired by Franco Carraro, Thomas Bach, and Anita DeFrantz, respectively. Their tasks were to examine and make recommendations concerning the composition and structure of the IOC, the IOC's role, and the host-city selection process.[102] Following the first meeting of the IOC 2000 Commission on June 1 and 2, the working groups met twice between July and September to facilitate the submission of their final reports to the Executive Commission of the IOC 2000 Commission on September 25.[103]

## Light at the End of the Tunnel?

The late Ralph Sabock, a professor from whom Stephen Wenn took a sport administration course during his PhD studies at Pennsylvania State University in the early 1990s, shared an adage with those individuals aspiring to a career in administration: "Better to be a fire preventer than a fire fighter." Although we cannot comment on its originality, it speaks to the wisdom of heading off crises before they occur through consistent internal monitoring of one's organization. Its usefulness in assessing the attitude of IOC executives in April and May 1999 is also readily apparent.

In the November 1998 through March 1999 period, Samaranch and his colleagues were forced into managing the crisis in reactive fashion, but in the aftermath of the 108th Extraordinary IOC Session in March, they utilized the genesis of the IOC Ethics and 2000 Commissions to encourage a shift in their crisis management roles. They were weary of firefighting and took tangible steps in April and May intended to place the organization on a more positive trajectory for the twenty-first century through meaningful policy initiatives. Brush fires still appeared. The ongoing Coles affair, David D'Alessandro's media campaign, and John McCain's hearings all provided distractions.[104] Still, Lausanne's gloomy working environment became brighter and more hopeful. Could IOC officials maintain this momentum?

# 6

# Back from the Abyss

### The Storm Clouds Part

Media coverage of the IOC and its activities improved in the wake of the 108th Extraordinary IOC Session in March, and the genesis of the IOC Ethics and 2000 Commissions secured some breathing room for the IOC to craft its reform proposals; however, there was a clear need to follow through with the reform process pledged to the athletes, sponsors, and general public. During the summer months of 1999, IOC leaders forged ahead with this mission despite a number of distractions. Their efforts ultimately yielded passage of fifty reform measures to the *Olympic Charter* at the IOC's 110th Session in Lausanne in December. Within days of the Session, Juan Antonio Samaranch skillfully defended the IOC's interests in the US market before the House Commerce Subcommittee on Oversight and Investigations headed by Fred Upton (R-MI). Samaranch's calm, adroit performance signaled that the IOC had stepped back from the abyss. John Hancock's decision to renew its TOP sponsorship deal for the 2001–4 quadrennium (TOP V), formally announced in February 2000 but first revealed to the IOC a week after Samaranch's Washington visit, and the optics of David D'Alessandro's return to the Olympic tent, prompted a collective sigh of relief in Lausanne. The IOC's focus could rest squarely on Sydney in anticipation of the gathering of the world's Olympians later in the year.

### The IOC's Reform Proposals Take Shape

One albatross for both the IOC and Sydney organizers who labored to meet sponsorship targets in advance of the 2000 Summer Olympics was Phil Coles.

Coles's case continued to draw attention in June 1999. Olympics minister Michael Knight, Australian Olympic Committee president John Coates, and Sydney Organizing Committee CEO Sandy Hollway were lined up against him and considered him an impediment to their efforts to guide the city's effort to stage a successful Olympics.[1] Knight was greatly perturbed that Coles retained a position on SOCOG's board as a result of his IOC membership despite having been issued a "most severe warning" for his acceptance of excessive hospitality from Salt Lake City.[2]

Coles's survival in March provided the prima facie evidence for the likes of John Hancock's David D'Alessandro and the IOC's media critics of a double standard in how the organization meted out justice. They judged Coles's actions as serious as the activities of Jean-Claude Ganga, Lamine Keita, Sergio Santander Fantini, and the others, and they complained that he was spared the ignominious dispatch experienced by his six IOC colleagues because of his high-profile status and likable nature. Subsequent revelations concerning the preparation of dossiers on some seventy IOC members by Coles and his partner, Patricia Rosenbrock, and their possession by Salt Lake City bidders, forced the IOC to review its earlier decision.[3] Word that Coles also breached IOC policy by taking two companions (rather than the permitted one) on a trip to Atlanta in July 1989, during that city's candidature for the 1996 Olympics (at an expense of $13,053 to Atlanta bidders), compounded his predicament.[4]

A three-person investigative committee composed of IOC Executive Board members Kéba Mbaye, Anita DeFrantz, and Marc Hodler determined in early June that Coles's conduct merited expulsion; however, they filed no written recommendation when it became clear that other members of the Executive Board, specifically Richard Pound and Un Yong Kim, did not concur with the assessment. Mbaye, DeFrantz, and Hodler did not wish to propose an action that would divide the Executive Board, so they worked to find a compromise approach.[5]

The IOC Executive Board did not recommend Coles's expulsion at its June meeting in Seoul, but did move to squelch the damaging and persistent media coverage of Coles's situation in the Australian press and mollify Michael Knight, who considered his continuing membership on SOCOG's board untenable. The Executive Board, through the IOC's director-general, François Carrard, issued him an ultimatum on June 11: he could resign his seat on SOCOG's board or face expulsion from the IOC. The Executive Board concluded that Coles was guilty of serious negligence, not for having generated the files on his IOC colleagues but for having not ensured their security.[6] He kept his IOC seat but was precluded from serving on any IOC commissions or working groups for two years. Richard Pound, a longtime friend of Coles, played an instrumental role in carving out the compromise deal. One Executive Board member concluded that "Dick Pound saved [Coles] and he owes him heaps."[7]

Coles battled gamely to the end and tried without success to discuss the ultimatum with Samaranch by phone. He sought a conference call with Samaranch and Michael Knight, but Samaranch refused to discuss the entreaty with him and handed the receiver to Carrard, who reiterated the terms of the Executive Board's decision.[8] It might have been Pound's phone call to Coles that finally convinced his friend that there was no room for

8. Australia's Phil Coles shares his excitement about the impending opening of the Sydney Olympics during the waning moments of the torch relay with spectators gathered at Sydney's iconic Bondi Beach. *Source:* Scott Barbour/Getty Images Sport/Getty Images.

negotiation.[9] His actions proved costly. Having already resigned from his paid position (A$140,000) with the Australian Olympic Committee, Coles now sacrificed the A$50,000 yearly stipend received for his service on SOCOG's board.[10] Kevan Gosper swiftly tried to consign his case to the background. "This has been a pretty painful event for a lot of people," observed Gosper. "It has been a very severe chapter for the IOC," he noted. "It is a very severe punishment. I hope we have closed the door on it now."[11]

During its deliberations in Seoul, the Executive Board reflected on other troubling aspects of the fallout from the scandal. François Carrard generated a good deal of discussion with his assertion that IOC members entering the United States would likely face questioning from the FBI concerning the Salt Lake City bid. Kéba Mbaye and Kevan Gosper pledged to refrain from traveling to the United States until the threat passed. Thomas Bach preferred a similar course of action, but his own professional duties prevented him from shutting down his travel to the United States. He expressed concern about his professional reputation if, upon arrival in the country in the company of a client, he received a summons. Anita DeFrantz agreed to prepare a memorandum, subject to the approval of the Executive Board, that would outline the current situation regarding the FBI's investigative efforts and possible interest in IOC members entering the United States.[12] When Samaranch shared with the media the unease of IOC members with the prospect of facing an FBI interview, Richard Pound offered that the fears were misplaced. "I think most of the ones that might have had a concern aren't traveling as IOC members anymore," stated Pound.[13]

The Executive Board also considered John Hancock's expression of interest in negotiating a renewal of its TOP sponsorship for TOP V. Gosper, only a week removed from his very public media spat with D'Alessandro, expressed surprise that the Marketing Department contemplated such negotiations, as D'Alessandro proved "less than helpful" during the crisis. Thomas Bach doubted that John Hancock would renew its TOP agreement. He offered that the IOC might be best advised to cut ties with John Hancock now rather than deal with the media backlash if D'Alessandro walked away. He, too, believed D'Alessandro's conduct compromised the IOC's efforts.[14] Pound, who invested much time in communicating to D'Alessandro the IOC's purpose and intent in managing the crisis, dissented.

Pound noted that "the IOC would lose the PR battle if they fired John Hancock for being critical." He also offered that D'Alessandro's most recent public commentary indicated that he "was trying to climb down from his previous position."[15] He was prepared to grant the IOC sufficient time to advance its reform agenda. Undoubtedly, Pound referred to the op-ed piece appearing in the *Sydney Morning Herald* the previous week in which D'Alessandro commented on the development of the IOC 2000 Commission and the IOC's stated intent to address its recommendations for "structural reform" by the close of 1999:

> We're still not happy with this pace; the scandal will be a year old by then. But the IOC is a group of volunteers from around the globe, and incapable of reacting as quickly as a business or government. The IOC is asking for another half a year, and we should grant it. . . . As we await the IOC's promised reforms, reserving judgment as to how successful they will be, we can't forget that the Olympic movement is far bigger than the IOC. The Games and the athletes need and deserve our direct support. It may be very smart business to give it.[16]

Although he did not advise his sponsor colleagues to renew their TOP agreements before examining the nature of the reform proposals offered and adopted later in the year, his previous strident tone softened noticeably. The Executive Board stayed the course and permitted events related to any possible renegotiation with John Hancock to unfold.[17]

Turin's (Italy) startling win over Sion, Switzerland, for the right to host the 2006 Olympic Winter Games overshadowed developments concerning the IOC's reform agenda at the IOC's 109th Session in Seoul.[18] The fifteen-member electoral college selected by IOC members at the Session (as a result of the change in site-selection procedures in light of the scandal) identified Sion, which had been given the highest marks of all six contending cities by the IOC Evaluation Committee, and Turin as the two finalist cities for consideration.[19] Turin's convincing win by a vote of fifty-three to thirty-six when all IOC members were polled raised eyebrows. The aggrieved Swiss delegation accused IOC members of punishing Sion for Marc Hodler's whistle-blowing activities. Denis Oswald, an IOC member and delegate with the Sion bid committee, concluded that "Sion wasn't the loser. Sion was a victim. Today, the IOC was the loser."[20] Jean-Loup Chappelet, Sion's technical director, lashed out at the IOC's decision: "The best should win. If the best doesn't win, it's not sports. It's deals, business, politics. . . . Of course, we're angry. It's obvious. It's one thing to be angry. It's another to have a fair process. Let's make the vote public so each member is responsible for his vote."[21]

Even the Italians sensed the "Hodler effect." "I think for the Swiss bid," observed Marco San Pietro, one of Turin's bid committee leaders, "it would have been better if Mr. Hodler hadn't made his allegation."[22] Still, the re-sounding nature of the victory, a seventeen-vote win, added San Pietro, diminished its importance.[23] None of this subtext dampened the enthusiasm of the members of the Turin delegation, who bathed each other in champagne and danced following Samaranch's official announcement of the result.

In Seoul IOC members received progress reports from Kéba Mbaye on behalf of those individuals responsible for steering the efforts of the fledgling Ethics Commission and Franco Carraro, Thomas Bach, and Anita DeFrantz, the chairs of the three working groups of the IOC 2000 Commission. Mbaye's formal proposals on the statutes and rules of the Ethics Commission and the IOC Code of Ethics were passed with little discussion; however, Uruguay's Julio César Maglione wondered whether the operational scope of the Code of Ethics should extend beyond the IOC, OCOGs, and NOCs affiliated with host or bid cities to the broader sporting community, including the likes of the NOCs and ISFs. Mbaye appreciated the Session's support and indicated that those persons who drafted the proposals similarly gave thought to Maglione's concerns but elected for the more restricted approach "in order to avoid being challenged over a lack of jurisdiction." As for the IOC 2000 Commission, the working groups planned to use the recent meetings of the commission on June 1 and 2 as a springboard for much work in July, August, and September. The IOC 2000 Executive Commission would study the recommendations in September and propose a slate of reforms to the Plenary Commission for its approval. Once agreed upon, the recommendations would be shared with all IOC members, who would then gather at an IOC Session in December to consider and approve them.[24]

## Will He or Won't He Go to Washington?

Juan Antonio Samaranch turned aside efforts of Senator John McCain to
have him travel to Washington in April to face questions concerning the Salt
Lake City scandal and the IOC's site-selection procedures before McCain's
Senate Committee on Commerce, Science, and Transportation. George
Mitchell, who headed an investigation of the Salt Lake City scandal for the
USOC, counseled McCain to grant the IOC the remainder of the year to
enact its planned reforms. Before pursuing legislation that would remove the
organization's tax-free status and reroute much of the US television money
from the IOC and its partner organizations to the USOC, the IOC deserved
an opportunity to enact promised reforms, stated Mitchell. McCain stood
down, but he maintained significant interest in developments by reviewing
monthly reports from USOC president Bill Hybl and IOC Executive Board
member Anita DeFrantz and holding discussions with Richard Pound and
NBC's Dick Ebersol, a key member of the IOC 2000 Commission.[25]

McCain was not the only Washington politician with an interest in the
IOC reform process. Fred Upton, chairman of the House Commerce Subcommittee on Oversight and Investigations, called for hearings on the 1996
Atlanta bid in October. Former US attorney general Griffin Bell's investigation, which revealed that Atlanta employed gifts to aid its effort to secure the
1996 Summer Olympics, spurred Upton's decision. Bell revealed that Atlanta
offered college scholarships to the daughters of Nigeria's Henry Adefope and
Hungary's Pál Schmitt. Both were declined.[26] Atlanta organizers revealed
that thirty-eight gifts, including ones given to Un Yong Kim, Pirjo Häggman, and Marc Hodler, exceeded the IOC's $200 limit.[27] Three of Atlanta's
inducements, observed Bell, might have breached US law. A $948 carburetor
kit given to Libya's Bashir Attarabulsi and a live English bulldog provided to
Cuba's Manuel Gonzalez Guerra might have violated US trade embargoes in
effect with both countries. Two Atlanta officials carried money into the United
States for a (non-US) IOC member in quantities that did not require a customs
declaration. The money was then given to the IOC member's US business.[28]
Atlanta, too, possessed dossiers on IOC members regarding their preferences
and personal characteristics—these details had been provided by an individual
with Anchorage's failed bid for the 1994 Olympic Winter Games.[29]

Bell concluded that Atlanta did not employ a "systematic vote-buying system" as had been constructed by Tom Welch and Dave Johnson in Salt Lake City, but IOC Executive Board member Jacques Rogge disagreed. Atlanta "had this kind of seducing attitude, even with people whose reputation, honesty, and character was absolutely beyond any doubt. It was a pattern of trying to seduce people—and not vice versa," said Rogge.[30] Upton charged that Atlanta's bid reflected a "culture of corruption" within the Olympic bid process and that "votes were for sale."[31] Like John McCain, his colleague from the north wing of the US Capitol, Upton expressed interest in questioning Juan Antonio Samaranch.[32]

At its meeting in early October, the IOC Executive Board vigorously debated the preferred course of action in light of this second request from a congressional committee for Samaranch to provide testimony. With Fred Upton musing publicly on the possibility of serving him with a subpoena in the absence of his consent to appear,[33] Samaranch sought the counsel of members of the Executive Board. Samaranch shared that Ken Duberstein, vice chairman of the Mitchell Commission, envisioned that an appearance in Washington would be a "painful process," while Henry Kissinger, one of the high-profile members of the IOC 2000 Commission, warned Samaranch that he "would be eaten alive." Thomas Bach, Richard Pound, and Kevan Gosper believed that Samaranch should head to Washington, but on the IOC's timetable, not Upton's. They concurred that the trip should follow the approval of the proposed reforms in December. Chiharu Igaya advised against going, even though he conceded that a refusal to accept the invitation might injure the IOC's image. However, if Samaranch deemed it advisable, then he subscribed to the schedule proposed by Bach, Pound, and Gosper. Un Yong Kim stated that Samaranch should testify at a time of the IOC's choosing and advised against setting that date right now. The only person to suggest that Samaranch should venture to Washington now as opposed to later was Anita DeFrantz.[34]

Jacques Rogge, Kéba Mbaye, and China's He Zhenliang dissented. Rogge feared "bad PR" and an "ambush" in Washington and said Samaranch should refuse to appear now or later. Mbaye concurred. If Samaranch accepted the invitation, commented Rogge, "it would then open the door for any government in the world to call the President to testify at a hearing." He Zhenliang told Samaranch not to be intimidated by threats to the IOC's share of US Olympic revenue, as the Games "would continue, with or without American dollars." He agreed with Rogge and Mbaye in their opposition to such a trip and thought that a decision "to submit to [Upton's] arrogance made the IOC ridiculous in the eyes of the world, and it would lose all the respect it currently enjoyed."[35]

Samaranch ultimately sided with the view expressed by Bach, Pound, and Gosper and announced at the press conference held at the close of the Executive Board meetings that he would testify before Upton's congressional panel at a date to be determined following the close of the 110th IOC Session scheduled for December 11 and 12.[36] Clearly, Samaranch hoped that the passage of the proposed IOC reforms at that time would remove a number of arrows from the quivers of his inquisitors on Capitol Hill. Carrard departed swiftly for Washington at the close of the Executive Board meetings to converse with Upton concerning the timing of Samaranch's visit.[37] Ultimately, the IOC and Samaranch settled on December 15 with Upton. In the interim, François Carrard and Anita DeFrantz represented the IOC during the October hearings held by Upton as a result of the release of Griffin Bell's report on the 1996 Atlanta bid.

Upton and his colleagues flogged the IOC for its shortcomings in managing the Olympic site-selection process during the hearing on October 14. Sound bites dominated the proceedings. Henry Waxman (D-CA) warned that if the IOC did not follow through with promised reforms in December, "Congress is not going to have the patience any more to leave the IOC to reform itself," and he expected a "strong bipartisan push in Congress for punitive sanctions against the IOC."[38] Waxman's Democratic colleague from Pennsylvania Ron Klink expressed his bewilderment that the IOC took no action when it was clear that the bid process had been compromised by "lavish gifts" and "possible vote buying" for years. Joe Barton (R-TX) demanded Samaranch's resignation, decried Atlanta's decision to spend twelve thousand dollars to fly the IOC president's wife and a friend to Atlanta and a number of US cities during its candidature, and likened the Olympic site-selection process to a "cesspool."[39]

Chairman Upton's assessment was equally scathing. Although he did not equate Atlanta's gift-giving campaign to Salt Lake City's with respect to its size and scope, Upton noted that the list of gifts included "Cabbage Patch dolls, shopping sprees, carburetor kits, brake pads, jewelry, children's clothes and shoes, golf clubs, Spode china, [and] computer parts." Atlanta bidders, observed Upton, also funded IOC member travel to Walt Disney World, Miami, Honolulu, New York, and Sea Island, Georgia. He identified a "culture of corruption . . . that encourages the practice of excessive lobbying of IOC members." "This activity—this culture—must stop," he intoned.[40] Upton shared Waxman's belief that a bipartisan effort "to clear up the taint we have found in the Olympics" would result from any effort of the IOC to back away from needed reforms.[41] Carrard defended the IOC and affirmed its intent to pass the proposed reforms but keenly anticipated his ride to Dulles International Airport and his return flight to Switzerland. It had not been a relaxing trip.

The Upton hearings highlight one of the major challenges facing the IOC during the late summer and fall months of 1999, that is, maintaining focus on the most important goal: pushing through the reform proposals by December. However, Washington was not the only source of distraction for Samaranch and his colleagues.[42] IOC leaders spent much of this time with one eye on Washington and the other affixed on Sydney.[43]

## Sydney's Ticketing Fiasco

Of the myriad responsibilities falling to those individuals tasked with mounting an Olympic festival, budgeting, venue construction and delivery, transportation planning, and security protocols are key files. Of a lesser profile, but often as complex and confounding for OCOGs, is the generation and streamlined execution of a ticketing policy. SOCOG's ticketing strategy angered Australian citizens in 1999, drew pointed criticism in the Australian press, and provided yet another flash point for Olympic-sponsor relations during the period of the Salt Lake City crisis.

Four aspects of Sydney's ticketing strategy resulted in a public and media backlash in Australia. First, SOCOG established an exclusive contract with News Ltd., owned by Rupert and Lachlan Murdoch, such that ticket order forms during the first month of the sales campaign could be obtained only as an insert in one of Murdoch's newspapers. This decision forced Australians to purchase a News Ltd. publication.[44] Second, SOCOG held back 840,000 tickets, many to the most prestigious events, to be sold as premium packages to Australia's well-heeled citizens for as much as three times their face value without informing the public. With some 80,000 Australians having lost out on receiving any tickets in the initial public offering, the public rage was palpable.[45] SOCOG absorbed many blows from the media before deciding to return 524,451 tickets to the second round of the public offering in October.[46] Third, the second round of the public offering of tickets was compromised by SOCOG's "first-in, first served" policy. Individuals who ordered tickets in the first round of the public offering were given the first opportunity to order tickets in the second round. Although this policy seemed reasonable, the results of the first round, complete with an order booklet for the second round of tickets, did not arrive at Australian homes at the same time. Those persons who received their booklets first, and were quick to respond, would be granted their ticket requests.[47] Meanwhile, those persons whose ticket books were delayed in Australia's postal system were "left standing at the starting line."[48] SOCOG bowed to public pressure in October and changed the basis of the second round offer to a random draw.[49] Fourth, some of the premium tickets, before the program was scrapped in December, were purchased by rivals of SOCOG or IOC sponsors. For instance, Kerry Packer, owner of Australia's Channel 9, purchased a suite at the Olympic Stadium for A$245,000 that enraged executives at Channel 7, the Olympic broadcast rights holder.[50] Sponsors, including Channel 7's head, Kerry Stokes, charged that SOCOG had established a ready-made opportunity for their rivals to engage in ambush marketing.[51] Paul Reading, the architect of the premium ticket plan, who moved forward with its execution without sharing its full details with the SOCOG Board, left SOCOG in December.[52] A red-faced Michael Knight was forced to issue a public apology for SOCOG's managerial approach to ticketing in order to fend off a formal investigation of the matter by the Australian Competition and Consumer Commission.[53]

IOC officials, with enough on their administrative agenda as the 110th IOC Session approached in December, monitored events related to Sydney's ticketing program but tried to downplay their seriousness. Richard Pound characterized the situation as a "local problem," while Juan Antonio Samaranch, following Reading's departure, commented that it was "a problem, but I think now it is solved. I like to see the positive side. Never before, one year before the games, have people been so interested in buying tickets."[54] The IOC's direct involvement in the ticketing fiasco was limited in terms of stretching its crisis management resources, even though Michael Payne was dispatched to Sydney to calm agitated sponsors in early December.[55] However, the same cannot be said for Reebok's decision to walk away from its Sydney 2000 supporter sponsorship deal less than a week before the 110th IOC Session.

### Reebok Terminates Its Sydney 2000 Supporter Contract

IOC leaders directed their energies toward the IOC's 110th Session set for Lausanne in December and the necessity of ushering through the fifty reforms proposed by the IOC 2000 Commission; however, another brush fire threatened Sydney's sponsor base in the waning days before this crucial gathering. Reebok, a Sydney 2000 supporter, terminated its A$10 million contract in light of SOCOG's decision to permit Canterbury (rugby shirts) and Bonds (baseball hats) to produce apparel for merchandising and distribution to SOCOG staff members, respectively.[56] In reality, writes Michael Payne, Reebok was in the midst of contracting the scope of its worldwide sponsorship exposure across many deals.[57] A day and a half of mediation conducted by Laurence Street, a former New South Wales chief justice, failed to move the parties closer to a solution. Reebok also spurned Payne's offer to assist in finding a solution before dropping its bombshell announcement.[58]

Although the Reebok deal had a value of only A$10 million (as part of a budget of A$2.5 billion),[59] SOCOG needed to stanch the bleeding incurred by the public outrage concerning the ticketing scandal and mushrooming sponsor unrest as a result of the premium ticket sales campaign. Reebok, as part of its agreement, was contracted to outfit Australia's Olympians. Much of this work had been completed. Reebok counted on no competitor company seeing an opportunity to mount and complete that operation in nine months. It would still be the Olympic team outfitter, without having to pay its sponsorship contract. The gambit failed, as Reebok executives underestimated their rivals in Portland, Oregon.

At the suggestion of the AOC's secretary-general, Craig McLatchey, Payne swiftly contacted Nike's vice president of global sports marketing, Ian Todd, as a means of gauging Nike's willingness to consider replacing Reebok.[60]

Todd asked for thirty minutes to poll his executive colleagues on the feasibility of carrying off the job of outfitting the Australian Olympic team. When Payne called back, Todd asked whether Payne could get SOCOG negotiators to Nike's Portland, Oregon, headquarters within twenty-four hours to discuss the nature of the task and the terms of a possible deal. Within six hours, McLatchey and SOCOG's marketing manager, Rod Read, were on their way to meet Todd and his team of negotiators. Conference calls between the negotiating teams in Portland, Michael Knight and John Coates in Australia, and Payne, Kevan Gosper, and Richard Pound in Lausanne occupied the next two days, as round-the-clock negotiations ensued. Adidas executives hovered in the wings if an opening to launch negotiations could be exploited.[61]

The IOC desired a deal on such a short time frame so Samaranch could announce it at the close of the 110th IOC Session. A breakdown in the latter stages of negotiations seemed to doom the process to fail, but Todd and Payne, with encouragement from Pound and Gosper, resolved that neither side should pass up the opportunity. Talks resumed. The breakthrough occurred after Samaranch opened the closing press conference of the IOC Session.[62] Nike would outfit Australian Olympians and Paralympians and SOCOG officials, a total of some twenty-eight hundred individuals, as well as Australia's Olympic teams in 2002 and 2004.[63] The deal charted a fascinating change in course for Nike, which theretofore made its name in Olympic circles with its ambush marketing practices.[64]

Although the deal was for only A$8 million,[65] SOCOG, AOC, and IOC officials barely contained their glee. "Nike is the goddess of victory . . . and now, Nike, the company, will be part of the great victories of the Australian team at the Olympics and Paralympics," crowed Michael Knight.[66] Breathing a sigh of relief given Sydney's recent struggles, Gosper, who sat on both the SOCOG Board and IOC Executive Board, noted, "We think it's probably one of the fastest negotiations that you can imagine that can be put in place internationally." "What this has demonstrated," he added, "is that sponsors still have the confidence in the Games and I believe that they have also been observing what the IOC has been doing to reform itself and get back on course." John Coates was happy as well. "We're very pleased to welcome Nike on board for 2002 and 2004," he announced. "It's important for us to be satisfied that at this late stage Nike can deliver [for Sydney]."[67] The Nike announcement both heartened SOCOG officials and marked a positive end to the 110th IOC Session, which achieved its principal aim—the approval of fifty reform measures to the *Olympic Charter* designed to position the IOC for the twenty-first century as a vibrant and transparent body rooted in sound ethical principles.

## The 110th IOC Session

Effective stage management of meetings of key stakeholders is a valuable skill for leaders of organizations who are dedicated to achieving institutional goals. Olympic historians are well familiar with Pierre de Coubertin's skillful management of the 1894 Sorbonne Conference. The baron convinced invited delegates to support his aim of establishing an international Olympic committee and reviving the Olympic Games after two earlier failed attempts, owing in no small measure to the effectiveness of his preparations for the meeting.[68] Samaranch, too, subscribed to the need to effectively stage-manage crucial meetings such as the one to be held in Lausanne in December 1999. Much like he had before the 108th Extraordinary IOC Session in March, Samaranch wrote to all IOC members as the Session approached to reiterate the importance of embracing the concept of reform and to lay the foundation for the dialogue necessary to achieve his goals. With his date with Fred Upton's congressional committee set for December 15, Samaranch required a strong signal from the IOC members that they understood the need for sweeping reforms. "To begin the new millennium in the best conditions," observed Samaranch, "the IOC must reform and adapt its structures. The whole world is watching us," he continued, "and is expecting resolute action. While we are the masters of our own organization, we cannot ignore worldwide public opinion."[69]

When IOC delegates settled into their seats in Lausanne's Palais de Beaulieu, Samaranch empathized with them and touched on the difficulties they faced during the year. He urged them to push the IOC over the finish line in terms of its effort to confront the shortcomings of the organization exposed by the Salt Lake City scandal. "This crisis has affected many of you. You have faced harsh criticism. You have gone through undeserved suffering and pain," stated Samaranch. "I have suffered too. We had to work very hard to solve this crisis. And now," offered Samaranch, "we are very close to succeeding. These are reasonable reforms," he noted. "The people of the world are watching. We can't disappoint them."[70]

Samaranch hammered home the themes of transparency, accountability, democracy, and responsibility in his opening remarks. He also leaned on the gravitas of Henry Kissinger, a former US secretary of state, during the opening moments of the Session. A key member of the IOC 2000 Commission, Kissinger implored them to adopt the recommendations that he and his colleagues tabled: "I am convinced that failure to proceed along these lines would create a crisis of public confidence which sooner or later, and sooner rather than later, would bring us together again facing the same sort of challenge." Kissinger conveyed his thoughts that the reform measures, while related to the Salt Lake City scandal in terms of the timing of their genesis, represented a set of best practices that any review panel such as the IOC 2000 Commission would have recommended in the absence of a scandal. "None of our recommendations were animated by any sort of judgment about what has happened in the past. We would have made essentially the same recommendations. Whether or not there were shortcomings in the conduct of some members," concluded Kissinger, "is not relevant."[71] Samaranch's approach paid dividends—all fifty reform proposals passed with little question and by overwhelming majority votes.

The two-day Session marked a victory for the embattled Samaranch, who steadfastly gripped the reins of power throughout 1999 despite intense pressure and frequent calls for his resignation.[72] Observers focused on the members' collective view on the continued need to preclude bid city visits. IOC members sided with Samaranch and voted to continue the ban. Renewable eight-year term limits for IOC members were approved, as was a maximum presidential tenure of twelve years (by virtue of an eight-year term, with the possibility of one four-year extension). The Session reduced the members' age limit from eighty to seventy but exempted current members from the rule. In an effort to make the IOC more broadly representative of key Olympic stakeholders, the size of the IOC was set at 115 members, with membership cohorts of prescribed sizes. Seventy members are now elected as individuals, while the remaining 45 members are drawn from the ranks of active athletes (15), NOC presidents (15), and ISF presidents (15). The Session empowered athletes, ISFs, NOCs, and individual IOC members to nominate candidates for IOC membership who would be reviewed by the elected Selection Committee (a 7-member committee composed of both IOC and non-IOC members). The Selection Committee was tasked with generating a detailed report for the IOC Executive Board, which, in turn, would nominate one or two candidates for each vacant post. Ultimately, the Session possessed the authority to elect candidates by a secret ballot.

While the media was most interested in reforms dealing with the IOC's structure, other important measures that were passed targeted the following: (1) the need for streamlined knowledge transfer between successive organizing committees, (2) establishing a maximum of 280 events at the Summer Olympics, (3) the need for the IOC to provide guidelines to organizing committees with respect to ticketing policy, (4) strengthening the role and scope of the operations of Olympic Solidarity, (5) expanding the Olympic oath to include reference to drug-free sport, (6) policies dedicated to improving the functionality of the IOC's internal and external communications programs, (7) disclosure of IOC finances and the distribution of IOC funds to the NOCs and ISFs, and (8) the generation of oversight responsibilities for NOCs concerning Olympic hosting bids mounted by cities in their territory. Girded by the passage of the reform proposals and the encouragement of his colleagues on the IOC Executive Board, Samaranch jetted off for Washington with Richard Pound and François Carrard to face what promised to be pointed questioning from Fred Upton's House Commerce Subcommittee on Oversight and Investigations.[73]

## Samaranch Faces US Congressional Inquisitors

Rarely has Juan Antonio Samaranch's demeanor exemplified an individual who thrived on interaction with the media,[74] particularly when the discourse is carried out completely in English.[75] Would a confrontation with aroused Washington politicians be any different? Samaranch possessed a measure of comforting satisfaction that the IOC approved unanimously sweeping reforms at the 110th General Session adjourned but a few days earlier. However, Henry Kissinger's warning that "he would be eaten alive" was never far from his thoughts as he dozed fitfully in his Concorde airliner seat during the Atlantic crossing on December 13 from London's Heathrow to New York's John F. Kennedy International Airport.[76] Upton and his colleagues aside, what treatment awaited him from a generally hostile American media? He could only hope that the visit of a seventy-nine-year-old Spanish aristocrat might be lost in the welter of "bigger news" on the American domestic front— focus on Y2K, Christmas, candidates, the upcoming presidential primaries, and Hillary Clinton's not uncontroversial run for a US Senate seat.

The whirlwind week continued as a short Delta shuttle flight from New York put Samaranch, Pound, and Carrard in the nation's capital for meetings on December 14 with the editorial board of the *Washington Post* (2:00 p.m.) and President Bill Clinton's drug czar, Barry McCaffrey (4:00 p.m.). A three-hour rehearsal geared toward preparing Samaranch for the types of questions he might face the next day preceded these meetings during the morning hours.[77] At 9:30 the next morning, December 15, the congressional hearings began. Samaranch settled into the witness chair, flanked on either side by a

9. Fred Upton (R-MI) chaired hearings of the House Commerce Sub-committee on Oversight and Investigations on the Olympic bid process in October and December 1999. *Source:* Douglas Graham/*Congressional Quarterly*/Getty Images.

translator, one to translate questions addressed to him in Spanish, the other to translate his answers into English. The IOC negotiated this concession as a condition of his appearance.[78] He shuffled the pages of his prepared opening statement (5,789 words), designed to reassure Congress that the IOC had "made good" on its promise to reshape the organization for the twenty-first century. Chairman Upton and six members of his House Commerce Subcommittee on Oversight and Investigations readied themselves for the confrontation they had been spoiling for since October.

An anticipatory buzz permeated the hearing chamber that was crowded with spectators, congressional staff, and media personnel armed with cameras, pencils and notebooks, laptop computers, and tape recorders. In the middle of it all sat Juan Antonio Samaranch opposite his questioners, who were seated behind a long table replete with a battery of microphones. Behind

10. Juan Antonio Samaranch delivers his opening remarks before facing questions from Fred Upton's House Commerce Subcommittee on Oversight and Investigations on December 15, 1999. Richard Pound is seated to Samaranch's right, while US IOC member Anita DeFrantz is shown above Samaranch's left shoulder. *Source:* Gary Hershorn/Reuters/Corbis.

Samaranch, for moral support, sat Carrard and Pound. The scene from Samaranch's perspective was akin to a heavyweight boxing title fight—he the com-
batant, the translators and IOC colleagues his cornermen. The only thing
missing was ring announcer Michael Buffer and his now famous "Let's get
ready to rumble" call.

Samaranch was sworn in, and he immediately launched into his opening
statement in English.[79] It was a thorough, comprehensive epistle that distilled
the events of the past year and contained a strong assertion of Samaranch's
personal view that the IOC met the challenge posed by the Salt Lake City
scandal. "The IOC has kept its word," said Samaranch in noting the passage of the fifty reform measures recently in Lausanne. "Once fully imple-
mented," he observed, "the reforms will result in a fundamentally renovated
IOC—one that is more transparent, more accountable, and more respon-
sive. . . . It is because these changes promise a better future for the Olympic
Movement that I believe the crisis will go down in history as a positive force
for the International Olympic Committee." Samaranch tackled many issues,
including the customary acceptance of gifts by the IOC president (who has
not been considered subject to the Hodler Rules), his wife's funded trip to
Atlanta, the 1996 Olympic bid process, and an admission of the IOC's failure
to adequately monitor the activities of its members and bid committees in the
post–Los Angeles (1984) era. "As the temptations rose, our policing of the situations that placed people at risk should have increased. We can now see our
practices were too weak to disallow those among us who could be tempted to
accept—and unfortunately demand—excesses." To those persons who might
decry his decision not to resign, Samaranch pointed to the vote of eighty-six
to two in favor of his staying in office by a secret ballot at the 108th Extraordinary IOC Session in March. He took this vote of confidence as a message to
apply himself to leading the IOC through this difficult period. He recalled, at
length, the nature of the reforms passed, the willingness of the IOC members
to expel six colleagues and approve sanctions against others when presented
with credible evidence, and the genesis and work of the IOC Ethics and 2000
Commissions. Samaranch concluded his comments and invited questions
from members of the subcommittee.

Upton wasted little time in raising the temperature in the room in expressing his skepticism concerning the IOC's reform process, declaring that "we

are here because the Olympic Games are too important to allow a culture of corruption to be whitewashed and perpetuated by a paper called reforms."[80] One after the other, the charges flew across the committee room: the IOC reforms were simply an exercise in "window dressing . . . a whitewash;" the newly created IOC ethics panel "lacks teeth"; anticorruption rules will not even apply "to the IOC president or his successor."[81] At times the dialogue got nasty, and personal, even a bit theatrical. Ridiculing Samaranch's desire to be addressed as "His Excellency," as well as drawing reference to the alleged luxury of his living expenses in Lausanne, Joe Barton called for his immediate resignation.[82] And, finally, Henry Waxman belabored a point that, possibly more than any other offered, really underpinned the entire proceedings, a matter on which the USOC and IOC had previously sparred: "a long term extension of Olympic television rights granted without competition to the NBC television network."[83]

Through it all Samaranch sat calmly, resolved in his conviction that the IOC fulfilled its promise to reform its house. Samaranch took counsel from lawyers Pound and Carrard, both of whom understood the art of dealing with aroused adversaries, in and out of the courtroom. In the end, after six hours of testimony (two full hours by Samaranch), members of the subcommittee could do little more than pledge to monitor closely the IOC's vow to change, and if the IOC did not change, Congress "would implement legislation that would ban American companies from financially supporting the Olympics."[84] There, it was out! The real motivation behind Congress's desire to confront Samaranch in Washington! Upton, Barton, and the others relished the opportunity afforded by the scandal to interrogate Samaranch on their turf with respect to Olympic financial issues.

Major American newspaper accounts of the hearing episode judged Samaranch's performance before the committee as generally effective. Samaranch blunted the committee's attacks, but the testimony of three important American allies provided critical support. Testifying on Samaranch's and the IOC's behalf were Henry Kissinger; Howard Baker, former US senator from Tennessee; and Kenneth Duberstein, former White House chief of staff. They knew the ways of Washington and would not be bullied. Kissinger and Baker were members of the IOC 2000 Commission, while Duberstein served on the Mitchell Commission. Kissinger reported that the IOC had "come as close to achieving [reforms] as possible, replacing corrupt members with enthusiastic athletes."[85] Baker pleaded for the lawmakers "to be patient. . . . Samaranch is well meaning . . . fully dedicated to reform." Duberstein observed that "Samaranch is living reform every day."[86]

Samaranch, along with Carrard and Pound, retired from the hearing chamber, relieved by the outcome. Clearly, the day's events justified Samaranch's strategy in dealing with Congress's demand for his appearance in terms of both its timing and its format. The ability to testify in Spanish contributed greatly to the calmness and control Samaranch exerted throughout his testimony, and the package of reforms Samaranch carried under his arm in the wake of the 110th IOC Session defanged his questioners. On his return flight to Switzerland, he reflected on what had been the most trying and eventful year of his IOC presidency. Better days, he hoped, lay ahead.

# 7
# Judgment Day(s)

### Closing the Book on the Salt Lake City Scandal

The sensational and scandalous revelations surrounding Salt Lake City's bid for the 2002 Olympic Winter Games resulted in wide public disbelief and embarrassed Olympic officials worldwide. When frantic finger-pointing subsided and investigations by several commissions and organizations were completed, the end results were a changing of the guard to lead SLOC, dishonored and discharged IOC members, federally indicted Salt Lake City Olympic bid leaders, and hesitant international corporate sponsors. In the end, however, two indelible exclamation points punctuated the Salt Lake City Olympic Winter Games record. First, the grandeur and quality of the Salt Lake City Olympic endeavor ranked it arguably as the best ever celebrated in the history of Olympic Winter Games. Second, what came to be called the "Great Olympic Bribery Trial," brought to an end almost a year after the celebration of the Games, closed the book on the Salt Lake Olympic experience.

### The Aborted First Trial

The judicial arm of the US government remained mute on the subject of the great Olympic scandal amid all the commotion.[1] In time, after the hullabaloo ceased over the scandal, in part as a result of the IOC's efforts to confront the issue and effect needed reform measures, but also owing to the world media's fatigue in regard to the matter, the US Department of Justice lodged legal proceedings against Tom Welch and David Johnson, the tandem responsible for heading Salt Lake City's bid.

By the spring of 2000, almost on the eve of the opening of the Sydney Summer Olympic Games, the Department of Justice filed a fifteen-count felony indictment against Welch and Johnson, charging them with conspiring to bribe IOC members into awarding the 2002 Winter Games to Salt Lake City with approximately one million dollars in improper gifts, scholarships, health care benefits, and cash payments. Federal authorities charged Welch and Johnson with conspiracy, mail fraud, wire fraud, and travel across state lines in aid of racketeering, under the felony provisions of the Travel Act. The bulk of the case, ten of the fifteen counts, accused Welch and Johnson of concealing the alleged bribes and defrauding bid and organizing committee trustees of the "right to control" bid expenses and the "right to honest services."[2] Suddenly, the words *Olympic* and *scandal* were once again linked in daily news reports.

Defendants Welch and Johnson engaged legal counsel to answer the charges—in the case of Welch, the prestigious law firm Zuckerman Spaeder in Washington, DC, and for Johnson, the respected Salt Lake City law firm Snow, Christensen, and Martineau. Lead counsel for Zuckerman Spaeder was William Taylor; for Snow, Christensen, and Martineau, Max Wheeler. In June 2001, some seven months prior to the opening of the Salt Lake Winter Olympics, defense counsel asked for a dismissal of the racketeering charges, arguing that the federal Travel Act, which was cited in alleging the defendants engaged in interstate transportation in aid of racketeering, was defective and insufficient and consequently weakened the conspiracy charge. Defense counsel also maintained that the state's commercial bribery law was improper and defective. Studying the appeal for dismissal in the spring of 2001, federal magistrate judge Ronald N. Boyce determined that federal prosecutors "provided sufficient information in the indictment to justify the charges under the Travel Act." Punctuating his decision to proceed with court action, Boyce stated that the allegations "would be corrupting the site selection process and [were] contrary to the IOC's integrity interests." They also rested "directly within the terms of [commercial bribery] statutes." As an exclamation point in his decision, Boyce proclaimed, "The Government will have to meet the requisite standard of proof and whether it can do so must await the evidence."[3] Judge Boyce's final statement, as it turned out, had prophetic consequences for all involved.

The trial of *Welch-Johnson v. the United States Government* was scheduled to begin in Salt Lake City on July 16, 2001, some seven months prior to the opening of the Salt Lake City Olympic Winter Games. Not since the Addam Swapp–Vickie Singer trial in 1988 had there been such a high-profile federal case tried in Utah.[4] Judge David Sam, a seventy-year-old veteran of the courts and a longtime resident of Salt Lake City, drew the assignment of presiding over the trial proceedings staged in the Frank E. Moss Federal Courthouse in downtown Salt Lake City. He was, at the time, a part-time, nearly retired judge. His reduced workload commenced in November 1999 when his wife became severely ill. When federal authorities filed charges against Welch and Johnson in July 2000, a computer system assigned the case a number and a judge by random lottery. Judge David Sam was thus chosen by the "luck of the draw." Despite his wife's eventual passing in September 2000, Sam did not step down. He presided over the most public and potentially damaging legal proceedings with which the modern Olympic Movement had ever been associated in its some one-hundred-year history.

As the opening of what was rapidly being termed the "Great Olympic Bribery Trial" approached, so, too, did the clamor for seating in the courtroom. The venue selected for the trial was Judge Dee Benson's courtroom on the third floor of the federal courthouse. Its capacity was 160 seats. With 50 to 60 seats reserved for the defense, the prosecution, computer technicians, witnesses, lawyers, staff from the US Attorney's Office, and the defendants' families and friends, approximately 100 seats remained for reporters and spectators. Some 30 print and broadcast agencies applied for the allotted 100 press credentials. Chief clerk of the US District Court in Salt Lake Markus Zimmer grappled with monitoring courtroom technology (laptop computers, tape recorders, satellite cables, and parking lot passes) and the overburdened space of the courtroom.[5]

Five days before the scheduled opening of the trial of *Welch-Johnson v. the United States Government*, defense counsel appealed to Judge Sam to rebut Boyce's previous ruling on four of the fifteen federal charges, in effect, those charges relating to the use of federal mail to defraud. Sam deliberated for two days. Then he dropped a bombshell. In a two-page order, he said Utah's commercial bribery law could not be stretched to bring federal charges under travel-in-aid-of-racketeering laws. Sam also called the state statute "ambiguous and unconstitutionally vague" as applied to the *Welch-Johnson* case.[6] Later, Judge Sam had more to say. In responding to the prosecution's interpretation of the State of Utah's "commercial bribery" charges, Sam vehemently declared, "When state lawmakers passed a commercial bribery law, they certainly did not mean it to apply to the Olympic lobbying effort. . . . [I]t broaches absurdity to believe that the Legislature intended to criminalize goodwill gifts or gestures, especially in the context of promoting Salt Lake City and the state of Utah on the world stage to host the Olympic Games." Further, the venerable judge could not resist offering a final rejoinder to the feds: "A federal criminal prosecution, where an individual's reputation and liberty are at stake, is not the place to experiment with novel interpretations of state law. . . . However well-intentioned, federal prosecutors are misguided in attempting to fit the proverbial round peg into a square hole."[7] There was little doubt where Judge Sam's feelings lay.

For the moment at least, champagne glasses were raised among defense counsel members. Digesting Judge Sam's decision, Bill Taylor, Zuckerman Spaeder's lead counsel for Welch, offered his assessment. "The law is on our side," said Taylor, "and it shouldn't come as a great surprise that a fair-minded judge would take a look at this case and dismiss it. It never was a bribery case, it's not now and it never should have been." Max Wheeler, counsel for Johnson, was equally jubilant. "The government should say, 'We gave it our best shot,' and be done with it. It's best for the nation, best for the Olympic movement and best for this community." Welch and Johnson, too, were exultant. "We are delighted by the court's ruling today," said the indicted in a joint statement. "We believe it confirms what we have said from the beginning: We committed no crime. . . . We hope Judge Sam will agree that this entire indictment must be dismissed so we and our families can resume our lives, and our community can celebrate the Winter Olympic Games without this cloud looming over it." On the other hand, the government had already spent three years and millions of dollars pursuing Welch and Johnson. And Judge Sam had still to rule on the defense motions to dismiss the remaining eleven counts. Justice Department spokesman Chris Watney, though acknowledging their case had been wounded by Sam's ruling, nevertheless suggested that the attorney general himself "might look at it."[8]

On July 18, Judge Sam postponed the July 30 trial date indefinitely. For all practical purposes, this set the case adrift until after Salt Lake's Olympic Winter Games, scheduled to be celebrated some six months later and, in fact, increased the odds that it would fade away completely. Defense attorneys stated that it would "be best for Utah and the nation if [the] Justice Department dropped all the charges." Others were not so sure. Former US attorney Brent Ward opined that "the public deserves to know the whole tawdry truth behind Salt Lake City's bid. If there is a dismissal or a plea bargain, it will deprive the public of a sense of closure."[9] Quiet descended for the time being, interrupted in November by Judge Sam's dismissal of all charges pending. Seemingly this event concluded the matter.

And so ended act 1 of the Great Olympic Bribery Trial. With Judge Sam's dismissal of all charges, the world's attention on Olympic matters turned to the Salt Lake Games. In the wake of the tragic events of September 11, 2001, a grieving nation badly needed a celebration of achievement and success to offset the distress of the New York City disaster and feelings of "what has this world we live in sunk to?" Enter, then, the Olympic pageant that unfolded almost immaculately, certainly gloriously, in Salt Lake City in February 2002.

## "Light the Fire Within":
## The Salt Lake City Olympic Winter Games

On July 24, 1847, forty-six-year-old Brigham Young and a wagon-train contingent of 148 Mormons emerged from the Wasatch Mountains through what would one day be called Emigration Canyon and looked out on a spectacular sight: the vista of the Great Salt Lake. Young gazed down on the valley sprawled out before them. Legend informs us that the president of the Mormon Church advised his flock: "This is the place." Here would be established a new Zion, a refuge for the persecuted followers of the Mormon faith, removed and secure in the wilderness of the American West.

A great city, originally called Deseret, rose near the south shore of Great Salt Lake. From the beginning, Brigham Young's envisioned sanctuary experienced encroachment from events of the "outside world." Mormon settlers had hardly abandoned their covered wagons and constructed rough-hewn frontier homes when gold was discovered in California in 1849. By the thousands, gold seekers trekked to California. Most traveled overland on foot, horseback, and wagon; others arrived by sailing ship via San Francisco. Both journeys were difficult, particularly the overland route. It took several weeks, sometimes months, to make the passage. There were few "stopping-off" places between the Mississippi River and the Pacific Coast. But one that did exist and grew rapidly was Deseret. Here, explorers, trappers, prospectors, settlers, and opportunists by the thousands paused to rest and replenish supplies. Many decided not to proceed but to put down roots in Utah. Thus, the first "foreign intrusion" on the Mormon sanctuary occurred. It was not the last. Twenty years later, the great transcontinental railroad was completed, joining the track of the Union Pacific with the rails of the Central Pacific near Promontory Point on the shore of Great Salt Lake, some two-score miles north of Deseret. The discovery of gold and the expansion of the railroad were the first events in the startling transformation of the citadel of Mormonism toward worldliness.

Mormons showed little inclination to abandon Utah's distinctive religious and social culture in the twentieth century; indeed, this desire to shelter the state from outside influence continues today. However, hosting the 2002 Olympic Winter Games offered the Church of Jesus Christ of Latter-day Saints a platform for casting the Mormon faith as a "mainstream" Christian belief system. Concluded historian Larry Gerlach, "The conventional belief that the LDS church wanted to exploit the winter Olympics for missionary purposes was correct in that self-promotion was a natural and reasonable impulse, but incorrect in that public relations, not proselytizing, was the church's principal objective."[10] That said, however, Gerlach also argued that the exposure of Utah's Mormon community and its relationship to Salt Lake's Winter Games to the world via 2.1 billion television viewers and some 1.5 million on-site Olympic patrons quite likely exceeded the combined impact of thousands of young missionaries who have labored intensively for more than a century and a half to extend the Mormon faith to the far corners of the globe.[11]

Salt Lake City's quest to secure hosting status for the Winter Olympics proved to be an odyssey punctuated by disappointment and significant frustration. Despite sound technical bid plans and a substantial history as a prominent winter ski resort area, it was beaten soundly by Grenoble (France),

Innsbruck (Austria), and Nagano (Japan) for the Winter Games of 1968, 1976, and 1998, respectively. With a technical bid unrivaled by any other candidate, the loss to Nagano was particularly galling. In the 1980s and 1990s, amid an Olympic climate of expanding wealth, ingratiation, and largesse, it took more than the best technical bid to win host distinction. One solid testament to this conclusion was the rapid obliteration of all bid committee documents by Nagano authorities following the culmination of the Eighteenth Olympic Winter Games.

Undaunted by their loss to Nagano, but far wiser as to the "new practicalities" of winning the bid, Salt Lake's resolute bid committee officials orchestrated and executed a full-scale and relentless gift-giving campaign designed to secure IOC members' votes at the IOC Session scheduled for Budapest in 1995. Much was on the line for Salt Lake: this meeting would determine whether the community had an opportunity to step onto the world stage as host city for the 2002 Olympic Winter Games or suffer the indignity of a fourth loss in Olympic Games bid competitions.

The loss to Nagano convinced Salt Lake City bid officials that a future bidding triumph required a not immodest expenditure of money, in the end some one million dollars, to cultivate needed votes. An expenditure of such an amount could hardly have flown under the radar in an atmosphere of intense public awareness with respect to "Olympic visits" by IOC members. Indeed, the parade of IOC members and their privileged entourages appearing regularly at an established pattern of parties, receptions, and galas under the guise of "evaluation visits" went neither unnoticed nor unnoted.

The IOC convened in Budapest in the summer of 1995 to determine the site of the 2002 Olympic Winter Games. Following the announcement of the IOC's deliberations, jubilant Salt Lake citizens celebrated wildly, reveling in having captured the necessary majority on the first ballot. Tom Welch was immediately named SLOC's president, while David Johnson was appointed as his top assistant. The storied Utah capital set to work to translate bid energies into actually organizing the Games entrusted to it.

For two full years after gaining the bid, Salt Lake City Olympic organizational efforts proceeded under Welch and Johnson's energetic and seemingly expert direction. In early July 1997, a disturbing event disrupted the entire organizational mission. Welch's wife brought court proceedings against him on charges of spousal abuse. Welch pleaded no contest, expressed his contrition, and promptly resigned from leading Salt Lake City's Olympic effort.[12] But Welch, a bishop in the LDS, and known in Utah as "Mr. Olympics," did not altogether disqualify himself from Olympic matters. He was retained as a consultant.[13] Frank Joklik, chairman of the former bid committee's board of trustees, replaced Welch as head of the organizing committee.

Following the "Olympic bribe" disclosures of late November 1998, and in the face of expanding allegations of bid committee wrongdoing, Joklik resigned in early January 1999.[14] SLOC searched frantically for a fresh "arm's-length" figure to rescue Salt Lake's mission to carry out its Olympic mandate. By March 1999, SLOC officials had found their man: Mitt Romney, Michigan born, Brigham Young University and Harvard Law School graduate, dedicated Mormon Church member and servant, and millionaire venture capitalist who resided in Boston.[15] Romney's business specialty focused on turning around firms suffering financial and management troubles. Was SLOC's situation not too different? Romney moved quickly and assertively to implement damage control and restore badly shaken confidence in Salt Lake's Olympic enterprise. Particularly was this critical with respect to SLOC's paid and volunteer staff and, even more important, the boardrooms of both prospective and already-in-place corporate sponsors, both domestically and in an international context.[16] Overall, it was a daunting task. But Romney, who once chuckled over the fact that "someone with as little athletic talent as I is running the Olympics," rose to the challenge and ended up organizing and executing the largest and most profitable Olympic Winter Games ever.[17]

Salt Lake City's Olympic Winter Games opened on February 8, 2002. Almost twenty-five thousand volunteers welcomed Olympic competitors and spectators from the world over. Seventy-seven countries sent athletes, some twenty-four hundred in total. They competed in fifteen Olympic winter sport disciplines, comprising seventy-eight Olympic events. Over the course of the following sixteen days, almost nine thousand media personnel reported the results, while television viewers worldwide together with on-site spectators thrilled to superb athletic performances. Countries the world over had much to celebrate, but nations in Europe and North America celebrated most often. Germany led the list, winning thirty-five medals, twelve of them the coveted gold. The United States followed closely, winning thirty-four medals, ten of them gold. Traditional winter sports powers Norway, Canada, and Russia followed in total medals won. But other countries rejoiced also in light of superlative performances: Switzerland for its great champion Simon Amman, who won both ski-jumping events, competitions traditionally dominated by the Scandinavian countries; Italy for Armin Zoeggeler's gold medal in men's luge; Great Britain for the dramatic upset victory of its women's curling team; and France for the gold medal won by its superb alpine skier Carole Montillet in the women's downhill. Foreshadowing future Asian impact on Olympic winter competitions, South Korea's Gi-Hyun Ko won gold in the women's 1,500-meter short-track speed skating, and, as well, its women's team won gold in the short-track 3,000-meter relay event. Capping those sterling performances was the victory of China's indomitable Yang Yang, who dominated the women's short-track sprint events, winning gold in both the 500- and 1,000-meter races.

For the USOC, which had some time ago committed itself to thinning its elaborate administrative infrastructure and concentrating considerable energies and resources toward achieving its highest-priority objective, winning Olympic medals, especially gold, it was the nation's most successful Olympic Winter Games ever.[18] Heroes abounded, among them Brian Shimer and crew for their gold medal effort in the four-man bobsled competition; Apolo Anton Ohno ("oh yes!"), triumphant in the men's 1,500-meter short-track speed-skating event; and Tristan Gale, who stood at the top of the medal podium following the women's skeleton competition.

Gale's counterpart in men's skeleton provided one of the more emotional moments of the Games. The final runs of men's skeleton, conducted in a surreal snowstorm, produced an upset winner, as Jimmy Shea emerged with the gold medal. Shea's grandfather Jack Shea, struck down and killed by an errant driver two months before the Salt Lake City Olympics opened, remains in the pantheon of all-time American Winter Olympic heroes as a double gold medal Olympian; noted motivational speaker to thousands of young, aspiring American Olympic athletes; and, before his untimely death at age ninety-three, the oldest living American gold medal Olympian.[19] Leaping from his sled after crossing the finish line of his victorious descent, young Shea tore his helmet from his head and dramatically pointed to the photograph of his grandfather mounted inside his headgear. For many of the more than two billion television viewers around the world, it was both a dramatic and a poignant Olympic moment.

There were some not-so-glorious moments that occurred during the Games. Doping episodes marred otherwise dramatic cross-country skiing and biathlon events. The biggest controversy, however, occurred in pairs figure skating. Quickly dubbed "Skategate" by the media, it involved a glaring example of judging misconduct, for which figure skating, in general, had long been accused.

On February 11, shortly after the opening of the Games, the Russian pair Elena Berezhnaya and Anton Sikharulidze was awarded the gold medal over Canada's Jamie Salé and David Pelletier. The Russians' performance reflected clear technical errors, evident even to the unsophisticated viewer. The Canadian performance appeared flawless. Media pundits and spectators alike were thunderstruck by the result; a vast public outcry called for an investigation of the judging scores. Meanwhile, a crestfallen but gracious Canadian pair mounted the victory podium to accept the silver medal. Within a few days, it was discovered that one member of the judging panel, the French judge, Marie-Reine Le Gougne, had been pressured by her national skating federation to favor the Russians. This type of politically motivated conduct in figure skating judging had been "whispered about" for years. An investigation of the incident resulted in the International Skating Union's suspension of Le Gougne for three years and, further, barred her from judging at the next Winter Games, scheduled for Turin in 2006. Finally, the ISU, in unprecedented action, recommended to the IOC that Salé and Pelletier be awarded a "second gold medal." On February 15, the IOC Executive Committee convened in emergency context and approved the ISU recommendation. Justice seemingly prevailed.[20]

For all gold medalists, of course, the significant financial bonuses from their national governments or NOCs, or both, and the well-entrenched phenomenon of wealth gained from marketing Olympic success added extra luster to their Olympian performances. One disappointed Olympic performer in that respect, however, was the Canadian cross-country skier Beckie Scott. Scott finished third in the 5-kilometer pursuit event; the gold and silver medalists were Russian women, Olga Danilova and Larissa Lazuktina, respectively. Both passed immediate postrace drug tests; however, both tested positive following a later event. After two years of legal proceedings, and a final Court of Arbitration for Sport decision to disqualify the two Russians and negate their entire Olympic performances, including their 5-kilometer pursuit result, Scott was upgraded to first place, thus entering the time-honored and prestigious roll of Olympic gold medalists. But the power that winning a gold medal immediately has in the commercial marketplace wanes rapidly. For Scott, the normal three- to six-month window of opportunity to capitalize on a gold medal's value in sponsorship had long passed; alas, the "corporate camp moved on" to focus on the Athens Summer Games of 2004. Elliot Kerr, Scott's agent, estimated the unfortunate delay cost his client $1 million in possible endorsements. "The reality is she was robbed of the marketing opportunity," said Kerr.[21] One "salvation" for Scott was the fact that she was elected an IOC member to Canada shortly afterward.

In the immediate aftermath of the Games, Mitt Romney and his SLOC team tackled the details concerning the financial "bottom line" of their endeavor. It was an awesome task. No one has ever been successful in determining the absolute monetary cost attached to bidding for, organizing, and executing an edition of the modern Olympic Games, Summer or Winter. And, in fact, this remained true for Salt Lake City. The "best guess" with respect to the 2002 Olympic Winter Games was somewhere between $2 billion (SLOC's pronouncement), and $3.5 billion (*Sports Illustrated*'s judgment). "Guestimates" are always the order of the day in determining "bottom lines." Final tallies really depend on which "bean counters" are counting which "beans." Invariably, organizing committees, loath to show a deficit, generally discount expenditures for infrastructure facilities and services that have the potential of both direct and long-term continuing benefit to the public. Their budgets, so the argument goes, are responsible only for carrying out the great festival, not investing in "bricks and mortar" for the benefit of public consumption in the long term. Of course, one of the major arguments put forth to both the IOC and local citizen groups by all Olympic Games bid committees is the fact that "their Games" will provide lasting "public use" legacies in the form of sports and recreational facilities, transportation and communication infrastructure, and enrichment of the economy, especially expansion of the tourism industry. In general, however, the costs inherent in maintaining and operating Olympic sports facilities after the Games have "left town" far outstrip revenues gained from their public use. In case after case, Olympic stadia stand ghostlike and underutilized and serve as vague (but very expensive) reminders of a glorious and wonderful time.

Nevertheless, the significant amount of "public moneys" from various layers of government (municipal, county, state, and federal) invariably channeled the host city's way for its Olympic project is seldom put forward by the organizing committee in its final accounting. But the Games could no more be staged without the aid of public funds in the form of tax moneys than they could without the help of privately generated revenues, especially the funds generated from the commercial realm. For instance, the final federal "public money" tab alone for the Salt Lake City endeavor was somewhere between $400 million (SLOC's judgment) and $1.5 billion (*Sports Illustrated*'s estimate).[22] In between those two figures, but heavily skewed toward the *Sports Illustrated* assessment, was the estimate by the federal government's General Accounting Office (GAO). The government's assessment of the final gross cost of the Games was $2.7 billion, almost half of which, some $1.3 billion, came from federal funds, more than double the federal spending for the 1996 Atlanta Games.[23] Such startling revelations left some Washington politicians angry. "I think it's a disgrace," thundered John McCain. "But this is logical when you start pork-barrel spending." Recognizing that "our government spends billions of dollars to maintain wartime capability," countered Mitt Romney in a letter to the GAO, "it is entirely appropriate to invest several hundred millions to promote peace."[24] Few could argue Romney's point.

Federal moneys to support the Salt Lake Games were one thing; the contributions from the IOC in the form of television rights revenues and commercial sponsorship fees were quite another. Salt Lake City's share of the worldwide television rights amounted to $443 million;[25] its share of The Olympic Partners moneys amounted to $131.5 million, producing, in total, $574.5 million, less than a quarter of the Games' cost.[26] Where did the balance come from?

Salt Lake City, in a not always harmonious partnership with the USOC, undertook the most energetic and ultimately the most successful domestic sponsorship initiative in the history of any Olympic Games, Winter or Summer. Named OPUS (Olympic Properties of the United States), the program generated a massive $877 million, of which SLOC reaped $599 million (60 percent), and its partner, the USOC, the remainder (40 percent). SLOC's share represented 43 percent of the entire revenue pot it raised for the Games. OPUS affiliations were divided into three categories: partners, sponsors, and suppliers. The six OPUS partners were all well-known national corporations: AT&T (long-distance telecommunications), Bank of America (retail banking services), General Motors (domestic automobiles and trucks), Qwest (local telecommunications and services), Havoline (retail oil and gas), and Budweiser (alcoholic and nonalcoholic beverages). Each paid tens of millions of dollars for the privilege of linking their products and services with the Olympic Movement's five-ring logo. The OPUS sponsors category numbered sixteen, among them such well-known national brands as Allstate (auto and home insurance), BlueCross BlueShield (health insurance), Delta (passenger and freight air transportation), Gateway (computer hardware), Hallmark (flowers and greeting cards), Seiko (timing devices), and Home Depot (retail home improvement). In addition, OPUS garnered the financial and "in kind" goods and services support of thirty-five local and national firms, from KSL Television/Radio and Garrett Metal Detectors to Kellogg's and General Mills, the noted cereal manufacturers. Even Bombardier, the giant Canadian manufacturer of airplanes, snowmobiles, and railway cars, joined SLOC's Olympic corporate sponsorship program. There is little doubt that in the absence of OPUS's spectacular success, the financial burden on the Salt Lake City and Greater Utah taxpayer might have been extremely severe. "The sponsors and partners supported us after the scandal, and after September 11th," exclaimed a delighted, and no doubt relieved, Mitt Romney at the end of the Games. "They came and invested more and helped make the Games a success. They were our greatest friends and allies."[27]

The sale of Olympic events tickets, licensing fees for sale of Olympic merchandise, and private donations formed the greater final dimension of revenue gathering for the organizing committee. Salt Lake 2002 set unprecedented Olympic Winter Games records in ticket and licensed goods sales. Utilizing the Internet as no previous Olympic Games ever had, Salt Lake sold 90 percent of its 1.6 million tickets on-line.[28] Ticket sales generated $183 million. SLOC established seventy associations with licensees to manufacture and sell Olympic-branded merchandise. Energetic licensing rights owners, feverish buying by consumers (particularly in the six-month period preceding the Games and the seventeen-day period of the Games themselves), together with an aggressive Olympic coin sales program generated a further $34 million. SLOC's marketing programs for corporate and business sponsorship, ticket sales, licensing, coin sales, and private donations,[29] together with the TOP and television rights fees contributions from the IOC, generated a final figure of approximately $1.39 billion, well short of the most conservative estimate of the cost of the Games. The balance (either $600 million or $2.1 billion) was covered by "public money" contributions.

### Finis: The Great Olympic Bribery Trial

With the Salt Lake City Games successfully staged, Utahans relaxed and basked in the afterglow of the city's performance before the gaze of on-site tourists and a worldwide television audience. There were, of course, countless congratulatory hugs and backslapping galore. A great sense of satisfaction prevailed. Scurrilous events associated with the bid process, all subject to examination by an engaged world media three years earlier, were forgotten. Indeed, they had disappeared from the radar screen. But had they?

Well over a year after the closing of Utah's Olympic Games, slumbering federal government action on the *Welch-Johnson* trial case issue awakened. In April 2003, the Tenth US Circuit Court of Appeals in Denver, Colorado, heard arguments by the Department of Justice for reopening the case. A three-person "hearing panel" voted two to one in favor of the request. "I can't understand why the government keeps going after Tom and I," stated a frustrated David Johnson to reporters. "I'd think they'd have better things to do. From the beginning, we've maintained that what was going on during the bid process was widely known. We didn't invent any part of it." In a particularly condemning statement, Johnson concluded his remarks by stating that "not only was the I.O.C. aware of what Welch and I were doing, they were teaching us the bid process."[30]

Once again, an exasperated Judge David Sam was assigned to try the case. He had tried his best to put the issue to rest by his dismissals in the summer and late fall of 2001. He, like most Utah citizens, was subsequently enraptured by the Games as they unfolded in the global citadel of Mormonism. There were only "good memories" for Sam. Now he was yet again asked to preside over a trial of two individuals who had, in the eyes of most Utahans, been vindicated by the success of the Games. He did not particularly relish the task before him, but dutifully, he soldiered on. And so, too, did the legal teams of both the prosecution (the Justice Department) and the defense (Zuckerman Spaeder and Snow, Christensen, and Martineau). At 8:30 a.m. on October 28, 2003, Judge Sam's gavel descended on his courtroom desk, signaling the opening of the Great Olympic Bribery Trial. For Welch and Johnson, there was a lot at stake—the litany of felony allegations, fifteen in all, including one count of conspiracy, five counts of wire fraud, five counts of mail fraud, and four violations of the United States Immigration and Travel Act laws, each punishable by a maximum five-year prison sentence, a $250,000 fine, or both. As the trial wore on, government attorneys John Scott and Richard Wiedis focused squarely on the issue of fraudulent conduct on the part of Welch and Johnson—that they concealed their activities from their overseers on the bid committee's board of trustees, activities that were alleged to have been in the form of cash payments, wire transfers, unaccounted expenditures, and secret deals.[31]

On December 4, 2003, after five weeks of argument and questioning of witnesses by prosecutors Scott and Wiedis, cross-examination by defense counsel, examination of more than a million pages of documents, and expenditure of millions of dollars in legal costs, the prosecution rested its case. The pathway for the prosecution was extraordinarily difficult. At times the testimony of its witnesses appeared to support the defendants' case rather than its own. For instance, in reference to the IOC's conduct in curtailing the culpable conduct of its members involved in the "core essence" of the trial, Richard Pound, the Justice Department's final witness summoned to testify on its behalf, feebly noted, "The IOC was certainly aware [of its members' conduct] but never could find out who was involved, so nothing could be done about it." Outside the courtroom, in an impromptu press scrum, Pound told reporters that he did not consider the bid committee's inducements to be bribes, simply "payments to encourage good feelings about Salt Lake. . . . [W]e had the fabulous Games that we thought we'd have in the first place," adding that he hoped the trial would bring an end to a case that "has caused embarrassment on a world-wide scale."[32]

With the prosecution's case rested, the twelve-member jury waited expectantly for the defense to present its arguments, examine its witnesses, and strive for a victory over what they considered from the start an ill-advised encroachment on the rights and reputations of two public-spirited, solid-citizen Utahans. In fact, day by day throughout the more than one-month proceedings led by the prosecution, the defense gained considerable confidence, supported in no small measure by what they considered prosecutorial error on numerous points. In the end, the defense presented but one succinct argument—the government had failed to prove its allegations. In a startling move, defense counsels Bill Taylor and Max Wheeler asked Judge Sam for immediate dismissal of all charges, in effect, a Rule 29 judgment of acquittal.[33] This dramatic turn of events reverberated in the half-empty courtroom—packed audiences had been the norm at the trial's outset. Aroused federal prosecutor Richard Wiedis urged Judge Sam to reject the request to drop the charges: "To dismiss this case now is to deprive the jury of its right to make a statement that Olympic corruption must be stopped."[34]

Faced with a ruling he could not avoid, Judge Sam chose caution, announcing to all present that he would deliberate overnight on the defense motion and reconvene the court at 9:00 the next morning. And so he did! At the appointed hour on Friday, December 5, before a courtroom once again filled to the rafters, Sam launched into his decision. First, he spoke to each count of the criminal conduct charges. Finally, he reached the "bottom line." "Due to the insufficiency of the evidence presented to support the crimes alleged and the inferential nature of that evidence, the Court, with respect and due deference for the province and the role of the jury, concludes that there is an unavoidable danger of confusion and speculation if this matter were subjected to a jury. . . . Therefore, it is hereby ordered that defendant Thomas K. Welch and defendant David R. Johnson are hereby acquitted of each and every count of the indictment."[35] Welch slumped in his seat, a stoic expression on his face; Johnson broke into tears and embraced his lawyer, Max Wheeler, in a prolonged hug. "Enough is enough," preached Sam.[36] "In my 40 years' experience with the criminal justice system, as a defense and prosecuting attorney, and as a Utah state judge and a United States District Court Judge, I have never seen a criminal case brought to trial that was so devoid of . . . criminal intent or evil purpose."[37] In a sop to the crestfallen Department of Justice legal team, Judge Sam applied a final bit of wisdom to his resolution: "The government always wins when justice is done," he said, "regardless of the outcome."

## A Final Word

And so the curtain fell on the final act of the Great Olympic Bribery Trial.[38] Sam's decision also closed the last chapter of the otherwise glorious 2002 Salt Lake City Olympic Winter Games, the first of the new millennium. Although the trial's abrupt end confounded many, few were shocked by Judge Sam's final decision. In fact, Sam's association with the case boded badly for the prosecution. That Sam was "an Olympic fan," and more especially a Salt Laker who found the entire case of the government ill-advised, can be seen in his preliminary dismissal of a portion of the charges against Welch and Johnson, his postponement of the proceedings until after the Olympic Games had been staged, and his final categorical dismissal of all charges in November 2001. Did Sam's affiliation with the LDS, some of whose members occupied the highest offices of the bid and organizing committees, influence his disposition?[39] Federal government authorities launched no appeal on the decision to reassign the case to Judge Sam. In the end, the case was not about religion, or Salt Lake City's image, no, not even the success of the state of Utah's most glorious historical event since Brigham Young led his flock through Emigration Canyon more than 150 years ago. To Judge Sam, the question of guilt boiled down to a single issue: in the case before him, did there exist "a continual course of organized criminal conduct . . . with intent to inflict economic harm or injure the property rights of another?" "No," opined the venerable judge! And that was the end of the matter.[40]

What brought the focus of Utahans, Americans, and the Olympic world on Salt Lake City's Frank E. Moss Federal Courthouse in December 2003? The story began with the ascension of Spain's Juan Antonio Samaranch to IOC member status and his subsequent rise to the position of IOC president. Samaranch orchestrated the expansion and diversification of the IOC's revenue base as a means of both supporting the financial needs of organizing committees tasked with establishing the infrastructure for hosting the Games and facilitating the wider dissemination of the Olympic ideals. His success in this regard represented a major element of what David Miller dubbed an "Olympic Revolution."[41] The IOC struggled to entice cities to pursue the opportunity to host the Olympic Games in the late 1970s, but under Samaranch, this challenge dissipated owing to the funding model introduced by

Peter Ueberroth, president of the 1984 Los Angeles Organizing Committee, the realization of enhanced revenues through Samaranch's initiative in establishing The Olympic Program (now The Olympic Partners), and the mushrooming value of Olympic television rights.

The opportunity to host the world's athletes, while simultaneously thrusting one's city onto the international stage and leveraging the event to enhance a community's infrastructure, energized civic leaders worldwide. The competitive environment of the Olympic bid process intensified. In their quest to win the favor of IOC members, some bid committees elected to offer inducements ranging widely in terms of both value and variety. And some IOC members "cashed in" on their status. Samaranch steered a wide berth around rumors of this discreditable conduct of some bidders and IOC members and did not establish any means of oversight concerning the conduct of IOC members during bid city visits instituted in the mid-1980s. In their use of gifts to lure IOC member votes, Tom Welch and David Johnson did not break new ground, and in protesting their innocence of any wrongdoing and stating to reporters during their own trial proceedings that they had merely played the game, they did not shade the truth. The proliferation of this gift-giving culture, which also invited the intervention of self-styled Olympic agents who promised IOC member votes in exchange for employment as bid consultants, established a festering crisis that exploded in Salt Lake City.

# 8

# Then and Now

## The Tempest Fades

In March 1999, on the eve of the IOC's 108th Extraordinary Session, Francisco Elizalde, IOC member from the Philippines, predicted a drawn-out struggle for the organization in its effort to establish a meaningful path for brand recovery. "It's very hard to undo the damage. It will linger. Let's talk reality," offered Elizalde. "Our image is kaput right now." Was Elizalde's prognostication accurate? The set of reforms proposed by the IOC 2000 Commission, subsequently accepted by IOC members at the 110th IOC Session in December 1999, and the establishment of the IOC Ethics Commission created the desired impression of an organization engaged in confronting its exposed shortcomings. Before the end of 1999, the IOC also benefited from Nike's decision to seize Reebok's abandoned sponsorship of the Sydney Olympic Games[1] and Samaranch's performance before US congressional authorities.[2] In February 2000, David D'Alessandro voiced his opinion that a TOP sponsorship remained a wise investment for John Hancock, which also sent a positive signal regarding the IOC's recovery efforts. This collective of factors, when combined with the satiation of the media's appetite resulting from the expulsion of six IOC members at the March Session and its less cacophonous coverage of the organization in its aftermath, placed the IOC and the Olympic Movement on an improved trajectory well before that which Elizalde predicted possible.

The Sydney Olympic Organizing Committee, backed up by an enthusiastic volunteer base some forty-seven thousand strong,[3] staged the 2000

Summer Olympics with skill and aplomb to glowing worldwide reviews. Sydney's success was central to the IOC's recovery process. In carrying out this task, SOCOG survived a revolving door into and out of the offices of its senior executives for four years after the award of the Games in 1993, withstood a ticketing scandal and the Reebok dispute, and navigated the difficult discussion of "reconciliation" between Australia's Indigenous and non-Indigenous peoples.[4] Transportation, a concern for organizers, especially in the wake of the difficulties experienced in Atlanta four years earlier, flowed smoothly during the Games. Sydney's hosting effort, and the fact that 88 percent of the Olympic tickets were sold,[5] reflected Australians' passion for sport. Organizers successfully leveraged the Games to advance Sydney's global status, promote Australian business, and secure additional tourism dollars.[6] Visitors to Sydney departed Australia with fond memories of the athletic competition, highlighted by heroics of Australia's own Ian Thorpe and Cathy Freeman, and Sydney's picturesque harbor and festive downtown atmosphere. Australia's success permitted the IOC to emerge from any lingering shadow of the Salt Lake City bid scandal.

## Samaranch's Exit, New Leadership, and Money Matters

The IOC gathered nine months following the close of the Sydney Olympics to select the successor to Juan Antonio Samaranch. Five candidates stood for election. They were Jacques Rogge (Belgium), Richard Pound (Canada), Anita DeFrantz (United States), Pál Schmitt (Hungary), and Un Yong Kim, the controversial South Korean. Some IOC members cringed at the prospect of a Kim presidency. Rogge, with Samaranch's support, won the election handily on a second ballot over Kim (fifty-nine to twenty-three).

Pound's third-place finish (twenty-two votes) behind Kim proved a difficult pill for the Canadian to swallow, especially in light of his knowledge of the findings of the Salt Lake City inquiry he chaired (and Samaranch's eleventh-hour intervention designed to save Kim from expulsion). Following the election, Pound resigned his roles as chairman of the IOC's Marketing Commission and WADA.[7] Upon reflection, and following discussions with Rogge, Pound resumed his work with WADA. Kim's second-place finish prompted observers to question the organization's commitment to reform in light of the Korean's past alleged transgressions. While accomplished and respected, Rogge owed his victory, or at least the plurality of his triumph, to his European background and Samaranch's support. The European bloc once again demonstrated its historic resistance to releasing its iron grip on the IOC presidency.

The European continent's dominance in Olympic affairs provides the IOC and its affiliated bodies with a long-term challenge. There are strong reasons for this assertion. Seven of the eight IOC presidents have hailed from Europe, and it took twenty-five rounds of voting for the only non-European, Avery Brundage, to triumph over Great Britain's Lord Burghley in 1952. Of the thirty-five ISFs sponsoring events on the Summer and Winter Olympic programs (as of September 2008), twenty were led by European presidents, and thirty-one had their headquarters on the Continent.[8] Europeans have exerted significant control over the award of Olympic festivals to bidding cities, ensuring that the majority of the Olympics have been staged on the Continent. Of the forty-seven Olympic festivals staged, twenty-nine (or 62

11. Juan Antonio Samaranch raises Jacques Rogge's hand and in so doing congratulates him on his election as IOC president at the IOC's Moscow Session in July 2001. Marc Hodler, Thomas Bach, and Kevan Gosper appear from left in the background. *Source:* Reuters/Corbis.

percent) have been in Europe. Two of the next four scheduled Games will occur there.[9] In selecting Rio de Janeiro to host the 2016 Olympic Games at its 121st IOC Session in Copenhagen in October 2009, for the first time granting hosting responsibilities for an Olympic festival to a South American city, while at the same time setting aside the aspirations of Madrid on the final ballot (sixty-six votes to thirty-two), perhaps the organization is (finally) signaling its understanding of the true ambulatory mission of the Olympic Games.[10] The IOC removed baseball and softball from the Olympic program in 2005 (for 2012 and beyond). European countries are not represented in great numbers in these sports. The IOC's European cohort dismissed their popularity in North America and Asia. Much American sentiment focused on Rogge having orchestrated their ouster.[11] Removing softball was particularly shortsighted. Handball and modern pentathlon, two sports that have no meaningful foundation outside Europe (and Scandinavia), survived the IOC's review of the Olympic program at the 117th IOC Session in Singapore. Power and influence in the Olympic Movement are clearly tilted toward Europe.

No one denies Europe's central importance to the establishment and nurturing of the Olympic Movement in its early years, but within the Olympic world as we open the twenty-first century, Europeans exhibit a troublesome sense of entitlement. Europeans raged when the foundation board of the World Anti-Doping Agency placed its headquarters in a non-European city, Montreal.[12] When Australia's John Fahey emerged as a late candidate to replace Richard Pound as chairman of WADA in 2007, the European candidate, a two-time Olympic fencing champion, France's Jean-François Lamour, cried foul and withdrew from the contest. Europeans sought a six-month postponement of the election so that they could locate a candidate. This appeal was denied.[13] Lamour threatened to establish a rival European Anti-Doping Agency.[14] Members of the Council of Europe, who were responsible for placing Lamour's candidacy forward, claimed that their response to Fahey's candidacy and Lamour's backpeddling reflected their belief that it was Europe's turn to lead WADA.[15] Power sharing hardly defines Europeans' approach to the IOC presidency.

When Juan Antonio Samaranch finally relinquished the IOC presidential reins in 2001, NBC's Dick Ebersol offered his thoughts on the leadership void created and the depth of the challenge facing his successor. "In the world of international sport, particularly the Olympics," stated Ebersol, "his passing from the scene after two decades has the importance of David Stern, Paul Tagliabue, and Bud Selig all resigning on the same day." Samaranch, in a reflective mood prior to Rogge's election, observed that "the IOC I leave my successor has nothing to do with the IOC I received in 1980." His agenda was sweeping. With the able assistance of Richard Pound and Michael Payne, he transformed the IOC from a staid, conservative organization that possessed a limited understanding of its ability to generate revenue to an economic juggernaut capable of generating four billion dollars on a quadrennial basis, primarily from television rights sales and corporate sponsorship deals. He assigned amateurism to the dustbin of history, encouraged increased competitive opportunities for women at Olympic festivals, fostered a closer connection between the IOC and the Paralympic Movement, and pursued efforts to make the Olympic program more attractive to the world's youth. Samaranch effected meaningful repair to the IOC's relationships with the International Sport Federations and National Olympic Committees that had deteriorated under Avery Brundage and received little attention from his predecessor, Lord Killanin. "Through sheer willpower," concluded Anita DeFrantz, "[Samaranch] has created the Olympic movement as it exists now."[16]

Olympic historians, too, credit Samaranch for the personal industry demonstrated in pursuing the implementation of his overall vision. However, his failure to confront the rumors of IOC member misconduct within the context of an increasingly bloated Olympic bid process, a crucial lapse in leadership that culminated in the Salt Lake City scandal, indifference to the doping issue, and inability to reach goals for increasing women's presence in the halls of decision making in international sport must also figure in any assessment of his legacy.

Rogge assumed the IOC presidency with a significant degree of goodwill, even from the IOC's harshest critics. The IOC benefited in the short term from the transition simply because Samaranch was no longer a lightning rod for criticism. He demonstrated a relaxed demeanor and more media-friendly attitude than his predecessor and set to work to establish a new management team in Lausanne in an effort to distance himself from assertions that the Samaranch-Rogge constellation would resemble a "ventriloquist and his doll," a charge buttressed by the fact that Samaranch planned to remain resident in Lausanne and take an active role in his new position as IOC honorary president for life.[17] Rogge established the fight against doping as the central aspect of his presidential agenda and has admirably maintained his focus on that issue; however, the infrastructure for that fight was established in 1999 with the formation of WADA. In this respect, the efforts of Richard Pound figure prominently in the assessment of gains made on this front in recent years. Admittedly, a second priority, downsizing the Games, especially the Summer Games program, posed a challenging proposition. Little progress has been made on this front; however, further growth has been restrained. Last, people hoping that Rogge would find a means of pursuing an enhanced role for women in Olympic decision making have been disappointed. It is problematic that the IOC's 15-member Executive Board is populated by but one woman. A mere 19 of the 110 active IOC members (or 17.3 percent as of March 2011) are women. Goals set in 1996 for female representation on executive boards of the world's NOCs and ISFs, and the IOC itself, remain unfulfilled goals for the majority of those bodies.[18]

As Rogge concluded his initial eight-year term, and launched himself into a four-year extension granted him at the 121st IOC Session in Copenhagen in 2009, it is difficult to identify anything that defines his presidency, certainly nothing along the lines of the revolutionary change orchestrated by his predecessor. He has been an effective caretaker.[19] There were no major missteps that jeopardized the IOC's overarching mission of brand recovery in the decade following the Salt Lake City scandal. The Games that unfolded on his watch have been successful (even though the financial debt accrued by the Greeks in 2004 was extremely large). One must assume that Rogge wishes to leave a presidential legacy, but clearly the substance of that legacy has yet to be revealed. Perhaps, in time, people will focus on the decision made on his watch that delivered the Olympic Games to South America and the concomitant extension of the Olympic brand to that region of the world. The oversight of successful Games in Beijing within a global environment that questioned the wisdom of delivering the Games to China and the advent of the Youth Olympics are noteworthy and will likely attract some attention when historians assess his efforts.

Will his legacy involve delivering peace to the Olympic Movement with respect to the distribution of global Olympic sponsorship and television revenues? This objective has consumed a good deal of his attention in recent years. When the IOC established the TOP sponsorship program in the mid-1980s, the United States Olympic Committee invoked the Amateur Sports Act to claim 15 percent of the total revenue. This share shifted to 20 percent in the mid-1990s.[20] The USOC argued that its exclusive ownership of the use of the Olympic rings in US territory precluded the IOC from establishing such a program without its consent. The advertising platform that the IOC and the major sponsors desired would have been greatly compromised (and far less lucrative for the IOC) without access to the US market. With the vast majority of TOP sponsors based in the United States, the USOC also claimed that this percentage share compensated it for lost revenue from its own domestic sponsorship program. The USOC also leveraged the Amateur Sports Act to acquire 10 percent of the value of the US Olympic television contract through the joint IOC-USOC Broadcast Marketing Agreement signed in 1986 (beginning with the 2004 Athens Olympics, the USOC received 12.75 percent).[21] The bottom line is that the USOC receives an extremely large sum of money when compared to the dollars shared by the other 204 National Olympic Committees (NOCs). In the 2005–8 quadrennial, the USOC received $298,154,000 from TOP ($106,078,000) and Olympic television funds ($192,076,000), as well as a portion of the $233,590,000 in television money distributed to the NOCs via Olympic Solidarity. The remaining 204 NOCs shared $159,492,000 from the TOP program.[22]

Despite European IOC members who resented the USOC's share of TOP revenue, until recent efforts yielded a more diversified composition of the TOP sponsor list by region, there had been no sustained campaign for altering the status quo in the 1980s and 1990s.[23] Television revenue and the manner of its distribution, however, had long posed a source of friction for the IOC and the USOC, in light of the USOC's repeated efforts to enhance the terms of the BMA through face-to-face negotiations or by calling upon its congressional allies. The IOC's interests in this protracted struggle were represented by Richard Pound, a North American, who believed the USOC was well compensated and required no further concessions. European IOC members did not call en masse for a reduction in the USOC's share of Olympic television revenue in the 1980s or 1990s. In 2008, however, European IOC members dropped the gloves and demanded change. The TOP sponsor list was no longer dominated by US-based multinational companies, they argued, and Europe and Asia had also been making substantial contributions to global Olympic television revenue for more than a decade. The USOC's privileged status conceded an "immoral amount of money [to the USOC] than what other people get," charged Holland's Hein Verbruggen.[24] Switzerland's Denis Oswald circulated a letter to various Olympic organizations in March 2008, decrying the situation as being "no longer morally acceptable."[25] Verbruggen and Oswald accused USOC officials of "footdragging" in discussions aimed at reaching an accord in advance of the receipt of revenues from the 2020 Olympics. Verbruggen admitted that "[he was] angry with these people."[26] "It's hard to negotiate," countered Anita DeFrantz, a member of the IOC and the USOC's Board of Directors, "when you are being called immoral."[27]

Rogge's effort at brokering an agreement involved striking a three-person team composed of Oswald, Mexico's Mario Vázquez Raña, and Norway's Gerhard Heiberg (who also serves as the chairman of the IOC Marketing Commission) to negotiate an accord with USOC chairman Peter Ueberroth. Ueberroth's public utterances revealed a rearguard strategy. The money accrued from the TOP program and the US television contract provides the USOC with 50 percent of its operating budget. He opposed simply reducing the USOC's percentage share of the money. Rather, he sought a plan to grow the revenue "pot" in exchange for a reduced percentage share in order to avert a decrease in the amount of money flowing to the USOC's headquarters in Colorado Springs.[28] "Handshake deals" Ueberroth reached with Heiberg were torpedoed when they were presented for consideration in Lausanne. "I think we had agreements in place three different times, but then what they agree to they don't want to agree to anymore," observed Ueberroth. "I think they would rather have disagreement than agreement."[29]

Ueberroth was motivated to find a solution, as he and others feared that IOC officials were employing Chicago's bid for the 2016 Olympics as the "stick" in negotiations. If the USOC proved intransigent, Chicago's bid might suffer when IOC members cast their ballots in late 2009.[30] But he was mindful of the money flowing into Olympic tills from the US market and refused to yield to the IOC's demands. Ueberroth stepped down from the USOC chairmanship when his term expired in October 2008 and handed this sensitive file to his successor, Larry Probst.[31]

## Chicago 2016's Copenhagen Collapse

The impasse between Ueberroth and IOC negotiators did little for the blood pressures of Chicago 2016 bid chairman Patrick Ryan and his colleagues, who were fully engaged in a pitched battle with Madrid, Rio de Janeiro, and Tokyo bid officials for the right to host the 2016 Summer Olympics. In March 2009, Probst, (now former) USOC vice president Bob Ctvrtlik, (then) acting USOC CEO Stephanie Streeter, and IOC negotiators set aside further discussion of the issue until 2013; however, both sides pledged to work toward an agreement at that time with a new formula governing distribution of Olympic revenues in 2020 and beyond. Probst's approach, commented Ryan, hit the proper chord with Heiberg and Rogge. He toned down the rhetoric of past discussions involving Ueberroth when the USOC intimated that it might withdraw its support from the TOP program without an agreement that recognized the contribution of the US market to Olympic revenues.[32] Rogge expressed optimism that Probst was someone with whom he could eventually broker a deal: "I think the chemistry is working extremely well between Mr. Probst and myself."[33] Postponing further discussion relieved Chicago of the specter of this dispute leading up to the vote on the site of the 2016 Olympics and protected this revenue stream for the USOC during what has proved a challenging economic period for the organization; however, it also secured for the IOC, principally its European cohort, an assurance that the USOC would negotiate.[34]

But it was a fragile truce. In July 2009, the USOC rattled Lausanne officials in announcing the launch of its planned Olympic television network (USON) in partnership with Comcast before resolving all matters of concern to the IOC, most important its impact on NBC, its longtime television partner.[35] "They know we have issues. I just find it frankly cavalier on the part of the USOC. It's just vintage USOC," concluded Richard Carrión, the clearly frustrated chairman of the IOC's Finance Commission. "I don't see how this can help [Chicago]," he concluded. Ueberroth, the USOC's former chairman and a point person for the organization in its effort to mount the new channel, shot back: "We started this two years ago. Everybody's known this [was] coming on and so we're not surprising anybody."[36] Jacques Rogge intervened in August 2009 and secured a pledge from Larry Probst that the

USOC would delay any further development of the channel until all matters of concern to the IOC had been resolved.[37]

With these matters set aside, Rogge dismissed the impact of the recent brush fires on Chicago's chances to secure the right to host the 2016 Summer Olympics.[38] However, the city's shocking first-ballot ouster at the vote on the site for the 2016 Olympic Games in October 2009 despite the lobbying of President Barack Obama and First Lady Michelle Obama during Chicago's final bid presentation challenges Rogge's reading of the IOC membership. Chicago's demise, in the aftermath of New York's second-ballot departure in the final vote on the site of the 2012 Olympics, created an interesting back-drop for future IOC-USOC discussions. Kevan Gosper was not the only per-son who worried about how the obvious snub to Chicago, and by extension the USOC, would influence an already strained relationship between the two organizations.[39] "It was horrible for the Olympic Movement," concluded Anita DeFrantz. Richard Pound, who experienced his share of frustration with USOC negotiators concerning the distribution of Olympic revenue in the 1980s and 1990s, considered the rebuke to be shortsighted: "This is not the way you deal with the United States of America," he warned. Pound expressed concern that a guaranteed eighteen-year gap between Olympic festivals on US soil (the USOC had no candidate in the race to host the 2018 Olympic Winter Games) might suppress available US corporate dollars. Without a solution to the IOC-USOC dispute, stated Pound, "there are lots of nightmare scenarios that could come back and bite everybody."[40]

A review of the last few months of the race reveals two critical moments for Chicago's hopes that played out against the backdrop of the ongoing ten-sion between the IOC and the USOC. First, in June 2009, Jacques Rogge downplayed one of the principal strengths of Chicago's candidacy when the bid committees made their final presentations to IOC members in Lausanne prior to the October gathering in Copenhagen. A Chicago win offered the IOC and the Olympic Movement the opportunity to cash in on the increased dollars available from an energized American commercial marketplace. With the world's economic troubles wreaking havoc on countries and posing a threat to transnational organizations such as the IOC, Chicago's advantage escaped few. Yet Rogge must have unsettled Ryan and his Chicago colleagues when he stated on the eve of the presentations, "Economics should not drive our decision. Frequently in the past we did not necessarily go for the richest city and I believe we were right to do that. Ultimately it is not the economics but leaving a sustainable legacy. When we leave, we want it to be a bonus for the city, the region and the country."[41] The words and the timing of their delivery could not have been drafted any better by Carlos Nuzman, Rio's bid committee president. Second, the soft underbelly of Rio's candidacy, public safety and security concerns resulting from the well-reported activities of Rio's criminal gangs, was shored up by the IOC Evaluation Commission in its final report released a mere month before IOC members convened in Copenhagen. "Recognising that it faces public safety challenges," wrote Chairwoman Nawal El Moutawakel and other commission members, "the City of Rio has taken a new approach with regard to local policing which engages the community in a range of social and sports programmes, already showing positive results." To an outsider, the words seem vague and puzzling. Members of Rio's gangs will drop their guns and knives and turn to sport and breakfast clubs? For IOC members, it said, don't let this be a reason not to support South America's and Brazil's aspirations; the Brazilians will find a way. The report also raised question marks concerning Chicago's public transportation plans and the city's financial guarantee that did not fully conform to the terms of a host-city contract.[42] Rio's path to victory was laid.

## Repairing the USOC-IOC Relationship Is a Major Priority

US corporations and television networks provide the IOC and its Olympic family constituents with vast sums of money through television rights and TOP sponsorships, but the percentage of the global contribution from these entities has been in decline. In the 1985–89 quadrennial, US networks provided $609 million of the $727.5 million (83.7 percent) secured from the world's television markets and a similarly large 77.8 percent of the $96 million generated by TOP. For the 2009–12 quadrennial, the US contribution to television rights and TOP funds on a percentage basis fell to 52.6 percent and 44 percent, respectively, at the outset of the current quadrennial period. These data underpin the arguments forwarded by the likes of Oswald and Verbruggen; however, it should be noted that TOP agreements signed in 2010 following the Vancouver Olympic Winter Games with US-based Procter & Gamble and Dow Chemical will elevate the latter percentage.[43] The status quo in terms of distribution of television and corporate sponsorship dollars is not defensible; however, finding the middle ground that will satisfy the USOC and those individuals lobbying for a reduction in the USOC's share of Olympic revenue poses a challenge for Jacques Rogge and negotiators on both sides of the table. The world's NOCs believe they deserve more consideration concerning the allocation of television and sponsorship dollars. The USOC received in the neighborhood of $300 million from global revenues in the 2005–8 quadrennial and projects to receive in excess of $400 million between 2009 and 2012.[44]

In commenting on these recent financial squabbles between IOC and USOC officials, a communications executive familiar with the dialogue behind closed doors observed, "It's almost like the USOC and IOC have been in marriage counseling. They love each other, they need each other, but they're sure good at not getting along."[45] Patrick Ryan, after having recovered from Chicago's humbling results in Copenhagen, conceded that the friction between the two bodies did not help the city's cause. Reflecting on the longstanding dispute over Olympic revenue, Ryan likened the IOC and USOC to the Hatfields and McCoys.[46] Still, he maintained a "team player" attitude in defending the efforts of the USOC on behalf of Chicago: "The U.S. Olympic Committee did a great job," Ryan said. "I don't think they had a thing to do with this [defeat]."[47] A major priority for Rogge, one that he has pursued with vigor especially in 2010 and 2011, is to establish the necessary interorganizational trust that will encourage dialogue dedicated to reaching a fair and equitable agreement concerning the distribution of Olympic revenue.[48] And at the end of the day, the discussants must not ignore the fact that the bill for hosting the Games still falls to host cities and their organizing committees.

In *Selling the Five Rings*, we detailed the friction between the USOC and the IOC on Olympic revenue matters in the 1980s and 1990s. In this most recent chapter of the relationship between officials in Lausanne and Colorado Springs, Rogge, Oswald, Vázquez Raña, Heiberg, Ueberroth, Probst, and Streeter were the key actors, replacing the likes of Juan Antonio Samaranch, Richard Pound, Michael Payne, Dick Schultz, and John Krimsky.

However, ongoing discussions do not involve Streeter, who stated a mere five days after Chicago's loss that she would not be a candidate for the USOC's CEO position on a permanent basis. Probst, too, came under fire from America's national sport governing bodies following the debacle in Copenhagen but has survived. The NSGBs chafed at the revelation in August 2009 that Streeter received a base salary of $560,000, 30 percent larger than her predecessor, Jim Scherr, and complained that Streeter and Probst, who both hailed from the corporate world, lacked the necessary knowledge of the workings of the IOC and the international sport community. "If you don't know what you don't know," stated USA Triathlon's CEO, Skip Gilbert, "you really can't lead from a dynamic position. So, realistically, today is the day to make the change," he observed in pressing for Probst's resignation.[49] Unabated support from the USOC's board of directors was central to Probst's survival.[50]

Dick Ebersol, given his company's financial investment in the Olympic Movement, qualified as more than a casual bystander with respect to discussions of the need for improvement in the USOC's functionality. He pinned responsibility for Chicago's loss on the USOC, an organization in need of "real leadership,"[51] and immediately advanced the names of Chuck Wielgus (CEO, USA Swimming) and Steve Penny (CEO, USA Gymnastics) as viable candidates for Streeter's former job. The financial benefit accrued by the USOC from Olympic television and corporate sponsorship funds when compared to the sums flowing to the other two-hundred-plus NOCs, stated Ebersol, poisoned relations between the IOC and the USOC. "I don't believe there will be another Olympics in the U.S. until the USOC really gets its act together," said Ebersol.[52]

The turnstile on the office door of the organization's CEO clearly hampered the USOC's operational effectiveness. Streeter's replacement, Scott Blackmun, an attorney and former acting CEO of the USOC (November 2000–October 2001), who was named to the post in January 2010, satisfied Ebersol and watchful NSGB leaders who feared the appointment of another individual from the corporate world. Stability and outreach will need to be central themes for his four-year term, as Blackmun, the USOC's seventh acting or permanent CEO since 2000,[53] must seek to repair relations with the IOC and facilitate improved communication with NSGBs in the United States.[54] During his inaugural press conference, he extended an olive branch to IOC officials with words that would have been welcomed in Lausanne: "At the end of the day, the IOC is the leader of the worldwide Olympic

Movement, and we need to respect that, and we need to spend some time listening," he said.[55]

An improved working relationship between the USOC and IOC is vital to the future health of the Olympic Movement. There were encouraging signs in early 2010 that Blackmun's arrival paid immediate dividends.[56] Respectful dialogue between USOC and IOC officials advanced their mutual desire for an improved rapport within months. In September 2010, the two sides reached agreement concerning the "Games cost" issue, specifically, the USOC's financial contribution to the operation of a number of IOC commissions, WADA, and the Court of Arbitration for Sport in Vancouver and London. In March 2011, the IOC appointed Probst and Blackmun to the International Relations and Marketing Commissions, respectively, providing them important platforms to enhance the USOC's level of engagement with Lausanne officials. The next step in this process will likely be the election of an IOC member from the United States to the Executive Board in the months ahead. Mere weeks later, both sides reported meaningful progress in discussions aimed at securing an agreement for the future distribution of television and TOP dollars, indicating the possibility of a positive resolution as early as July 2011.[57] However, in early September 2011, a solution still eluded the two parties. The USOC also decided not to put forward a US candidate city for the 2020 Olympics. Clearly, work still remains for Jacques Rogge, Larry Probst and Scott Blackmun, and their respective leadership groups.

## The IOC's Reform Agenda

In the wake of the 110th IOC Session in December 1999, heightened interest in the amount of money channeled to Colorado Springs on a quadrennial basis coincided with the implementation of measures to enhance financial transparency within the Olympic Movement. The IOC released the data concerning dollars distributed to the USOC, ISFs, NOCs, and OCOGs such that IOC members who had previously been unaware concerning such matters were now informed. However, improved financial accountability and transparency mandated through reform initiatives approved in 1999 extended beyond the release of these figures. Bid cities were directed to submit detailed accounting of the sources of their funds, the Olympic Solidarity program was subject to an improved auditing process, and independent, external auditors were tasked with analyzing the IOC's quadrennial financial records before their release. Interested parties can now follow discussions at IOC Sessions via closed-circuit television.[58]

The second significant reform thrust targeted the structure of the IOC and membership criteria. Eight-year term limits were imposed on members, and new members were subject to an age limit of seventy years of age. It is difficult to conclude that an age limit and term limits will reduce the prospect for corruption within the bid process, given that their absence in the 1990s did not contribute to the Salt Lake City crisis in any way. Rather, Samaranch orchestrated the admission of some IOC members as a means of increasing the reach of the Olympic Games without due regard to character issues. Now, a Nominations Committee generates candidates for membership, vets them, and makes recommendations to the IOC members, who must approve any candidate in a vote at an IOC Session.[59] And the Ethics Commission, a permanent body composed of a majority of non-IOC members, yet another product of the reform process, responds to any cases brought to its attention concerning the conduct of IOC members in the context of both their professional and their sport administration lives. Seventy members achieve their standing on individual grounds as per past practice (but now representation is limited to a maximum of only one member from any country via attrition). Finally, though some IOC members once enjoyed an affiliation with an NOC or ISF and some even participated in a past Olympic festival, the present 115-member IOC now includes 15 NOC presidents, 15 ISF presidents, and 15 athletes who are no more than four years removed from Olympic competition.[60]

In attempting to enhance the representation of these constituencies, especially the ISFs and NOCs, Samaranch, who seized the crisis as a means of furthering this long-held goal, introduced a system in which the independence of members nominated by the ISFs and NOCs is potentially compromised. The newly minted ISF representatives have already lobbied to expand the IOC in such a way that all ISFs on the Olympic program would be granted an IOC member. One could expect similar demands from the NOCs if the IOC granted this degree of representation to the ISFs. The IOC, states Richard Pound, would become "as cumbersome as the United Nations and equally paralyzed" when confronted with difficult issues.[61] The potential for this "balkanization" of the IOC bears close monitoring.

The IOC 2000 Commission wisely suggested that the IOC explore tangible methods of knowledge transfer from one organizing committee to its successor. This transfer of knowledge includes sharing thoughts concerning best practices and the logistical challenges involved in delivering the Games, as well as providing information concerning how to develop critical relationships with the major corporate sponsors in order to maximize the value of their involvement. TOP sponsors had grown weary of educating each new set of organizers who entered the preparatory stages for their festival bearing a "tabula rasa" concerning sponsors' needs and capabilities. They lobbied the IOC while the reform agenda was being shaped to place priority on lessening the allocation of sponsors' resources to this educative process. The IOC listened to the counsel of its corporate partners.[62]

Bid city visits, the primary forum for the type of exchange that sparked the Salt Lake City crisis, were banned by IOC members at the 110th IOC Session. Although there have been periodic suggestions from the IOC rank and file that visits should be reinstituted, the ban remains in effect. While it is true that you do not have to meet someone face-to-face in the twenty-first century to facilitate a bribe, the optics of IOC members flying around the world at the expense of bid cities or the IOC itself are not positive. In 2002 Kevan Gosper bluntly rejected the protestations of some IOC members who believed the ban demonstrated a lack of trust on the part of the IOC leadership and made their ability to render an informed choice very difficult. "I'm dead against [bid city visits]," stated Gosper. "It's inconsistent with world practice to have 130 people going around to visit candidatures. It's overly costly, and it was the procedure that almost brought us down after 100 years." Jacques Rogge stated that bid city visits "are a waste of money."[63] He dismissed recent lobbying by Malaysia's Prince Tunku Imran, who argued in Beijing that members should have been able to travel in groups to the 2016 candidate cities as a means of enhancing their knowledge base prior to committing to a particular site.[64] Rogge countered that IOC members can glean sufficient information from the IOC Evaluation Commission, composed of a select number of IOC members, NOC and ISF officials, and athletes, that subjects all aspects of candidate-city bids to rigorous on-site analysis and files detailed reports. Rogge and the IOC leadership have given no indication that the ban on bid city visits will be withdrawn in the short or medium term.

## Reflections on Beijing

In 2001 Beijing's selection as host city for the Games of the XXIXth Olympiad sparked much controversy in light of China's human rights record and its relationships with Tibet and Taiwan. The late Tom Lantos (California), the ranking Democrat on the US House of Representatives' International Relations Committee, decried the IOC's decision. "It truly boggles the mind," said Lantos. "This decision will allow the Chinese police state to bask in the reflected glory of the Olympics despite having one of the most abominable human rights records in the world." Henry Kissinger, US secretary of state under Richard Nixon, played a central role in opening diplomatic relations between China and the United States. He disagreed with Lantos's analysis. "This is a very important step in the evolution of China's relationship with the world. It will have a positive impact," concluded Kissinger. The IOC's director-general, François Carrard, understood the backlash in some quarters of the world's media. Still, "it is not up to the IOC to interfere in [China's approach to human rights]," observed Carrard. "But we are taking the bet that seven years from now, we sincerely and dearly hope we will see many changes in China."[65]

While those engaged in politics and diplomacy debated the wisdom of the IOC's action, coaches and athletes pondered the prospect of challenging environmental conditions for the athletes given the city's air-pollution levels and traditional August climate. Indeed, the fifteen members of the IOC's Athletes' Commission, who also possessed IOC member voting rights, effectively split their votes for and against Beijing.[66] Toronto, Canada, offered a strong technical bid and a much safer choice for the IOC less than two years removed from the Salt Lake City bid scandal. However, justifying the award of a third Olympic festival to Canada (Montreal in 1976 and Calgary in 1988), a comparatively small Olympic nation, before granting the same honor and responsibility to China, the most populous nation on earth, proved too difficult.

When the IOC convened for its 112th Session in Moscow in July 2001, members knew that as of that date, only two of the previously staged twenty-four Summer Olympic festivals had taken place in an Asian city (Tokyo in 1964 and Seoul in 1988). With European IOC members, who held more than 40 percent of the votes, united in their desire for a European center to host the 2012 Summer Olympics, and the Games committed to Athens in 2004, Beijing's other rivals, Paris and Istanbul, stood little chance. Moreover, Vancouver-Whistler's active bid for the 2010 Olympic Winter Games likely moved some of them to pledge their future support to the Canadian bid, while lining up with Beijing's bid for the 2008 Summer Olympics. Both Albertville (1992) and Turin (2006) benefited from the use of the Winter Games as a consolation prize for nations disappointed at their loss in a Summer Games bid competition (Paris in 1992 and Rome in 2004). So, too, did Vancouver gain from Toronto's loss.[67] Most European members were comfortable with the prospect of an Athens-Turin-Beijing-Vancouver rotation in setting the foundation for a European city in 2012.

Beijing officials, to their credit, did not cry foul in the public arena following revelations during the Salt Lake City crisis concerning the deal John Coates consummated with Francis Nyangweso and Charles Mukora on the eve of the vote for the 2000 Summer Olympics, a vote Beijing lost by the narrowest of margins (forty-five votes to forty-three). Instead, Chinese officials improved the caliber of the plan proposed in 1993. Media coverage of Coates's last-minute lobbying efforts, and demonstrated Chinese restraint, secured an additional measure of sympathy for Beijing in the latter stages of the bid competition. The Chinese required little help given the clear predisposition of the majority of IOC members; however, a wayward comment from Toronto's mayor, Mel Lastman, provided some self-inflicted damage in the waning days of Toronto's campaign. Lastman stated that attending an Olympic meeting in Africa concerned him because he imagined himself "in a pot of boiling water with all these natives dancing around me."[68]

The coalescence of these factors resulted in Beijing's comfortable second-ballot victory over Toronto, fifty-six votes to twenty-two. Paris (eighteen) and Istanbul (nine) trailed the two front runners. When outgoing IOC president Juan Antonio Samaranch announced the final voting results, thousands of Beijing's citizens gathered in Millennium Square erupted in celebration, while fireworks set the city's skyline ablaze, green laser beams probed the night sky, and ballerinas and lion dancers mixed with the jubilant crowd.[69] Still, the ease of Beijing's win startled Norway's Gerhard Heiberg: "Toronto made an excellent presentation here, but more members than we anticipated had already made up their minds that it was time to go to China."[70]

When the festive atmosphere in Beijing subsided, the Chinese, undeterred by the level of international media scrutiny, proceeded with the expected degree of industry (and financial investment) to provide both a first-rate experience for Beijing's Olympians and to present the desired image of the country to the world. Athletes raved about the Olympic Village. The Bird's Nest (National Stadium) and Water Cube (aquatics facility) represent two of the most impressive architectural designs ever pursued in conjunction with hosting an Olympic festival, albeit at a cost of $423 and $146 million, respectively. An expenditure of some $43 billion gave Beijing a facelift of staggering proportions, especially when one considers that only one-quarter of the budget was directed to building new, or renovating existing, athletic facilities, with much of the rest allocated for infrastructural improvements. Resulting from its host-city status, Beijing now stands as a modern, booming capital in Asia, having benefited from a shift in the infrastructural development agenda away from the country's financial hub, Shanghai.[71]

We will not see the scale of financial investment witnessed in Beijing in future host cities. Beijing's budgetary commitments far outstripped the most expensive Olympic festival in history held four years earlier in Athens (a reported $15 billion). London's (2012) planned costs rose to $17.7 billion in 2008.[72] Successive host cities labored to outdo, outspend, outperform, and upstage their predecessor, often with an unnecessary long-term financial burden. The depth of China's financial commitment in staging such a spectacular event and the project to remake Beijing might curb the competitiveness that gripped these communities. If so, Beijing, whose $43 billion outlay prompted jaws to drop and provoked questions concerning the need for such lavish expenditure, did the IOC and the Olympic Movement a favor. It is doubtful that any host city can surpass Beijing's effort in terms of grandeur, so maintaining a focus on the needs of the athletes and ensuring tighter controls on the size of the organizing committee's budget represent a wise course of action for all future host cities.

James Kynge, former China bureau chief for the *Financial Times* and author of *China Shakes the World: A Titan's Rise and Troubled Future—and the Challenge for America,* concluded that for China, the Olympics were "not about sport and generosity in victory and defeat, but about showing the world that China is a powerful country that needs respect."[73] Deyan Sudjic, director of London's Design Museum, in assessing Beijing's architectural refit, shared Kynge's sentiments. The Beijing Olympics, stated Sudjic, offered Chinese government authorities an opportunity "to make a defiant and unmistakable statement that the country has taken its place in the world," and they seized it.[74]

However, there were missteps. One of the more significant miscalculations by Chinese authorities occurred in the context of the international torch relay. Protests, a number marred by violence, took place during the ITR staged prior to the Beijing Olympics. These episodes revealed the hubris of Chinese officials, who failed to anticipate the vehicle it offered those individuals who would use the media spotlight to decry China's human rights record, lobby for Tibet's independence, and criticize its unwillingness to support the United Nations' desire to confront the genocide in Darfur (through the wielding of its veto authority within the UN Security Council).[75]

Richard Pound asserted that the nature of these protests, specifically the ones plagued by violence, cost the protesters "the moral high ground." However, he also conceded the IOC Executive Board's support for the ITR, especially in light of a prior recommendation of the Olympic Games Study Commission (2003), supported unanimously by the IOC Session, to refrain from staging international torch relays, represented a failure in the IOC's risk-assessment protocol.[76] When Pound critiqued the Executive Board's decision to ignore the earlier recommendation of the Olympic Games Study Commission during the 120th IOC Session in Beijing, "a lot of people looked at their shoes."[77] An ITR in the future is a dim prospect.

Members of the international press corps eager to dissect the Beijing experience spent a measure of their time highlighting other perceived failings of the Chinese organizers and sport officials. Chinese authorities replaced the young girl chosen to sing at the opening ceremony because of her physical appearance. A "prettier" child lip-synched the singing of the originally cast young girl. They also employed computer-enhanced images of fireworks for the television audience. Both actions drew criticism. Accusations that the Chinese entered underage female gymnasts, and did so with the complicity

of government agencies that produced false documents, caused embarrassment, even though international gymnastics officials found no wrongdoing
following an investigation. A number of fatalities among construction work-
ers who toiled on some of Beijing's state-of-the-art athletic facilities and the
rigors of training for, and performing in, the opening ceremonies were noted.
The decision of the Chinese to block access to certain Internet sites during
the Games also drew derisive comment from the media and clearly pointed to
a breakdown in communication between the Beijing Organizing Committee
(BOCOG) and the IOC. This failure underscored insufficient attention, on
the part of IOC officials tasked with drawing up the host-city agreement, to
the need for clear language between the parties. Questions remain concerning the number of Beijing citizens who lost their homes as a result of Olympic
construction and the banning of individuals identified as "antagonistic elements" from the Games.[78] Even IOC president Jacques Rogge struggled to
explain how all three designated protest zones in Beijing remained empty for
the duration of the Games. All seventy-seven applications to stage a protest
were denied by Chinese authorities.[79]

The hoped-for gains in China's commitment to human rights, in the
short term, were unrealized.[80] James Kynge's analysis of China's gradual economic transformation revealed that such returns on the human rights front
were unrealistic, as the country could not "[turn] on a sixpence."[81] Critics
contend that the commitment to economic change, ideas first introduced
by Deng Xiaoping in the late 1970s, later consolidated through the successful pursuit of membership in the World Trade Organization in 2001,[82] was
simply not matched by similar initiative with regard to human rights. The
human rights issue continues to tarnish China's reputation as a member of
the world's community of nations. Indeed, the jury will not return a verdict
on the influence of the Beijing Olympics on the country's human rights
record for a number of years.

The opportunity to host the Games and the prospect of watching Olympians in competition energized the Chinese people. Internet demand and in-
person ticket requests in the opening hours of ticket sales in November 2007
caused the ticketing computer system to crash.[83] The final batch of tickets
for domestic sale made available in late July 2008 prompted clashes between
police and some of the 40,000–50,000 individuals who waited in line at the

main ticket office, some for two days before walking away with their prized ducats.[84] BOCOG's success in recruiting in excess of 400,000 volunteers (in contrast to Athens's 45,000) is added testament to the enthusiasm of Beijing's citizens. Chinese pride swelled as years became months, and months became days, before Beijing welcomed the world's Olympians.

Though China viewed the Games with intense fervor, so, too, did the international television audience based on viewership data released within days of the close of the festival. The world's cumulative television audience was 20 percent larger (4.7 billion) than the record-setting audience that followed events in Athens (3.9 billion). In the American market, NBC reveled in the news that the Beijing Olympics stood as the most watched event in America's television history.[85]

Controversy lingers concerning some of the methods employed by Beijing's organizers and China's commitment to human rights;[86] however, by almost any past set of metrics, the Beijing Olympics must be deemed successful in terms of their on-site delivery. With the notable exception of the random (and fatal) attack on Todd Bachman, the father-in-law of Hugh McCutcheon, the head coach of the US men's volleyball team, the Games' environment proved safe and secure for athletes, officials, and spectators.[87] Organizers transported athletes, coaches, and media personnel to venues with efficiency. Spectators opted for taxicabs or the subway and experienced little difficulty in moving about the city. World records tumbled at the Bird's Nest and at the Water Cube, the two flagship athletic facilities. Air quality, an issue that prompted Jacques Rogge to express concern in October 2007 that Beijing's pollution levels might wreak havoc with the event schedule, was acceptable, though noxious at times.[88] An aggressive pre-Beijing commitment to drug testing kept a good number of cheaters at home; however, it would be naive to suggest that Beijing, much like most recent Olympic festivals, was 100 percent clean.[89] Despite the opinion of some Olympic correspondents who found the Games joyless or without the festive, celebratory atmosphere of past Olympic festivals, there is little doubt that the Chinese delivered for the Olympic Movement's most important constituency—the athletes.[90] Beijing staged a successful festival despite intense media scrutiny, and in the process justified the IOC's confidence in Chinese organizers signaled in 2001 when the 2008 Olympic Games were awarded to the People's Republic of China.[91]

Thirteen years after the Salt Lake City scandal, the IOC enjoys a diversified major sponsor complement, TOP, across the world, making it less dependent on US multinational corporations than in earlier years.[92] Then, too, the IOC boasts burgeoning numbers of television viewers, as it basks in the afterglow of Beijing's efforts. Enthusiastic Canadians and international visitors flocked to Vancouver's Winter Olympic venues in February 2010, and television networks delivered 47 percent more global television coverage than had been produced in Turin four years earlier.[93] Interest in hosting a future Olympic festival echoes in the council chambers of the world's major cities, both those places whose reputations are well established as well as those who seek to elevate their global stature. Jacques Rogge and his IOC colleagues anticipate memorable Games in London (England, 2012), Sochi (Russia, 2014), Rio de Janeiro (Brazil, 2016), and Pyeongchang (South Korea, 2018).

## The Road Traveled and the Way Ahead

During the halcyon days of the Samaranch presidency in the late 1980s and 1990s, Olympic festivals offered the prospect of a profit for host cities and a lever for civic leaders to advance infrastructural improvements in their communities. Boycotts were consigned to the past, the numbers of Olympic television viewers soared, newly minted countries scrambled to seek IOC recognition through the establishment of an NOC, burgeoning Olympic revenues supported an expansion of the IOC educational mission, and ISFs clamored for a place or an enhanced position on the Olympic program. These successes bred a degree of complacency and arrogance in the IOC's presidential leadership that contributed directly to the Salt Lake City crisis. The grave threat to the integrity and image of the IOC fixed an anchor to Samaranch's personal legacy. The size and weight of that anchor will be debated by future historians who examine his stewardship.

Peter Ueberroth's economic blueprint for the 1984 Los Angeles Olympics and the IOC's demonstrated acumen in securing significant revenue from television rights negotiations and the TOP sponsorship program energized community leaders in many world cities to chase the Olympic rings. Olympic bid competitions became hotly contested. This altered bid environment evolved at a time when Samaranch desired to expand the reach of the Olympic Movement. In doing so, he invited into the Olympic tent the likes of Jean-Claude Ganga, whose personal ethics became a matter of public disgust. Bid committees operating in this high-stakes atmosphere plied IOC members with gifts and other inducements and ignored guidelines established by the IOC to limit the value of gifts that could be provided (and accepted). Most IOC members resisted these approaches, but some cashed in on their status. A lack of oversight of the IOC-member bid city visit protocol first enunciated in 1986, together with Samaranch's failure to pursue the rumors of embarrassing conduct by a number of individual IOC members, contributed to the genesis of a simmering crisis. The givers and the takers established a dangerous dynamic, a powder keg that placed the IOC in a precarious position. A document leaked to a local Salt Lake City television reporter and Marc Hodler's exhausted patience with the conduct of a number of his colleagues provided the tinderbox.

In this book, we detailed the genesis of the Salt Lake City crisis and the IOC's response to the conflagration that ensued in the international media. This twofold mission revealed an organization at both its worst and its best. Samaranch abrogated his leadership responsibilities in not pressing forward to uncover the depth and breadth of the compromised nature of the bidding process. IOC Executive Board members chose not to pointedly express the levels of their concern when the so-called Hodler Rules did not restrain the conduct of the givers and the takers. Clearly, the leadership, indeed the entire IOC membership, failed in the execution of its oversight mandate. It neither fully grasped the manner in which the bidding terrain changed as a result of the growth of the Olympic Movement and the new reality of Olympic economics nor seemingly understood the severity of the threat that inaction posed. However, when the crisis broke, Lausanne officials, once they found their feet, responded effectively. The scandal exposed an understaffed and ill-prepared media communications operation in Lausanne, yet over the ensuing weeks and months, members of the Executive Board, most notably Richard Pound, director-general François Carrard, marketing director Michael Payne, and other members of the IOC headquarters support staff performed ably under very trying conditions.

Samaranch did not immediately grasp the gravity of the threat following initial media reports in Salt Lake City and experienced some difficult
and awkward moments in his interaction with the media in the early stages
of the crisis. However, for his principal constituents, the rank-and-file IOC
members, he ultimately displayed a resolute and determined demeanor. In
February 1999, Samaranch convened the World Conference on Doping in
Sport, assuming he would, as IOC president, take his rightful place as the
head of a fledgling global anti-doping agency. The subsequent public and
outright dismissal of this presumption by government officials and prominent sport leaders in attendance clearly wounded his pride. Despite this
bruising to his ego, Samaranch rallied. In March 1999, he stage-managed
the 108th Extraordinary IOC Session effectively and conveyed in frank language to those members assembled the challenge facing the organization.
He guided the IOC's reform mission with purpose during the remainder of
the calendar year. He also performed well in defending the IOC's reforms
during his appearance before a US congressional subcommittee in December 1999.

Central to the IOC's ultimate success in staving off the threat to the
IOC's autonomy was the time-consuming and ultimately successful work of
Richard Pound and Michael Payne in the 1980s and 1990s in carefully nurturing the Olympic brand. Corporate sponsors held firm, demonstrated faith
in the power and resilience of the Olympic brand, and permitted the IOC to
pursue its brand-recovery operations through the work of the IOC 2000 and
Ethics Commissions unfettered by an unbridled crisis in public confidence
that most surely would have resulted if the sponsors abandoned their TOP
agreements. A steeply ascending learning curve defined the IOC's exercise in
crisis management in 1998 and 1999; the central actors would neither elect
to relive those days nor deny the rewarding feeling that accompanied the
knowledge that their personal industry and commitment facilitated the IOC's
success in salvaging the five rings.

The way ahead for Jacques Rogge and his IOC colleagues offers both
challenges and opportunities. The recent global economic downturn and
debt burdens faced by a number of European nations in particular offer possible short-term challenges in terms of revenue generation and the recruitment of bid cities. The IOC must find the means necessary to enhance the

voice of women in Olympic decision making. The will to provide enhanced opportunities for female athletes to compete in the Olympic arena witnessed in recent years must be applied in such a way as to provide the keys to IOC boardrooms to more qualified, eager, and committed female sport officials. Their contributions would enhance the operation of the Olympic Movement. Jacques Rogge targeted doping as a priority for his presidential agenda, and recent years have witnessed gains in this area for those persons committed to a level playing field for all athletes; however, there can be no lessening in the determination of the IOC, NOCs, and ISFs to confront the cheaters.[94] Gene therapy provides the next front on which this battle for "clean" sport will be contested. While the IOC has increased its concern for environmental issues when considering Olympic host-city bids, it has not invested sufficient energies in protecting the property rights of citizens in host cities, such as Atlanta and, most recently, Beijing. Though challenged by Chinese authorities, estimates exist that 1.2–1.5 million Beijing residents were displaced to facilitate the construction of Olympic facilities.[95] The bid process, irrespective of the advances in its regulation tied to the reforms passed in 1999, remains susceptible to the influence of money. Samsung (a South Korean conglomerate led by Kun-Hee Lee, an IOC member) offered to sponsor some National Olympic Committees during the period in time when South Korea lobbied for votes in the 2010 bid competition. When combined with Lee's earlier stated pledge to assist Pyeongchang's bid, Samsung's approach raised eyebrows and prompted denials from Pyeongchang officials that the company's dialogue with the NOCs was connected to the bid.[96] The Slavkov affair of 2004 also demonstrated that self-styled Olympic agents lurk in the shadows.[97] Oversight of the bid process must remain a high priority in order to protect the integrity of the Olympic Movement.[98]

While the challenges exist, so, too, do the opportunities. The Olympic Games offer the IOC a noteworthy vehicle for the promotion of sport, ethics, fair play, and peace. The IOC's mission must be carried forward with an enhanced degree of energy and an emphasis on how best to deliver on the promotional possibilities of the Olympic Games. Although not unanimously supported by IOC members, the newly instituted Youth Olympics, staged for the first time in Singapore in 2010, offer an opportunity to connect with the world's youth. A sizable number of Olympians have committed to promoting sport in developing regions through Johann Olav Koss's Right to Play organization, and it is incumbent upon the IOC to match that passion through a revitalized and more efficient Olympic Solidarity program. The IOC and Vancouver Organizing Committee's (VANOC) decision to expel Right to Play from the Olympic Village in 2010 (it had been given a promotional booth in the village in recent years) because of a sponsor conflict was counterproductive and delivered the wrong message.[99] This situation begged for an inspired solution and, given the mission of the Olympic Movement, offered Jacques Rogge an opportunity to demonstrate leadership. Excessive nationalism, a troubling undercurrent within the Olympic Movement, could be addressed by having athletes enter the Olympic Stadium for the opening ceremony by sport affiliation as opposed to trooping in some two-hundred-plus national teams or dispensing with the use of national anthems in medal ceremonies in favor of the "Olympic Hymn." Admittedly, both options would elicit howls of protest from the IOC's television partners, who are wedded, accurately, to the belief that nationalistic displays translate into larger numbers of television viewers and the NOCs worldwide that cherish their moment before a global television audience in the opening ceremonies as currently constituted.

The Olympic Movement purports to be a global institution, but this claim's merit rests largely on the fact that 205 NOCs are affiliated with the IOC. However, the claim is diminished by restrictions imposed on the ambulatory nature of the Olympic Games that no longer are defensible and the unwillingness of the European bloc to entrust non-Europeans (with the exception of Avery Brundage) to lead the IOC. The recent award of the 2016 Summer Olympics to Rio de Janeiro is a truly historic event. South Americans, heretofore prevented from hosting an Olympic festival and demonstrating their love of sport and their athletic traditions to a global television audience, will enjoy such an opportunity. If the Olympic Movement is in fact a "global" institution, the close of Rogge's presidential tenure must witness the installation of a qualified non-European as the next IOC president and a focused effort on preparing the ground for delivering the Olympic Games to Africa. Jacques Rogge will secure a lasting imprint on the IOC and the Olympic Movement if he convinces his colleagues to take these two necessary steps and reaches an anticipated accord with the USOC, and its new leadership tandem, Larry Probst and Scott Blackmun, concerning the distribution of Olympic television and corporate sponsorship money.

These issues are some of the major challenges and opportunities that provide possible grist for Jacques Rogge's agenda, indeed his presidential legacy, as he moves forward with the four-year extension to his presidency through 2013.[100] But these thoughts remain simply our ideas. Jacques Rogge needs to set out *his* vision for the Olympic Movement and carry through with its implementation by leveraging the power of the Olympic brand whose resilience and strength were tested and confirmed in the cauldron of the Salt Lake City crisis.

*Appendix*

*Notes*

*Bibliography*

*Index*

*Appendix*

# Salt Lake City Scandal Time Line, 1998–1999

**Legend**

| | |
|---|---|
| AHC | Ad Hoc Commission |
| DD | David D'Alessandro |
| IOC | International Olympic Committee |
| JAS | Juan Antonio Samaranch |
| MRP | Michael Payne |
| RWP | Richard Pound |
| SLOC | Salt Lake City Olympics Organizing Committee |
| SOCOG | Sydney Olympics Organizing Committee |
| TOP | The Olympic Partners (Worldwide Olympic sponsors) |
| WADA | World Anti-Doping Agency |

**November 1998**

• RWP receives a phone call from a member of the Salt Lake City media. Individual informs him that a document has been leaked that indicates Sonia Essomba, daughter of the late IOC member René Essomba (Cameroon), received Salt Lake City bid committee funds to assist with her college education in the United States. Pound alerts JAS regarding the prospect of trouble for the IOC.

• Reporter Chris Vanocur (KTVX-TV, Channel 4, Salt Lake City) breaks the story concerning tuition support granted to Sonia Essomba.

• Salt Lake City bid committee officials deny wrongdoing.

## December 1998

- JAS assigns internal investigative responsibilities to the IOC Juridical Commission, led by Senegal's Kéba Mbaye.
- SLOC shares bid documents with the IOC Executive Board.
- JAS appoints RWP chair of the AHC. The AHC replaces the Juridical Commission as the body responsible for conducting the IOC's internal investigation.
- AHC launches its investigation.
- Marc Hodler reveals his concerns about IOC member conduct and the bid process to reporters gathered in Lausanne for the meetings of the IOC Executive Board.
- Past bid committee officials from unsuccessful cities reveal approaches from Olympic "agents" who promised access to groups of IOC members in exchange for payment.
- RWP informs representatives of corporate sponsors who sit on the IOC's Marketing Commission of the IOC's pledge to confront the issue.
- JAS, RWP, and MRP open lines of communication with TOP sponsor CEOs.
- RWP travels to Salt Lake City to initiate on-site investigation.

## January 1999

- AHC pores over files provided by SLOC officials.
- David Johnson, SLOC vice president, and Frank Joklik, SLOC president, resign.
- Deedee Corradini, Salt Lake City's mayor, announces she will not seek reelection.
- Australian media report John Coates's 1993 deal with Charles Mukora and Francis Nyangweso on the eve of the vote on the site of the 2000 Summer Olympics.
- Corporate sponsors issue statements of support for the IOC, but clearly indicate the level of their collective concern in private communications with IOC officials.
- DD, president and CEO of John Hancock, warns the IOC of the need to confront problems with the flawed and compromised bid process.
- AHC identifies thirteen IOC members for possible censure. These members are asked to respond via written communication to issues raised as a result of the AHC investigation.
- Two IOC members, Pirjo Häggman and Bashir Attarabulsi, resign.
- The IOC Executive Board recommends the expulsion of seven IOC members, a warning for one member, and a continuation of the investigation of three other cases.

- The IOC Executive Board confirms Sydney and Salt Lake City as sites of the 2000 and 2002 Olympic festivals and announces new rules for the 2006 Olympic Winter Games bid competition. Samaranch suspends IOC-member bid city visits.
- A study by Datops and Sportsweb reveals that late January is the high-water mark for media coverage of the crisis in terms of volume of articles appearing on a per-day basis.
- JAS faces many calls in the media for his resignation. He refuses to submit his resignation.
- Hill & Knowlton's presence felt in Lausanne in terms of the IOC's interaction with the media.
- Charles Mukora, IOC member to Kenya, resigns.
- Eight of eleven TOP sponsors pledge their continued support for the 2000 Sydney Olympics.

**February 1999**

- World Anti-Doping Conference lays the groundwork for the establishment of the WADA; however, the gathering in Lausanne offers a platform for the media and government representatives to grill IOC officials concerning the ethical shortcomings of some IOC members.
- JAS believes some unnamed IOC members and headquarters staff members are destabilizing his leadership.
- The IOC Executive Board backs away from its plan to remove IOC member voting privileges for the upcoming vote on the site for the 2006 Olympic Winter Games.
- SLOC releases the investigative report filed by its Board of Ethics. Ten additional IOC members, including Australia's Phil Coles, fall under scrutiny.
- DD suspends negotiations with NBC for advertising time on Sydney 2000 telecasts and removes Olympic rings from his company's stationery.
- Corporate sponsors unload their frustrations on RWP and MRP at sponsors' summit meeting. They are disturbed by new allegations of IOC-member misconduct stemming from the report of SLOC's Board of Ethics, the pace of the reform process, and the volume of negative press concerning the Olympic Movement.
- JAS phones all TOP sponsor CEOs to reassure them of his commitment to reform.
- DD expresses his dissatisfaction with the slow pace of the reform process in a series of media interviews. He publishes an op-ed piece in the *New York Times* that is very critical of the IOC's efforts to date.

• DD's public assertions irritate JAS, MRP, and Kevan Gosper.

• AHC holds a series of conference calls during the month and convenes late in the month in Lausanne to prepare for the 108th Extraordinary IOC Session.

## March 1999

• Corporate sponsors speculate on the extent of the damage resulting from a refusal on the part of rank-and-file IOC members to expel the six IOC members recommended for such sanction by the AHC and IOC Executive Board.

• IOC members James Easton (United States) and Tomas Sithole (Zimbabwe) issue public statements encouraging their colleagues to approve the recommendations.

• IOC leaders worry that IOC members not situated at the vortex of the crisis, in Europe, North America, and Australia, might not understand the seriousness of the crisis.

• JAS claims in an interview with a Spanish newspaper that the depth of the IOC's problems has been exaggerated. The blowback from the international media is strong, and Samaranch is accused of minimizing the issue.

• JAS sends a letter to all IOC members laying out the issues and imploring them for their support.

• Samaranch fears a "palace revolt."

• Un Yong Kim, who remains under investigation, confronts François Carrard, IOC director-general, during a meeting in Lausanne between the IOC Executive Board and SLOC president Mitt Romney and his team.

• The IOC Executive Board decides to hold 108th Extraordinary IOC Session and the consideration of the cases of the six implicated IOC members behind closed doors. The media claim a lack of transparency. IOC leaders believe it is necessary to shield the IOC from any attempt on the part of Jean-Claude Ganga to embarrass the organization with accusations.

• The IOC Executive Board debates the extent to which corporate sponsors are steering the reform process.

• JAS opens the IOC's 108th Extraordinary IOC Session with these sobering words: "There has never been an occasion on which a President of the IOC has needed to express his opinion, in relation to an issue which so profoundly affects the present and future of the Olympic Movement as much as the current crisis. . . . It is my conviction that unless we act quickly, decisively and unanimously, at this Extraordinary Session, the damage which may be done to the Olympic Movement and to the IOC as a result of the recent disclosures will be very, very serious."

- JAS calls for support of new procedures for the selection of the host city for the 2006 Olympic Winter Games, the establishment of an Ethics Commission, and a comprehensive review of the *Olympic Charter* by a proposed IOC 2000 Commission.
- JAS receives an overwhelming vote of confidence from IOC members (eighty-six to two, one ballot spoiled).
- Agustin Arroyo (Ecuador), Zein El Abdin Ahmed Abdel Gadir (Sudan), Jean-Claude Ganga (Congo), Lamine Keita (Mali), Sergio Santander Fantini (Chile), and Seiuli Paul Wallwork (Samoa) are expelled from the IOC.
- International media, and many Olympic observers, charge that the organization established a double standard—one for Ganga and his colleagues and one for the more powerful and influential such as Un Yong Kim and Phil Coles, who survive the purge, albeit with severe censures.
- IOC members approve new procedures for the selection of the host city for the 2006 Olympic Winter Games and the IOC 2000 Commission. Provisional approval given to the establishment of the IOC Ethics Commission, with its structure to be considered at the June IOC Session in Seoul. IOC members support the formation of the World Anti-Doping Agency.
- International media not convinced that the IOC has enacted real change. Real change, reporters say, will come only if Samaranch resigns.
- DD comments that "absolutely nothing breathtakingly performance-oriented happened" at the IOC's 108th Extraordinary Session.
- John McCain, chairman of the Senate Commerce Committee, announces hearings on the IOC's tax-exempt status in the United States.
- RWP and MRP brief TOP sponsor CEOs via conference call following the close of the IOC Session.
- New allegations dog Australia's Phil Coles after the close of the IOC Session. Media reports include assertions that Coles and his ex-wife accepted expensive jewelry from an individual affiliated with the 1996 Athens bid committee.
- JAS indicates he will not appear at hearings on the IOC's tax-exempt status to be held by the Senate Commerce Committee in Washington, chaired by John McCain.

**April 1999**

- Composition of the IOC Ethics Commission announced.
- Sponsors receive morals clause in future contracts. This clause permits sponsors to walk away from future agreements if the IOC suffers another scandal owing

to breach of ethics. The IOC receives same rights in the event of an ethical lapse by a sponsor.

• John McCain holds hearings of the Senate Commerce Committee on the IOC's tax-exempt status. The hearings amount to a shot across the IOC's bow and a pledge that Washington will monitor the progress of the IOC's reform agenda. Anita DeFrantz and Jim Easton, US IOC members, face tough questioning in JAS's absence.

• George Mitchell, who had earlier filed an investigative report on behalf of the USOC, refers to the IOC's efforts as a work in progress. He signals some optimism with respect to the IOC's commitment to enacting meaningful reform.

• TOP sponsors begin to respond to the IOC's call for detailed suggestions on possible reform measures. McDonald's and Xerox are among the first to respond.

**May 1999**

• The IOC Ethics Commission holds its first meeting.

• The IOC Executive Board determines that mandate of the IOC 2000 Commission will be addressed by three working groups that will examine the IOC's role, its structure, and the host-city bid process, respectively.

• Remaining TOP sponsors weigh in with their thoughts on necessary reform measures. IOC member term limits, accountability, and financial transparency rank highly in their respective recommendations.

• This month marks an intense period of communication between DD, who once again castigates JAS and the IOC for its lethargic pace of reform, and RWP, who seeks to temper DD's public criticism.

• Phil Coles remains in the media spotlight. Attention focuses on dossiers kept by Coles and his partner, Patricia Rosenbrock, on the habits and preferences of IOC members that ended up in the hands of the Salt Lake City bid committee.

• Coles charges that Olympics minister Michael Knight is orchestrating his ouster from SOCOG.

**June 1999**

• NBC's Dick Ebersol unloads on DD for his high-profile critique of JAS and the IOC. DD dismisses Ebersol's criticism: "If I were Dick Ebersol and had hitched my career to the Olympics, I'd be pretty scared too," states DD.

• The IOC 2000 Commission convenes in Lausanne for its first meeting.

• The IOC 2000 Commission Working Groups (1. composition, structure, and organization of the IOC—Carraro; 2. role of the IOC—Bach; and 3. designation of Olympic Games host cities—DeFrantz) hold initial meetings.

- Coles given an ultimatum by the IOC Executive Board. If he wishes to retain his IOC seat, he must resign from the SOCOG Board. Coles opts to remain an IOC member, but loses his right to serve on any commissions or working groups for two years.
- The IOC Session approves rules and statutes of the IOC Ethics Commission.
- The IOC Session selects Turin to host the 2006 Olympic Winter Games. Sion (Switzerland) charges that its loss to Turin in the race for the right to host the 2006 Olympic Winter Games is payback for Marc Hodler's actions in December 1998.

## July 1999

- All three IOC 2000 Commission Working Groups meet, the first on July 10, the second on July 17–18, and the third on July 13.

## August 1999

- John McCain ponders the need for additional hearings of the Senate Committee on Commerce, Science, and Transportation as a means of maintaining pressure of the IOC to pass needed reform measures by the end of 1999.
- IOC Working Group 2 meets (August 30–31).

## September 1999

- IOC Working Group 3 meets (September 2).
- IOC Working Group 1 meets (September 10).
- Griffin Bell report on Atlanta, 1996 bid, released.
- The IOC 2000 Executive Commission meets to consider and adopt final reports of the working groups.

## October 1999

- The IOC Executive Board discusses whether JAS should accept invitation from Fred Upton (R-MI) to testify before his House Commerce Committee on Investigations and Oversight. Decision is made that Samaranch will appear before a congressional committee, but not before IOC reforms are passed at the 110th IOC Session scheduled for December.
- Upton hearings proceed on October 14. François Carrard represents IOC interests in Washington.
- Michael Knight apologizes for SOCOG's management of ticketing for the Sydney Olympics.
- The IOC 2000 Plenary Commission approves report and recommendations of the IOC Executive Board (with minor modifications).

**November 1999**

- JAS and Lausanne officials prepare for the 110th IOC Session.

**December 1999**

- Paul Reading, architect of the premium tickets program in Sydney, leaves SOCOG.
- Reebok terminates its Sydney 2000 supporter contract. Nike seizes opportunity to replace its rival as a Sydney sponsor.
- The 110th IOC Session approves fifty changes to the *Olympic Charter.*
- JAS travels to Washington. He testifies before Fred Upton's House Commerce Committee on Investigations and Oversight.
- DD informs RWP that John Hancock will renew its TOP sponsorship for 2001–4. Formal announcement occurs in February 2000.

# Notes

### Introduction

1. For a blow-by-blow description of how KTVX Channel 4 (Salt Lake City) reporter Chris Vanocur broke the story on the bid committee's funneling of money to Sonia Essomba, see Alicia C. Shepard, "An Olympian Scandal: How a Local TV News Story in Salt Lake City Led to the Disclosure of Far-Reaching Corruption in the Way Olympic Sites Are Chosen."

2. Steve Buffery, "IOC Gives Six the Heave-Ho."

3. Jim Caple, "Let the Fun and Games Begin."

4. For Amsterdam, see "And the Heat Is Turned Up Concerning Salt Lake City's Bid," *Toronto Star*, Jan. 20, 1999. For Nagano, see "Nagano Games Tainted by Scandal," *Toronto Star*, Jan. 18, 1999. For Quebec City, see "Votes for Sale: The Olympic Meddlers," *Australian* (Sydney), Dec. 19, 1998. For Atlanta, see Bill Brubaker, "Ex-Official Admits Violation; Atlantans Allegedly Broke Gift Rules," *Washington Post*, Feb. 19, 1999.

5. "Le Tour de Farce Comes to Sorry End," *Irish Times* (Dublin), Aug. 1, 1998; "Day by Day in the Doping Drama," *Guardian* (Manchester), Aug. 3, 1998. None of this surprised John Hoberman, author of *Mortal Engines: The Science of Performance and the Dehumanization of Sport,* who later wrote, "Cycling has been the most consistently drug soaked major sport in the 20th and 21st centuries. While weight lifting and shot-putting have also been thoroughly drug dependent, they are minor cults compared with the cycling carnival that plays across Europe every year." Hoberman, "Dopers on Wheels: The Tour's Sorry History." For Hoberman's examination of doping in high-performance sport, see his *Mortal Engines*. Pantani, suffering from depression, died as a result of drug abuse in 2004.

6. "Le Tour de Farce Comes to Sorry End."

7. Caitlin Jenkins, "Establishing a World Anti-Doping Code: WADA's Impact on the Development of an International Strategy for Anti-Doping in Sport," 75. For a recent and thorough analysis of doping and sport, and the IOC's involvement in the issue over time, see Thomas M. Hunt, *Drug Games: The International Olympic Committee and the Politics of Doping, 1960–2008.*

8. "Sport: Olympic Moves to Combat Drugs," *BBC Online*, Aug. 20, 1998, http://news.bbc.co.uk/1/hi/sport/154586.stm.

9. John W. Kingdon, *Agendas, Alternatives, and Public Policies*, 94–95. For Lachance's observation, see Jenkins, "Establishing a World Anti-Doping Code," 75–76 (brackets added).

10. Michael Payne (former director, IOC Marketing), interview with Stephen Wenn and Scott Martyn, June 18, 2007, Lausanne, Switzerland.

11. For the Executive Board's consultation with the Ad Hoc Commission, see *Minutes of the Ad Hoc Executive Board Meeting*.

12. Jonathan Calvert, "How to Buy the Olympics," *Observer* (London), Jan. 6, 2002, http://observer.guardian.co.uk/sport/issues/story/0,,676494,00.html; Jo Thomas, Kirk Johnson, and Jere Longman, "The Rise and Fall of Olympic Ambitions Tactics May Have Been Pointless," *New Orleans Times-Picayune*, Mar. 14, 1999.

13. Samaranch's opening address can be reviewed in *Minutes of the 108th Extraordinary IOC Session*, Annex #1, 25–39.

14. Payne interview. Payne confirmed that the 108th Extraordinary IOC Session provided a measure of breathing room for the embattled members of the IOC's leadership team.

15. Bill Mallon, "The Olympic Bribery Scandal." Mallon's summary of the changes can be found on pp. 21–24.

16. Robert Barney, Stephen Wenn, and Scott Martyn, *Selling the Five Rings: The International Olympic Committee and the Rise of Olympic Commercialism*, 268–70.

17. Mallon, "The Olympic Bribery Scandal," 24.

18. Michele Simpson, "Reebok Pulls Multi Million-Dollar Olympic Games Sponsorship"; "Nike Takes Up Where Reebok Left Off." Reebok cried foul when the Sydney Organizing Committee reached agreement with an Australian company (Bonds) that would provide baseball caps to SOCOG personnel as part of a sponsorship deal. Reebok also took issue with Canterbury, a sportswear company, producing rugby shirts as part of its merchandising deal. Reebok claimed that these contracts violated the exclusivity terms within its A$10 million deal. For the reaction in Lausanne to Nike's decision, we relied on the view of Michael Payne. Payne interview.

19. Payne interview. Looking back, David D'Alessandro believes the IOC addressed the most egregious IOC member activities and that some of the processes put into place marked progress for the IOC, such as enhanced athlete input, term limits for its members, and improved financial transparency. D'Alessandro to Stephen Wenn, July 14, 2009.

20. Selena Roberts, "Olympics: As Countdown Kicks Off, Bribery Trial Looks Likely," *New York Times*, Feb. 9, 2001, http://www.nytimes.com/2001/02/09/sports/olympics-as-countdown-kicks-off-bribery-trial-looks-likely.html; Lester Munson, "Back on the Docket: Details Revealed of Case vs. Salt Lake City Olympics Organizers"; Paul Foy, "Judge Tosses Salt Lake Bribery Case," *USA Today.com*, Dec. 5, 2003, http://www.usatoday.com/sports/olympics/winter/2003-12-05-bribery-trial_x.htm.

21. Harry Gordon briefly reviews the main events in the Salt Lake City crisis in the context of preparations for the Sydney Olympics in *The Time of Our Lives: Inside the Sydney Olympics—Australia and the Olympic Games, 1994–2002*, 98–108.

22. The full program can be accessed via the Internet. The crisis served as the core element of a case study at the Harvard Business School. See John A. Clendenin and Stephen A. Greyser, *Tarnished Rings? Olympic Games Sponsorship Issues*. The seven-page case study was prepared in its original form in 1999.

23. Crisis management literature identifies two types of organizational crises: sudden and simmering. A sudden crisis denotes events such as accidents, breakdowns in machinery required for the production of goods, or acts of terrorism. "Simmering events," state Peter Ruff and Khalid Aziz, "cover situations that lurk beneath the organization's surface and can erupt into a crisis at any time." A simmering crisis, adds Lerbinger, builds "up over time until a threshold is reached. When this build-up is gradual and small, managers may be unaware of an approaching crisis. . . . When a crisis follows this slow, cumulative pattern, the crisis threshold is likely to be defined by outsiders: the media, the government, whistle blowers, or public watchdogs of organizational behavior." Conventional wisdom states that the vast majority of organizational crises are "sudden." However, an in-depth examination of major organizational crises between 1990 and 1998 conducted by the United States Institute of Crisis Management demonstrated that 86 percent of crises result from "simmering events." Ruff and Aziz, *Managing Communications in a Crisis*, 3–4; Otto Lerbinger, *The Crisis Manager: Facing Risk and Responsibility*, 7.

24. Jerry W. Markham, *A Financial History of Modern U.S. Corporate Scandals: From Enron to Reform*, 5–6, 3, 20.

25. Ibid., xv–xviii. See also George W. Dent Jr., "Corporate Governance: Still Broke, No Fix in Sight," 60; Richard A. Epstein, "Scrapping Sarbox"; and Elizabeth Webb, "Sarbanes-Oxley Compliance and Violation: An Empirical Study."

26. For treatment of the transition to multifestival television rights packages, see Barney, Wenn, and Martyn, *Selling the Five Rings*, 258–62.

27. For an analysis of the escalation of lobbying involved in the Olympic site-selection process in the aftermath of the 1984 Los Angeles Olympics, and the IOC's burgeoning gift culture, see Doug Booth, "Lobbying Orgies: Olympic City Bids in the Post-Los Angeles Era."

## 1. The Man from Barcelona

1. David Miller, *Olympic Revolution: The Biography of Juan Antonio Samaranch*. For Samaranch's quote concerning his impending retirement, see Alan Abrahamson, "Passing the Torch," *Los Angeles Times*, July 9, 2001, http://articles.latimes.com/2001/jul/09/sports/sp-20281?pg=2.

2. Lord Killanin, *My Olympic Years*, 20. For an exploration of critical developments within the IOC during the Killanin presidency, as well as the greater Olympic Movement,

spurred by Killanin that charted out the IOC's path to commercial riches in the 1980s and 1990s, see Scott Martyn and Stephen Wenn, "A Prelude to Samaranch: Lord Killanin's Path to Olympic Commercialism."

3. Following the Games of the XXth Olympiad in Munich, Avery Brundage has been quoted as having "reluctantly predicted that Lord Killanin's term might see the collapse of the Movement in the course of the next two Olympiads." See David Miller, "Evolution of the Olympic Movement," 9.

4. Ibid.

5. Jere Longman, "Juan Antonio Samaranch Dies at 89; Led I.O.C.," *New York Times*, Apr. 21, 2010, http://www.nytimes.com/2010/04/22/sports/22samaranch.html?ref=sports&page wanted=print.

6. Miller, *Olympic Revolution*, 20.

7. Jere Longman, "Samaranch's Legacy: An Olympic Savior or a Spoiler?," *New York Times*, Sept. 10, 2000.

8. Alan Abrahamson, "The One and Only Juan Antonio Samaranch."

9. Abrahamson, "Passing the Torch."

10. Andrés Merce Varela, "The Journey of a Great President." The Real Club de Tenis Barcelona 1899 is a private tennis club located in Barcelona, Spain. Since moving to its current location in the northwest of the city in 1953, the club has hosted the Open Godó tournament, a part of the ATP World Tour's 500 Series. The facility has eighteen clay courts, including a stadium court with a capacity of seventy-two hundred and show court for two thousand spectators.

11. The Spanish Civil War devastated Spain from July 17, 1936, to April 1, 1939. It began after an attempted coup d'état against the government of the Second Spanish Republic, then under the leadership of President Manuel Azaña, by a group of Spanish Army generals, supported by the conservative Confederación Española de Derechas Autónomas, Carlist groups, and the fascistic Falange Española de las JONS. The conflict ended with the victory of the rebel forces, the overthrow of the Republican government, and the founding of a dictatorship led by Generalissimo Francisco Franco. See Stanley G. Payne, *Fascism in Spain, 1923–1977*. For information on the Franco regime, see Stanley G. Payne, *The Franco Regime, 1936–1975*. According to various sources, Samaranch was drafted into the Popular Front army of the existing government during the conflict and served as a medic. John E. Findling reports that information on his activities during this time is limited, and those sources available tend to differ, but Samaranch apparently deserted and hid in Barcelona for the remaining months of the conflict. Findling, "Juan Antonio Samaranch," 487. The "Popular Front" or "the government" received weapons and volunteers from the Soviet Union, Mexico, the international socialist movement, and the International Brigades. They ranged from centrists who supported a moderately capitalist liberal democracy to revolutionary anarchists and communists; their power base was primarily secular and urban, but also included landless peasants. For information on

the Spanish Civil War, in particular the combatants, see Antony Beevor, *The Battle for Spain: The Spanish Civil War, 1936–1939*.

12. See Vyv Simson and Andrew Jennings, *Dishonored Games: Corruption, Money, and Greed at the Olympics*, 65.

13. Fékrou Kidané, "Samaranch and Olympism," 19.

14. Wayne H. Bowen, *Spain During World War II*, 19. General José Moscardó (1878–1956) was the military governor of Toledo Province during the Spanish Civil War. He sided with the Nationalist army fighting the Republican government and is most notable for the defense and holding of the Alcázar of Toledo against Republican forces.

15. Simson and Jennings, *Dishonored Games*, 65.

16. See Mundial de Hockey Vigo 2009, "Roller Hockey World Championship Official Website: History."

17. "Samaranch: IOC Will Win War on Drugs."

18. Simson and Jennings, *Dishonored Games*, 66.

19. Findling, "Juan Antonio Samaranch," 488.

20. Merce Varela, "Journey of a Great President," 11. The Diputació de Barcelona was less constrained by bureaucracy, providing Samaranch with a more effective forum for his efforts.

21. The Mediterranean Games are a multisport games held every four years, mainly for nations bordering the Mediterranean Sea, generally incorporating Europe, Africa, and Asia. The idea of these games was proposed at the 1948 Summer Olympics by Mohammed Taher Pasha, chairman of the Egyptian Olympic Committee, and they were inaugurated in October 1951, in Alexandria, Egypt. The first ten games took place always one year preceding the Olympics. However, from 1993 on, they were held the year following the Olympic Games. The Second Mediterranean Games were held in the Olympic Stadium and Palace of Sport of Barcelona, from July 16 to July 25, 1955. The stadium, originally constructed in 1929, was specifically renovated for the occasion. The number of participants at the games reached nine hundred (all men).

22. Taking advantage of the infrastructure constructed in advance of Barcelona's bid for the 1936 Olympic Games, the games were a complete success. At the closing ceremony, the IOC vice president, Armand Massard, made an official announcement indicating that, in light of the successful staging of the Mediterranean Games, Barcelona had the capacity to stage a brilliant Olympic Games, providing all the necessary guarantees were in place. See Scott Martyn, "The Struggle for Financial Autonomy: The IOC and the Historical Emergence of Corporate Sponsorship, 1896–2000," 242.

23. Richard Pound, *Inside the Olympics: A Behind-the-Scene Look at the Politics, the Scandals, and the Glory of the Games*, 231.

24. Findling, "Juan Antonio Samaranch," 488.

25. "Administrative History/Biographical History: Juan Antonio Samaranch."

26. "First Anniversary Obituary of Francisco Samaranch Castro," *La Vanguardia Española*, Apr. 25, 1958, http://hemeroteca.lavanguardia.es/preview/1958/04/25/pagina-22/32753000/pdf.html.

27. "Administrative History/Biographical History."

28. Adam Przeworski, *Democracy and the Market*, 8.

29. Omar G. Encarnación, "Spain after Franco: Lessons in Democratization," 36.

30. The December 1979 Soviet incursion into Afghanistan spurred US president Jimmy Carter to issue an ultimatum to the Soviet government that the United States would boycott the Moscow Olympics if their troops were not withdrawn from the country by 12:01 a.m. eastern standard time on February 20, 1980. The official announcement confirming the boycott was made on March 21. In all, sixty-one nations boycotted the Moscow Olympic Games, reducing the number of participating nations to eighty, the lowest number since 1956.

31. See, for instance, Andrew Jennings and Vyv Simson, *The Lords of the Rings: Power, Money, and Drugs in the Modern Olympics*, 59–71.

32. Michael Payne, *Olympic Turnaround: How the Olympic Games Stepped Back from the Brink of Extinction to Become the World's Best Known Brand—and a Multi-Billion-Dollar Global Franchise*, 7.

33. Pound, *Inside the Olympics*, 232. In Osto Mora's case, it was a return to the role of FINA president. He served two terms in this capacity, 1968–72 and 1976–80, with the Fédération Internationale de Natation, the international sport federation for aquatic sports.

34. M. Payne, *Olympic Turnaround*, 10.

35. Ibid., 14.

36. "Notes on the Work of the Television Sub-Committee." See also Stephen Wenn, "Growing Pains: The Olympic Movement and Television, 1966–1972," 15. Numerous IOC members were concerned that the modern Olympic Movement derived some 98 percent of its revenue from the sale of television rights during the 1970s. Well before Samaranch formed a commission to investigate new sources of revenue generation, the subject engendered discussion inside the halls of IOC decision making. For an analysis of the Samaranch-Dassler dealings, see Barbara Smit, *Sneaker Wars: The Enemy Brothers Who Founded Adidas and Puma and the Family Feud That Forever Changed the Business of Sports*, 163–74.

37. For a full discussion of the emergence of commercialism in the modern Olympic Movement, see Barney, Wenn, and Martyn, *Selling the Five Rings*.

38. Ibid., 203.

39. Deane Neubauer, "Modern Sport and Olympic Games: The Problematic Complexities Raised by the Dynamics of Globalization," 19, 20.

40. Ibid. (brackets added).

41. Ibid., 19.

42. For Brundage, see Stephen Wenn, "An Olympian Squabble: The Distribution of Olympic Television Revenue, 1960–1966." For Killanin, see Martyn and Wenn, "Prelude to Samaranch," 44–48.

43. Samaranch, who retained control of negotiating European television contracts with Marc Hodler during his presidency, protected the European Broadcasting Union (EBU) in negotiations. Samaranch spurned the advances of private networks and sacrificed millions of dollars in arguing that EBU was the only entity capable of giving blanket coverage of the Games to the European continent. In late 2008, in light of the increasing penetration of private networks into Europe's television markets, the IOC stepped away from its long-standing partnership with EBU during negotiations for the European rights to the 2014 Olympic Winter Games and 2016 Summer Olympics. In early 2009, SportFive, an international sports-rights marketing agency owned by France's Lagardère Group, secured these rights across forty European countries, excluding France, Germany, Italy, Spain, Turkey, and Great Britain. The sale price—$342 million. Subsequent negotiations yielded an additional $250 million from the Italian (Sky Italia) and Turkish (FOX Turkey) markets, and $100 million from Spain. The IOC hoped that ongoing negotiations in the three other prime European markets, Germany, France, and Great Britain, would push the total value of European rights to $1.2 billion, a noticeable (projected) improvement on the $746 million that EBU paid for the 2010 Vancouver-Whistler Olympic Winter Games and the 2012 London Olympics. "SportFive Bags European Rights for 2014 and 2016 Olympics"; Stephen Wilson, "Spanish TV Secures Olympic Rights for $100M." The disappointment of EBU officials was palpable and predictable. Volker Herres, ARD's programming director (ARD is an EBU-affiliated network in Germany), charged that the IOC had "completely exaggerated the value of the broadcast rights." He labeled the IOC's decision to walk away from its relationship with EBU as a "strategic mistake." If ARD was shut out of the Olympics, warned Herres, it would revisit its programming plans for smaller Olympic sports in non-Olympic years. A retreat from this commitment would cripple those sports. Thomas Bach, one of the IOC's negotiators, brushed off the attempt at "blackmail." "German Broadcaster Threatens to Drop Small Sports in Olympics Standoff," *NYTimes.com*, Feb. 7, 2009, http://www.nytimes.com/2009/01/27/technology/27iht-rights.4.19720862.html. Fritz Pleitgen, EBU's president, stated, "We very much regret the decision of the IOC. We have worked with the IOC . . . to deliver the Olympic Games to the broadest possible audience, and ensured maximum exposure of the Olympic Games, and also Olympic Sports between the Games. We note that there are different views about the future monetary broadcast value of the Games. EBU members were surprised by the high financial expectations of the IOC. We regret that, it seems, little account is taken of the additional high level of investment by the EBU in rights for, and the production and quality editorial coverage of, World-, European- and National Championships, across many Olympic Sports." Matthew Glendinning, "IOC Rejects EBU Bid for 2014–2016 Olympic Games Rights."

44. M. Payne, *Olympic Turnaround*, 14.

45. Miller, *Olympic Revolution*, 4.

46. M. Payne, *Olympic Turnaround*, 15.

47. Findling, "Juan Antonio Samaranch," 490. For a full discussion on diplomacy, see Geoff R. Berridge, *Diplomacy: Theory and Practice*.

48. M. Payne, *Olympic Turnaround*, 277; Miller, *Olympic Revolution*, 5. Financial indiscretions involving conflict of interest forced Robert Helmick's resignation from both the USOC and the IOC in the autumn of 1991. For additional information, see Thomas C. Hayes, "Ethics Report Criticizes Helmick," *New York Times*, Nov. 25, 1991.

49. International Olympic Committee, *Press Kit: The Samaranch Years, 1980–2001*. Having communicated his three priorities, Samaranch presented his means of accomplishing them at the Olympic Congress in Baden-Baden in January 1981. On the occasion of the closing ceremony of the congress, he communicated the five-part agenda of this action plan: to strengthen unity of the Olympic Movement; fight against doping; fight against racial discrimination; open the Olympic Games to all the best athletes, including professionals; and increase women's participation both on the field of play and in sports administration. Juan Antonio Samaranch, "Closing Speech by IOC President Mr. Juan Antonio Samaranch."

50. See *Minutes of the Meeting of the IOC Executive Board* (May 28, 1985), 177–78. At the 148th meeting of the IOC Executive Board, Juan Antonio Samaranch, representing the IOC, and Horst Dassler, representing International Sports Leisure Marketing Aktiengesellschaft, signed the TOP I (1985–88) agreement. For a complete explanation of the emergence of the TOP program, see Martyn, "Struggle for Financial Autonomy."

51. Longman, "Samaranch's Legacy"; Miller, *Olympic Revolution*, 3.

52. Pound, *Inside the Olympics*, 256–60.

53. According to Richard Pound, the former World Anti-Doping Agency president, Samaranch tried to sweep doping under the carpet to protect other IOC interests. "Samaranch wasn't interested in the issue," Pound told Reuters in an October 2007 telephone interview. "There was no money available for research and Samaranch wasn't interested in using the Olympic leverage against the international federations to make them do their job," he stated. "He was never willing to do that." Furthermore, Pound argues that if it were not for the 1998 Festina team cycling scandal at the Tour de France, things in the Olympic Movement would not have changed. Pound, *Inside the Olympics*, 235; Steve Keating, "Samaranch 'Not Interested in Doping': Pound," Reuters.com, Oct. 24, 2007, http://www.reuters.com/article/sportsNews/idUSL244888320071024. See also Richard Pound, *Inside Dope: How Drugs Are the Biggest Threat to Sports, Why You Should Care, and What Can Be Done about Them*; and John Hoberman, "Olympic Drug Testing: An Interpretive History."

54. Commodification refers to a reduction "in the value of any act or object to only its monetary exchange value, ignoring historical, artistic or relational added values." Michael R. Real, "Is TV Corrupting the Olympics? The (Post) Modern Olympics—Technology and the Commodification of the Olympic Movement," 7.

55. Moscow (1980) welcomed 5,179 athletes compared to Sydney's (2000) 10,651. In Sydney's case, add 16,033 media personnel, and the challenge when you factor in Olympic tourists is clear. The immense organizational, logistical, and financial challenges inherent in hosting a Summer Olympic festival, owing to the unbridled growth of the Olympic program under Samaranch, have eliminated the possibility of extending hosting opportunities to major

centers in emerging nations and even taxes those cities with the infrastructure to stage them. One can understand the pleadings of those individuals who say the Games are too big, too complex, too expensive, too much of a risk for the host city and feature too many sports, too many athletes, and too many representatives of the media.

56. Pound, *Inside the Olympics*, 264; Bert Roughton Jr., "Olympics Chief Ends 21-Year Reign," *Palm Beach (FL) Post*, July 16, 2001 (brackets added); Greg Garber, "Samaranch's Legacy: Controversy, Corruption."

57. Juan Antonio Samaranch with Pedro Palacios, *Memorias Olímpiacos*. A WorldCat Library database search listed only eighteen subscribing institutions in possession of the work, including Yale, Harvard, the University of Toronto, the University of Wisconsin, and the Library of Congress. It is published in Chinese, but we located no other translations. Samaranch also coauthored a book with a French journalist based on a series of interviews as the Centennial Games in Atlanta approached. Juan Antonio Samaranch and Robert Parienté, *The Samaranch Years, 1980–1994: Towards Olympic Unity, Entrevues*.

58. Abrahamson, "Passing the Torch"; Garber, "Samaranch's Legacy: Controversy, Corruption." Juan Antonio Samaranch Jr. had been a member of the Spanish Olympic Committee since 1989 and was a vice president of the International Modern Pentathlon Union at the time of his election to the IOC.

59. Jacquelin Magnay, "Samaranch Trapped by His Love of Power," *Age* (Melbourne), July 10, 2001. Even Samaranch conceded that extending his term beyond the 1992 Barcelona Games might have been unwise in the final analysis: "Maybe, yes, that was a mistake," he observed.

60. In commenting on Samaranch's lengthy term as IOC president, and the troubles encountered in the latter years of his tenure in Lausanne, Richard Pound noted, "It's a little like the story of the baboon climbing the pole. The higher the baboon climbs, the more undesirable are the parts exposed." Longman, "Juan Antonio Samaranch Dies at 89."

61. James Pearce, "Juan Antonio Samaranch 'Leaves Lasting Olympic Legacy,'" *BBC Sport*, Apr. 21, 2010, http://news.bbc.co.uk/sport2/hi/olympics_games/8634243.stm.

62. Readers might wish to consult Jere Longman's concise, informative, and evenhanded analysis of Samaranch's life and career in Olympic leadership published mere hours after his passing. Longman, "Juan Antonio Samaranch Dies at 89."

63. "Samaranch: IOC Will Win War on Drugs." The second "worst" moment was the Soviet-led boycott of the 1984 Los Angeles Olympics.

## 2. A Gathering Storm

1. Stephen Wilson, "Corruption Scandal Likely to Force Changes in the IOC," *Kitchener-Waterloo Record* (Canada), Dec. 17, 1998. It was later learned that Stephanie Pate, Tom Welch's former secretary, under pressure from SLOC trustee Ken Bullock and a US West lobbyist, the late Dave Watson, to provide information damaging to SLOC vice president Dave Johnson, gave Bullock the document. Bullock denied Pate's version of events. Vanocur

has never revealed who delivered the document into his possession. Linda Fantin, "Olympics Trial Like a Bad Rerun," *Salt Lake Tribune*, Apr. 27, 2003. Unless otherwise indicated, such as above, all *Salt Lake Tribune* articles were retrieved from the newspaper's archival (online) database. Chris Vanocur is the son of veteran political and diplomatic correspondent with *NBC News* and *ABC News* Sander Vanocur.

2. Mike Gorrell, "Panel Paid Tuition for IOC Voter's Relative; SLOC Says Practice Is Common," *Salt Lake Tribune*, Nov. 26, 1998. Salt Lake City captured fifty-four votes on the first ballot, thereby securing the right to host the 2002 Olympic Winter Games over Ostersund, Sweden (fourteen votes); Sion, Switzerland (fourteen votes); and Quebec City, Canada (seven votes).

3. Mike Gorrell, "Bribery Accusations Are Unfair, S.L. Olympic Officials Say," *Salt Lake Tribune*, Dec. 6, 1998.

4. Gorrell, "Panel Paid Tuition for IOC Voter's Relative."

5. Lisa Riley Roche, "Were SLOC Payments a Bribe for 2002 Bid?," *Deseret Morning News*, Nov. 25, 1998; Lisa Riley Roche, "Details of Bid Payments Urged," *Deseret Morning News*, Nov. 26, 1998; "SLOC Stir: Fishy but Irrelevant," *Salt Lake Tribune*, Dec. 6, 1998; Lisa Riley Roche, "Did IOC Buy African Votes?" *Deseret Morning News*, Dec. 9, 1998; "Report: Boosters Paid for Scholarships for IOC Children," Associated Press, Nov. 25, 1998; "Political Leaders Call on SLOC for Full Disclosure on Scholarships," Associated Press, Nov. 26, 1998; "SLOC Asked for Data on Scholarships," Associated Press, Nov. 26, 1998; Mike Carter, "IOC Member: Salt Lake Olympic Payments Weren't Legitimate," Associated Press, Dec. 9, 1998.

6. Christopher Price and Patrick Harverson, "Sema Seals Olympic Games Contract," *Financial Times* (London), Dec. 8, 1998; Payne interview (see introduction, n. 10).

7. Barney, Wenn, and Martyn, *Selling the Five Rings*, ix. The authors were completing some research at Pound's office that day for the above book. Pound would later report in his 2004 book, *Inside the Olympics*, that he had been tipped off by a Salt Lake City reporter that a document had surfaced indicating that Salt Lake City bidders had supplied the dependent of an IOC member with college tuition assistance. When the reporter asked Pound for advice on what to do with the document, Pound responded that he was not aware of any money distributed by Salt Lake City bidders, but if he thought it to be a credible lead, it should be pursued. Pound alerted Samaranch that "there might be trouble coming." Pound, *Inside the Olympics*, 197.

8. Roche, "Details of Bid Payments Urged."

9. Guy Boulton, "SLOC Gets Blindsided by Scandal; Lack of Damage Control a Public-Relations Disaster," *Salt Lake Tribune*, Dec. 13, 1998; "Scandal Catches SLOC in Media Disaster," *Salt Lake Tribune*, Dec. 13, 1998. Fred Fogo, a communications and public relations instructor at Salt Lake City's Westminster College, criticized Joklik's efforts to manage the media, concluding, "Frank Joklik comes across as a Prussian general who appears to be irritated that he's been called away from reviewing the troops." Peter Valcarce, a public relations

expert and political strategist, stated that SLOC's approach created its media nightmare. The decision to steadfastly maintain that the money had been targeted for humanitarian aid bred skepticism. Joklik, a former head of Kennecott Corporation, had not managed the situation (and the media) well. "It's just this attitude that I've been successful in business and how dare you question me," observed Valcarce.

10. Pound, *Inside the Olympics*, 198.

11. Ibid.

12. Mike Gorrell, "SLOC Cash to Students under Fire; Critic Says Payments Smell Like Bribes to IOC for Votes; SLOC Payments to IOC Relatives under Suspicion," *Salt Lake Tribune*, Dec. 9, 1998.

13. "If he [Samaranch] had not appointed Dick Pound, who sponsors and advertisers respect most," commented John Hancock Mutual Life Insurance CEO David D'Alessandro (who shepherded John Hancock into the TOP program), "I wouldn't be surprised to see half the sponsors gone." Jere Longman, "Finnish IOC Member Resigns over Scandal," *New York Times*, Jan. 20, 1999.

14. Pound, *Inside the Olympics*, 256–60.

15. "By giving Pound the high-profile job of prosecuting IOC members, Samaranch may have—wittingly or unwittingly—ruined his [presidential] ambitions." Stephen Wilson, "No Samaranch Successor in Sight," *AP Online*, Feb. 27, 1999 (brackets added). "Originally Pound was Samaranch's hand-picked successor, but the two fell out over Samaranch's successful lobbying in 1995 to extend the age limit of members to 80, thus ensuring himself a few extra years in power. . . . Many people believe that Samaranch appointed Pound to examine the scandal to stymie the Canadian's presidential hopes. He was expected to put the rest of the membership offside and create antagonism among those he investigated." Jacquelin Magnay, "Pound of Flesh," *Sydney Morning Herald*, Mar. 20, 1999.

16. Pound's description of Samaranch's successful campaign for the IOC presidency provides but one example of Samaranch's backroom skills. Pound, *Inside the Olympics*, 230–33, 265–67.

17. Ibid., 214.

18. Mike Carter, "IOC Official Slams Scholarships; He Says Voters' Kin Got Gifts Because S.L. Had 'Lost Twice and Wanted to Win'; IOC Criticizes SLOC for Scholarships," Associated Press, Dec. 10, 1998; Mike Gorrell, "IOC to Investigate Olympic Payments; Salt Lake Bid Committee's Financial Assistance Called Bribe by Member of IOC Executive Board; IOC Will Investigate Olympic Payments," *Salt Lake Tribune*, Dec. 11, 1998.

19. Wilson, "Corruption Scandal Likely to Force Changes in the IOC." James E. Shelledy, editor of the *Salt Lake Tribune*, believed Hodler's comments in Lausanne stoked the media fire and pushed the scandal to a new level. "In my mind," offered Shelledy, "the story would have dead-ended with KTVX's letter had not Marc Hodler lost bladder control in front of the entire news media in Lausanne. How far this single scholarship controversy would have gone with just that, I don't know." Shepard, "Olympian Scandal."

20. "World: Europe Olympic 'Vote Buying' Scandal"; Mike Gorrell, "IOC Official: Games Are for Sale," *Salt Lake Tribune*, Dec. 13, 1998; Christopher Clarey, "Olympics: Senior Official Says Votes on Sites Were Sold," *New York Times*, Dec. 13, 1998.

21. "Scandal Shadows Salt Lake's Olympics," *Hamilton Spectator* (Ontario), Dec. 16, 1998. The article cites Hodler's comment as having been made on December 12.

22. Gorrell, "IOC Official: Games Are for Sale." This thought was confirmed by Michael Payne during a personal interview with him in his Lausanne office on June 18, 2007.

23. "IOC Official Says Allegations Based on Hearsay," *Kitchener-Waterloo-Record* (Canada), Dec. 19, 1998.

24. *Minutes of the Meeting of the IOC Executive Board* (Dec. 11–13, 1998), 54. See also "Hodler Says He Went Public to Avoid Cover-Up," Associated Press, Dec. 16, 1998.

25. *Minutes of the Meeting of the IOC Executive Board* (Oct. 10–11, 1986), 38.

26. *Report to the International Olympic Committee by the Toronto Ontario Olympic Council on the Candidature of the City of Toronto to Host the Games of the XXVI Olympiad.*

27. *Minutes of the Meeting of the IOC Executive Board* (Dec. 4–6, 1991), 12.

28. *Minutes of the Meeting of the IOC Executive Board* (Feb. 1–3, 1992), 51; *Minutes of the 98th IOC Session*, 31.

29. Hodler referred to the Executive Board meetings in Lausanne as some of the "blackest days of his life," but he clearly enjoyed the mantle of "IOC whistleblower" in consenting to numerous interviews in the wake of the meetings and asserting that "no revolution has been possible without scandal." *Minutes of the Meeting of the IOC Executive Board* (Dec. 11–13, 1998), 54; Pound, *Inside the Olympics*, 214; Wilson, "Corruption Scandal Likely to Force Changes in the IOC."

30. Thierry C. Pauchant and Ian I. Mitroff, *Transforming the Crisis-Prone Organization: Preventing Individual, Organizational, and Environmental Tragedies*, 74.

31. Ibid.

32. Ibid., 74–75. According to Pauchant and Mitroff, fixation "is the mechanism by which individuals become rigidly attached to a particular course of action for dealing with a threatening reality, so attached that they cannot change to a more appropriate course of action as the situation demands."

33. Longman, "Samaranch's Legacy" (see chap. 1, n. 7).

34. Garber, "Samaranch's Legacy: Controversy, Corruption" (brackets added).

35. Payne interview.

36. Longman, "Samaranch's Legacy."

37. Pauchant and Mitroff, *Transforming the Crisis-Prone Organization*, 74.

38. Payne interview.

39. Fernand Landry and Magdalene Yerlès, *The International Olympic Committee—One Hundred Years: The Idea—the Presidents—the Achievements; The Presidencies of Lord Killanin [1972–1980] and of Juan Antonio Samaranch [1980–]*, 216–17.

40. Payne interview (brackets added).

41. Randy Starkman, Ashante Infantry, and Jack Lakey, "Pound Faces Olympian Task in Probe," *Toronto Star*, Dec. 17, 1998.

42. *Minutes of the Meeting of the IOC Executive Board* (Dec. 11–13, 1998), 57. "In [Pound's] view, they could not go into a doping conference on a platform of Olympic ethics without putting the IOC's house in order first" (brackets added).

43. Starkman, Infantry, Lakey, "Pound Faces Olympian Task in Probe" (brackets added).

44. Mike Carter, "IOC Probe Possible: City Officials Admit Paying Internship to Son of IOC member," *Hamilton Spectator* (Ontario), Dec. 18, 1998.

45. Jere Longman, "Olympics: More Reports of IOC Favors Emerge in Utah," *New York Times*, Dec. 18, 1998.

46. Randy Starkman and Ashante Infantry, "Games Bribery Scandal Grows," *Toronto Star*, Dec. 19, 1998. See also Lisa Riley Roche, "Libyan Denies Dad Sold Vote," *Deseret Morning News*, Dec. 19, 1998.

47. Stephen Wilson, "Rival Cities Want $22M," *Sun-Herald* (Sydney), Dec. 20, 1998. Note that the $22 million figure was converted to US$14 million.

48. "IOC Mafiosi Should Be Held Accountable," *Toronto Star*, Dec. 20, 1998.

49. *IOC Marketing Commission: Report to the IOC Executive Board*, 2.

50. *Minutes of the Meeting of the IOC Marketing Commission*, 1; Pound to Douglas Ivester, chairman, Coca-Cola Company, Dec. 15, 1998, PFRWP.

51. Ibid.

52. Guy Boulton, "IOC Official Apologizes; Pound Expresses Regret That S.L. Was Tainted by Scandal; Pound Offers Apology to Salt Lake City," *Salt Lake Tribune*, Jan. 22, 1999.

53. *IOC Marketing Commission: Report to the 109th IOC Session*, 2.

54. Stephen Wenn and Scott Martyn, "Storm Watch: Richard Pound, TOP Sponsors, and the Salt Lake City Bid Scandal" and "'Tough Love': Richard Pound, David D'Alessandro, and the Salt Lake City Olympics Bid Scandal," 189.

55. *Minutes of the Ad Hoc Executive Board Meeting*, 2.

56. Maureen Clark, "Vote-Buying of IOC Claimed an Organizer for Anchorage's Bid for the Winter Olympics Says He Was Solicited for Bribes by Agents of the IOC," *Greensboro (NC) News and Record*, Dec. 15, 1998.

57. "Votes for Sale" (brackets added) (see introduction, n. 4).

58. Janine Watson, "We Used to Joke about Bribes and Gifts for Members; Clean Up the Olympics; Stringer Calls for Corruption Probe," *Manchester Evening News*, Dec. 15, 1998.

59. "And the Heat Is Turned Up" and "Nagano Games Tainted by Scandal" (see introduction, n. 4).

60. Payne interview.

61. *Minutes of the Meeting of the IOC Executive Board* (June 13–15, 1999), 9–10; Payne interview. From the outside looking in, David D'Alessandro viewed Hill & Knowlton's performance as "not effective." D'Alessandro to Wenn, July 14, 2009.

62. Mike Gorrell, "Joklik Hopes His Sacrifice Will Push Forward; Joklik Hopes His Sacrifice Will Save Games," *Salt Lake Tribune*, Jan. 9, 1999. See also Dan Egan, "Once Best and Brightest, Is Johnson a Fallen Star? Johnson's Olympic Dream Tumbles," *Salt Lake Tribune*, Jan. 9, 1999. Welch was unaware if Joklik knew of cash payments to IOC members, but indicated that Joklik was fully apprised of the NOC Assistance Program that had been the source of funds for Essomba and the others. See Mike Gorrell, "Welch Says Board Had Access to All Dealings: Joklik Insists Members 'Screened' from Improper Payments; Welch Says Board Had Access to All Information," *Salt Lake Tribune*, Jan. 11, 1999.

63. "Corradini's Wise Decision," *Salt Lake Tribune*, Jan. 12, 1999.

64. Mike Gorrell, "USOC Member Resigns; LaMont Leaves Amid Story of Welch 'Business Relationship'; USOC Member Resigns; Fifth Probe Is Opened," *Salt Lake Tribune*, Jan. 15, 1999. LaMont had not revealed consultant contracts he had signed with Welch as well as two 2004 bid committees, Rome and Istanbul, to the USOC. He testified against Welch and Johnson at their conspiracy, fraud, and racketeering trial that he had provided $3,000 of Salt Lake's money to the son of Austin Sealy, an IOC member from Barbados. LaMont pleaded guilty to conspiracy and felony tax fraud resulting from having withheld more than $24,800 in taxes from the Internal Revenue Service. See Lisa Riley Roche, "Ex-USOC Official Grilled," *Deseret Morning News*, Nov. 20, 2003; Lisa Riley Roche, "Oly Witness Sticks to His 'Bribe' Claim," *Deseret Morning News*, Nov. 25, 2003; and Linda Fantin, "Games Scandal Figures to Be Sentenced," *Salt Lake Tribune*, Sept. 16, 2004.

65. Greg Burton, "Escorts: Investigators Look for Link to Bid Committee," *Salt Lake Tribune*, Jan. 16, 1999.

66. Jacquelin Magnay and Glenda Korporaal, "African Link in Vote Bid by Sydney," *Age* (Melbourne), Dec. 15, 1998.

67. John Lehmann and Nicole Jeffery, "Inquiry Clouds Games," *Australian* (Sydney), Jan. 25, 1999; Glenn Stanaway, "Under Fire: Sydney's Main Players," *Courier-Mail* (Brisbane), Jan. 26, 1999; Jacquelin Magnay, "The Skilled Survivor May Soon Be Facing His Toughest Test," *Age* (Melbourne), Jan. 25, 1999.

68. Ben English, "Bribe Inquiry to Include Sydney," *Daily Telegraph* (Sydney), Jan. 20, 1999.

69. Michael Evans and Glenda Korporaal, "IOC Asked to Repair Games Image," *Sydney Morning Herald*, Jan. 19, 1999.

70. Kevan Gosper, blindsided by Coates's comments to the press, was extremely concerned about Sydney's status. Jacquelin Magnay, "Gosper Feared Losing Games," *Age* (Melbourne), Jan. 26, 1999; "We May Lose the Games," *Sunday Herald Sun* (Melbourne), Jan. 24, 1999; Glenn Stanaway, "Ill-Prepared Gosper Defends Sydney's 'Lunge to the Line,'" *Daily Telegraph* (Sydney), Jan. 25, 1999. For a detailed analysis of Kevan Gosper's efforts to defend Sydney from further investigation at the Executive Board meetings in late January, see Glenn Stanaway, "Forty-Eight Hours That Rocked Kevan Gosper," *Daily Telegraph* (Sydney), Jan.

26, 1999; and Matthew Stevens, "Putting an Apple on His Own Head, Gosper Survives the Crossbows," *Australian* (Sydney), Jan. 26, 1999.

71. Jere Longman, "Potential Olympic Sponsors Said to Be Uneasy," *New York Times,* Jan. 21, 1999.

72. D'Alessandro to Wenn, July 14, 2009.

73. For an analysis of the Pound-D'Alessandro relationship, see Wenn and Martyn, "'Tough Love.'"

74. Wenn and Martyn, "Storm Watch," 178–79, 183–84. For repeated expression of D'Alessandro's criticism of the pace of the IOC reform process, see D'Alessandro to Pound, May 10, 19, 24, 1999, PFRWP. For the characterization of the IOC's institution of reform measures as "lethargic," see David D'Alessandro, "With Sponsorship Money on the Line, the IOC Must Take Radical Steps," *NYTimes.com,* Feb. 14, 1999, http://www.nytimes.com.library/sports/other/021499oly-sponsor.html.

75. Pound, *Inside the Olympics,* 158–59.

76. Ruth Shalit, "Chain Saws, Drugs, and Lesbians: Olympic Advertising Deserves a Gold Medal—in Confusion"; D'Alessandro to Wenn, July 14, 2009.

77. D'Alessandro to Wenn, July 14, 2009.

78. Ibid. Samaranch's attitude alarmed D'Alessandro. His view that "IOC members would not have been tempted if Salt Lake City officials had not offered" inducements dismissed the accepted fact that a bribe required a "briber and a bribee," stated D'Alessandro. In an e-mail to Stephen Wenn on July 17, 2009, D'Alessandro absented Richard Pound from his assessment of the institution's grasp of the severity of the matter: "I would only add that Dick Pound had a better understanding of our strategy. He was more inclined to push the IOC into reforms on a timely basis. He knew what was at stake for the IOC; he understood the media and U.S. Congress were not going to back off until significant governance changes were made."

79. Ibid.

80. Ibid.; D'Alessandro to Wenn, July 17, 2009.

81. Jere Longman, "Corporate Backer Tells IOC to Come Clean," *New York Times,* Jan. 13, 1999.

82. Longman, "Potential Olympic Sponsors Said to Be Uneasy."

83. Boulton, "IOC Official Apologizes."

84. Jere Longman, "Corruption Is Extensive, IOC Official Finds," *New York Times,* Jan. 22, 1999.

85. Randy Starkman, "IOC Bigwigs' Heads Buried Deep in the Sand," *Toronto Star,* Jan. 23, 1999.

86. Randy Starkman, "A Pound of Prevention," *Toronto Star,* Jan. 23, 1999.

87. "13 IOC Members Caught in Scandal's Web," *Seattle Post-Intelligencer,* Jan. 15, 1999.

88. Marc Fisher and Bill Brubaker, "IOC Focus Turns Inward; Amid Olympic Corruption Charges, 13 Members Investigated," *Washington Post,* Jan. 23, 1999.

89. Rob Hughes, "Haggman Resigns in Bribes Scandal—Olympics," *Times* (London), Jan. 20, 1999; Mike Dodd, "Finnish IOC Member Steps Down Reports: Bid Cities Gave Her Husband Jobs," *USA Today*, Jan. 20, 1999; Steve Buffery, "Scarred by Scandal: Ex-IOC Member Haggman Tries to Rebuild Her Life." Häggman maintained (a claim supported by Bjarne) that she knew nothing about her ex-husband's pursuit of work in Utah but that the stress suffered as a result of her treatment by the Finnish media forced her to abandon her hopes of retaining her IOC membership. Questions were also raised about Bjarne's work for Ontario's Ministry of Natural Resources during Toronto's candidature for the 1996 Olympics. While the ministry was to have paid the rent for their stay in northern Ontario (they were married at the time), it reneged, and Toronto's bid committee provided the funds. "Second Head Rolls in Bribes Scandal," *Herald Sun* (Melbourne), Jan. 23, 1999. For background on Suhel Attarabulsi's financial support from Salt Lake City, see Roche, "Libyan Denies Dad Sold Vote."

90. Stephen Wilson, "IOC Members Vow Cleanup Campaign," Associated Press, Jan. 23, 1999 (brackets added); "Interview: Anita DeFrantz, Vice President of the International Olympic Committee, Speaks Out about Removing Those Who Abuse Their Authority Within the IOC"; Stephen Wilson, "While Another Quits, Samaranch Stands Firm," *Dallas Morning News*, Jan. 23, 1999.

91. "On Their Marks: Games Chiefs Poised for Major Cleanup," *Toronto Star*, Jan. 24, 1999.

### 3. Survival Mode

1. "On Their Marks."
2. *Minutes of the Ad Hoc Executive Board Meeting*, 1, 3.
3. Ibid., 1–4.
4. Ibid., 8, 4–6, 15. This money supplemented a previously signed agreement with eleven African nations, including Kenya and Uganda. Regardless of the result of the vote, Coates, president of the Australian Olympic Committee, had pledged to deliver Australian coaching expertise and the opportunity to use Australian training facilities to African athletes hailing from these countries.
5. Ibid., 4.
6. Ibid., 15, 16 (brackets added).
7. "IOC Cleans House 6 Kicked Out in Influence-Peddling Scandal," *Kitchener-Waterloo Record* (Canada), Jan. 25, 1999.
8. Robin McDowell, "U.S. Olympic Committee Says IOC Purge Is a Good Start," Associated Press, Jan. 24, 1999.
9. "Olympic Committee Targets Six: IOC Members Accepted $800,000 in 'Inducements,'" *Hamilton Spectator* (Ontario), Jan. 25, 1999.
10. "Text of Samaranch Inquiry and Findings Speech," *Deseret News*, Jan. 25, 1999. The *Times* (London) considered the sacrifice of the six members in concert with a vote of confidence

as "a cynical attempt to save [Samaranch's] career." See Simon Haydon, "Olympics—'Culture of Presents' Normal, Samaranch," Reuters News, Jan. 25, 1999 (brackets added).

11. Stephen Wilson, "Six Olympic Committee Members Ousted," *Augusta (GA) Chronicle*, Jan. 25, 1999.

12. Stanaway, "Under Fire: Sydney's Main Players" (see chap. 2, n. 67).

13. Ibid.

14. Clinton delivered his State of the Union address in January 1999 under the shadow cast by the Senate trial presided over by the chief of the US Supreme Court, William Rehnquist. Peter Baker and Juliet Eilperin, "Both Sides Lay Out Cases for Senators; Scope and Factual Basis Are Debated in Filings," *Washington Post*, Jan. 12, 1999; "Clinton Blasts Impeachment Process on Eve of Senate Trial," Agence France-Presse, Jan. 13, 1999; Elaine S. Povich and Ken Fireman, "The Impeachment Trial; A Cancer on the Body Politic; Bipartisanship Has Broken; GOP Senators Discuss Witnesses Despite Deal," *New York Newsday*, Jan. 15, 1999; Morton M. Kondracke, "Ruff Defense, State of the Union Boost Clinton," *Roll Call*, Jan. 21, 1999.

15. Fraud and favoritism in the distribution of EC contracts were at the root of the charges made by Dutch civil servant Paul van Buitenen, who took on Marc Hodler's role, that is, whistle-blower, in this scenario. Kevin Cullen, "Corruption Scandal Jolts European Union," *Boston Globe*, Jan. 11, 1999; Stephen Castle and Katherine Butler, "European Union Crisis: MEPs Retreat in Battle with Santer," *Independent* (London), Jan. 14, 1999. The twenty-person commission, including Santer, fought on; however, a scathing report filed by an investigative panel forced Santer and his colleagues to resign in March 1999. Neil King Jr. and Julie Wolf, "EU's Executive Commission Steps Down after Report Finds It Bungled Finances," *Wall Street Journal*, Mar. 16, 1999.

16. "British Minister in Row over Loan from Cabinet Colleague," Agence France-Presse, Dec. 22, 1998; Paul Routledge, "I Knew the Loan Deal Secret First . . . but I Was Prepared to Save," *Daily Mirror* (London), Jan. 2, 1999; "The Casting-Out of Mandelson," *Economist* (London), Jan. 2, 1999.

17. Datops and Sportweb, "International Olympic Committee—Summary of the Media Crisis: International Media Crisis, Dec. 1998–June 1999," 3, 6, 14, 15.

18. "Slack Boss Must Go," *Herald Sun* (Melbourne), Jan. 27, 1999; "Sweep the Olympics," *Chicago Sun-Times*, Jan. 26, 1999; "Samaranch in Denial, but He Must Resign," *Atlanta Journal-Constitution*, Jan. 31, 1999; "Olympic Empire Head Must Quit," *Waikato Times* (Hamilton, New Zealand), Jan. 27, 1999.

19. Rita Delfiner, "Olympic Mess Spurs Calls for Lord of the Rings to Resign," *New York Post*, Jan. 27, 1999.

20. Stephen Wade, "Newspapers Want Samaranch to Resign," Associated Press, Jan. 25, 1999; James Christie, "IOC Head Draws Fierce Criticism," *Globe and Mail* (Toronto), Jan. 26, 1999.

21. "IOC's Samaranch Turns into Media Scapegoat," *Business Day* (Thailand), Jan. 27, 1999; Haydon, "Olympics—'Culture of Presents' Normal"; Wade, "Newspapers Want Samaranch to Resign."

22. Michael Wilbon, "To Get to the Bottom of the Scandal, Look to the Top," *Washington Post*, Jan. 25, 1999.

23. Delfiner, "Olympic Mess Spurs Calls."

24. Tom Ross, "(Olympics) IOC Members Stand by Samaranch," Agence France-Presse, Jan. 25, 1999.

25. Stephen Wilson, "International Olympic Committee Chief Goes on Offensive," Associated Press, Jan. 25, 1999; Ross, "(Olympics) IOC Members Stand by Samaranch."

26. Jere Longman, "Feisty Samaranch Takes on Scandal and Critics," *New York Times*, Jan. 26, 1999.

27. John Powers, "Showing Olympic Mettle Samaranch Is Staunch," *Boston Globe*, Jan. 26, 1999.

28. Ross, "(Olympics) IOC Members Stand by Samaranch"; Christie, "IOC Head Draws Fierce Criticism"; John Partridge, "Pound Denies Capitalizing on Scandal: Investigator's Role Would Hurt Any Presidential Aspirations, IOC Member Believes," *Globe and Mail* (Toronto), Jan. 27, 1999.

29. Christie, "IOC Head Draws Fierce Criticism."

30. *Minutes of the Ad Hoc Executive Board Meeting*, 16.

31. Robert Sullivan et al., "How the Olympics Were Bought: Salt Lake City Finally Got the Games, and Now the Allegations—and the Investigations—Are Spreading"; Christopher Dickey, Andrew Murr, and Russell Watson, "No More Fun and Games: Juan Antonio Samaranch Comes under Fire as Head of the International Olympic Committee"; E. M. Swift, "Breaking Point: Years of Greed and Corruption Have Caught Up at Last with the International Olympic Committee."

32. Andrew Selesky, "African Backlash in Olympic Scandal," Associated Press, Jan. 26, 1999.

33. "Africans: Purge 'Conspiracy,'" *Raleigh News and Observer*, Jan. 27, 1999.

34. Lori Shontz, "Let Scandal End Samaranch Reign," *Pittsburgh Post-Gazette*, Jan. 30, 1999.

35. Ian Darby, "Deals to Survive Olympic Scandals," *Marketing*, Jan. 28, 1999; Gregg Krupa, "So Far, Sponsors Are Buying It," *Boston Globe*, Jan. 26, 1999.

36. James Christie, "Koss Delivers Blow to Samaranch: Athletes Leader Doesn't Want IOC Boss to Become First Head of Antidoping Body," *Globe and Mail* (Toronto), Feb. 3, 1999.

37. "Olympics Chief under Fire," *BBC News Online*, Feb. 2, 1999, http://news.bbc.co.uk/1/hi/sport/ 270611.stm.

38. Gregory Katz, "Drug Czar Urges Olympic Reforms: Scandal-Tainted IOC Needs to Establish Separate Testing Body," *Dallas Morning News*, Feb. 3, 1999; "Olympics Chief under Fire."

39. Stephen Wilson, "Disputes Emerge on Eve of Drug Summit," Associated Press, Feb. 1, 1999.

40. Pound, *Inside the Olympics*, 72; Tom Humphries, "IOC Will Not Direct New Testing Body," *Irish Times* (Dublin), Feb. 3, 1999, http://canthrow.com/internationalnews/feb041999.sthml; Gregory Katz, "IOC Chief Feels the Heat of Scandal's Flames: Power Won in Golden Olympic Years Challenged During Anti-Drug Summit," *Dallas Morning News*, Feb. 5, 1999.

41. "An Olympic-Sized Family Feud Rages at Lausanne Conference," *Deseret News*, Feb. 4, 1999. The *Wall Street Journal* article was reprinted in the *Deseret News*; Randy Starkman, "Intrigue at Fever Pitch as Olympic Moguls Face Congress on Corruption: Weeding Out IOC's Woes," *Toronto Star*, Feb. 6, 1999.

42. A. Craig Copetas and Roger Thurlow, "The Olympics under Fire—End of an Empire?" *Wall Street Journal Europe*, Feb. 4, 1999. The origin point for the faxes is identified in "Olympic News: Around the Rings." Jacques Rogge thought the perpetrator of the smear campaign to be "desperate, and perhaps a little bit evil to do this."

43. Starkman, "Intrigue at Fever Pitch."

44. Copetas and Thurlow, "Olympics under Fire" (brackets added).

45. William Drozdiak, "At IOC Breakfast, Gripes, Grievances Are Served; Members Say They're Being Unfairly Punished," *Washington Post*, Feb. 5, 1999.

46. Ibid. (brackets added).

47. Stephen Wilson, "IOC Facing Membership Revolt," Associated Press, Feb. 3, 1999.

48. *Minutes of the 108th Extraordinary IOC Session*, 8–11, Annexes #9 (62–63) and #10 (64–65). The electoral college was composed of the IOC president, the IOC doyen, eight IOC members selected by the IOC Session, the chairman of the IOC Evaluation Commission, an appointed representative of the Association of International Winter Sport Federations, an appointed representative of the Association of National Olympic Committees, and three athletes elected by the Olympic athletes in the Nagano Olympic Winter Games. For the context of the original Pescante-Easton initiative, see Wilson, "IOC Facing Membership Revolt."

49. Glenn Stanaway, "Now a Word to Our Sponsors," *Sunday Telegraph* (Sydney), Jan. 24, 1999.

50. Steve Bailey, "The *Boston Globe* Downtown Column," *Boston Globe*, Feb. 3, 1999.

51. Larry Siddons, "Sponsors to IOC: Clean Up This Scandal Fast," Associated Press, Feb. 12, 1999.

52. Melissa Turner, "Olympics Sponsorship Worries: IOC Aware Corporate Partners Are Getting Skittish over the Scandal—IOC Tries to Stroke Sponsors," *Atlanta Journal-Constitution*, Feb. 12, 1999; James Christie, "IOC Officials Busy Reassuring Sponsors," *Globe and Mail* (Toronto), Feb. 12, 1999; Glenda Korporaal, "Olympic Man's Nightmare Stretch," *Sydney Morning Herald*, Feb. 18, 1999.

53. "John Hancock Uses Its Ad Clout to Pressure IOC: Company Chief Hints It's Time for Samaranch to Go," *Milwaukee Journal Sentinel*, Feb. 10, 1999; David D'Alessandro, "Backtalk: How to Save the Olympics," *New York Times*, Feb. 14, 1999.

54. D'Alessandro, "Backtalk."

55. Joan Vennochi, "An Olympic-Sized Ethical Dilemma," *Boston Globe*, June 8, 1999. This article accompanied a letter sent by fax by D'Alessandro to Pound, June 8, 1999, PFRWP.

56. Scott Bernard Nelson, "The Name's the Same for Top Two"; Jeffrey Krasner, "Two Eras: Before David, after David"; Christopher Rowland, "Signature Brand to Remain a Driving Force in the Sports Scene." Golf sponsorships, stated D'Alessandro, allowed CEOs to brag to their friends at their country clubs. "They can beat their chests for a weekend, and hand out a giant check with Greg Norman looking at them cross-eyed." Boston's ATP tennis tournament, he noted, was second-rate. "Players can pick and choose now because they have so many tournaments. Longwood attracts a fair amount of has-beens and never-weres." John Powers, "Untarnished Gold: D'Alessandro Finds Marathon Safer Bet than Olympics," *Boston Globe*, Apr. 15, 1999.

57. Pound, *Inside the Olympics*, 158.

58. D'Alessandro, "Backtalk"; Stephen Wilson, "Senior IOC Exec Rebukes US Sponsor," Associated Press, Feb. 22, 1999.

59. Payne interview.

60. Pound, *Inside the Olympics*, 159.

61. Payne interview.

62. D'Alessandro to Wenn, July 14, 2009. In the early 1990s, John Hancock shifted its Olympic dollars from a USOC sponsorship (held for a brief period of time) to a TOP sponsorship. Enhancing the company's international profile, noted D'Alessandro, could not be pursued through an USOC sponsor agreement, as a sponsor's marketing operations were limited to the domestic market. He was also discouraged at the time by the degree of tension between officials with the USOC and the Atlanta Organizing Committee. In order to accommodate John Hancock's desire to move to a TOP sponsorship, the USOC traded the insurance category to the IOC for a number of other categories. In 1992, at the outset of John Hancock's involvement in TOP, 95 percent of its consumer revenue was provided by internal agents who owned the company. By the end of the decade, this dependency had been reduced to 30 percent. D'Alessandro viewed the TOP relationship, at the end of the day, as "very positive." He summarized his thoughts on the value of a TOP sponsorship prior to the 2002 Salt Lake City Olympic Winter Games. "The Olympic rings help John Hancock reinforce certain essential things about our brand over and over, in every line of business and every market: that we're willing to support something our customers consider a great cause and that we're a big player. In truth," said D'Alessandro, "the rings suggest that we are a much bigger player than we actually are, given the company they put us in. The 10 other TOP sponsors include corporations . . . whose market capitalization dwarfs ours." *Salt Lake City 2002 Marketing Report*, 69.

63. Joseph B. Treaster, "Insuring Games' Future: John Hancock Exec Fights for Investment," *Denver Post*, Apr. 11, 1999; Shalit, "Chain Saws, Drugs, and Lesbians."

64. Treaster, "Insuring Games' Future."

65. D'Alessandro to Pound, Feb. 22, 1999, PFRWP.

66. Robert Melnbardis, "IOC's Pound Says Reforms Will Reassure Olympic Sponsors," Reuters News, Feb. 25, 1999.

67. Pound, *Inside the Olympics*, 159. While D'Alessandro informed Pound of his decision in December, the public announcement was not made until February 2000.

68. Payne interview.

69. Pound, *Inside the Olympics*, 159.

70. Payne interview.

71. Richard Pound, "Daily Message Log, 1999"; Richard Pound, "Personal Day Planner, 1999"; Pound, *Inside the Olympics*, 159.

72. Stephen Wilson's wire report, dated February 22, titled "IOC Member Criticizes John Hancock Chief for Public Attacks," was sent by fax, along with a letter from D'Alessandro to Pound on the same day. Both documents can be found in PFRWP.

73. Glenda Korporaal and Wire Services, "Samaranch Assures Key Sponsors about Reforms," *Sydney Morning Herald*, Mar. 12, 1999.

74. "Notes for Telephone Call Between IOC President and McDonald's Corporation, Tuesday, 16 February 1999, 16:00"; "Notes for Telephone Call Between IOC President and the Coca-Cola Company, Wednesday, 17 February 1999, 16:00." Handwritten notes on the typed pages indicate these talking points were sent by fax by Michael Payne to Richard Pound.

75. Coca-Cola should have followed this institutional advice—move quickly to solve a crisis—later in the year. In June 1999, a group of Belgian schoolchildren fell ill after consuming tainted Coke. It was later shown that some product had been compromised by disinfectant (phenol) that had been used to treat wooden pallets employed in transporting Coca-Cola from its Dunkirk, France, plant to Belgium. The disinfectant, in trace amounts, was on the outside of the cans. In addition, two Belgian plants had not sufficiently tested the quality of carbon dioxide used to produce the carbonation in Coca-Cola at those locations, thereby contributing more "tainted" beverages (the chemicals that compromised the carbon dioxide were carbonyl sulfide and hydrogen sulfide) to the Belgian consumer market. "Coke Identifies Taint Source." Even though independent research later showed that the outbreak had been likely fueled by mass hysteria, as opposed to product tainted to a point that would have produced illness (the symptoms struck people after drinking what they reported to be foul-smelling Coke), Coca-Cola officials did not move swiftly enough to address concerns. Coca-Cola reported $103 million in lost sales owing to their products being withdrawn from the shelves in five European countries. Furthermore, the situation cost President Douglas Ivester his job later in the year when he announced his resignation. See David Ignatius, "A Global Marketplace Means Global Vulnerability" (this article appeared first in the *Washington Post* on June 22, 1999); "Business: The Company File—Belgium Bans Coca-Cola," *BBC Online*, June 14, 1999, http://news.bbc .co.uk/1/hi/world/Europe/369089.stm; Sarah Boseley, "Coca-Cola Health Scare Was 'Mass Hysteria,'" *Guardian* (Manchester), July 2, 1999, http://guardian.co.uk/print/0,3858,3879929-103526,00.html; N. Deogun et al., "Anatomy of a Recall: How Coke's Control Fizzled Out in Europe," *Wall Street Journal*, June 29, 1999; and B. Nemery et al., "The Coca-Cola Incident in

Belgium—June 1999." Nemery and his colleagues concluded that the hysteria, or mass socio-genic illness, concerning Coke products stemmed from recent dioxin and PCB problems with chickens in Belgium and lingering concerns about BSE (mad cow disease) in Europe.

76. Larry Siddons, "IOC Commission Recommends Warnings for Kim, Coles," Associated Press, Mar. 12, 1999.

77. Mark Coultan and Jacquelin Magnay, "Phil Is Grilled Just in Time for Dinner," *Sydney Morning Herald*, Mar. 3, 1999.

78. Larry Siddons, "IOC Defends Corruption Probe," Associated Press, Mar. 14, 1999.

79. Pound, *Inside the Olympics*, 220.

80. "IOC Did Not Encourage Corruption—Gosper," *Illawarra Mercury* (Australia), Mar. 4, 1999; Beverley Smith, "Watchdog Pound Denies Whitewash IOC Report Recommends Only One More Expulsion," *Globe and Mail* (Toronto), Mar. 13, 1999; Siddons, "IOC Defends Corruption Probe."

81. Stefan Fatsis, "Olympics Gets Vote of Confidence from GM, Its Biggest U.S. Sponsor," *Wall Street Journal—Asia*, Feb. 15, 1999; "SKorea's Samsung Worried by Olympic Scandal," Agence France-Presse, Feb. 15, 1999; Nalita Ferrez, "Games Sponsor Goes for Gold," *Illawarra Mercury* (Australia), Feb. 16, 1999; Stefan Fatsis, "Olympic Sponsors Study Their Options Amid Scandal," *Wall Street Journal*, Mar. 10, 1999.

82. IOC *Marketing Commission: Report to the IOC Executive Board*, 2–3.

83. Fatsis, "Olympic Sponsors Study Their Options."

84. Steve Keating, "Olympics: Let's Stop IOC Bleeding, Says Pound," Reuters News, Feb. 28, 1999; Siddons, "IOC Defends Corruption Probe."

**4. Two Days Lausanne Stood Still**

1. William H. Starbuck, Arent Green, and Bo L. T. Hedberg, "Responding to Crises," 173.

2. A. Craig Copetas and Roger Thurow, "Tightening Rings: Olympic Investigations Sprawl Far Abroad, Vexing a Stressed IOC," *Wall Street Journal*, Mar. 3, 1999.

3. "(Olympics) Sponsors Worried about IOC Double Standards," Agence France-Presse, Mar. 13, 1999 (brackets added). A representative of Xerox stated, "We're certainly monitoring the situation." Meanwhile, a Kodak official concluded that the company was "committed to the spirit of the Olympics but we're disturbed about what's going on. We expect the IOC to fix the problem."

4. Jere Longman, "Defiance and Gloom as IOC Convenes," *New York Times*, Mar. 15, 1999.

5. Jere Longman, "IOC Expulsion Vote Key for Samaranch," *New York Times*, Mar. 17, 1999.

6. Jere Longman, "Reform Process Could Change Entire IOC Structure," *New York Times*, Feb. 20, 1999.

7. Ibid. (brackets added).

8. Payne interview (see introduction, n. 10). Noted Norway's Gerhard Heiberg: "The real problem always comes back to IOC members having different sets of values, and they look upon what's happening now as unimportant. I've spoken to many of these members and gotten them to think about their actions and voting to change the IOC's structure. I would not characterize my lobbying as successful." Copetas and Thurow, "Tightening Rings."

9. Pound, *Inside the Olympics*, 219.

10. On March 7, 1999, Stephen Wilson (Associated Press) wrote, "At the IOC's marble headquarters in Lausanne, Switzerland, a sort of siege mentality has set in. Samaranch has stopped doing interviews and made no public appearances or statements in recent weeks. But Samaranch has kept busy, conferring with his aides and IOC members, laying the groundwork for the March Session, the most crucial in his 19 years as president. Aides say Samaranch, who appeared tired and disheartened a month ago, is more upbeat and determined to fight on and save his legacy." Wilson, "Samaranch Still Wields Big Stick: Embattled Olympic Boss Has Some Powerful Allies," *Milwaukee Journal Sentinel*, Mar. 7, 1999.

11. Erica Bulman, "Samaranch Raps Critics; IOC Officials Testify," *Pittsburgh Post-Gazette*, Mar. 1, 1999 (brackets added).

12. James Christie, "Pound Weighs Future of IOC: Corruption Investigator Considers More Expulsions," *Globe and Mail* (Toronto), Mar. 2, 1999.

13. "Samaranch Says He Erred by Not Acting Earlier Against Bidding Abuses," Associated Press, Mar. 12, 1999.

14. Stephen Wilson, "Samaranch Prepares IOC Members for 'Painful' Decisions," Associated Press, Mar. 11, 1999.

15. Larry Siddons, "IOC Chief Calls 'Fearful' Sponsors," Associated Press, Mar. 10, 1999.

16. John Powers and Mitchell Zuckoff, "IOC Faces Its Day of Reckoning: Difficult Decisions on Tap This Week," *Boston Globe*, Mar. 14, 1999.

17. "With Vote Approaching, Samaranch Worries about Palace Revolt," *Newark Star-Ledger*, Mar. 16, 1999; Larry Siddons, "Investigators Review New Information as Expulsions Vote Nears," Associated Press, Mar. 16, 1999; Copetas and Thurow, "Tightening Rings."

18. Copetas and Roger Thurow, "Tightening Rings."

19. Mike Dodd, "Kim Hits Boiling Point with IOC Panel," *USA Today*, Mar. 18, 1999; Glenn Stanaway, "Clash Kicks Off Olympic Crisis Talks," *Courier-Mail* (Brisbane), Mar. 18, 1999; "Korean IOC Member Takes Threatening Stance," *Kitchener-Waterloo Record* (Canada), Mar. 17, 1999. Dodd reported that Carrard used the words "I'm leaving" and shouted them in Samaranch's direction. The report from the Associated Press appearing in the *Kitchener-Waterloo Record* indicates that Carrard employed the words "I quit."

20. Romney with Robinson, *Turnaround*, 147.

21. Erskine McCullough, "(Olympics) Secret Trial Mocks IOC Transparency Pledge," Agence France-Presse, Mar. 16, 1999.

22. "IOC Official Flees as Kim Strikes Tae Kwon Do Stance," Associated Press, Mar. 17, 1999. Kim provided a letter of apology to Carrard and Pound for his outburst.

23. *Minutes of the Meeting of the IOC Executive Board* (Mar. 15–16, 19, 1999), 5–7. Kevan Gosper sought confirmation that all Executive Board members preferred staging the votes at the conclusion of the six speeches as opposed to conducting each vote at the close of an individual speech.

24. McCullough, "(Olympics) Secret Trial."

25. *Minutes of the Meeting of the IOC Executive Board* (Mar. 15–16, 19, 1999), 23 (brackets added), 24.

26. Ibid., 46 (brackets added).

27. *Minutes of the 108th Extraordinary IOC Session*, Annex #1, 25. Mere days before the Session, British IOC member Craig Reedie warned, "If [Samaranch] is going to retain the presidency and remain in power, he has to resolve this. The ball is in his court." Stephen Wilson, "Samaranch Reputation on Line at Watershed IOC Meeting," Associated Press, Mar. 13, 1999 (brackets added).

28. *Minutes of the 108th Extraordinary IOC Session*, Annex #1, 25–26, 27–32. Samaranch mentioned the successes of the Olympic Congresses of 1981 and 1994 in enhancing the IOC's relationships with the NOCs and ISFs, while also noting steps taken to improve the voice of athletes within the organization. He spoke in glowing terms of the IOC's recognition of both China and Chinese Tapei, while also crediting the IOC with a role in tearing down apartheid in sport and improving the representation of women in the IOC and in Olympic competitive venues. He also noted the successful efforts to tackle boycott threats and address the IOC's dependence on television revenue. The Olympic Museum and Studies Centre (opened in 1993) offered opportunities to examine Olympic culture and history, while the IOC's involvement in the reconstruction of the Sarajevo Olympic Stadium was a project in which members could take much pride. Though not an exhaustive list of events and accomplishments raised by Samaranch in his speech, the above demonstrates that he provided his audience with a comprehensive personal treatment of his work on behalf of the organization since his election in 1980.

29. Ibid., 34, 33.

30. Ibid., 34–35.

31. Ibid., 36, 38. For Samaranch's ideas concerning the proposed IOC 2000 Commission, see ibid., 36–37.

32. *Minutes of the 108th Extraordinary IOC Session*, 1, 3.

33. Ibid., Annex #3, 42, 43.

34. Ibid., 44.

35. Calvert, "How to Buy the Olympics" (see introduction, n. 12). Calvert reported that Gadir's room service bill in Berlin was £1,000. Although we do not have access to the dates of his visit, an online currency converter (OANDA.com, the Currency Site) yields a sum of $1,825.35 when contemporary (May 31, 1992) exchange rates are used. We have made a reasonable assumption that he made the visit in the year before the vote on the 2000 Summer Olympics.

36. The Board of Ethics of the Salt Lake Organizing Committee for the Olympic Winter Games of 2002, *Report to the Board of Trustees*, 38–39. Gadir requested the funds through Muttaleb Ahmad, one of the bid committee's consultants, who had been hired to lobby IOC members from the Middle East and North Africa. For details on Ahmad, the director-general of the Olympic Council of Asia, see p. 24. Page numbers cited for this source are in keeping with the html version of the document retrieved from the Internet on June 1, 2000.

37. *Minutes of the 108th Extraordinary IOC Session*, Annex #4, 45, 46.

38. Calvert, "How to Buy the Olympics"; Thomas, Johnson, and Longman, "Rise and Fall of Olympic Ambitions" (see introduction, 12). Salt Lake City bid officials referred to his visits as "Ganga time."

39. *Minutes of the 108th Extraordinary IOC Session*, Annex #5, 48. Ganga insisted that the trip had also been offered to him, but that all three preferred not to travel to Las Vegas. Only his wife took the trip after others insisted.

40. Calvert, "How to Buy the Olympics."

41. Swift, "Special Report"; Larry Siddons, "Ousted African Official Says IOC Rules Aimed at Angels and Saints," Associated Press, Mar. 15, 1999.

42. Mike Dodd, "Plot Against the Third World," *USA Today*, Mar. 16, 1999.

43. Roger Cohen and Jere Longman, "Master of the Games: Olympic Chief's Expansion Goals Left Little Zeal to Pursue Abuses," *New York Times*, Feb. 7, 1999.

44. Jere Longman, "African Expelled from IOC Lobbies for His Reinstatement," *New York Times*, Mar. 16, 1999.

45. *Minutes of the 108th Extraordinary IOC Session*, Annex #5, 47, 48.

46. Ibid., 49.

47. Powers and Zuckoff, "IOC Faces Its Day of Reckoning."

48. "Fourth IOC Official Resigns Amid Bribery Scandal." *Le Matin* is a Swiss daily newspaper.

49. *Minutes of the 108th Extraordinary IOC Session*, Annex #6, 50–52.

50. Ibid., Annex #7, 53–54.

51. Ibid., 55.

52. Board of Ethics, *Report to the Board of Trustees*, 37–38.

53. *Minutes of the 108th Extraordinary IOC Session*, Annex #7, 54–56.

54. Ibid., Annex #8, 57.

55. Board of Ethics, *Report to the Board of Trustees*, 15.

56. *Minutes of the 108th Extraordinary IOC Session*, Annex #8, 57.

57. Board of Ethics, *Report to the Board of Trustees*, 15.

58. *Minutes of the 108th Extraordinary IOC Session*, Annex #8, 58–60 (brackets added).

59. *Minutes of the 108th Extraordinary IOC Session*, 4–6.

60. Pound, *Inside the Olympics*, 219.

61. Drut experienced the "new reality" concerning IOC member conduct a number of years later. The IOC suspended Drut in late 2005 after he was found guilty in the French court

system of having accepted a "fictitious job" at a construction company in the early 1990s, a benefit that lasted for nearly three years. In 2006 France's President Jacques Chirac granted a presidential pardon to Drut, a gold medalist in the 110-meter hurdles in Montreal (1976), which permitted his return to the IOC. Drut had received a fifteen-month suspended sentence and a fine of sixty thousand dollars. "Guy Drut Given Presidential Pardon." Chirac claimed that Drut's return to the IOC was "fully essential for France and the defense of its interests in the domain of sports."

62. Pound, *Inside the Olympics*, 219.

63. *Minutes of the 108th Extraordinary IOC Session*, 5–6 (brackets added).

64. Ibid., 6–7.

65. Magnay, "Pound of Flesh" (see chap. 2, n. 15).

66. Christopher Clarey, "6 Olympic Officials Are Forced Out but the IOC President Receives a Convincing Vote of Confidence," *International Herald Tribune*, Mar. 18, 1999.

67. Glenda Korporaal, "Samaranch Smelling of Roses," *Sydney Morning Herald*, Mar. 19, 1999.

68. Ibid.; Bob Ford, "The Dirty Half-Dozen Hit Back at IOC Chiefs," *Daily Telegraph* (Sydney), Mar. 19, 1999.

69. "Extinguishing the Flame?"

70. "IOC Banishes Its Sullied Six; Samaranch Gets Vote of Confidence; Hints at Retirement," *Los Angeles Daily News*, Mar. 18, 1999 (brackets added).

71. Korporaal, "Samaranch Smelling of Roses"; Ford, "Dirty Half-Dozen Hit Back at IOC Chiefs."

72. The Coles saga, and in particular Australian reaction, is dealt with in detail by Doug Booth in Doug Booth, "Gifts of Corruption? Ambiguities of Obligation in the Olympic Movement."

73. Magnay, "Pound of Flesh."

74. Booth, "Gifts of Corruption?," 53–55. Coles allegedly accepted jewelry valued at more than A$9,000 for his ex-wife from an individual affiliated with the Athens 1996 bid committee and provided Salt Lake City bidders with dossiers on his IOC colleagues' characteristics and tendencies.

75. Pound, *Inside the Olympics*, 220.

76. Steven Downes, "Kim Will Dish Dirt on IOC to Save His Skin—Olympics," *Sunday Times* (London), Mar. 21, 1999 (brackets added).

77. Magnay, "Pound of Flesh."

78. Pound, *Inside the Olympics*, 220.

79. Lynn Zinser, "Official Quits and the IOC Avoids Expulsion Vote," *New York Times*, May 21, 2005; "Appeal by IOC Vice President Rejected," Associated Press Newswires, Sept. 17, 2004; "Appeals Court Upholds Conviction of IOC Vice President Kim," Agence France-Presse, Sept. 16, 2004; "Kim Un-Yong Gets 30 Months in Prison," *Korea Times* (Seoul), June 4, 2004. The Korean Olympic Commission pressured Kim for his resignation from the IOC

because it feared that his determination to fight Jacques Rogge and the Executive Board, which had voted thirteen to zero in February in support of his expulsion, would damage Pyeongchang's chances for the 2014 Olympic Winter Games. Korean government authorities later denied that Kim had been paroled after one year in prison in exchange for his resignation from the IOC. "Cheong Wa Dae Denies Alleged Involvement in Ex-IOC Deputy Head's Resignation," *Yonhap English News* (Seoul), June 22, 2005. In IOC documents, the fine was listed at approximately $763,000. *International Olympic Committee Ethics Commission, Decision Containing Recommendations N° D/01/05.*

80. Jere Longman, "Censure of Top Delegate Raises Doubts on Reform," *New York Times,* Mar. 13, 1999.

81. "Extinguishing the Flame?"

82. Booth, "Gifts of Corruption?," 66.

83. Korporaal, "Samaranch Smelling of Roses."

84. Ibid.

85. *Minutes of the 108th Extraordinary IOC Session,* 8. The composition of the electoral college and voting procedures are located in Annexes #9 (62–63) and #10 (64–65).

86. Ibid., 8–10.

87. Ibid., 11–12.

88. The proposed composition of the Ethics Commission and its terms of references are located in Annex #11 (66–68).

89. Slavkov was expelled by the IOC in Singapore (July 2005) following revelations that a BBC show, *Panorama,* filmed him on hidden camera discussing how votes could be bought for the 2012 Summer Olympics bid competition. "Despite His Defence, Slavkov Kicked Out of IOC," *Today* (Singapore), July 8, 2005.

90. For this series of interventions, see *Minutes of the 108th Extraordinary IOC Session,* 12–13.

91. Ibid., 13–14.

92. Ibid., 15. In 2011 the IOC Ethics Commission is comprised of nine members (including its chair), and no more than four of the Commission members may hold membership in the IOC. IOC members serving in this capacity as of May 2011 are Francisco Elizalde, Craig Reedie, Beckie Scott, and Leo Wallner.

93. Ibid., 15–16.

94. Ibid., 16.

95. Ibid., 17–18.

96. Ibid., 20–22. Kumar and Nyangweso asked for a forceful public statement of their lack of any involvement in corrupt activities. Both had been cleared of any wrongdoing by the Ad Hoc Commission and Executive Board. Kumar had been accused of accepting airfare compensation for a family member from Salt Lake City bidders. Salt Lake City investigators failed to note that "A. Kumar" as listed in their documents was, in fact, Kumar himself. Nyangweso completed an agreement before the 1993 vote on the site of the 2000 Olympic

Games with John Coates, president of the Australian Olympic Committee. The money was an extension of an existing agreement in support of African athletes. The money was duly transferred to the Ugandan NOC. Gosper and Pound confirmed that Nyangweso had been rapidly cleared of any wrongdoing; however, the media was not always quick to accept and publicize good news.

97. Bert Roughton and Melissa Turner, "As Reform's Shape Goes, So Will IOC's; Movement Faces Future in Which Its Business Will Be Conducted in Spotlight of the World's Scrutiny," *Atlanta Journal-Constitution*, Mar. 21, 1999.

98. Brennan as cited in Lisa Riley Roche, "IOC Event Fails to Live Up to Hype," *Deseret Morning News*, Mar. 21, 1999; Tom Knott, "Good Reform: Send Samaranch to Feed the Pigeons," *Washington Times*, Mar. 22, 1999; "Olympic Cleanup Falls Short of the Mark," *Toronto Star*, Mar. 20, 1999; "Lords of the Rings," *Sydney Morning Herald*, Mar. 20, 1999; Cathy Harasta, "IOC Cleanup Offers More of Usual Games," *Dallas Morning News*, Mar. 20, 1999 (brackets added).

99. Roche, "IOC Event Fails to Live Up to Hype" (parentheses in original). Roche wrote that "IOC officials sound frustrated when they try to defend the actions in the special session. One staffer compared the reform effort to turning the Titanic around. . . . [H]e said changing the course of the century-old institution with European sensibilities is going to take time."

## 5. Managing the Crisis

1. Payne interview (see introduction, n. 10).

2. "(Olympics) Sponsors and US Senator Rip Samaranch for Non-Reforms," Agence France-Presse, Mar. 19, 1999; See also "McD's Greenberg Sees Record Year, Vows to Support Olympics."

3. "IOC OKs Reform Plan; McCain Unimpressed," *Newark Star-Ledger*, Mar. 19, 1999.

4. Larry Siddons, "IOC to Meet with Sponsors for First Time Since Special Scandal Assembly," Associated Press, Mar. 29, 1999.

5. Larry Siddons, "Sponsors Seek Concessions for 'Damage' from Salt Lake Scandal," Associated Press, Mar. 30, 1999.

6. Chris Michaud, "IOC, Corporate Sponsors Meet to Discuss Changes," Reuters News, Mar. 30, 1999. The sponsors did press Pound and Payne for concessions such as enhanced access to street signage during the upcoming Sydney Olympics as a result of the scandal, but no commitments were received. Siddons, "Sponsors Seek Concession."

7. For examples of these letters from TOP sponsor officials, see Charles B. Fruit, vice president, director of media and marketing assets, Coca-Cola Company, to Pound, June 11, 1999; George Fisher, chairman and chief executive officer, Eastman Kodak Company, to Pound, May 10, 1999; and Jackie S. Woodward, director of global sports marketing, McDonald's Corporation, to Pound, Apr. 28, 1999, PFRWP.

8. "(Olympics) IOC Ethics Commission Members Named," Agence France-Presse, Apr. 9, 1999. Other individuals appointed to the commission were: IOC members Kéba Mbaye,

Kevan Gosper, and Chiharu Igaya and outside members Howard Baker (former US senator), Robert Badinter (French senator), Kurt Fürgler (former three-term president of Switzerland), and Charmaine Crooks (Canadian five-time Olympian and silver medalist in track and field in Los Angeles [1984]).

9. "Morals Clause to Give Sponsors an Out," Associated Press, Apr. 14, 1999. This clause provided the same rights to the IOC—to walk away from a sponsor if the sponsor's business practices damaged the Olympic brand. M. Payne, *Olympic Turnaround*, 240.

10. Mike Gorrell, "IOC Attempts to Move Forward," *Salt Lake Tribune*, Mar. 19, 1999; "IOC Opens Its Books to the Public," *Pittsburgh Post-Gazette*, Mar. 19, 1999. As of December 1998, an interim financial report revealed the IOC's net worth to be $136 million. Samaranch received no salary, but his living expenses for 1998 totaled $204,000. Executive Board members received $1,000 for expenses tied to attending a scheduled meeting, not including first-class travel, meal, and accommodation costs, which were also covered. IOC members were also flown first class to general Session meetings and had their accommodation costs covered, but received a meal allowance for breakfast only. They received a per diem allowance of $105 when attending a meeting in Lausanne and $150 when meetings were held away from Lausanne.

11. Booth, "Lobbying Orgies," 212. Only one of the trips occurred while Salt Lake City was a candidate city.

12. Magnay, "Pound of Flesh" (see chap. 2, n. 15).

13. Ibid. Some IOC members challenged this finding by the Ad Hoc Commission. They claimed he asked Tom Welch to arrange for accommodations for his daughter and son-in-law for a vacation in early 1995.

14. Booth, "Gifts of Corruption?," 53, 52. Coates eventually sided with those individuals seeking Coles's resignation. John Zubrzycki, David Tanner, and Trudy Harris, "Games Chief Dumps Coles—Now Even Coates Backs Call to Quit," *Australian* (Sydney), May 6, 1999.

15. "Coles Must Make the Final Sacrifice," *Sun-Herald* (Sydney), Mar. 14, 1999.

16. "(Olympics) Fax Links IOC member to Corruption Probe," Agence France-Presse, Mar. 19, 1999; Michael Millett and Jacquelin Magnay, "Revealed: The Jewels Coles Has Never Seen," *Age* (Melbourne), Mar. 19, 1999; Stephen Wilson, "IOC to Investigate Jewelry Claims," *AP Online*, Mar. 19, 1999.

17. Jacquelin Magnay, "Ex-Wife Turns Up Heat on Coles," *Age* (Melbourne), Mar. 20, 1999.

18. John Salvado, "OLY—Coles Finally Moves onto the Front Foot," Australian Associated Press, May 6, 1999. Coles broke down during a radio interview with Radio 2UE's John Laws.

19. "OLY—Knight Seeks Documents," Australian Associated Press, May 4, 1999; "Time to Go Says Knight," *Daily Telegraph* (Sydney), May 5, 1999; Martin Parry, "(Olympics) Prime Minister Wades into Olympic Scandal," Agence France-Presse, May 6, 1999; Zubrzycki, Tanner, and Harris, "Games Chief Dumps Coles."

20. Bruce McDougall and Tom Salom, "It's a Conspiracy—Coles," *Daily Telegraph* (Sydney), Mar. 24, 1999. A number of businessmen who held positions on the Melbourne bid committee including John Ralph, Ron Walker, and Peter Clemenger summarily dismissed Coles's claim. See also Russ Bynum, "Australian Olympic Official Responds," *AP Online*, May 6, 1999.

21. Krystyna Rudzki, "OLY—Fahey Tells Knight to Change Law to Get Rid of Coles," Australian Associated Press, May 9, 1999.

22. Booth, "Gifts of Corruption?," 54.

23. Matthew Moore, "And the Loser Is," *Sydney Morning Herald*, May 8, 1999. For Coles's denials, see also Jacquelin Magnay and Lyall Johnson, "Coles Defiant as Critics Close In," *Age* (Melbourne), May 7, 1999; Salvado, "OLY—Coles Finally Moves onto the Front Foot."

24. Ibid. Coles and his detractors debated the number of Sydney officials who had access to the files. Any of some forty individuals, claimed Coles, might have slipped the files to Salt Lake City, but others such as Michael Knight indicated that the confidential files would have been available to a much more select group of people, including Coles. "OLY—Knight Seeks Documents"; Sophie Tedmanson, "We Were Betrayed, Says Bid Worker," *Daily Telegraph* (Sydney), May 6, 1999.

25. Moore, "And the Loser Is."

26. Michael Evans and Glenda Korporaal, "Knight to Release Coles Dossiers," *Sydney Morning Herald*, May 12, 1999; Stephen Wilson, "IOC Member Offered a Compromise," *AP Online*, June 13, 1999.

27. Steve Penells, "Furore over Coles' Calls to Atlanta," *West Australian* (Perth), May 7, 1999.

28. "US Bid Clue Leads to Mystery," *Australian* (Sydney), May 6, 1999.

29. Philippe Naughton, "Olympics: IOC's Coles Tells Sydney—Give Me a Fair Go," Reuters News, May 5, 1999.

30. Parry, "(Olympics) Prime Minister Wades into Olympic Scandal"; Wayne Smith, "Coles Claims Games Plot," *Courier-Mail* (Brisbane), May 6, 1999. Coles's appearance at the International Triathlon World Cup event in Sydney in early May is illustrative of his troubles and damaged image. International Triathlon Union executives informed Coles, who was scheduled to award the women's event gold medal, that his duties had been reassigned. ITU officials ignored his presence during the event, and he remained isolated in a corporate compound, kept company by Doug Donaghue, a member of the Australian Olympic Committee's Board, and SOCOG member Bob Elphinston. One ITU official commented, "Never before have I seen Phil looking for someone to talk to." Jacquelin Magnay and Glenda Korporaal, "Coles Left Out on Cold as IOC Meets to Determine His Fate," *Sydney Morning Herald*, May 3, 1999.

31. Philip Hersh, "Major Sponsor Blasts IOC Reforms," *Chicago Tribune*, May 5, 1999. This article was sent to Pound by Michael Payne. See M. Payne to Pound, May 11, 1999, PFRWP.

32. "John Hancock Urges IOC Resignation," *AP Online*, Mar. 22, 1999.

33. Hersh, "Major Sponsor Blasts IOC Reforms."

34. Stephen Wilson, "NBC Sports Chief Dick Ebersol Rips John Hancock Boss," Associated Press, June 1, 1999. D'Alessandro sent this AP report to Pound along with a fax message. See D'Alessandro to Pound, June 1, 1999, PFRWP.

35. Amy Shipley, "Sponsor Pushing for IOC Reforms," *Washington Post*, Apr. 21, 1999.

36. "'Phooey,' Romney Says of John Hancock Poll," Associated Press Newswires, May 13, 1999.

37. M. Payne to Pound, May 11, 1999.

38. Pound to D'Alessandro, May 10, 1999, PFRWP. Pound did not agree with the decision to expand the size of the IOC 2000 Commission, but did not share these thoughts with D'Alessandro. Samaranch believed the only means of facilitating the passage of the reform proposals involved appointing more rank-and-file IOC members to the IOC 2000 Commission. The media's reaction, stated Pound, would be severe, as the IOC would be seen to be diminishing the influence of non-IOC members on the reform process. Pound to Samaranch, Apr. 19, 1999, PFRWP.

39. Ibid. (brackets added).

40. Ibid.

41. D'Alessandro to Pound, May 19, 1999, PFRWP.

42. Ibid. D'Alessandro believed that the IOC should begin its search for Samaranch's replacement (without suggesting an immediate change) and that the organization should submit itself to the Anti-Bribery Convention of the Organization for Economic Cooperation and Development. The latter action would permit legal action against those persons who tried to bribe IOC members, as the IOC members themselves would be designated foreign public officials.

43. Pound to D'Alessandro, May 21, 1999, PFRWP.

44. Ibid.

45. D'Alessandro to Pound, May 24, 1999, PFRWP.

46. Ibid. D'Alessandro referenced a phone conversation with Pound in the letter.

47. Ibid.

48. Ibid.

49. Pound to D'Alessandro, May 28, 1999, PFRWP.

50. Ibid.

51. The original draft and final copy of D'Alessandro's article "The Games Must Go On" are located in PFRWP.

52. Richard Sandomir, "Ebersol Defends His Investment from Scandal-Induced Criticism," *New York Times*, June 2, 1999.

53. Stephen Wilson, "NBC Sports Chief Assails Sponsor," *AP Online*, June 1, 1999.

54. D'Alessandro to Pound, June 1, 1999, PFRWP. For an overview of the dispute, see Paul Tharp, "NBC, John Hancock in Olympic Feud," *New York Post*, June 2, 1999; and Gregg

Krupa, "NBC Chief Again Hits Hancock: Questions Motive for Olympic Reform Call," *Boston Globe*, June 4, 1999.

55. Wilson, "NBC Sports Chief Assails Sponsor."

56. Sandomir, "Ebersol Defends His Investment."

57. "John Hancock Ready to Talk to NBC."

58. Rosemary Windsor-Williams to Pound, Apr. 30, 1999, PFRWP.

59. Nancy J. Wiese to Pound, May 13, 1999, PFRWP; D'Alessandro to Pound, May 19, 1999.

60. Woodward to Pound, Apr. 28, 1999.

61. Fisher to Pound, May 10, 1999.

62. This concern can be clearly inferred from Pound's response to a letter received from Carl F. Gustin Jr., Kodak's senior vice president and chief marketing officer. Pound to Gustin, May 31, 1999, PFRWP.

63. Fisher to Pound, May 10, 1999.

64. Fruit to Pound, June 11, 1999.

65. Michael J. Klingensmith to Pound, May 21, 1999, PFRWP; Pound to Klingensmith, May 31, 1999; Pound to Fisher, May 13, 1999; Pound to Windsor-Williams, May 21, 1999; Pound to Nancy J. Wiese, May 31, 1999; Pound to Woodward, June 3, 1999; Pound to Fruit, June 21, 1999, PFRWP.

66. Stephen Wilson, "IOC Launches Post-Scandal Reform Process," Associated Press Newswires, May 31, 1999.

67. Barney, Wenn, and Martyn, *Selling the Five Rings*, 159, 165.

68. Ibid., 168–75.

69. The USOC benefited for the first time from this enhanced share in conjunction with money distributed from TOP III (1993–96).

70. Pound to Samaranch, Sept. 26, 30, 1985, "Seoul 1988 TV-General 1985 II" File, IOCA.

71. The IOC and the Seoul and Calgary Organizing Committees each contributed five million dollars to facilitate the fifteen-million-dollar payment. For details on the genesis of the BMA, see Barney, Wenn, and Martyn, *Selling the Five Rings*, 211–26.

72. "Because of fears during the late 1800s that monopolies dominated America's free market economy, Congress passed the Sherman Antitrust Act in 1890 to combat anticompetitive practices, reduce market domination by individual corporations, and preserve unfettered competition as the rule of trade." Under section 2 of the act, signed into law by President Benjamin Harrison, collusive bidding is banned. Cornell University Law School, "Antitrust: An Overview." In order for the television networks to submit a pooled bid, a strategy underpinned by an agreement to share the rights to an Olympic festival, they required relief from the Sherman Antitrust Act. The US television networks contemplated such an approach to government authorities during protracted and frustrating negotiations with Soviet organizers of the 1980 Moscow Olympic Games. Network executives were incensed by the price that the

Soviets sought to exact from the US market. The Columbia Broadcasting System (CBS) was the first to withdraw from the process involved in obtaining a waiver and abandoned its effort to acquire the US television rights. The NBC and ABC were left to battle for the Moscow television rights when the pooled-bid approach collapsed following CBS's withdrawal. NBC captured the television rights for eighty-five million dollars. Barney, Wenn, and Martyn, *Selling the Five Rings*, 138–45.

73. Barney, Wenn, and Martyn, *Selling the Five Rings*, 247–48.

74. Ibid., 248–50. Pound understood that the IOC had created the environment that might result in the collaboration of politicians, the USOC, and US television network executives. The IOC's pursuit of maximum television revenue from the US market (in negotiations led by Pound) and the glaring absence of such an approach in negotiations with European television officials (managed by Samaranch) angered American officials. Pound used the near disaster of the McMillen bill to press Samaranch to increase the sum of money accruing from future European television contracts.

75. Ibid., 254–59, 261–62.

76. Ibid., 263.

77. Pound to the authors, May 12, 1999.

78. *Minutes of the Meeting of the IOC Executive Board* (Oct. 5–10, 1996), 15–16. The financial impact of this decision was mitigated by a parallel decision to elevate the IOC's share of Olympic television revenue to 51 percent from the previously assigned 40 percent beginning in 2004. Barney, Wenn, and Martyn, *Selling the Five Rings*, 260–61. The IOC's 51 percent share was apportioned in equal 12.75 percent shares to the IOC, USOC, NOCs, and ISFs.

79. "(Olympics) Sponsors and US Senator Rip Samaranch"; Randy Harvey, "Unimpressed McCain Keeps Heat on IOC," *Los Angeles Times*, Mar. 19, 1999; "Senator John McCain Statement, Chairman of the Committee on Commerce, Science, and Transportation, Investigation of Olympic Scandals Hearing."

80. "Statement of Senator George J. Mitchell, Chairman of the Special Bid Oversight Commission of the United States Olympic Committee Before the Committee on Commerce, Science, and Transportation."

81. Jim Slater, "(Olympics) Samaranch Refuses to Testify at US Hearing on IOC Scandal," Agence France-Presse, Mar. 30, 1999.

82. Jason Nisse, "Marketing Man's Olympian Feat of Crisis Management—Business of Sport—Interview—Michael Payne," *Times* (London), Apr. 14, 1999.

83. Stevens ran into legal difficulties in July 2008 when he was indicted for failing to report a relationship with Veco Energy on his Senate disclosure forms. The company allegedly paid for extensive renovations to his home, while at the same time Veco captured a number of federal contracts with Stevens's assistance. Having served in the US Senate for forty years, Stevens's indictment was big news in Washington. "Grand Jury Indicts Alaska Senator"; David Stout and David M. Herszenhorn, "Alaska Senator Is Indicted on Corruption Charges," *New*

*York Times*, July 29, 2008, http://www.nytimes.com/2008/07/30/washington/30stevens.html. In an interesting twist, Stevens, who lost his bid for reelection to the Senate in November 2008, was relieved of his legal problems in April 2009 when federal judge Emmet Sullivan set aside his October 2008 conviction because of suspected prosecutorial misconduct. The US attorney general, Eric Holder, dismissed Stevens's indictment and indicated that the government would not pursue a new trial. "Sen. Ted Stevens' Conviction Set Aside." Stevens died in a plane crash on August 9, 2010.

84. Stephen Wilson, "Europeans Chafe at Olympic Policy," *AP Online*, Apr. 23, 1999. See also Christopher P. Lu, counsel, Democratic staff, to D'Alessandro, May 18, 1999; and *Summary of the International Olympic Committee Reform Act of 1999*. The Sydney, Salt Lake City, and Athens festivals were exempt from the bipartisan legislation proposed by Waxman and Lazio.

85. "American IOC Member Criticizes U.S. Politicians," *Las Vegas Sentinel-Review*, Mar. 21, 1999. Possible actions in Washington might very well have privileged the USOC in terms of the distribution of Olympic revenue. Given the friction between the IOC and USOC, it might seem odd that an American Olympic leader would adopt this critical posture. One must recall that as a result of the IOC's tradition of co-opting members, an American member, such as Easton, represents the IOC in the United States, not the USOC in Lausanne.

86. Amy Shipley, "With Senate Hearing Set, IOC Member Apologizes to McCain," *Washington Post*, Apr. 11, 1999.

87. Larry Siddons, "Panel: IOC Doing OK on Reform," *AP Online*, Apr. 11, 1999. Mitchell's fellow committee members Donald Fehr, Jeff Benz, and Roberta Cooper Ramo delivered similar messages to the press in the days before McCain's Senate committee's hearings.

88. "Statement of Senator George J. Mitchell."

89. Larry Siddons, "Senate Panel Lashes IOC," *AP Online*, Apr. 14, 1999.

90. "Senator John McCain Statement."

91. *Minutes of the Meeting of the IOC Executive Board* (May 4, 1999), 16–17. For McCain's request, see McCain to Samaranch, Apr. 20, 1999, Annex #8, 55; and Linda Fantin, "McCain Wants Samaranch to Send Monthly Reports: Claims 'Significant Skepticism' by American People," *Salt Lake Tribune*, Apr. 21, 1999.

92. George Vecsey, "Samaranch Wise to Duck the Senator," *New York Times*, Apr. 15, 1999. See also Greg Gatlin and Ralph Ranalli, "McCain: Give Olympic Committee Some Time Before Revoking Tax Exempt Status," *Boston Herald*, Apr. 24, 1999.

93. *Minutes of the Meeting of the IOC Executive Board* (Feb. 1, 1999), 13–14.

94. *Minutes of the Meeting of the IOC Executive Board* (Mar. 15–16, 19, 1999), 47–49.

95. Mallon, "The Olympic Bribery Scandal," 18–20; *Statutes of the IOC Ethics Commission*; "IOC Approves New Rule on 'Nominal Value' Gifts," Associated Press Newswires, June 20, 1999.

96. While originally ensnared in the Italian match-fixing scandal in 2006, Franco Carraro, who served as the president of the Italian Football Federation at the time, received no

sanction from the IOC Ethics Commission. Carraro resigned his post with the FIGC. The FIGC's tribunal found him guilty of attempting to alter the results of a match and precluded him from serving the FIGC in an administrative capacity for four and a half years. On appeal Carraro's penalty was reduced to a warning plus an €80,000 fine. Carraro appealed this decision to the Italian Olympic Committee, which indicated it had no jurisdiction to address the fine, but concluded that Carraro's activities "fell within the complete politico-administrative discretion of the Federal Chairman." CONI dismissed the warning, but took no action with respect to the fine. Carraro pursued relief in the Regional Administrative Court of Latium, but requested a decision from the IOC Ethics Commission in light of CONI's decision. *International Olympic Committee Ethics Commission, Decision N° D/04/06.* On the recommendation of the Ethics Commission in 2006, the IOC Executive Board issued a reprimand to France's Guy Drut and suspended his right to chair any IOC commission for five years. The Paris Criminal Court found Drut guilty of holding a fictitious job between 1990 and 1992 with a company caught up in a corruption probe regarding the distribution of construction projects in the Ile de France region. He received a sentence of fifteen months (suspended) and a €50,000 fine. When the case was first brought to the Ethics Commission in 2005, Drut's IOC membership was suspended. He then successfully pursued an amnesty decree from the French president, Jacques Chirac, who proclaimed the decision necessary in order to retain Drut's IOC seat for France. *International Olympic Committee Ethics Commission, Decision on Interim Measures N° D/06/05; International Olympic Committee Ethics Commission, Decision with recommendations N° D/02/06;* "Drut Given Presidential Pardon." The IOC Session expelled Mohamed (Bob) Hasan, an IOC member from Indonesia, on the recommendation of the Ethics Commission and Executive Board in 2004 as a result of embezzling $134 million and $87 million in 1989 and 1996, respectively. Hasan, chairman of the Indonesian Forest Concessionaires Association, funneled the money to Mapindo, a company in which he had a 51 percent ownership share. *International Olympic Committee Ethics Commission, Decision N° D/01/02;* "IOC Expel Indonesian Member," *BBC Online,* Aug. 10, 2004, http://news.bbc.co.uk/sport1/hi/olympics_2004/3551430.stm. On June 3, 2004, the Seoul Central District Court sentenced Un Yong Kim to two and a half years in jail and fined him a sum of approximately $763,000 as a result of his guilt on embezzlement and corruption charges regarding the World Taekwondo Federation, the "Kukkiwon" (headquarters of the WTF), and the General Assembly of International Sports Federations. On appeal the jail term was reduced to two years. Kim resigned from the IOC before the Session considered the recommendation for his expulsion at the 117th IOC Session in Singapore in 2005. He was paroled shortly after submitting his resignation. *International Olympic Committee Ethics Commission, Decision Containing Recommendations N° D/01/05;* Zinser, "Official Quits and the IOC Avoids Expulsion Vote"; "Cheong Wa Dae Denies Alleged Involvement" (see chap. 4, n. 79). In some respects, the case of South Korea's Yong Sung Park paralleled the case of Guy Drut in terms of its process. In February 2006, Park received a three-year jail term (suspended for five years) and a fine of approximately $8 million as a result of having embezzled, along with a number of other officials and family members, approximately $32 million from the Doosan Group. He served as the conglomerate's chairman at the time of the criminal acts between 2001 and 2004. The IOC Ethics Commission suspended his IOC membership three days after the release of the court's decision. When the Seoul High Court upheld the original decision in July 2006, Park submitted an amnesty request to the president of South Korea. The jail term was eliminated as a result of the amnesty decree issued by Roh Moo-hyun in February 2007. Realizing that the withdrawal of the sentence did nothing to remove from the record the acts committed, the Ethics Commission issued a reprimand and suspended his right to serve on any IOC commission for a five-year term. *International Olympic Committee Ethics Commission, Decision with Recommendations N° D/02/07.* On two occasions, the Executive Board, through recommendations of the Ethics Commission, "reminded" Richard Pound to temper his public comments concerning allegations of doping violations by athletes whose guilt had not been established (Lance Armstrong and Floyd Landis). In the case of Armstrong's complaint, the Ethics Commission recommended that "the Executive Board remind Mr Richard Pound, IOC member, of the obligation to exercise greater prudence consistent with the Olympic spirit when making public pronouncements that may affect the reputation of others." *International Olympic Committee Ethics Commission, Decision with Recommendations N° D/01/07; International Olympic Committee Ethics Commission, Decision with Recommendations N° D/01/08.* Henri Sérandour, the president of the French National Olympic Committee (CNOSF) from 1993 to 2008, whose IOC membership expired at the close of 2007 because he reached the retirement age of seventy, received a reprimand from the Ethics Commission and a suspension of his right to sit on any IOC commission for five years in October 2007. The Executive Board approved the recommendation in December 2007. The sanctions stemmed from the Paris Regional Court's decision in October 2006 that Sérandour awarded the firm Les Pléiades two (CNOSF) contracts without a required bid or tender process. Sérandour took unilateral decisions to award these contracts to the company, which also happened to have recently employed his wife (March 2001). He contracted Les Pléiades to produce a mural of French Olympic medalists (April 2001) and to revise and maintain the CNOSF's website (June 2001). The court imposed a three-month suspended jail term and a €20,000 fine in October 2006. The Ethics Commission took action at the point he abandoned his appeal of the court's decision in September 2007. *International Olympic Committee Ethics Commission, Decision with Recommendations N° D/03/07.* Ivan Slakov was expelled from the IOC in 2005 following an investigation by the Ethics Commission into his contact with self-styled Olympic agent Goran Takac and an interview caught on a hidden camera by an undercover production team from the British Broadcasting Corporation in which the two discussed ways in which they could influence IOC member votes. The interview with individuals posing as representatives of London's East End business community who had a vested interest in London's capturing the Olympics in 2012 was televised on the *Panorama* show in early August 2004. *International Olympic Committee Ethics Commission, Decision with Recommendations N° D5/04.* John Krimsky, the USOC's former deputy secretary general and managing director of business affairs (1986–99), who represented that organization in its negotiations with the

IOC's Richard Pound concerning Olympic revenues in the late 1980s and 1990s, resigned his seat on the IOC's Olympic Philately, Numismatics, and Memorabilia Commission in December 2007. Krimsky faced child pornography charges in the United States. He elected to resign before the Ethics Commission considered a suspension of his committee membership. *International Olympic Committee Ethics Commission, Decision with Recommendations Nᵒ D04/07*; "Former USOC Fundraiser Faces Child Pornography Charges," *USA Today.com*, Dec. 6, 2007, http://usatoday.com/sports/olympics/2007–12–06–264044991_x.htm.

97. Pound to Samaranch, Apr. 19, 1999. Participative leadership as defined by Johns and Saks involves permitting employees' input regarding "work-related decisions" as a means of improving the motivation of one's workforce and the quality of its work and enhancing the possibility that employees will accept change. Gary Johns and Alan M. Saks, *Organizational Behaviour: Understanding and Managing Life at Work*, 283. In drawing together matters on the IOC's timeline concerning its work in establishing the IOC Ethics and 2000 Commissions, the authors were assisted by Stephanie Eckert. See Eckert, "Reforming the Rings: An Evaluation of the IOC's Reform Process Following the Salt Lake City Bid Scandal."

98. Ibid. Samaranch was indebted to Richard Pound for his industriousness concerning the television and corporate sponsorship portfolios during his presidency. Pound's labors played a significant role in furthering Samaranch's effort to transform the financial basis of the Olympic Movement. He also understood Pound's credibility with the international media. This reality and Pound's demonstrated ability to tackle difficult jobs explain his selection of Pound to lead the IOC's internal investigation of the Salt Lake City scenario. There are two schools of thought with respect to Samaranch's decision to impose himself on the presidential campaign staged in 2001 for the purpose of electing his successor. First, Pound scuttled his own aspirations by opposing Samaranch's effort to raise the mandatory retirement age of IOC members in 1995 so that he could extend his presidency. Samaranch abandoned any thought of supporting Pound in the future, and he moved over time in the direction of grooming his successor, and the individual he selected was Jacques Rogge. He assisted Rogge in elevating his profile, given that he had only been on the IOC since 1991, by assigning him the task of chairing the Co-ordination Commission for the 2000 Sydney Olympic Games and ushering him onto the IOC Executive Board. The second line of thinking is that Samaranch had made no such determination by 1999 about whom he might support in the future. If so, it is clear that while Samaranch greatly respected Pound's abilities, episodes such as their difference of opinion concerning the composition of the IOC 2000 Commission further compounded Samaranch's thinking that Pound lacked the nuanced sense of diplomacy that he believed central to the leadership of the IOC. It was just one more example, for Samaranch, of why Pound was not the appropriate individual to support when the IOC members would eventually search for his successor.

99. *Minutes of the Meeting of the IOC Executive Board* (May 4, 1999), 2–4.

100. Pound to Samaranch, Apr. 19, 1999.

101. *Minutes of the Meeting of the IOC Executive Board* (May 4, 1999), 8.

102. Ibid., 34; *Report by the IOC 2000 Commission to the 110th IOC Session.*

103. *Report by the IOC 2000 Commission,* 1–2.

104. Duncan MacKay, "Samaranch Again under Fire after Turin Decision," *Irish Times* (Dublin), June 21, 1999; Clare Nullis, "Much Soul-Searching for Swiss after Olympic Loss," Associated Press Newswires, June 22, 1999. Turin defeated Sion fifty-three to thirty-six for the right to host the 2002 Olympic Winter Games. The vote was held at the IOC's 109th IOC Session in Seoul in June.

### 6. Back from the Abyss

1. Michael Evans and Jacquelin Magnay, "The Final Fall of Phil Coles," *Sydney Morning Herald,* June 15, 1999; Keith Tremayne, "Olympics Chiefs Abandon Coles—Calls for His Resignation," *Hobart Mercury* (Australia), May 6, 1999. In April 1999, SOCOG cut A$75 million from its budget in light of difficulties securing corporate support in a negotiating environment compromised by the Salt Lake City scandal. SOCOG lowered its sponsorship target from A$863 million to A$813 million and raised its contingency fund by A$25 million. SOCOG had successfully signed sponsorship deals totaling A$643 million, so the challenge involved the need to locate the remaining A$170 million. "Over the past few months," stated Michael Knight, "the focus in the media and elsewhere on the IOC problems has left us with a period that was incredibly difficult to pitch to sponsors." Jacquelin Magnay, "$75M Slashed from Olympic Spending," *Age* (Melbourne), Apr. 23, 1999. The IOC countered that Sydney's original sponsorship target was ambitious, and the IOC questioned its decision to raise its target by an additional $100 million. Pound succinctly summarized the IOC's opinion in a letter to John Hancock's David D'Alessandro. Sydney was using the scandal as a means of dealing with domestic criticism. The IOC informed Sydney that the elevated target figure could be achieved, "if at all, only at the expense of clutter, lower levels of sponsor service and by impinging on the edges of categories already granted, thus diminishing the assurances given to the original waves of sponsors. You [D'Alessandro] have experienced some of the effects of this already. SOCOG recognized the problem with this budget last summer, not as a result of the current troubles. This is a domestic 'political' budget and the political escape route has now been to blame the IOC for a problem that was SOCOG-created in the first place." Pound to D'Alessandro, May 28, 1999, PFRWP (brackets added).

2. Erskine McCullough, "Beleaguered Aussie IOC Member Escapes Expulsion over Salt Lake Scandal," Agence France-Presse, June 14, 1999.

3. Evans and Magnay, "Final Fall of Phil Coles."

4. McCullough, "Beleaguered Aussie IOC Member Escapes Expulsion."

5. Jacquelin Magnay, "You Know It's Over When Juan Won't Take Your Call," *Sydney Morning Herald,* June 15, 1999.

6. McCullough, "Beleaguered Aussie IOC Member Escapes Expulsion."

7. Magnay, "You Know It's Over When Juan Won't Take Your Call." In a less than ringing endorsement of his IOC colleagues, Pound informed Sydney's *Daily Telegraph* that "there

wouldn't be too many IOC members around" if expulsion awaited those persons who collected "information on fellow delegates to help Games bid committees." Lee Benson, "IOC Waited for the Time to Hit Back," *Deseret News*, June 21, 1999.

8. Magnay, "You Know It's Over When Juan Won't Take Your Call."

9. Jacquelin Magnay, "IOC's Cold War," *Sydney Morning Herald*, June 19, 1999.

10. Jacquelin Magnay and Matthew Moore, "Phil Coles Sin—Binned," *Sydney Morning Herald*, June 15, 1999. For a sympathetic view of Coles and his conduct, one that qualifies as an effort to "rehabilitate" the Australian IOC member, according to Gordon MacDonald, see Gordon, *Time of Our Lives*, 109–26. See also Gordon MacDonald, review of *Time of Our Lives* by Gordon, 104. In exchange for his resignation as director of international relations for the AOC, Coles received one year's salary and allowances. Gordon, *Time of Our Lives*, 121.

11. McCullough, "Beleaguered Aussie IOC Member Escapes Expulsion." Coles's discomfort and embarrassment were compounded the following year when controversy flared up in relation to his role in the Olympic torch relay. In October 1999, Coles learned he would carry the flame along Sydney's iconic Bondi Beach, a veritable second home for Coles, who had celebrated a fifty-year membership in the North Bondi Surf Club. In July 2000, the plans changed. Coles was informed he would not have this responsibility, but he would carry the flame on some of the Bondi neighborhood's streets. Harry Gordon refers to this decision on the part of torch-relay organizers, and by extension SOCOG, as "petty and spiteful." Australian talk radio was consumed with discussion of the issue for a number of days and eventually the SOCOG Board in a six-to-five decision, with Michael Knight and Kevan Gosper abstaining, determined that Coles would be accorded the honor of carrying the torch along the beach with a stopping point in front of the North Bondi Surf Club. On September 14, 2000, Coles carried the torch aloft at this location before a crowd numbering some fifty thousand. Gordon, *Time of Our Lives*, 123–26.

12. *Minutes of the Meeting of the IOC Executive Board* (June 13–15, 1999), 6–8.

13. Randy Starkman, "Fear of FBI Overstated: Pound," *Toronto Star*, June 19, 1999.

14. *Minutes of the Meeting of the IOC Executive Board* (June 13–15, 1999), 30, 31.

15. Ibid., 31. By the fall, Pound envisioned that a deal with John Hancock might send a very positive message to those people monitoring the IOC's reform process. "Notwithstanding the remarks by the CEO of John Hancock earlier in the year, a renewal could, correctly positioned, send an important and positive signal to the market place on the overall 'Olympic Recovery.'" *Minutes of the Meeting of the IOC Executive Board* (Oct. 1–4, 1999), 30. Pound had responded to Gosper's observation that D'Alessandro was a "fair weather friend."

16. David D'Alessandro, "Sponsors Must Keep the IOC's Feet to the Fire," *Sydney Morning Herald*, June 8, 1999.

17. There is little doubt that the possibility of John Hancock's continued sponsorship of the Olympic Movement was a keenly debated subject in IOC marketing circles and had been for a period of time. In an e-mail dated May 12 to Pound, Payne, and Chris Welton, Meridian Management's Terrence Burns expressed his suspicion that John Hancock was trying to step

back from a TOP V (2001–4) deal in order to pursue a sponsorship agreement directly with Salt Lake City. "Now, more than ever," wrote Burns, "we have to pre-empt them and go our separate ways." He predicted a "PR battle royale" if this path was followed, but believed the IOC would have the silent support of other TOP partners. The IOC would not approve any sponsorship deals with John Hancock and could defend the decision by stating that "TOP is an elite club and not all companies have the wisdom or wherewithal to be players in the Game, and from time to time, we will trim associations which do not further our brand development goals." He conceded his was a "rather strong position—but, why wait for them to make us look like chumps, and, why give them SLC as an opportunity on a silver platter?" Burns to Pound, Payne, and Welton, May 12, 1999, PFRWP. Michael Payne still harbored a good deal of resentment for D'Alessandro's frequent public criticism and condemnation of the IOC's reform efforts. Payne expressed his frustrations to John Hancock's vice president of corporate communications, Stephen Burgay. D'Alessandro's comments "have created significant damage to the Olympic Movement around the world, but that is a cross we are obliged, for the time being, to bear. . . . Hopefully, in time, David and you will both recognise that the IOC has responded decisively and extremely quickly to the developments of the beginning of the year. The reforms will be far-reaching, and, the Olympic Movement and the IOC will come through these difficult times as a far stronger and better organisation. . . . Once the dust settles, I hope that we will be able to have a drink together, and focus on building and promoting the Olympic Movement, not tearing it down." Payne to Burgay, June 15, 1999, PFRWP.

18. Samaranch banned bid city visits in light of the revelations concerning Salt Lake City in December 1998, a decision opposed by all six cities who claimed that voters needed to experience a city in order to understand its vision for the Games as well as its ability to organize them. Erskine McCullough, "Olympic Bidders in 60 Minute Gamble," Agence France-Presse, June 18, 1999.

19. Mike Gorrell, "Tale of Two Cities: Turin, Sion in Close Contest for 2006 Winter Games," Salt Lake Tribune, June 19, 1999.

20. Reid G. Miller, "Italy's Turin Wins 2006 Winter Olympics," Associated Press Newswires, June 19, 1999.

21. Mike Gorrell, "2006 Upset Vote Adds to IOC Mess," Salt Lake Tribune, June 20, 1999.

22. Miller, "Italy's Turin Wins 2006 Winter Olympics."

23. Gorrell, "2006 Upset Vote Adds to IOC Mess."

24. Minutes of the 109th IOC Session, 1–5.

25. Larry Siddons, "McCain Vows to Keep Nose Inside Samaranch's Tent," Deseret News, June 27, 1999.

26. "Atlanta Admits Wrong Doings: Organizers Might Have Broken Three Other Laws."

27. Melissa Turner, "Payne's Foundation Reveals Gifts Given to IOC Members: Report to Congress Lists More than 3 Dozen Items Exceeding Limits," Atlanta Journal-Constitution, June 2, 1999.

28. "Atlanta Admits Wrong Doings"; Turner, "Payne's Foundation Reveals Gifts."

29. "Atlanta Releases Dossiers on 'Sleaze Bags' at IOC," *Salt Lake Tribune*, Sept. 18, 1999.

30. Ibid.

31. Linda Fantin, "Samaranch a Witness in Atlanta Investigation?," *Salt Lake Tribune*, Sept. 22, 1999; "IOC Says It'll Hold Off Deciding If Samaranch Will Testify in D.C.," *Deseret News*, Sept. 23, 1999.

32. "IOC Says It'll Hold Off Deciding."

33. David Pace, "House Chairman Will Push IOC to Clean Up Its Act," Associated Press Newswires, Sept. 21, 1999.

34. *Minutes of the Meeting of the IOC Executive Board* (Oct. 1–4, 1999), 8–10.

35. Ibid., 10, 20 (brackets added).

36. "Samaranch to Go to USA in December," Agence France-Presse, Oct. 3, 1999.

37. "US Congressman Meets with IOC's Carrard but Nothing Set for Samaranch," Agence France-Presse, Oct. 7, 1999.

38. Lee Davidson, "Congress Threatens IOC If Major Reforms Aren't Enacted," *Deseret News*, Oct. 15, 1999; David Pace, "Panel Questions Olympic Committee Commitment to Reform," Associated Press Newswires, Oct. 14, 1999.

39. Davidson, "Congress Threatens IOC"; Pace, "Panel Questions Olympic Committee Commitment."

40. Lee Davidson, "IOC 'Culture of Corruption' Attacked," *Deseret News*, Oct. 14, 1999.

41. Davidson, "Congress Threatens IOC."

42. John McCain, who earlier pledged to hold off further action until the close of the IOC Session in December, called for a hearing of the Senate Committee on Commerce, Science, and Transportation on October 20 to apply pressure on the IOC. McCain responded to news that the IOC might postpone its December Session until 2000. Mark Tewksbury, a Canadian athlete and Olympic gold medalist (Barcelona, 1992), was the point person for OATH (Olympic Advocates Together Honorably), an organization dedicated to IOC reform. Tewksbury's recent meeting with McCain might have served as the stimulus for McCain's reversal. Tewksbury did not favor US legislation that would compromise the sums of money flowing to the Olympic Movement but saw the need for the threat: "The only thing right now that is going to hold the IOC accountable is somebody pinching the purse strings. . . . [S]omebody needs to be waving the loaded gun around," he stated. Lisa Riley Roche, "McCain Keeping Pressure on IOC for Reform," *Deseret News*, Aug. 2, 1999. In the end, McCain redirected the focus of the hearings to the IOC's effort to combat doping. A parade of witnesses including former US Olympians Nancy Hogshead and Frank Shorter and President Bill Clinton's drug czar, Barry McCaffrey, characterized the IOC's efforts as too little, too late. For McCaffrey, the IOC's stated intent with respect to establishing a worldwide doping agency was "more public relations ploy than public policy solution." Hogshead commented that, "to date, the evidence is lacking that [the IOC] has the will or the ability

to do what needs to be done" (brackets added). Shorter lamented the IOC's unwillingness to confront the doping issue in a meaningful way before 1999: "The level playing field of the Olympic Games has been chemically elevated. Taking illegal drugs is now the price of entry into the competition, and the teenage athletes of the world know this. They no longer have a choice." Senator Ron Wyden (D-OR) was similarly unimpressed, referring to the IOC's effort as "all wind-up and no pitch." Lee Davidson, "IOC Anti-Doping Plans Flawed, McCaffrey Says," *Deseret News*, Oct. 20, 1999.

43. While we focus our attention on the ticketing and Reebok-Nike affairs because of their clearer connection to the IOC, it should be noted that SOCOG also found itself embroiled in a controversy at this time concerning plans for the opening ceremony. The marching band controversy drew much attention in the Australian media. Ceremonies director Ric Birch planned for a performance of an international marching band composed of five hundred Australians, two hundred Japanese, and thirteen hundred Americans. The band's planned performance comprised a mere seven minutes of the three-hour ceremony. However, the marching band community in Australia took issue with the decision to contract foreigners at the expense of opportunities that should have been granted to Australian youth. The domestic talk-back radio community drove SOCOG to "disinvite" the foreign performers. However, World Projects Corporation, the company in charge of putting together the international contingent, took SOCOG to court for breach of contract. Eventually, an out-of-court settlement was reached whereby SOCOG had to pay WPC an additional A$1 million in a compromise agreement that resulted in a revised distribution of spots in the band composed of individuals from twenty countries. The four-hundred-member strong Australian contingent would be the largest group. "Deal Struck in Sydney Olympics Opening Ceremony Row," Agence France-Presse, Aug. 16, 1999; Gerald Henderson, "Calls to Arms Often Have Built-in Recoil," *Sydney Morning Herald*, Aug. 17, 1999; "SOCOG's Gold Medal Bungle," *Canberra Times*, Aug. 19, 1999.

44. Alex Mitchell, "Homebush Ambush," *Sun-Herald* (Sydney), May 9, 1999. News Ltd. was involved in another sponsor controversy later in 1999. AMP, one of the kingpins of Australia's financial industry, secured the sponsorship rights to the Olympic torch relay. However, by December 1999, AMP grew restive about the value of the deal, specifically in relation to perceived encroachment on its sponsorship rights by News Ltd. AMP sought mediation with SOCOG as a means of having its concerns addressed. Matthew Moore, "And Now . . . a Word from Our Sponsors," *Sydney Morning Herald*, Dec. 11, 1999; Leonie Lamont, "Seven Kept in Dark on Packer's Stadium Suite," *Age* (Melbourne), Dec. 11, 1999.

45. Matthew Horan, "Game Is Up on Ticket Bungles," *Sunday Telegraph* (Sydney), Oct. 17, 1999. See also Kelvin Bissett and Evie Gelastopoulos, "Milk the Rich Ticket Strategy," *Daily Telegraph* (Sydney), Oct. 16, 1999; Susan Briggs, "Aust SOCOG Prepares for Outrage over Olympic Ticket Allocations," Australian Associated Press, Oct. 24, 1999; "Ticket Boss Leaves Olympic Panel," *AP Online*, Dec. 7, 1999; and "Australians Misled over Olympic Ticket Sales, Says Irate PM," Agence France-Presse, Oct. 25, 1999.

46. Jacquelin Magnay and Michael Evans, "But Wait, There's More," *Sydney Morning Herald*, Oct. 26, 1999; "Olympics Tickets Released," *West Australian* (Perth), Nov. 12, 1999.

47. Evie Gelastopoulos and Carly Chynoweth, "Sorry but No Change: Games Chief Firm on Tickets," *Daily Telegraph* (Sydney), Oct. 12, 1999.

48. Horan, "Game Is Up on Ticket Bungles."

49. "SOCOG Bows to Ticketing Pressure," *Australian* (Sydney), Oct. 19, 1999.

50. Peter Charlton, "Five-Ringed Circus," *Courier-Mail* (Brisbane), Dec. 10, 1999; Lamont, "Seven Kept in Dark on Packer's Stadium Suite"; "SOCOG Drops Controversial Ticket Plan," Associated Press Newswires, Dec. 8, 1999. In an effort to recoup a portion of the A$35 million shortfall resulting from the termination of the premium tickets program, SOCOG decided to sell tickets to the dress rehearsal for the opening ceremony. The anticipated sellout would provide A$20 million for Sydney organizers based on the ticket pricing plan established. "SOCOG Now Charging to See Rehearsal," *Illawarra Mercury* (Australia), Dec. 11, 1999.

51. Michael Evans, "Secret Tickets Programs Threaten Sponsors' Deals," *Sydney Morning Herald*, Oct. 27, 1999. Said a Telstra (a Team Millennium partner) spokesperson, "We understand you [SOCOG] have to make money—you don't do that by undermining your sponsors. . . . We have invested sizably in the success of the Games through our sponsorship and we see hospitality as part of that. We expect SOCOG to protect, not erode, our sponsorship rights" (brackets added).

52. Michael Knight refused to address whether Reading had resigned or been fired. John Salvado, "Ticketing Debacle Claims First Scalp," *Adelaide Advertiser* (Australia), Dec. 9, 1999.

53. "Sydney Olympic Games Organisers Apologise for Ticketing Fiasco," Agence France-Presse, Oct. 29, 1999.

54. "Ticket Boss Leaves Olympic Panel." Samaranch referred to the ticketing situation as a "small scandal." Gay Alcorn, "Tickets Fiasco Just a 'Small Scandal,'" *Sydney Morning Herald*, Dec. 17, 1999. Interestingly, while SOCOG claimed that the IOC knew, and approved, of the premium ticket plan, the IOC, through the Sydney Coordination Commission chairman, Jacques Rogge, denied such knowledge. Rogge indicated that the forty-page ticketing document submitted to the IOC in May 1998 contained no details on that particular line item, leading IOC officials to conclude that premium packages referred to an aspect of SOCOG's hospitality program. Matthew Moore and Jacquelin Magnay, "Offshore Games Windfall," *Sydney Morning Herald*, Oct. 29, 1999.

55. Stephanie Peatling, "When Reebok Revolted Nike Said: We'll Just Do It," *Sydney Morning Herald*, Dec. 14, 1999.

56. Krystyna Rudzki, "OLY: Nike and Olympics Just Do It on a New Sponsorship Deal," Australian Associated Press, Dec. 13, 1999.

57. M. Payne, *Olympic Turnaround*, 158.

58. "Just Did It: Nike's Deal to Seal Games," *Australian* (Sydney), Dec. 14, 1999; M. Payne, *Olympic Turnaround*, 159.

59. Moore, "And Now . . . a Word from Our Sponsors."

60. "Just Did It: Nike's Deal to Seal Games."

61. M. Payne, *Olympic Turnaround*, 159–60; Rudzki, "OLY: Nike and Olympics Just Do It"; Rudzki, "OLY: Nike and Olympics Just Do It."

62. M. Payne, *Olympic Turnaround*, 160.

63. Peatling, "When Reebok Revolted."

64. Even before the split between SOCOG and Reebok, work had commenced on Nike's Sydney village, a warehouse just beyond the boundaries of Olympic Park. Nike planned at this location, as had been its practice at past games, to entertain the Olympians it sponsored as well as Nike retailers. Tom Salom, "Nike in $8M Deal to Clothe Athletes," *Herald Sun* (Melbourne), Dec. 14, 1999. Nike's most brazen promotional campaign unfolded during the 1996 Centennial Olympics in Atlanta. Nike billboards were commonplace on Atlanta's streetscape, some with a direct challenge to Olympic philosophy: "You do not win silver, you lose gold." Other Nike ads attacked the thematic approach adopted by numerous Olympic sponsors: "We don't sell dreams, we sell shoes." The campaign touched off a row between the IOC and USOC marketers, who sought to protect the Atlanta Games and the Olympic message, and Nike. When Pound, Payne, and the head of the USOC's marketing portfolio, John Krimsky, met with Nike chairman and founder Phil Knight's special assistant, Howard Slusher, in an attempt to convince Nike to step back from its campaign, tempers were short. Krimsky and Slusher challenged each other to sort things out, one on one, in the halls of the Marriott Marquis Hotel. "Both men were of equal stature, similar egos and of questionable fitness," recalled Payne. "The impending boxing match had definite entertainment value, if doubtful sporting discipline, but was probably not going to resolve the issue." As the Games unfolded, it became clear to Nike that Olympic athletes did not appreciate its campaign and the message. Nike also understood that the IOC contemplated recruiting a group of Olympic silver medalists to challenge Nike in public fashion. Nike responded by changing the tone of its advertising messages and ceased efforts to convince spectators to carry Nike advertising signs into Olympic venues. Payne met with Nike executives at the close of the Games in order to ward off the possibility of a confrontation between the IOC and Nike in the future. M. Payne, *Olympic Turnaround*, 138–41.

65. Salom, "Nike in $8M Deal to Clothe Athletes." The deal directed three million dollars to SOCOG. Nike also agreed to provide uniforms for Australia's Olympic teams for Salt Lake City (2002) and Athens (2004).

66. Deborah Cameron and Stephanie Peatling, "Games Clothing Victory to Nike," *Sydney Morning Herald*, Dec. 14, 1999.

67. "Sydney Olympics Act Quickly in Confidence-Building Sponsor Move," Agence France-Presse, Dec. 13, 1999. SOCOG's troubles were reflected in polls concerning SOCOG's performance. An AC Nielsen poll conducted in association with the *Sydney Morning Herald* in early December revealed that 59 percent of the respondents disapproved of Michael Knight's leadership efforts, a staggering 40 point increase from a year earlier. A mere 16 percent of the respondents believed SOCOG was doing a good job (a drop of 27 points from a

year earlier), while 43 percent indicated that its performance was poor (an increase of 32 points from a year earlier). A spokesperson for Michael Knight brushed off the poll. Given "a relentless two months of bad publicity," it was expected. "You don't have to be Einstein," said the spokesperson, to understand the poll results; however, the individual quickly added that "the only poll that counts is the vote of the community after the Games are over." Philip Cornford, Stephanie Peatling, and Leonie Lamont, "Rich Olympics: Cut-Price Seats for Bill Gates," *Sydney Morning Herald*, Dec. 11, 1999.

68. Allen Guttmann picks up the story: "As the day of the Sorbonne conference approached, Coubertin orchestrated his themes brilliantly. On the very eve of the conference, he published an essay in the Revue de Paris in which he eloquently urged the revival of the Olympic Games. He arranged for the seventy-eight delegates from nine countries to convene in an auditorium whose walls had recently been adorned with suitably neoclassical murals by the painter Pierre Puvis de Chavannes. The delegates were seduced by ear as well as by eye. On the opening day, June 16, they heard a performance of the ancient 'Hymn to Apollo,' discovered the previous year at Delphi, translated into French by Théodore Reine, set to music by Gabriel Fauré, and sung by Jeanne Remacle. Fauré was also called upon to conduct a choral group accompanied by harps. The discussions on amateurism began on Sunday and continued for several days. Like all of Coubertin's conferences, this one had a full program of festive entertainments, exhibitions, and displays. Catching the dazzled delegates at a propitious moment, the canny baron proposed the revival of the Olympic Games. Why not? On June 23, the obliging delegates voted unanimously to support Coubertin's plan." Guttmann, *The Olympics: A History of the Modern Games*, 14. For the definitive treatment of Coubertin's launch of the modern Olympic Movement, see David C. Young, *The Modern Olympics: A Struggle for Revival.*

69. Jim Byers, "A Year Later, IOC Struggles to Find Balance: As Scandal Fades, Olympic World Wrestles Reform," *Toronto Star*, Dec. 9, 1999.

70. Stephen Wilson, "Olympic Committee Approves Rules on Age Limits for Members," *Sunday Herald* (Glasgow), Dec. 12, 1999.

71. Ibid. Kissinger noted later that the experience of serving on the IOC 2000 Commission prompted personal reflection concerning his support of the 1980 Olympic boycott. "Now that I've gotten to know athletes, it was a rather harsh punishment for [young] people who spent a lot of time to prepare with probably only one chance to compete. Today, I would be thinking again about it." "1980 Boycott Decision Wrong Says Kissinger," *Salt Lake Tribune*, Dec. 12, 1999. See also *Minutes of the 110th IOC Session*, 3–6.

72. A complete list of the proposed (and ultimately accepted) reform proposals can be found in *Report by the IOC 2000 Commission.*

73. Following the close of the Session, the IOC Executive Board convened to assess the events of the past forty-eight hours and reflect on the events of the past year. Richard Pound singled out the IOC's staff for praise: "Thanks and recognition were due in particular to the younger IOC staff, many of whom could doubtless be earning more elsewhere, but who were

with the IOC because of their commitment to the organization and the Olympic Movement. These people had a very difficult time in 1999, not through what they themselves had done, but because of events caused by the actions of IOC members. He hoped that these staff would now appreciate the real commitment on the part of the organization for which they worked." Pound's thoughts were echoed by Kevan Gosper and François Carrard. Carrard noted the Session's importance in regard to staff morale. Mbaye told Samaranch that he "had nothing more to fear and could hold his head high in the defence of the IOC" in Washington. He Zhenliang predicted tough questioning for Samaranch, but he offered the following words from a Chinese poet: "I shall face with a cold, hard stare the thousand fingers pointing to attack me." Rogge cautioned that while "the Session votes had been a sign of unity . . . work was still needed to win the hearts and minds of colleagues who had voted for the sake of discipline or a sense of unity." In wishing Samaranch well on his Washington mission, Rogge quoted Jean de la Fontaine: "The spittle of toads never reaches the light of the stars." Bach believed Samaranch's leadership had been exemplary: "To turn around such an organization as the IOC without losing a third of its membership or its support only added to the achievement." While Pound was convinced some people waiting in Washington were poised to "treat the IOC and its President unfairly," Samaranch had the ammunition in the form of the just-passed IOC reforms to deal with the questioning. *Minutes of the Meeting of the IOC Executive Board* (Dec. 8–10, 13, 1999), 67–70.

74. Readers may recall Samaranch's disastrous interview with Bob Simon of CBS's popular investigative news program *60 Minutes* aired during the Nagano Olympic Winter Games in February 1998. During those proceedings, an extremely ill-at-ease and baffled IOC president left the impression that the world's leading sports organization was in the hands of a bewildered septuagenarian, better off in a retirement home than occupying a formidable seat of power.

75. Catalan and Spanish are Samaranch's "first" languages, French his "second."

76. *Minutes of the Meeting of the IOC Executive Board* (Oct. 1–4, 1999), 8.

77. Pound, "Travel Log—1999." Hill & Knowlton personnel and a lawyer from O'Melveny and Myers's Washington office managed the preparation process and counseled Samaranch on the standard process involved in congressional hearings. Pound and Carrard were present.

78. Ibid. To her credit, US IOC member Anita DeFrantz suggested this method of delivering Samaranch's message. Obviously, this process gave Samaranch a great advantage and, in effect, did much to slow, interrupt, and blunt the rapid-fire accusations and statements of his questioners.

79. For a complete text of Samaranch's prepared opening statement, see Juan Antonio Samaranch, "The Olympic Site Selection Process: A Review of the Reform Effort."

80. For Upton's remarks, see "In the Hot Seat: Samaranch Defends Olympic Reforms in House Grilling," *Salt Lake Tribune*, Dec. 16, 1999. Following Samaranch's "opening statement" in English, the entire question-answer discourse between Samaranch and congressional subcommittee members reverted to translated Castilian Spanish.

81. See "Samaranch Unruffled by Charges in Congress," *Globe and Mail* (Toronto), Dec. 16, 1999.

82. For but one of several newspaper accounts of Congressman Barton's remarks, see "Samaranch Also Speaks Stengelese," *New York Times*, Dec. 16, 1999.

83. For Waxman's remarks, see "Lawmaker Suggests NBC Donation Was Bribe for Contract," *Salt Lake Tribune*, Dec. 16, 1999. The reference to an "NBC Donation" refers to an original, spontaneous donation of five hundred thousand dollars to the construction of the Olympic Museum in Lausanne made by NBC's Dick Ebersol on the occasion of a speech delivered on the evening of the long-term "Sunset" television contract signing. NBC later increased the donation by an additional half-million dollars. It might be noted that the US Home Office of the FOX Television Network, a competitor of NBC, is located in Waxman's congressional district.

84. This remark was made by Congressman Waxman. See "IOC's Samaranch Weathers Storm on Capitol Hill," *Japan Economic Newswire*, Dec. 16, 1999.

85. See "In the Hot Seat."

86. See "Samaranch Sparkles in Washington," *Los Angeles Times*, Dec. 16, 1999.

### 7. Judgment Day(s)

1. The US government is the party most responsible for the federally granted authority to conduct Olympic matters in the United States. Although Congress is the ultimate authority, US Public Law 95–606, known as the Amateur Sports Act of 1978, cedes to the USOC the exclusive rights within the United States to govern Olympic matters, including the rights to all Olympic-related "terminology and designations."

2. Linda Fantin, "Judge Misread Case Law, Oly Defendants Say," *Salt Lake Tribune*, July 12, 2001.

3. Mike Gorrell, "Judge Lets Racketeering Charges Against Welch, Johnson Stand," *Salt Lake Tribune*, June 12, 2001 (brackets in original).

4. On the night of January 16, 1988, a bomb exploded in the Church of Latter-day Saints located in the rural community of Marion, Utah. The chapel was severely damaged. Local police responding to the incident found footprints in the snow leading to a farm owned by Vickie Singer, the mother of Addam Swapp's two wives. Police surrounded the farmhouse, requesting a surrender of the occupants. Besides Swapp himself, a well-known grouser against Mormon Church policy, they included his brother Jonathan, Vickie Singer, and brother-in-law John Timothy Singer. Federal authorities were summoned, and further surrender requests were made by telephone. Armed with pistols, rifles, and knives, the Swapp-Singer group remained defiant. A stalemate ensued. Ten days into the ordeal, with the press sensationalizing the latest updates, a letter of appeal to surrender from Governor Norman Bangerter was delivered to Swapp. Their response was to fire shots at lights, generators, and loudspeakers set up by the authorities. Finally, on January 28, the twelfth day of the standoff, representatives of the Bureau of Alcohol, Tobacco, Firearms, and Explosives, together with

members of the FBI Hostage Rescue Team and Utah State Corrections Department dog handlers, moved to end the confrontation. In a melée of shots subsequently fired by both sides, law enforcement officer Fred House was killed and Addam Swapp wounded. The besieged group then surrendered. Addam Swapp, in a trial conducted in federal district court and concluded a year later (January 26, 1989) was convicted of manslaughter and sentenced to not less than one year nor more than fifteen years in the Utah State Prison. Two years after that, on January 23, 1991, the US Court of Appeals for the Tenth Circuit successfully argued that the federal trial court had erred when deferring Swapp's sentence on count 2 of the charges (the use of a deadly and dangerous weapon). The result was that Swapp received an additional five-year sentence. "Westlaw Results: 808 P.2d 115." The Addam Swapp episode turned out to be a small but alarmingly similar event to the fifty-one-day standoff between federal authorities and David Koresh and his Branch Davidian followers. In late February, throughout March, and well into April 1993, officials of the US Bureau of Alcohol, Tobacco, Firearms, and Explosives surrounded and besieged the Branch Davidian ranch-house complex near the city of Waco, Texas. The end of that horror resulted in the entire complex being burned to the ground; seventy-two Davidians perished, twenty-one of them children.

5. Linda Fantin, "Seating Scarce for Bribery Trial," *Salt Lake Tribune*, July 5, 2001. The harassed Zimmer noted to the Salt Lake press corps that he had sought guidance from colleagues in Denver and Sacramento on how they handled public and media interest in the trials of Unibomber Ted Kaczynski and Oklahoma City bomber Timothy McVeigh. Although the Olympic trial was not projected to attract the attention as did those high-profile murder cases, they dwarfed anything in Utah's recent history. In the end, Zimmer did his best to accommodate media demands. "We're a public service organization," proclaimed Zimmer, "and the press has every right to be there."

6. Linda Fantin, "Judge Dumps Key Oly Charges," *Salt Lake Tribune*, July 17, 2001.

7. "Judge Blasts 'Misguided' Oly Charges," *Deseret News*, Aug. 10, 2001.

8. Fantin, "Judge Dumps Key Oly Charges."

9. Linda Fantin, "Bid Trial May Wait for Games," *Salt Lake Tribune*, July 19, 2001 (brackets added).

10. Larry Gerlach, "The Mormon Games: Religion, Media, Cultural Politics, and the Salt Lake Winter Olympics," 11.

11. Ibid., 1–52.

12. Welch was also head of the Salt Lake Bid Committee in its unsuccessful effort to gain the Winter Games in 1998 (awarded to Nagano). In fact, Welch had been party to Salt Lake Olympic Winter Games bidding activities since 1985.

13. Welch received a sentence in the Utah State Court of one year's probation and mandatory family counseling. In a controversial but nevertheless emphatic decision, Welch was retained on the organizing committee as a consultant at a monthly fee of ten thousand dollars until closure of the Games and awarded a deferred compensation package of one million

dollars. See Mike Dodd, "SLOC Looking for Leader: Welch Steps Down as Controversy Escalates," *USA Today*, July 31, 1997.

14. Frank Joklik, proclaimed "a giant in our city" by the Salt Lake Area Chamber of Commerce, was, at the time, a seventy-year-old retired president of Kennecott Copper Corporation. See "Joklik Hopes His Sacrifice Will Push Games Forward," *Salt Lake Tribune*, Jan. 9, 1999.

15. Mitt Romney—youngest son of the late George Romney, hugely successful president and CEO of American Motors in the 1950s, governor of Michigan in the 1960s, and a Republican Party presidential primary candidate in 1968—established the highly successful venture-capital firm Bain Capital in 1984.

16. In fact, in-place sponsors, keeping their eyes on the prospect of the massive world audience sure to materialize for the Olympics, in general stood fast. Michael Payne pointed specifically to the IOC's rapid course of action in investigating improprieties and revamping its *Olympic Charter* when he announced in late March 1999 that not only had no (TOP) sponsors withdrawn, but he was seeking new ones and had raised the quadrennial TOP sponsorship fee to more than fifty million dollars. See William Echikson and Richard Siklos, "Scandal? What Scandal? Olympic Sponsors Aren't Fazed by Allegations of Corruption."

17. Neither a particularly avid nor a skilled sports participant in his youth, Romney's link with school athletic endeavors was usually as team manager. When Romney's leadership of Olympic matters in Salt Lake City became public, congratulatory correspondence was quick to fill his mailbox. In receiving one such missive, an e-mail note from the former ice hockey coach of his high school alma mater, the Cranbrook Preparatory School for Boys (Bloomfield Hills, Michigan), where, as student manager of the hockey team in the early 1960s he had taped ankles and sticks, sliced oranges, handed out towels, and retrieved pucks shot into the outdoor rink's surrounding snowbanks, Romney responded by proclaiming the irony of it all: "I chuckle thinking about you out on the rink marshalling the boys around. . . . Say, don't you think it's one of life's little ironies that someone with as little athletic talent as I is running the Olympics?" Romney to David Barney, e-mail message, Aug. 12, 2001. We are grateful to David Barney for sharing this anecdote with us.

18. US athletes captured thirty-four medals in Salt Lake City (ten gold, thirteen silver, and eleven bronze), a total exceeded by US Olympians in 2010, who won thirty-seven medals in Vancouver (nine gold, fifteen silver, and thirteen bronze).

19. Jack Shea won two gold medals in speed skating (500 meters and 1,000-meter sprints) at the 1932 Olympic Winter Games organized by Lake Placid. He was also the first individual in Olympic history to stand atop the medal podium when it was first introduced in Olympic context in February 1932. For details of that significant Olympic episode, see Robert Barney, "The Great Transformation: Olympic Victory Ceremonies and the Medal Podium."

20. "Golden Moment: Canadian Duo Receives Pairs Skating Medals."

21. See "Scott Feels No Animosity Toward Russian Cheaters: Delay Costs $1 Million," *London Free Press*, Dec. 19, 2003.

22. On the question of federal expenditure for the Games, as the festival neared its conclusion, Cindy Gillespie, Romney's top aide for federal liaison affairs (Gillespie served a similar role under Billy Payne's presidency of the 1996 Atlanta Games), told reporters in Salt Lake City, "When the final report comes out, what you will actually see will be a little over $400 million. That increase is primarily support that's been provided post–Sept. 11." See "Winter Games to Cost U.S. Government $400 Million," Reuters News, Feb. 17, 2002. According to an in-depth investigation carried out by *Sports Illustrated*, the total federal government financial involvement in the Games came to $1.5 billion. The cost dimensions listed by *Sports Illustrated* included security, parking lot and highway construction and renovation, a light-rail transit system, infectious disease monitoring, weather forecasting, housing, transportation, airport improvement, drug testing, and beautification. See Donald R. Barlett and James B. Steele, "Snow Job: Thanks to Utah Politicians and the 2002 Olympics, a Blizzard of Federal Money—a Stunning $1.5 Billion—Has Fallen on the State, Enriching Some Already Wealthy Businessmen." *Sports Illustrated* pointed to Utah's congressional delegation (two senators and three congressmen) as a unit deploying the "skill, grace, and precision of a hockey team on a power play" in quests for federal funding of projects, tapping in the end some three dozen federal agencies, offices, and departments, from the Agriculture Department to the Office of National Drug Control Policy. If *Sports Illustrated*'s assessment is correct, then the federal government allocations for the Salt Lake Games would equate to an expenditure of $625,000 for each of the twenty-four hundred athletes who competed.

23. See Julia Campbell, "Vaulting Costs: Olympic Games Cost U.S. Taxpayers More than Ever." In a telling article, Campbell cited General Accounting Office figures in breaking down the federal government's contribution of $1.3 billion: (1) building venues, federal services, and Olympic infrastructure, each 1 percent; (2) spectator transport, 6 percent; (3) safety and security services, 13 percent; (4) mass transport, 28 percent; and (5) highway construction, a whopping 51 percent.

24. Ibid.

25. According to IOC figures, 2.1 billion viewers spent some 13.1 billion hours watching the Games on television sets located in 160 different countries. The various broadcasters worldwide recorded 10,416 hours of Olympic Games programming. The world's foremost viewing area in terms of number of hours watched was Asia (49 percent), followed by Europe (31 percent), North America (11 percent), Central America and South America (7.5 percent), Oceania-Australasia (1 percent), and Africa (0.5 percent). See *Salt Lake 2002 Marketing Report*, 16–17.

26. These figures can be found in *Marketing Matters: The Olympic Marketing Newsletter*, 5.

27. See *Salt Lake 2002 Marketing Report*, 92, 7.

28. In all, 1,605,524 tickets were available; 1,525,118 (almost 95 percent) were sold. Ibid., 27.

29. By far the largest of these gifts was a donation of eight million dollars by the George S. and Dolores Doré Eccles Foundation. The Eccles donation underwrote the cost of the

specially designed two-million-dollar Olympic flame cauldron, as well as enhancements to the opening and closing ceremonies. See Lisa Riley Roche, "Eccles Family Paying for the Games Cauldron," *Deseret News*, Nov. 29, 2001.

30. See "Appeals Court Reinstates Salt Lake Bribery Case," *New York Times*, Apr. 23, 2003.

31. Lex Hemphill, "Government Case Shifts Its Focus to Fraud," *New York Times*, Nov. 28, 2003.

32. Mike Gorrell, "Olympic Trial: Judge Could Wrap Up Matters Today," *Salt Lake Tribune*, Dec. 4, 2003 (brackets added).

33. Rule 29: Motion for a Judgment for Acquittal is a request by the defense to dismiss criminal charges on the grounds that the government has not presented enough evidence to sustain a conviction. The court can rule on the motion immediately, proceed with the trial and decide the motion before sending the case to a jury, or wait until the jury returns a verdict. If the judge grants the motion before the case goes to jury, the decision cannot be appealed, because the defendants cannot be tried twice for the same crime. See "Motion for a Judgment of Acquittal: Rule 29," 2.

34. As cited by Alan Abrahamson, "Judge Drops Olympic Bid Case," *Los Angeles Times*, Dec. 6, 2003.

35. For the verbatim text of Judge David Sam's reflections and final verdict, see "Transcript of Judge Sam's December 5th Dismissal of the Olympic Case," *Salt Lake Tribune*, Dec. 5, 2003.

36. Linda Fantin, "Olympic Bribery Case Dismissed," *Salt Lake Tribune*, Dec. 5, 2003.

37. Abrahamson, "Judge Drops Olympic Bid Case."

38. Those persons who followed closely events in Salt Lake City might contend that the "final" curtain did not fall until September 2004 when Alfredo LaMont and David Simmons, both of whom pleaded guilty to tax-law violations in 1999, avoided jail time. Their sentencing hearing was delayed until after the Welch-Johnson trial, where they served as witnesses. Simmons's telecommunications firm employed John Kim, the son of Un Yong Kim, but did so with money for his salary funneled from Salt Lake City. LaMont received money from Salt Lake City in his role as a consultant for the bid while employed as the director of international relations for the USOC. Still, the media attention focused on this event paled in comparison to the coverage given to events in Judge Sam's courtroom. "Olympics Scandal Cases Closed."

39. There is no doubt as to Judge Sam's Mormon background and membership in the LDS. Educated at Brigham Young University and the University of Utah (Law School), Sam married his late wife, Betty Jean Brennan, in 1957 in the Salt Lake City LDS Temple. Sam not only taught religion as an adjunct faculty member at BYU, but also served as an institute director in the LDS in both Colorado and Oregon. He and Betty were scheduled to lead the Romania Bucharest Mission in 1998, but had to withdraw because of her unfortunate diagnosis with amyotrophic lateral sclerosis (Lou Gehrig's disease). See "Obituary: Betty Jean Brennan Sam,"

*Deseretnews.com*, http://dn.desnews.com/archives/internal.html; and "David Sam, District of Utah," http://faculty.rwu.edu/dzlotnick/profiles/sam.html. Betty Sam died in August 2000.

40. Barry Tarlow, "Let the Games Begin." *Champion Magazine*, which published Tarlow's article, is the official publication of the National Association of Criminal Defense Lawyers.

41. Miller, *Olympic Revolution*.

## 8. Then and Now

1. Deborah Cameron, "Reebok Gives $10M Contract Royal Order of the Boot," *Sydney Morning Herald*, Dec. 9, 1999; "Reebok Sues SOCOG over Sponsorship Deal," Associated Press Newswires, Dec. 8, 1999; "Nike in $8M Deal to Clothe Athletes," *Herald Sun* (Melbourne), Dec. 14, 1999; "Sydney Olympics Act Quickly in Confidence-Building Sponsor Move" (see chap. 6, n. 67).

2. For an assessment of Samaranch's efforts in Washington, see Barney, Wenn, and Martyn, *Selling the Five Rings*, 267–77.

3. London East Research Institute, *A Lasting Legacy for London? Assessing the Legacy of the Olympic and Paralympic Games*, 20.

4. Glenda Korporaal, "Pemberton Goes for Gold with Qantas Float," *Sydney Morning Herald*, May 27, 1995; Glenda Korporaal, "Mal, the Next Olympic CEO," *Sydney Morning Herald*, Aug. 21, 1995; Rachel Gibson, "Surprise Resignation for Olympics Chief," *Age* (Melbourne), Mar. 6, 1996; Glenda Korporaal, "SOCOG Seeks Senior Helper," *Sydney Morning Herald*, May 6, 1996; "Games Debacle Angers Minister," *Australian* (Sydney), Sept. 4, 1996; "Knight to the Rescue for 2000 in September 1993," *Daily Telegraph* (Sydney), Sept. 7, 1996; "SOCOG Must Show Stability," *Daily Telegraph* (Sydney), Oct. 29, 1996; Matthew Moore, "Knight Steps into Games Crisis," *Sydney Morning Herald*, Nov. 27, 1996; Matthew Moore, "Bureaucrat, Businessman Given Top Olympics Job," *Sydney Morning Herald*, Dec. 18, 1996; "Sydney Olympics Boss Hemmerling Resigns," Reuters News, Mar. 26, 1997; Matthew Moore, "Olympic Jitters as Knight Kills Off Another Chief," *Sydney Morning Herald*, Mar. 27, 1997; Matthew Moore, "Knight of the Long Knives," *Sydney Morning Herald*, Mar. 29, 1997; Robert Galvin, "Olympics: Turmoil at the Top for Sydney Games," Reuters News, Apr. 3, 1997; "SOCOG Drops Controversial Ticket Plan" (see chap. 6, n. 50); "Ticket Decision Could Cost Sydney," *AP Online*, Dec. 9, 1999; Deborah Cameron, "Angry Sponsors Get Their Man," *Sydney Morning Herald*, Dec. 9, 1999; Catriona Elder, Angela Pratt, and Cath Ellis, "Running Race: Nationalism and the Sydney 2000 Olympic Games."

5. *Olympic Marketing Fact File*, 2008, 38. Ticket sales generated $551 million for SOCOG, outstripping the Atlanta Organizing Committee's ticket revenue ($425 million) by $126 million. The *Fact File* also reveals (p. 18) that Sydney's domestic sponsorship partners possessed a good deal of enthusiasm for Australia's opportunity to host the Olympic Games, providing $492 million in revenue (compared to ACOG's $426 million).

6. *A Lasting Legacy for London?*, 18, 20, 36, 39; Jill Haynes, "Socio-economic Impact of the Sydney 2000 Olympic Games," 5–7.

7. "Rogge Wins IOC Presidency; Pound Resigns from IOC Posts."

8. These data were compiled through a search of the IOC website and subsequent Internet research to ascertain the nationality of a number of the IF presidents. The research was conducted on September 25, 2008. Thirteen of the thirty-five federations had their headquarters in Lausanne. An additional six were also located in Switzerland. The data included baseball and softball even though they will not be contested in London. At the time, both were served by presidents from the United States (Harvey Schiller and Don Porter). Baseball is based in Lausanne, while softball's headquarters are in Plant City, Florida. For the 1952 presidential election, see Allen Guttmann, *The Games Must Go On: Avery Brundage and the Olympic Movement,* 114. After twenty-five rounds of voting, Brundage triumphed by a final count of thirty to seventeen.

9. In September 2008, 42 of the 111 IOC members (37.8 percent) hailed from European countries. However, most Olympic observers concede that much of the power and decision-making authority resides in the Executive Board. In May 2011, 7 of the 15 members of the Executive Board were European, including the president, and 2 of the 4 vice presidents.

10. Samaranch, who was not keen to accept responsibility for Madrid's demise, claimed days after the vote that he counseled Madrid officials to delay their bid until 2020. He understood the challenge and difficult optics of a London (2012), Sochi (2014), Madrid (2016) rotation. Madrid pressed forward with the bid for 2016. Madrid's bid committee CEO Mercedes Coghen was unwilling to give much credit to the South Americans following their triumph in Copenhagen. She maintained that Madrid presented the best bid and that Rio was chosen "because it was somewhere new." Meanwhile, Tokyo's governor, Shintaro Ishihara, said that Brazil's president, Luiz Inácio Lula da Silva, "made quite daring promises to the people of Africa" and that Nicolas Sarkozy, France's president, pledged his support for the Rio bid if Brazil purchased French-made military aircraft. "I don't know how relevant these promises were but they seem in violation of IOC rules," observed Ishihara. "This is part of the discomfort I have with the bid process," he commented. Tokyo, stated Ishihara, was caught within a web of IOC politics as Samaranch lobbied for Madrid, while Rogge seemed committed to Rio. Not content with criticizing Rio, and offering that "invisible dynamics" sunk Tokyo's bid, Ishihara also took a swipe at US president Barack Obama. "Prime Minister (Yukio) Hatoyama's speech was much better than Obama's, whose speech seemed to be just for granted whereas Mr. Hatoyama's speech had substance," noted Ishihara. Rio issued a sharp rebuke to Ishihara and indicated its intent to send a formal note of complaint to the IOC. This summary was constructed through the use of a number of sources: "Samaranch: I Told Madrid to Wait until 2020"; "Ishihara Blames Tokyo 2016 Failure on Politics," *Star Online* (Malaysia), Oct. 4, 2006, http://thestar.com.my/sports/story.asp?file=/2009/10/4/sports/20091004132612&sec=sports#; and "Rio 2016 Refutes Tokyo's Claims of 'Invisible Dynamics.'"

11. Bill Briggs, "Rogge Looking Like Rogue to Many after IOC Vote," *Denver Post,* July 10, 2005; David Lassen, "Baseball, Softball Fall Victim to Eurocentric Nature of IOC," *Fort Wayne (IN) Journal Gazette,* July 10, 2005; Jesper Fjeldstad, "Games Snub Anger," *Adelaide Sunday Mail* (Australia), July 10, 2005.

12. Richard Pound, "The Future of the Olympic Movement: Promised Land or Train Wreck?," 6.

13. Juliet Macur, "Pound Exits Amid Strain in Vote for WADA Chief," *New York Times*, Nov. 18, 2007.

14. Glenn Milne, "Aussie Coup on Anti-Doping Top Sports Job Set to Go to Fahey," *Sunday Mail* (Brisbane), Sept. 30, 2007. *L'Equipe* referred to the effort of the US, New Zealand, and Australian governments to sideline Lamour as an "Anglo-Saxon putsch." See also Samuel Petrequin, "French Candidate Lamour Bows Out of Race for New WADA Chief," Associated Press Newswires, Oct. 16, 2007; James Christie, "WADA Comes under Fire from Former French Sport Minister," *Globe and Mail* (Toronto), Oct. 17, 2007; Paul Kelso, "Drugs Body in Disarray after Leadership Row," *Guardian* (Manchester), Nov. 17, 2007; "Fahey's Enemies in Veto Attempt," *Australian* (Sydney), Nov. 17, 2007; and Macur, "Pound Exits Amid Strain in Vote for WADA Chief."

15. Jeremy Whittle, "Diplomatic New Anti-Doping Champion Fahey Says He's Backed by His Board, If Not European News Media," *International Herald Tribune*, Mar. 1, 2008.

16. Abrahamson, "Passing the Torch" (see chap. 1, n. 1).

17. James Christie, "IOC Belittles Job by Pound," *Globe and Mail* (Toronto), July 16, 2001.

18. In 2008 fewer than one-third of the NOCs and ISFs had achieved the goal of having 20 percent of the seats on their executive bodies filled by women. This goal, set in 1996, was to be reached by 2005. "Promotion of Women Sport Leaders."

19. However, whispers in Lausanne are that Rogge lacks a grand vision for the Olympic Movement. Rogge is "Juan Antonio Lite, a guy who never had an original thought in his head, but ruffled no feathers," concluded the *Montreal Gazette*'s Jack Todd in a blunt assessment of the Belgian's efforts. Todd, "Time for the IOC to Jettison Rogge; Olympic Chief Should Apologize to Sprinter Bolt—on His Way Out the Door," *Montreal Gazette*, Aug. 25, 2008. Rogge's image suffered in Beijing. The decision by the Chinese to block access of the Olympic press corps to certain Internet sites during the Games damaged Rogge's reputation, especially in light of IOC Press Commission chairman Kevan Gosper's initial comments that a deal to permit such action must have been brokered by his superiors without his knowledge. Even though Gosper recanted this assertion following a conference with Rogge, the IOC appeared weak as a result of not having ensured that such censorship did not occur. His public criticism of Jamaican Usain Bolt's conduct following his world record–setting performance in the 100-meter sprint also left observers thinking he was a bit of a "stuffed shirt." See, for instance, Rick Broadbent, "Deluded Jacques Rogge Fails to See the Champion in Usain Bolt," *Times Online*, Aug. 22, 2008, http://www.timesonline.co.uk/tol/sport/olympics/article4578959.ece#.

20. Contrary to the frequently reported 20 percent in the media, in the post-Athens years, the actual revenue flowing to the USOC fell between 15 percent and 20 percent, as the USOC now pays a commission for the operation of the TOP program and agreed to take a lesser percentage on two TOP sponsors agreements that are tied heavily to VIK for the OCOGs.

21. IOC-USOC relations concerning television and corporate sponsorship revenues in the 1980s and 1990s are detailed in Barney, Wenn, and Martyn, *Selling the Five Rings*, 203–65. With respect to the Broadcast Marketing Agreement, the 10 percent payments to the USOC commenced with the 1992 Olympic festivals in Albertville and Barcelona. However, the first moneys received by the USOC as a result of the Broadcast Marketing Agreement flowed in conjunction with the 1988 Calgary Olympic Winter Games and Seoul Summer Olympics. The IOC and Calgary and Seoul Organizing Committees each paid the USOC five million dollars in order to ensure that US television advertisers and the US Olympics television rights holders could employ the Olympic rings on US telecasts. ABC held the rights for the Calgary Games, while NBC secured the rights for the Seoul Olympics, launching its ultimately successful pursuit of the mantle of America's Olympic Network in the 1990s. NBC has enjoyed an uninterrupted run as the US Summer Olympics rights holder since 1988 and has also delivered the Winter Olympics to American homes since 2002. NBC had locked up the US Olympic television rights through the 2012 London Olympics and recently secured these same rights through the 2020 Summer Olympics when it purchased the four-festival package (2014, 2016, 2018, and 2020) for approximately $4.4 billion. Michael McCarthy, "NBC Wins Rights to Olympics through 2020; Promises More Live Coverage," *USA Today. com*, June 7, 2011, http://content.usatoday.com/communities/gameon/post/2011/06/olympic-tv-decision-between-nbc-espn-and-fox-could-come-down-today/1.

22. There is some discrepancy in the existing literature concerning the USOC's share of television and corporate sponsorship dollars. Philip Hersh reported that the USOC received more than all of the other 204 NOCs combined. Hersh, "IOC Official Rips USOC's Share of Olympic Funding," *Chicago Tribune*, June 3, 2008, http://www.chicagotribune.com/sports/chi-us-olympic-revenues-share,0,1220316.story. Amy Shipley revealed that the USOC received "more than $300 million from the IOC; the rest of the more than 200 national Olympic committees combined got $373 million." Shipley, "Deteriorating USOC-IOC Relations Threaten Both Organizations," *Washington Post*, Dec. 22, 2009, http://www.washingtonpost.com/wpyn/content/article/2009/12/21/AR2009122101900.html?hpid=artslot. A query to the IOC Reference Service resulted in the numbers provided in the text. IOC Reference Service e-mails to Wenn, Jan. 14, 15, 2010.

23. Initial TOP sponsors for the TOP VII (2009–12) cycle were Acer (Taiwan), Atos Origin (France), Coca-Cola (United States), General Electric (United States), McDonald's (United States), Omega (Switzerland), Panasonic (Japan), Samsung (South Korea), and Visa (United States). The IOC hoped to recruit one or two additional TOP sponsors for the Van-couver-London cycle (prior to the Vancouver Olympic Winter Games), but failed to do so. In this regard, it faced decisions of Eastman Kodak (digital camera category assumed by Panasonic), Lenovo (replaced by Acer), Manulife, and Johnson and Johnson to refrain from renewing their TOP agreements for TOP VII. "IOC Loses TOP Sponsor." See also "IOC Confident of Hitting Sponsorship Revenue Targets," *Canadian Press*, Nov. 18, 2008, http://www.tsn.ca/olympics/story/?id=256367&lid=sublink011&lpos=headlines_main. With one more sponsor,

noted Gerhard Heiberg, chairman of the IOC Marketing Commission, TOP would reach its one-billion-dollar target for the current cycle. However, the global economic crisis stalled progress toward this goal. "We are in discussions with several companies in different product lines, and we are pursuing this of course," observed Heiberg. "In the current financial climate, it is not the best time to conclude big deals at the moment, so we are taking it a little easy."

24. "IOC, USOC to Revisit Olympic Revenue Sharing."

25. "Dispute over Olympic Revenue Sharing May Impact Chicago Bid," *USA Today.com*, June 3, 2008, http://www.usatoday.com/sports/olympics/2008–06–03-chicago-share_N.htm.

26. Hersh, "IOC Official Rips USOC's Share of Olympic Funding"; "Dispute over Olympic Revenue Sharing."

27. Hersh, "IOC Official Rips USOC's Share of Olympic Funding." The USOC counterargument is that the key to TOP's financial success is the access to the US market granted to TOP sponsors in connection with their use of Olympic marks and logos. The USOC maintains that the percentage share of TOP revenue it receives compensates it for lost domestic sponsorship revenue; however, the strength of the argument was weakened by the increasing number of TOP sponsor companies whose headquarters were located outside the United States.

28. Ibid.

29. Philip Hersh, "IOC-USOC Deal: Some Ado about Nothing," *Chicago Tribune*, Apr. 1, 2009, http://newsblogs.chicagotribune.com/sports_globetrotting/2009/04/lets-make-a-few-things-clear-about-the-net-result-so-far-of-the-volatile-revenue-sharing-negotiations-between-the-us-o.html.

30. Hersh, "IOC Official Rips USOC's Share of Olympic Funding."

31. Katie Thomas, "Wrenching Shake-Up of the U.S. Olympic Committee," *New York Times*, June 28, 2009, http://nytimes.com/2009/06/28/sports/28usoc.html. For details on Probst, the chairman of the board of directors of Electronic Arts, see "Lawrence F. Probst III Appointed Chairman of U.S. Olympic Committee."

32. Hersh, "IOC-USOC Deal."

33. Tripp Mickle, "IOC, USOC Break Revenue-Sharing Stalemate."

34. Juliet Macur, "Olympic Committees Compromise in Revenue-Sharing Dispute," *New York Times*, Mar. 28, 2009, http://nytimes.com/2009/03/28/sports/28olympics.html; Matt Cutler, "IOC and USOC Reach Revenue Distribution Agreement."

35. Richard Sandomir, "Olympics Channel Draws Rebuke from the IOC," *New York Times*, July 9, 2009, http://www.nytimes.com/2009/07/09/sports/09olympics.html.

36. "IOC Official Expresses Frustration with New USOC TV Network" (brackets added).

37. "USOC Delays Olympic Television Network—Boost for Chicago 2016."

38. Stephen Wilson, "Rogge: USOC Issues Won't Harm Chicago's 2016 Bid." In April 2010, the USOC abandoned the plan for an Olympic television network. Philip Hersh, "U.S. Olympic Network Cuts to Black Before Ever Seeing Light," *Chicago Tribune*, Apr. 21, 2010, http://newsblogs.chicagotribune.com/sports_globetrotting/2010/04/us-olympic-network-cuts-to-black-before-ever-seeing-light.html.

39. "Rio de Janeiro Wins 2016 Olympic Games." Denis Oswald, for one, was succinct in his analysis of Chicago's loss. Oswald labeled it "a defeat for the USOC, not Chicago." "Television Revenue Not Important Insists Rogge."

40. Shipley, "Deteriorating USOC-IOC Relations Threaten Both Organizations." Pound expanded on his thoughts in a January 2010 interview with Reuters: "The risk for the IOC—if it plays this badly—is that the U.S. will say, 'ok so you don't like the share we take we won't take any.' But just remember, whatever broadcaster you license needs our permission to use the word Olympic. We'll make a separate deal on our own. And it's important to us and to you that there be a Games once in-a-while in the United States. So whenever you want a Games in one of our cities, come tell us and we'll find a city and we'll put on a great Games. But we are not going to go on getting kicked in the nuts and being eliminated in the first and second round in these contests that are not based on the merits of the bid. That would not be something I would ever want to hear. . . . For a long time 80 percent of the total resources for the Olympic movement were coming out of the United States. You have to pay attention to that. The United States could say, 'look we're out of the Olympic business for now.' We're not going to bid for 2018 or 2020 or 2022 maybe 2024, but that's 14 years there won't have been a Games in (North) America. You're going to run out of places like Dubai and Bulgaria and so on. If you only go to places like that you're [sic] brand is really going to take a beating. There will be no interest in America and therefore no television rights, no sponsorship. If the U.S. television rights shrink by half not only do you lose a billion dollars there is probably a knock on effect in other markets.' The USOC could easily shoot itself in the foot here, but so could the IOC." Steve Keating, "IOC Keen to See Where Blackmun Steers USOC," *Reuters.com*, Jan. 6, 2010, http://ca.reuters.com/article/SportsNews/idCATRE6055QA20100106?sp=true.

41. "Rogge Says Economics Should Not Drive 2016 Vote," *USA Today.com*, June 16, 2009, http://www.usatoday.com/sports/olympics/2009–06–16-ioc-meetings-rogge_N.htm.

42. *Report of the 2016 IOC Evaluation Commission: Games of the XXXI Olympiad*, 85, 81–82.

43. Tripp Mickle, "IOC Shifts from Dependence on U.S. Revenue"; "IOC Officially Announces Dow Sponsorship Deal"; "IOC Announces Sponsorship Deal with Consumer Products Giant Procter & Gamble."

44. "Dispute over Olympic Revenue Sharing."

45. Brian Cazeneuve, "U.S. Against the World: A New TV Network Exacerbates Olympic Tensions."

46. "Chicago Bid Boss Says Regional Voting, IOC-USOC Friction Costly," *Reuters. com*, Oct. 6, 2009, http://blogs.reuters.com/sport/2009/10/06/chicago-bid-boss-says-regional-voting-ioc-usoc-friction-costly/.

47. Eddie Pells, "USOC Still Looking for Answers in Wake of Chicago's Embarrassment in Vote for 2016 Olympics" (brackets added).

48. For a suggested method of enhancing Olympic-generated revenue available to the OCOGs, see Stephen Wenn and Tim Elcombe, "A Path to Peace: Some Thoughts on Olympic Revenue and the IOC/USOC Divide."

49. Philip Hersh, "USOC's Acting CEO Stephanie Streeter Won't Seek Permanent Post," *Chicago Tribune*, Oct. 7, 2009, http://www.chicagotribune.com/sports/chi-08usoc-treeter oct08,0,5049875.story.

50. Eddie Pells, "USOC Board Votes in Support of Streeter, Probst."

51. "Streeter's Tenure Marked by Missteps." Dick Ebersol resigned as chairman of NBC Universal Sports and Olympics in May 2011. Richard Sandomir and Bill Carter, "Dick Ebersol Resigns from NBC Sports," *New York Times*, May 19, 2011, http://www.nytimes.com/2011/05/20/sports/dick-ebersol-resigns-from-nbc-sports.html?pagewanted=all. He returned as a senior adviser in August 2011.

52. Laura Walden, "Obama and Chicago Victims of USOC Politics with IOC." With respect to the lingering dispute between the USOC and IOC over Olympic revenue, and the manner in which it is likely to undercut host bids from other US cities, Ebersol pulled no punches: "The IOC, which is heavily Eurocentric as just under half the voters are European, and are very, very disappointed in the relationship that they have with the United States Olympic Committee. They find it very hard to believe that the USOC takes almost 13% of all the US television money off the top and they take 20% sponsorship money. . . . We've got to get it worked out between our US Olympic Committee and the other Olympic Committees of the world and the IOC or we won't see another Olympic Games in the United States for a long, long time."

53. Larry Probst is the organization's sixth acting or permanent chair since 2000: Bill Hybl, 1996–2000; Sandy Baldwin, 2000–2002; Marty Mankamyer, 2002–3; Bill Martin, 2003–4; Peter Ueberroth, 2004–8; and Probst, October 2008–present. "Like the Entrance to Macy's the Revolving Door Spins at the USOC," *Colorado Springs Gazette*, Oct. 22, 2009, http://gazetteolympics.freedomblogging.com/2009/10/22/like-the-entrance-to-macys-the-revolving-door-spins-at-the-usoc/2319/.

54. Hersh, "Streeter Won't Seek Permanent Post"; Walden, "Obama and Chicago Victims"; Alan Abrahamson, "Scott Blackmun: Arguably the USOC's Last Best Chance"; Philip Hersh, "USOC Critics Hail Choice of Blackmun as CEO," *Los Angeles Times*, Jan. 5, 2010, http://latimes.com/olympics_blog/2010/01/usoc-critics-hail-choice-of-blackmun-as-ceo.html. USOC CEOs during this tumultuous time were Dick Schultz, 1995–2000; Norm Blake, February 2000–November 2000; Scott Blackmun, November 2000–October 2001; Lloyd Ward, October 2000–March 2003; Jim Scherr, March 2003–March 2009; and Stephanie Streeter, March 2009–January 2010. "Like the Entrance to Macy's."

55. Abrahamson, "Scott Blackmun."

56. Stephen Wilson, "IOC and USOC Look to Resolve Financial Issue," *USA Today*, Apr. 27, 2010, http://www.usatoday.com/sports/olympics/2010–04–27–2872487469_x.htm. Denis Oswald commented on "the very positive spirit" of recent discussions with the USOC, and Scott Blackmun expressed his understanding that a resolution was necessary for the USOC in its effort to reestablish positive relations with the IOC.

57. "USOC and IOC Reach Agreement in Financial Dispute," *USA Today.com*, Sept. 9, 2010, http://www.usatoday.com/sports/Olympics/2010–09–09-usoc-ioc-agreement_N.htm.

The USOC transferred eighteen million dollars to Lausanne. All NOCs except the USOC had contributed to such a Games cost fund in the past. For the Probst and Blackmun appointments, see "USOC Execs Named to Key IOC Roles." For progress in talks on revenue sharing, see Stephen Wilson, "IOC, USOC Hope for Deal by July on Revenue Sharing."

58. Mallon, "The Olympic Bribery Scandal," 23.

59. Ibid., 21. Seven members constitute the Nominations Committee. The group must include at least one athlete who has been elected by his or her peers to the IOC, three IOC members, and three members elected by the Ethics Commission.

60. Ibid.

61. Pound, "Future of the Olympic Movement," 7, 8.

62. Mallon, "The Olympic Bribery Scandal," 22; Nancy J. Wiese to Pound, May 13, 1999; D'Alessandro to Pound, May 19, 1999; Fruit to Pound, June 11, 1999, PFRWP.

63. "Baseball, Softball, Pentathlon Will Be Discussed" (brackets added).

64. "IOC President Rejects 2016 Bid City Visits Proposal."

65. "Great Call of China: IOC Awards 2008 Games to Favored Beijing" (brackets added).

66. Brian Cazeneuve, "China Scores Decisive Victory."

67. The Canadian Olympic Committee's decision to support a bid for the 2010 Olympic Winter Games fostered debate in that country, as many questioned the merit of constructing a second set of world-class winter training facilities (separated merely by the Canadian Rockies) before exhausting all efforts to bring the same level of infrastructure into play for the nation's summer athletes.

68. "Great Call of China."

69. Ibid.

70. Cazeneuve, "China Scores Decisive Victory."

71. Clifford Coonan, "Let the Games Begin," *Irish Times* (Dublin), Dec. 29, 2007. There is concern of a post-Olympics economic slowdown in China. Simon Rabinovitch, "Beijing's Priority: Supporting Growth Rate in a Slowing Economy," *International Herald Tribune*, Aug. 26, 2008.

72. "Greece's 2006 Budget Seeks to Slash Bloated Deficit," Associated Press Newswires, Nov. 21, 2005. Greece's deputy minister of culture pegged the total cost at $15.35 billion. Jane Merrick, "Security Bill for London's 2012 Olympics to Hit £1.5Bn—Triple the Original Estimate," *Independent* (London), Sept. 28, 2008, http://www.independent.co.uk/news/uk/politics/security-bill-for-londons-2012-olympics-to-hit-16315bn–triple-the-original-estimate-944766.html. In February 2011, London organizers stated that their budget remained at £9.3 billion, as had been the case in September 2008. With the devaluation of the British pound against the US dollar since 2008, this figure translates into $15.14 billion in April 2011. "2012 London Olympics 'Still on Budget,'" *BBC News London*, Feb. 14, 2011, http://bbc.co.uk-england-london-12445712.

73. "The Great Pall over China," *Irish Times* (Dublin), Nov. 24, 2007.

74. John Farndon, *China Rises: How China's Astonishing Growth Will Change the World*, 152. Victor Cha, director of Asian studies and the D. S. Song Chair at Georgetown University,

summarized the aims of the Chinese government. China, wrote Cha, "seeks to use the Olympics to enhance internal credibility and control, showcase its economic growth, delegitimize Taiwan, improve its international stature, extinguish memories of the 1989 Tiananmen Square massacre, and establish the People's Republic of China (PRC) as a global player—a formidable list of objectives." Cha, "Beijing's Olympic-Sized Catch-22," 107.

75. Cha reported that China did shift its approach in relation to Darfur as a result of international pressure during the run-up to the Olympics such that it appointed an envoy to the region in May 2007 and expended significant energy to secure Sudan's acceptance of the deployment of a 26,000-strong UN-backed peacekeeping force to the region. None of it was sufficient to prevent US filmmaker Steven Spielberg from resigning his post as artistic adviser to the Beijing Olympics. Cha, "Beijing's Olympic-Sized Catch-22," 115–17. Critics remained focused on China's continuing trade relationship with Sudan's government headed by Omar al-Bashir.

76. Pound, "Future of the Olympic Movement," 2, 3.

77. Pound used this description in response to a question during an audience discussion after his keynote address at the Ninth International Symposium for Olympic Research in Beijing, in August 2008.

78. Anita Chang, "Report: China Will Bar 'Antagonistic Elements' from Olympics," Associated Press Newswires, Nov. 9, 2007. See also "Man Resisting Eviction for Beijing Olympics Forcibly Removed," *Kyodo News* (Japan), Nov. 8, 2007; "The Great Pall over China"; and Mark Spector, "Olympic Façade Couldn't Hide China's Flaws," *National Post* (Canada), Aug. 24, 2008, http://www.nationalpost.com/story.html?id=746198. Estimates range between 1.25 and 1.5 million people.

79. "Rogge: London Should Play Up Its Diversity," *International Herald Tribune*, Aug. 24, 2008, http://www.iht.com/articles/ap/2008/08/24/sports/AS-OLY-Rogge-London.php.

80. "With End of Games Come Queries over China's Future," *Nikkei Weekly* (Japan), Sept. 1, 2008.

81. "The Great Pall over China" (brackets added).

82. For China's economic transformation, and the path to admission to the WTO, see Jonathan Story, *China: The Rise to Market—What China's Transformation Means for Business, Markets, and the New World Order*, 2, 140–73.

83. Jane McCartney, "Millions Frustrated as Olympic Ticket System Fails at First Hurdle," *Times* (London), Nov. 1, 2007. The international embarrassment suffered as a result of the computer failure cost Rong Jun, the Beijing Organizing Committee's director of ticketing, his job. "Beijing Replaces Director of Ticketing Following Computer Chaos," Associated Press Newswires, Nov. 30, 2007.

84. Charles Whelan, "Olympics: Chaos in Final Rush for Beijing Olympic Tickets," Agence France-Presse, July 25, 2008; Maureen Fan, "Olympic Ticket Tumult in Beijing," *Washington Post*, July 26, 2008; Clifford Coonan, "Melee in Beijing as Tickets for Games Go on Sale," *Irish Times* (Dublin), July 26, 2008.

85. "2 Out of 3 People in World Watched Olympics," *TheStar.com* (Toronto), Sept. 5, 2008, http://olympics.thestar.com/2008/article/491460.

86. "Mourning Old Beijing: Untold Stories of Chinese Loss and Punishment for Olympics," *Daytona Beach News Journal*, Aug. 25, 2008. A critic of China's human rights record, Naomi Klein, a Canadian social commentator and antiglobalization activist, sounded an alarm concerning the massive expenditure on Olympic security in the buildup to the Beijing Olympics. The extensive security infrastructure established through financial arrangements with US-based hedge funds, and corporations such as Google, Cisco, and General Electric, will remain after the Games. The Olympics, she says, were supposed to bring forward positive change with respect to the country's human rights record. "Instead," she asserts, "the Olympics have opened a backdoor for the regime to massively upgrade its systems of population control and repression." Klein, "China Unveils Futuristic Police State at Olympics."

87. The murder of Todd Bachman, the father-in-law of the US men's volleyball team coach, Hugh McCutcheon, during a sightseeing outing to the historic Drum Tower, cast a pall over the Games. "Stabbing Victim Father of '04 Olympian, Father-in-Law of Coach." While Usain Bolt and Michael Phelps garnered most of the headlines for their athletic feats, few stories competed with the emotion linked to the focus and determination of McCutcheon's crew in their successful pursuit of the gold medal.

88. Charles Hutzler, "UN, IOC Say Beijing's Foul Air Is a Problem, May Delay Some Events," Associated Press Newswires, Oct. 25, 2007; "IOC President Says Air Pollution May Spoil Beijing Games," Xinhua News Agency, Oct. 25, 2007. A halt on all construction projects in Beijing and a decision to remove half of Beijing's vehicles from the city's roadways on a daily basis represented two of the strategies employed to confront the air-quality issue.

89. Christopher Bodeen, "WADA Chief Praises Beijing Olympics Preparations, Help in U.S. Steroids Raids," Canadian Press, Sept. 27, 2007; Dave Stubbs, "Nowhere to Run: Doping Cheats Facing Stern Test, Says Pound," *National Post* (Canada), Aug. 5, 2008. As the Beijing Games approached their end, more than forty-six hundred drug tests had been administered, resulting in six positive tests. Pre-Games testing prevented thirty-nine athletes, twenty-two of whom were Bulgarian and Greek weightlifters, from taking part in the 2008 Beijing Olympics. "Beijing a Watershed Games in Anti-Doping Fight," Canadian Press, Aug. 23, 2008, http://www.ctv.ca/servlet/ArticleNews/story/CTVNews/20080823/beijing_doping_080823/20080823?s_name=beijing2008.

90. As the Games closed, Sebastian Coe seized on what would be one of London's missions in the absence of the ability to match Beijing's spending. "We are going to work on generating a party atmosphere," commented Coe. "Rogge: London Should Play Up Its Diversity."

91. There are concerns that China's economic boom of recent years will slow in the wake of the Games and that the Chinese government will need to deal with a rising inflation rate and reduced trade surplus. See "With End of Games Come Queries over China's Future."

92. The IOC, like many business entities, suffered losses as a result of the economic recession of 2008 that dragged into 2009. In May 2009, Jacques Rogge reported that the IOC

lost $34 million in the value of its investments, or approximately 8 percent off its reserves since January 2008. The IOC was also exposed to a loss ($4.8 million) as a result of the Bernie Madoff scandal; however, there remains some hope that a portion of that loss is recoverable. "Rogge Says Economic Downturn Cuts US$34 Million Form IOC Coffers," Canadian Press, May 5, 2009, http://ctvolympics.ca/news-centre/newsid=10329.html. In June 2009, Rogge reported that the IOC's reserves recovered 4.2 percent of their value in the first five months of 2009 as a result of an improved stock market and rested at $429 million. Stephen Wilson, "Jacques Rogge: IOC Reserves Up 4.2%," Canadian Press, June 12, 2009, http://www.ctvolympics.ca/news-centre/newsid=11772.html?cid=rssctv.

93. "By the Numbers: The Vancouver 2010 Olympic Winter Games."

94. "IOC to Retest Samples." The IOC announced its intent to retest doping samples from Beijing for a drug discovered by the French Anti-Doping Agency in its effort to retest samples from the Tour de France. The drug CERA is a blood booster and has been described as "a new generation of the endurance-enhancing hormone, EPO." This decision was encouraging and sent the appropriate signal concerning the IOC's (and Rogge's) commitment. Observers were heartened by the results of these tests announced in April 2009. Six athletes, including the 1,500-meter gold medalist, Bahrain's Rashid Ramzi, and the silver medalist in the cycling road race, Italy's Davide Rebellin, tested positive (A samples). The hope is that athletes will not engage in doping activities if they can subsequently be shamed given that samples can be retained for eight years after the competition date. Stephen Wilson, "All Six Athletes Identified in Doping Cases from Beijing Olympics."

95. The 1.5 million estimate issued by the Geneva-based Centre on Housing Rights and Evictions in June 2007 was disputed by Beijing officials. BOCOG and China's Foreign Ministry responded that the number of citizens who had been relocated and compensated was a mere 6,037. Lindsay Beck, "Beijing to Evict 1.5 Million for Olympics: Group," *Reuters.com*, June 5, 2007, http://www.reuters.com/article/worldNews/idUSPEK12263220070605.

96. Martin Ziegler, "Olympics: Vancouver Favourite to Win Race for 2010 Winter Games," *Independent* (London), July 2, 2003, http://www.independent.co.uk/sport/general/olympics-vancouver-favourite-to-win-race-for-2010-winter-games-585449.html; James Christie, "Pyeongchang's Stunning Rise," *Globeandmail.com*, July 4, 2003, http://www.theglobeandmail.com/servlet/story/RTGAM.20030704.wolpr04/BNStory/National.

97. A sting operation launched by the producers of BBC's *Panorama* television show in 2004 ended the IOC career of Bulgaria's Ivan Slavkov. Posing as representatives of business interests in London's East End, a number of BBC journalists drew Slavkov and reputed "Olympic agent" Goran Takac into a discussion of how they (Slavkov and Takac) might be able to influence some IOC members to support London's bid. While Slavkov neither asked for nor received money from the Londoners, the discussion taped with a hidden camera on July 1 and televised on August 4 clearly demonstrated that Slavkov would share in the prospective contract. Takac informed IOC vice president Vitaly Smirnov of the contact with

the London delegation in April 2004. Smirnov passed the information to IOC president Jacques Rogge in May. Rogge told Smirnov to inform Takac that he should approach the IOC Ethics Commission immediately. Takac did not take this advice. Slavkov, caught red-handed on the *Panorama* broadcast, claimed after the fact that he and Takac had set a trap for the people from London. He and Takac sought to root out this type of corruption in the bid process; however, the Ethics Commission deemed his claim not credible. His IOC colleagues expelled him, on the recommendation of the Ethics Commission and Executive Board, at the IOC's 117th IOC Session in Singapore in July 2005. Takac, Gabor Komyathy, Mahmoud El Farnawani, and Muttaleb Ahmad, individuals whose names surfaced in conjunction with the Salt Lake City scandal in their capacity as self-styled Olympic agents, were labeled personae non gratae in the Olympic world as a result of the BBC's telecast and the Ethics Commission's deliberations. *International Olympic Committee Ethics Commission, Decision with Recommendations N° D5/04.*

98. Of recent note, Vancouver 2010 CEO John Furlong revealed in his recently published assessment of the bidding for, and staging of, the Vancouver Olympic Winter Games that he had secured an arrangement with Moscow's mayor, Yuri Luzhkov, to acquire the "six or seven" Russian-controlled votes prior to the host-city election in 2003. Furlong was in error in terms of the number of votes because only three Russian members were active in 2003 and voted. In exchange for Vancouver staging a bid workshop for Moscow officials who were in pursuit of the 2012 Summer Olympics, a prize eventually secured by London, Luzhkov promised the votes. The IOC launched an investigation of the matter in early 2011 but determined that no rules had been breached since IOC members had not taken part in the discussions between Luzhkov and Furlong. John Furlong with Gary Mason, *Patriot Hearts: Inside the Olympics That Changed a Country*, 46–47; "IOC Clears Furlong of Wrongdoing." Interestingly, the final vote in 2003 was fifty-six for Vancouver over Pyeongchang, at fifty-three.

99. The IOC and VANOC removed Right to Play's platform for the recruitment of Olympians to support the organization's cause in the Olympic Village because VANOC enjoys a major sponsorship with General Motors, while Mitsubishi is delivering significant sponsorship dollars to Right to Play. Randy Starkman, "Right to Play Group Now on the IOC's Hit List," *Toronto Star*, Oct. 3, 2008, http://olympics.thestar.com/2008/article/510933. Johann Olav Koss expressed his regrets, even while negotiations continued: "VANOC brought it [the sponsor conflict] up with the IOC. We know that. We have no interest to harm the Olympic movement. It's been our wonderful partner for all these years and we hope we can be partners in the future. It's been exceptionally important because the Olympics mean so much for kids we're working with," stated Koss.

100. Rogge officially announced his intention to seek a second term of office in late October 2008. While expressing some concern about the prospect of the worldwide economic slowdown having an impact on the Olympic Movement and Olympic host cities in 2012 and

2014, he reiterated his intent to champion the fight against doping in sports: "Doping is still the major threat for sport," stated Rogge. He also noted his desire to promote increased youth involvement in sport. "Had the Beijing Games been a total failure," noted Rogge, "I would not have considered running. The Games were a great success. So were the others under my watch in Salt Lake City, Athens, and Turin. My motivation is to continue on the path I have followed." "Rogge: IOC Finances Solid Ahead of Second Term as President."

# Bibliography

**Archival Sources**

"Administrative History/Biographical History: Juan Antonio Samaranch." In *Juan Antonio Samaranch Fonds, 1957–2001: CH IOC-AH PT-JAS*. 2006. http://www .olympic.org/Documents/OSC/Resources/Archives/English/AH%20-%20Appendix %207-%20eng%20.PDF.

Board of Ethics of the Salt Lake Organizing Committee for the Olympic Winter Games of 2002. *Report to the Board of Trustees*. Salt Lake City: SLOC, Feb. 8, 1999.

Datops and Sportweb. "International Olympic Committee—Summary of the Media Crisis: International Media Crisis, Dec. 1998–June 1999." PFMRP.

*IOC Marketing Commission: Report to the IOC Executive Board*. Lausanne, Mar. 16, 1999. PFRWP.

*IOC Marketing Commission: Report to the 109th IOC Session*. Seoul, June 17–20, 1999. PFRWP.

*Minutes of the Ad Hoc Executive Board Meeting*. Lausanne, Jan. 24, 1999. PFRWP.

*Minutes of the Meeting of the IOC Executive Board*. Lausanne, May 28, 1985. IOCA.

*Minutes of the Meeting of the IOC Executive Board*. Lausanne, Oct. 10–11, 1986. IOCA.

*Minutes of the Meeting of the IOC Executive Board*. Lausanne, Dec. 4–6, 1991. IOCA.

*Minutes of the Meeting of the IOC Executive Board*. Courcheval, Feb. 1–3, 1992. IOCA.

*Minutes of the Meeting of the IOC Executive Board*. Lausanne, Oct. 5–10, 1996. IOCA.

*Minutes of the Meeting of the IOC Executive Board*. Lausanne, Dec. 11–13, 1998. PFRWP.

*Minutes of the Meeting of the IOC Executive Board*. Lausanne, Feb. 1, 1999. PFRWP.

*Minutes of the Meeting of the IOC Executive Board*. Lausanne, Mar. 15–16, 19, 1999. IOCA.

*Minutes of the Meeting of the IOC Executive Board.* Lausanne, May 4, 1999. PFRWP.

*Minutes of the Meeting of the IOC Executive Board.* Seoul, June 13–15, 1999. PFRWP.

*Minutes of the Meeting of the IOC Executive Board.* Athens, Oct. 1– 4, 1999. PFRWP

*Minutes of the Meeting of the IOC Executive Board.* Lausanne, Dec. 8–10, 13, 1999. PFRWP.

*Minutes of the Meeting of the IOC Marketing Commission.* Munich, Dec. 15, 1998. PFRWP.

*Minutes of the 98th IOC Session.* Courcheval, Feb. 5–6, 1992. IOCA.

*Minutes of the 108th Extraordinary IOC Session.* Lausanne, Mar. 17–18, 1999. IOCA.

*Minutes of the 109th IOC Session.* Seoul, June 17–20, 1999. IOCA.

*Minutes of the 110th IOC Session.* Lausanne, Dec. 11–12, 1999. IOCA.

"Notes for Telephone Call Between IOC President and McDonald's Corporation, Tuesday, 16 February 1999, 16:00." PFRWP.

"Notes for Telephone Call Between IOC President and the Coca-Cola Company, Wednesday, 17 February 1999, 16:00." PFRWP.

"Notes on the Work of the Television Sub-Committee." June 23, 1974. "TV Divers, 1974–1985" Binder. IOCA.

Pound, Richard. "Daily Message Log, 1999." PFRWP.

———. "Personal Day Planner, 1999." PFRWP.

*Report by the IOC 2000 Commission to the 110th IOC Session.* Lausanne, Dec. 11–12, 1999. http://multimedia.olympic.org/pdf/en_report-588.pdf.

*Report to the International Olympic Committee by the Toronto Ontario Olympic Council on the Candidature of the City of Toronto to Host the Games of the XXVI Olympiad.* London, Ontario: International Centre for Olympic Studies, Jan. 9, 1991.

*Summary of the International Olympic Committee Reform Act of 1999.* PFRWP.

**Other Sources**

Abrahamson, Alan. "The One and Only Juan Antonio Samaranch." *Universal Sports.com,* May 8, 2009. http://www.universalsports.com/news-blogs/blogs/blog=alanabrahamsonsblog/postid=316324.html.

———. "Scott Blackmun: Arguably the USOC's Last Best Chance." *UniversalSports.com,* Jan. 6, 2010. http://www.universalsports.com/blogs/blog=alanabrahamsonsblog/postid=387006.html.

"Atlanta Admits Wrong Doings: Organizers Might Have Broken Three Other Laws." *CBSnews.com,* Sept. 16, 1999. http://www.cbsnews.com/stories/1999/09/16/sports/main62640.sthml.

Barlett, Donald R., and James B. Steele. "Snow Job: Thanks to Utah Politicians and the 2002 Olympics, a Blizzard of Federal Money—a Stunning $1.5 Billion—Has Fallen on the State, Enriching Some Already Wealthy Businessmen." *Sports Illustrated.cnn.com*, Dec. 10, 2001. http://sportsillustrated.cnn.com/vault/article/magazine/MAG1024516/index.htm.

Barney, Robert. "The Great Transformation: Olympic Victory Ceremonies and the Medal Podium." *Olympika: The International Journal of Olympic Studies* 7 (1998): 89–112.

Barney, Robert, Stephen Wenn, and Scott Martyn. *Selling the Five Rings: The International Olympic Committee and the Rise of Olympic Commercialism*. Rev. ed. Salt Lake City: Univ. of Utah Press, 2004.

"Baseball, Softball, Pentathlon Will Be Discussed." *ESPN.com*, Nov. 24, 2002. http://espn.go.com/oly/news/2002/1124/146538.html.

Beevor, Antony. *The Battle for Spain: The Spanish Civil War, 1936–1939*. London: Penguin Books, 2006.

Berridge, Geoff R. *Diplomacy: Theory and Practice*. 3rd ed. Houndmills, UK, and New York: Palgrave Macmillan, 2005.

Booth, Doug. "Gifts of Corruption? Ambiguities of Obligation in the Olympic Movement." *Olympika: The International Journal of Olympic Studies* 8 (1999): 42–68.

———. "Lobbying Orgies: Olympic City Bids in the Post–Los Angeles Era." In *Global Olympics: Historical and Sociological Studies of the Modern Games, Research in the Sociology of Sport*, edited by Kevin Young and Kevin B. Wamsley, 3:201–25. Amsterdam: Elsevier, 2005.

Bowen, Wayne H. *Spain During World War II*. Columbia: Univ. of Missouri Press, 2006.

Buffery, Steve. "IOC Gives Six the Heave-Ho." *SlamSports.com*, Mar. 18, 1999. http://www.canoe.ca/SlamOlympicScandalArchive/mar18_ buffery.html.

———. "Scarred by Scandal: Ex-IOC Member Haggman Tries to Rebuild Her Life." *SlamSports.com*, Mar. 28, 1999. http://www.canoe.ca/SlamOlympicScandal Archive/mar28_buffery.html.

"By the Numbers: The Vancouver 2010 Olympic Winter Games." Accessed Mar. 26, 2010. http://vancouver2010.com/olympic-news/n/the-vancouver-2010-olympic-winter-games-by-the-numbers_297556Ko.html.

Campbell, Julia. "Vaulting Costs: Olympic Games Cost U.S. Taxpayers More than Ever." *ABC News.com*, Sept. 25, 2000. http://abcnews.go.com/section/us/DailyNews/olympicspending.

Caple, Jim. "Let the Fun and Games Begin." *ESPN.com*, Feb. 7, 2002. http://sports.espn.go.com/espn/print?id=1323982&type=Story.

Cazeneuve, Brian. "China Scores Decisive Victory." *CNNSI.com*, July 13, 2001. http://
sportsillustrated.cnn.com/inside_game/cazeneuve/news/2001/07/13/cazeneuve_
2008/.

———. "U.S. Against the World: A New TV Network Exacerbates Olympic Tensions." *SportsIllustrated.cnn.com*, July 27, 2009. http://sportsillustrated.cnn.com/
vault/article/magazine/ MAG1158146/index.htm.

Cha, Victor. "Beijing's Olympic-Sized Catch-22." *Washington Quarterly* 31 (Summer 2008): 105–23.

Clendenin, John A., and Stephen A. Greyser. *Tarnished Rings? Olympic Games
Sponsorship Issues.* Harvard Business School Case 599–107. Rev. ed. Boston:
Harvard Business School Publishing, 2004.

"Coke Identifies Taint Source." *CNN Money*, June 25, 1999. http://money.cnn
.com/1999/06/25/worldbiz/coke_phenol/.

Cornell University Law School. "Antitrust: An Overview." Accessed Nov. 14, 2008.
http://topics.law.cornell.edu/wex/antitrust/.

Cutler, Matt. "IOC and USOC Reach Revenue Distribution Agreement." *Sport Business International*, Mar. 30, 2009. http://www.sportbusiness.com/print/169110.

Darby, Ian. "Deals to Survive Olympic Scandals." *Marketing* (Jan. 28, 1999).

"David Sam, District of Utah." Accessed Mar. 22, 2010. http://faculty.rwu.edu/
dzlotnick/profiles/sam.html.

Dent, George W., Jr. "Corporate Governance: Still Broke, No Fix in Sight." *Journal
of Corporation Law* 31 (Fall 2005): 39–76.

Dickey, Christopher, Andrew Murr, and Russell Watson. "No More Fun and Games:
Juan Antonio Samaranch Comes Under Fire as Head of the International Olympic Committee." *Newsweek*, Feb. 1, 1999.

"Drut Given Presidential Pardon." *ESPN.com*, June 1, 2006. http://sports.espn.go
.com/espn/wire?section=oly&id=2457956.

Echikson, William, and Richard Siklos. "Scandal? What Scandal? Olympic Sponsors Aren't Fazed by Allegations of Corruption." *Business Week*, Mar. 22, 1999.

Eckert, S. "Reforming the Rings: An Evaluation of the IOC's Reform Process Following the Salt Lake City Bid Scandal." Honors senior thesis, Wilfrid Laurier
Univ., 2007.

Elder, Catriona, Angela Pratt, and Cath Ellis. "Running Race: Nationalism and the
Sydney 2000 Olympic Games." *International Review of the Sociology of Sport*
41, no. 2 (2006): 181–200.

Encarnación, Omar G. "Spain after Franco: Lessons in Democratization." *World
Policy Journal* 18 (Winter 2001–2): 35–44.

Epstein, Richard A. "Scrapping Sarbox." *Chief Executive* 231 (Jan.–Feb. 2008): 56–58.

"Extinguishing the Flame?" *Online News Hour: Olympic Scandal Fallout*, Mar. 18, 1999. http://www.pbs.org.newshour/bb/sports/jan-june 99/comeback_3.18.html.

Farndon, John. *China Rises: How China's Astonishing Growth Will Change the World*. London: Virgin Books, 2007.

Findling, John E. "Juan Antonio Samaranch." In *Historical Dictionary of the Modern Olympic Movement*, edited by John E. Findling and Kimberly D. Pelle, 487–94. Westport, CT: Greenwood Press, 2004.

"Fourth IOC Official Resigns Amid Bribery Scandal." *CNN.com*, Jan. 27, 1999. http://www.cnn.com/WORLD/africa/9901/27/ioc.01/.

Furlong, John, with Gary Mason. *Patriot Hearts: Inside the Olympics That Changed a Country*. Vancouver: Douglas and McIntyre, 2011.

Garber, Greg. "Samaranch's Legacy: Controversy, Corruption." *ESPN.com*, July 12, 2001. http://assets.espn.go.com/oly/columns/garber_greg/1225329.html.

Gerlach, Larry. "The Mormon Games: Religion, Media, Cultural Politics, and the Salt Lake Winter Olympics." *Olympika: The International Journal of Olympic Studies* 1 (2002): 1–52.

Glendinning, Matthew. "IOC Rejects EBU Bid for 2014–2016 Olympic Games Rights." *SportBusiness.com*, Dec. 3, 2008. http://www.sportbusiness.com/news/168397/ioc-rejects-ebu-bid-201416-olympic-games-rights.

"Golden Moment: Canadian Duo Receives Pairs Skating Medals." *CNNSI.com*, Feb. 18, 2002. http://sportsillustrated.cnn.com/olympics/2002/figure_skating/news/2002/02/17/canadian_medals_ap/.

Gordon, Harry. *The Time of Our Lives: Inside the Sydney Olympics—Australia and the Olympic Games, 1994–2002*. Brisbane: Univ. of Queensland Press, 2003.

"Grand Jury Indicts Alaska Senator." *CNN.com*, July 29, 2008. http://www.cnn.com/2008/POLITICS/07/29/stevens.indictment/index.html.

"Great Call of China: IOC Awards 2008 Games to Favored Beijing." *CNNSI.com*, July 13, 2001. http://sportsillustrated.cnn.com/olympics/news/2001/07/13/beijing_games_ap/.

Guttmann, Allen. *The Games Must Go On: Avery Brundage and the Olympic Movement*. New York: Columbia Univ. Press, 1984.

———. *The Olympics: A History of the Modern Games*. Urbana: Univ. of Illinois Press, 1994.

"Guy Drut Given Presidential Pardon." *ESPN.com*, June 1, 2006. http://sports.espn.go.com/espn/wire?section=oly&id=2457956.

Haynes, Jill. *Socio-economic Impact of the Sydney 2000 Olympic Games.* 2001. http://olympicstudies.uab.es/pdf/wp094_eng.pdf.

Hoberman, John. "Dopers on Wheels: The Tour's Sorry History." *NBCSports.com,* Sept. 20, 2007. http://nbcsports.msnbc.com/id/19462071/.

―――. *Mortal Engines: The Science of Performance and the Dehumanization of Sport.* New York: Free Press, 1992.

―――. "Olympic Drug Testing: An Interpretive History." In *Global Olympics: Historical and Sociological Studies of the Modern Games, Research in the Sociology of Sport,* edited by Kevin Young and Kevin B. Wamsley, 3:249–65. Amsterdam: Elsevier, 2005.

Hunt, Thomas M. *Drug Games: The International Olympic Committee and the Politics of Doping, 1960–2008.* Austin: Univ. of Texas Press, 2010.

Ignatius, David. "A Global Marketplace Means Global Vulnerability." *Global Policy Forum,* June 1999. http://globalpolicy.org/globaliz/special/globvuln.htm.

International Olympic Committee. *Press Kit: The Samaranch Years, 1980–2001.* Lausanne: IOC Publications, 2001.

*International Olympic Committee Ethics Commission, Decision Nᵒ D/01/02.* Mohamed (Bob) Hasan, May 7, 2002. http://multimedia.olympic.org/pdf/en_report_872.pdf.

*International Olympic Committee Ethics Commission, Decision with Recommendations Nᵒ D5/04.* Ivan Slavkov, Oct. 25, 2004. http://multimedia.olympic.org/pdf/en_report_1271.pdf.

*International Olympic Committee Ethics Commission, Decision with Recommendations Nᵒ D04/07.* John Krimsky, Dec. 7, 2004. http://multimedia.olympic.org/pdf/en_report_1272.pdf.

*International Olympic Committee Ethics Commission, Decision Containing Recommendations Nᵒ D/01/05.* Un Yong Kim, Feb. 4, 2005. http://multimedia.olympic.org/pdf/en_report_913.pdf.

*International Olympic Committee Ethics Commission, Decision on Interim Measures Nᵒ D/06/05.* Guy Drut, Nov. 29, 2005. http://multimedia.olympic.org/pdf/en_report_1023.pdf.

*International Olympic Committee Ethics Commission, Decision with recommendations Nᵒ D/02/06.* Guy Drut, June 15, 2006. http://multimedia.olympic.org/pdf/en_report_1075.pdf.

*International Olympic Committee Ethics Commission, Decision Nᵒ D/04/06.* Franco Carraro, Dec. 15, 2006. http://multimedia.olympic.org/pdf/en_report_1100.pdf.

*International Olympic Committee Ethics Commission, Decision with Recommendations N° D/01/07.* Lance Armstrong v. Richard Pound, IOC Member and WADA Chairman, and the World Anti-Doping Agency (WADA), Feb. 2, 2007. http://multimedia.olympic.org/pdf/en_report_1127.pdf.

*International Olympic Committee Ethics Commission, Decision with Recommendations N° D/02/07.* Yong Sung Park, Mar. 20, 2007. http://multimedia.olympic.org/pdf/en_report_1164.pdf.

*International Olympic Committee Ethics Commission, Decision with Recommendations N° D/03/07.* Henri Sérandour, Oct. 30, 2007. http://multimedia.olympic.org/pdf/en_report_1271.pdf.

*International Olympic Committee Ethics Commission, Decision with Recommendations N° D/01/08.* Floyd Landis v. Richard Pound, IOC Member and WADA Chairman, and the World Anti-Doping Agency (WADA), Jan. 21, 2008. http://multimedia.olympic.org/pdf/en_report_1328.pdf.

"Interview: Anita DeFrantz, Vice President of the International Olympic Committee, Speaks Out about Removing Those Who Abuse Their Authority Within the IOC." *NBC News: Today,* Jan. 22, 1999.

"IOC, USOC to Revisit Olympic Revenue Sharing." *CBSSports.com,* June 4, 2008. http://sportsline.com/worldsports/story/10852373.

"IOC Announces Sponsorship Deal with Consumer Products Giant Procter & Gamble." *Yahoo! News Canada,* July 28, 2010. http://ca.news.yahoo.com/s/capress/100728/business/oly_ioc_sponsor.

"IOC Clears Furlong of Wrongdoing." *Sportsnet.ca,* Mar. 12, 2011. http://www.sportsnet.ca/Olympics/2011/03/12/ioc_clears_furlong_/.

"IOC Loses TOP Sponsor." *Around the Rings,* Nov. 17, 2008. http://www.aroundtherings.com/articles/view.aspx?id=30969.

"IOC Official Expresses Frustration with New USOC TV Network." *Street & Smith's SportsBusiness Daily,* July 9, 2009. http://www.sportsbusinessdaily.com/article/131587.

"IOC Officially Announces Dow Sponsorship Deal." *Olympics—NOW.com,* July 17, 2010. http://www.olympics-now.com/2010/07/17/ioc-officially-announces-dow-sponsorship-deal.

"IOC President Rejects 2016 Bid City Visits Proposal." *GamesBids.com,* Aug. 6, 2008. http://www.gamesbids.com/eng/olympic_bids/1216133577.html.

"IOC to Retest Samples." *GlobeSports.com,* Oct. 8, 2008. http://www.globesports.com/servletstory/RTGAM.20081008.wsptoly1008/GSStory/Glob . . .

Jenkins, C. "Establishing a World Anti-Doping Code: WADA's Impact on the Development of an International Strategy for Anti-Doping in Sport." Master's thesis, Univ. of Windsor, 2006.

Jennings, Andrew, and Vyv Simson. *The Lords of the Rings: Power, Money, and Drugs in the Modern Olympics.* Toronto: Stoddart, 1992.

"John Hancock Ready to Talk to NBC." *SlamSports,* Feb. 16, 2000. http://www.canoe.com/SlamOlympicScandal/feb15_joh.html.

Johns, Gary, and Alan M. Saks. *Organizational Behaviour: Understanding and Managing Life at Work.* 6th ed. Toronto: Pearson–Prentice Hall, 2005.

Kellerman, Barbara. *Bad Leadership: What It Is, How It Happens, Why It Matters.* Boston: Harvard Business School Press, 2004.

Kidané, Fékrou. "Samaranch and Olympism." *Olympic Review* 39 (June–July 2001): 18–20.

Killanin, Lord. *My Olympic Years.* London: Secker and Warburg, 1983.

Kingdon, John W. *Agendas, Alternatives, and Public Policies.* 2nd ed. New York: Longman, 2003.

Klein, Naomi. "China Unveils Futuristic Police State at Olympics." *AlterNet.com,* Aug. 8, 2008. http://www.alternet.org/story/94278/?page=entire.

Krasner, Jeffrey. "Two Eras: Before David, after David." *Boston.com,* Sept. 29, 2003. http://www.boston.com/business/articles/2003/09/29/two_eras_before_david_after_david/.

Kynge, James. *China Shakes the World: A Titan's Rise and Troubled Future—and the Challenge for America.* Boston: Houghton Mifflin, 2006.

Landry, Fernand, and Magdalene Yerlès. *The International Olympic Committee—One Hundred Years: The Idea—the Presidents—the Achievements; The Presidencies of Lord Killanin [1972–1980] and of Juan Antonio Samaranch [1980–]).* Vol. 3. Lausanne: IOC, 1996.

"Lawrence F. Probst III Appointed Chairman of U.S. Olympic Committee." *TeamUSA.org,* Oct. 2, 2008. http://teamusa.org/news/article/6999.

Lerbinger, Otto. *The Crisis Manager: Facing Risk and Responsibility.* Mahwah, NJ: Lawrence Erlbaum Associates, 1997.

London East Research Institute. *A Lasting Legacy for London? Assessing the Legacy of the Olympic and Paralympic Games.* London: Greater London Authority, 2007.

MacDonald, Gordon. Review of *The Time of Our Lives: Inside the Sydney Olympics—Australia and the Olympic Games, 1994–2002,* by Harry Gordon. *Olympika: The International Journal of Olympic Studies* 13 (2004): 103–5.

Mallon, Bill. "The Olympic Bribery Scandal." *Journal of Olympic History* 8, no. 2 (2000): 11–27.

*Marketing Matters: The Olympic Marketing Newsletter* 21 (June 2002).

Markham, Jerry W. *A Financial History of Modern U.S. Corporate Scandals: From Enron to Reform*. London and Armonk: M. E. Sharpe, 2006.

Martyn, Scott. "The Struggle for Financial Autonomy: The IOC and the Historical Emergence of Corporate Sponsorship, 1896–2000." PhD diss., Univ. of Western Ontario, 2000.

Martyn, Scott, and Stephen Wenn. "A Prelude to Samaranch: Lord Killanin's Path to Olympic Commercialism." *Journal of Olympic History* 16 (July 2008): 40–48.

"McD's Greenberg Sees Record Year, Vows to Support Olympics." *Nation's Restaurant News* (Mar. 29, 1999).

Merce Varela, Andrés. "The Journey of a Great President." *Olympic Review* 39 (June–July 2001): 10–15.

Mickle, Tripp. "IOC, USOC Break Revenue-Sharing Stalemate." *Street and Smith's SportsBusiness Journal* (Mar. 30, 2009). http://www.sportsbusinessjournal.com/article/62128.

———. "IOC Shifts from Dependence on U.S. Revenue." *Street and Smith's SportsBusiness Journal* (Oct. 12, 2009). http://www.sportsbusinessjournal.com.article/63810.

Miller, David. "Evolution of the Olympic Movement." In *From Moscow to Lausanne*, 9–21. Lausanne: International Olympic Committee, 1990.

———. *Olympic Revolution: The Biography of Juan Antonio Samaranch*. London: Pavilion Books, 1992.

"Motion for a Judgment of Acquittal: Rule 29." In *Federal Criminal Code and Rules*, amended Jan. 2003, 2. Washington, DC: Thompson-West Group, 2003.

Mundial de Hockey Vigo 2009. "Roller Hockey World Championship Official Website: History." Accessed Mar. 6, 2009. http://www.mundialvigo2009.com/camp eonato.php?lang=en&s=5.

Munson, Lester. "Back on the Docket: Details Revealed of Case vs. Salt Lake City Olympics Organizers." *SI.com*, May 1, 2003. http://sportsillustrated.cnn.com/inside_game/lester_munson/news/2003/05/01/holding_court/.

Nelson, Scott Bernard. "The Name's the Same for Top Two." *Boston.com*, Sept. 29, 2003. http://www.boston.com/business/articles/2003/09/29/the_names_the_same_for_top_two.

Nemery, B., B. Fischler, M. Boogaerts, D. Lison, and J. Willems. "The Coca-Cola Incident in Belgium—June 1999." *Food and Chemical Toxicology* 40, no. 11 (2002): 1657–67.

Neubauer, Deane. "Modern Sport and Olympic Games: The Problematic Complexities Raised by the Dynamics of Globalization." *Olympika: The International Journal of Olympic Studies* 17 (2008): 1–40.

"Nike Takes Up Where Reebok Left Off." *ABC News Online*, Dec. 13, 1999. http://www.abc.net.au/news/olympics/1999/12/Item19991213090654_1.htm.

*Olympic Marketing Fact File, 2008*. Lausanne: IOC Television and Marketing SA, 2008."Olympic News: Around the Rings." *SportBusiness.com*, ca. late Jan. 1999. http://sportbusiness.com/news/130621/olympic-news-p-around-the-rings-p-ed-hula-editor.

*Olympic Reform: A Ten Year Review*. Toronto: Univ. of Toronto, May 19–20, 2009. http://www.ac-fpeh.com/Olympic_Reform/.

"Olympics Scandal Cases Closed." *Around the Rings*, Sept. 16, 2004. http://www.aroundtherings.com/article/view.aspx?id=27937.

Papamiltiades, Mary Charalmbous. "IOC: Factors That Fostered the Development of the Most Publicized Crisis in Its History—the Salt Lake Scandal." *Journal of Olympic History* 15 (Nov. 2007): 54–69.

Pauchant, Thierry C., and Ian I. Mitroff. *Transforming the Crisis-Prone Organization: Preventing Individual, Organizational, and Environmental Tragedies*. San Francisco: Jossey-Bass, 1992.

Payne, Michael. *Olympic Turnaround: How the Olympic Games Stepped Back from the Brink of Extinction to Become the World's Best Known Brand—and a Multi-Billion-Dollar Global Franchise*. London: London Business Press, 2005.

Payne, Stanley G. *Fascism in Spain, 1923–1977*. Madison: Univ. of Wisconsin Press, 1999.

———. *The Franco Regime, 1936–1975*. Madison: Univ. of Wisconsin Press, 1988.

Pells, Eddie. "USOC Board Votes in Support of Streeter, Probst." *Yahoo! News*, Oct. 8, 2009. http://news.yahoo.com/s/ap/20091010/ap_on_sp_ol/oly_usoc_turmoil.

———. "USOC Still Looking for Answers in Wake of Chicago's Embarrassment in Vote for 2016 Olympics." Oct. 3, 2009. http://blog.taragana.com/sports/2009/10/03/usoc-still-looking-for-answers-in-wake-of-chicagos-embarrassment-in-vote-for-2016-olympics-34010/.

Pound, Richard. "The Future of the Olympic Movement: Promised Land or Train Wreck?" In *Pathways: Critiques and Discourse in Olympic Research—Ninth International Symposium for Olympic Research*, edited by Robert K. Barney,

Michael K. Heine, Kevin B. Wamsley, and Gordon H. MacDonald, 1–19. London: Univ. of Western Ontario, 2008.

———. *Inside Dope: How Drugs are the Biggest Threat to Sports, Why You Should Care, and What Can Be Done about Them.* Mississauga, Ontario: John Wiley and Sons, 2006.

———. *Inside the Olympics: A Behind-the-Scene Look at the Politics, the Scandals, and the Glory of the Games.* Toronto: John Wiley and Sons, 2004.

"Promotion of Women Sport Leaders." http://www.olympic.org/uk/organisation/missions/women/activities/leaders_uk./asp.

Przeworski, Adam. *Democracy and the Market.* New York: Cambridge Univ. Press, 1991.

Real, Michael R. "Is TV Corrupting the Olympics? The (Post) Modern Olympics—Technology and the Commodification of the Olympic Movement." Accessed July 8, 2001. http://www.rohan.sdsu.edu/faculty/mreal/OlympicAtl.html.

*Report of the 2016 IOC Evaluation Commission: Games of the XXXI Olympiad.* Sept. 2009. http://www.turin2006.com/Documents/Reports/EN/en_report_1469.pdf.

"Rio de Janeiro Wins 2016 Olympic Games." *FOXNews.com,* Oct. 2, 2009. http://www.foxnews.com/story/0,2933,559181,00.html.

"Rio 2016 Refutes Tokyo's Claims of 'Invisible Dynamics.'" *GamesBids.com,* Oct. 6, 2009. http://www.gamesbids.com/eng/olympic_bids/rio_2016/1216134756.html.

"Rogge: IOC Finances Solid Ahead of Second Term as President." *TSN.ca,* Oct. 30, 2008. http://www.tsn.ca/olympics/story/?id=254221&lid=sublink01&lpos=headlines_main.

"Rogge Wins IOC Presidency; Pound Resigns from IOC Posts." *CBC.ca,* July 16, 2001. http://www.cbc.ca/olympics/2001/07/16/iocprez010716.html.

Romney, Mitt, with Timothy Robinson. *Turnaround: Crisis, Leadership, and the Olympic Games.* Washington: Regnery, 2007.

Rowland, Christopher. "Signature Brand to Remain a Driving Force in the Sports Scene." *Boston.com,* Sept. 29, 2003. http://www.boston.com/business/articles/2003/09/29/signature_brand_to_remain_a_driving_force_in_sports_scene/.

Ruff, Peter, and Khalid Aziz. *Managing Communications in a Crisis.* Burlington, VT: Gower, 2003.

*Salt Lake City 2002 Marketing Report.* Lausanne: IOC, 2002.

"Samaranch: IOC Will Win War on Drugs." *CNNSI.com,* July 3, 2001. http://sportsillustrated.cnn.com/olympics/news/2001/07/03/samaranch_drugs_ap/.

"Samaranch: I Told Madrid to Wait until 2020." *MoreThanTheGames.com,* Oct. 6, 2009. http://www.morethanthegames.co.uk/121st-ioc-session/066545-samaranch-i-told-madrid-wait-until-2020.

Samaranch, Juan Antonio. "Closing Speech by IOC President Mr. Juan Antonio Samaranch" [Baden-Baden, Sept. 28, 1981]. In *The 11th Olympic Congress in Baden-Baden, 1981*, 3:107–8. Lausanne: IOC, 1982.

———. "The Olympic Site Selection Process: A Review of the Reform Effort." *FDCH e-Media*, Dec. 15, 1999.

Samaranch, Juan Antonio, with Pedro Palacios. *Memorias Olímpiacos*. Barcelona: Editial Planeta SA, 2002.

Samaranch, Juan Antonio, and Robert Parienté. *The Samaranch Years, 1980–1994: Towards Olympic Unity, Entrevues*. Lausanne: IOC, 1995.

"Sen. Ted Stevens' Conviction Set Aside." *CNN.com*, Apr. 7, 2009. http://www.cnn.com/2009/POLITICS/04/07/ted.stevens.

"Senator John McCain Statement, Chairman of the Committee on Commerce, Science, and Transportation, Investigation of Olympic Scandals Hearing." *FDCH e-Media*, Apr. 14, 1999.

Shalit, Ruth. "Chain Saws, Drugs, and Lesbians: Olympic Advertising Deserves a Gold Medal—in Confusion." *Salon.com Business*, Sept. 30, 2000. http://archive.salon.com/business/col/shalit/2000/09/30/olympic_ads/print.html.

Shepard, Alicia C. "An Olympian Scandal: How a Local TV News Story in Salt Lake City Led to the Disclosure of Far-Reaching Corruption in the Way Olympic Sites Are Chosen." *American Journalism Review* (Apr. 1999). http://www.ajr.org/article_printable.asp?id=505.

Simpson, Michele. "Reebok Pulls Multi Million-Dollar Olympic Games Sponsorship." *National Business Review* (Dec. 10, 1999).

Simson, Vyv, and Andrew Jennings. *Dishonored Games: Corruption, Money, and Greed at the Olympics*. New York: SPI Books, 1992.

Smit, Barbara. *Sneaker Wars: The Enemy Brothers Who Founded Adidas and Puma and the Family Feud That Forever Changed the Business of Sports*. New York: Harper Perennial, 2009.

"SportFive Bags European Rights for 2014 and 2016 Olympics." *France24.com*, Feb. 18, 2009. http://www.france24.com/en/20090218-sportfive-acquire-european-rights-2014-2016-olympics-television-broadcasting.

"Stabbing Victim Father of '04 Olympian, Father-in-Law of Coach." *ESPN.com*, Aug. 10, 2008. http://sports.espn.go.com/oly/summer08/news/story?id=3526793.

Starbuck, William H., Arent Green, and Bo L. T. Hedberg. "Responding to Crises." In *Corporate Crisis Management*, edited by Stephen Andriole, 155–88. Princeton, NJ: Petrocelli Books, 1985.

"Statement of Senator George J. Mitchell, Chairman of the Special Bid Oversight Commission of the United States Olympic Committee Before the Committee on Commerce, Science, and Transportation." *FDCH e-Media*, Apr. 14, 1999.

*Statutes of the IOC Ethics Commission.* Apr. 2006. http://multimedia.olympic.org/pdf/en_report_692.pdf.

Story, Jonathan. *China: The Rise to Market—What China's Transformation Means for Business, Markets, and the New World Order.* London: Prentice Hall–Financial Times, 2003.

"Streeter's Tenure Marked by Missteps." *ESPN.com*, Oct. 7, 2009. http://sports.espn.go.com/oly/news/story?id4539035.

Sullivan, Robert, et al. "How the Olympics Were Bought: Salt Lake City Finally Got the Games, and Now the Allegations—and the Investigations—Are Spreading." *Time*, Feb. 1, 1999.

Swift, E. M. "Breaking Point: Years of Greed and Corruption Have Caught Up at Last with the International Olympic Committee." *Sports Illustrated*, Feb. 1, 1999.

Tarlow, Barry. "Let the Games Begin." *Champion Magazine*, Sept.–Oct. 2004, 52. http://www.zuckerman.com/files/News/27fe15c9–29F1–4d90–a53e–073d32e70c63/Presentation/NewsAttachment/40026a67-dcb2–4feb-a1f3–91e8e1e3d6d/RICO%20Report%20-%2081ar%20Brown%20and%20William%20Taylor%20Olympic%20Games.pdf.

"Television Revenue Not Important Insists Rogge." *MoreThanTheGames.com*, Oct. 5, 2009. http://www.morethanthegames.co.uk/121st-ioc-session/056536-television-revenue-not-important-insists-rogge.

"2 Out of 3 People in World Watched Olympics." *TheStar.com*, Sept. 5, 2008. http://olympics.thestar.com/2008/article/491460.

"USOC Delays Olympic Television Network—Boost for Chicago 2016." *GamesBids.com*, Aug. 16, 2009. http://www.gamesbids.com/eng/olympic_bids/chicago_2016/1216134594.html.

"USOC Execs Named to Key IOC Roles." *ESPN.com*, Mar. 11, 2011. http://sports.espn.go.com/oly/news/story?id=6206406.

Walden, Laura. "Obama and Chicago Victims of USOC Politics with IOC." *Sports Features Communications*, Oct. 3, 2009. http://www.sportsfeatures.com/index.php?section=olympicarticleview&title=Ebersol:%20Obama%20and%20Chicago%20victims%20of%20USOC%20politics%20with%20IOC&id=45977.

Webb, Elizabeth. "Sarbanes-Oxley Compliance and Violation: An Empirical Study." *Review of Finance and Accounting* 7, no. 1 (2008): 5–23.

Wenn, Stephen. "Growing Pains: The Olympic Movement and Television, 1966–1972." *Olympika: The International Journal of Olympic Studies* 4 (1995): 1–22.

———. "An Olympian Squabble: The Distribution of Olympic Television Revenue, 1960–1966." *Olympika: The International Journal of Olympic Studies* 3 (1994): 27–47.

Wenn, Stephen, and Tim Elcombe. "A Path to Peace: Some Thoughts on Olympic Revenue and the IOC/USOC Divide." *SAIS Review of International Affairs* 31 (Winter–Spring 2011): 117–33.

Wenn, Stephen, and Scott Martyn. "Storm Watch: Richard Pound, TOP Sponsors, and the Salt Lake City Bid Scandal." *Journal of Sport History* 32 (Summer 2005): 167–97.

———. "'Tough Love': Richard Pound, David D'Alessandro, and the Salt Lake City Olympics Bid Scandal." *Sport in History* 26 (Apr. 2006): 64–90.

"Westlaw Results: 808 P.2d 115." Accessed Jan. 15, 2009. http://Westlaw@westlaw.com.

Wilson, Stephen. "All Six Athletes Identified in Doping Cases from Beijing Olympics." *CTVOlympics.ca*, Apr. 29, 2009. http://www.ctvolympics.ca/news-centre/newsid=10042.html?cid=rsstsn.

———. "AP Source: IOC Negotiating with 2 US Sponsors." *Product Design and Development*, June 4, 2010. http://www.pddnet.com/news-ap-ioc-and-usoc-look-to-resolve-financial-issue-042710/.

———. "IOC, USOC Hope for Deal by July on Revenue Sharing." *Yahoo! News*, Apr. 7, 2011. http://news.yahoo.com/s/ap/21000407/ap_on_sp_ol/oly_ioc_usoc.

———. "Rogge: USOC Issues Won't Harm Chicago's 2016 Bid." *Southern California Public Radio*, Sept. 17, 2009. http://www.scpr.org/news/2009/09/17/rogge-usoc-issues-wont-harm-chicagos-2016-bid.

———. "Spanish TV Secures Olympic Rights for $100M." *Yahoo! Sports.com*, Sept. 4, 2009. http://news.yahoo.com/s/ap/20090904/ap_on_sp_ol/oly_ioc_spanish_tv_rights.

"World: Europe Olympic 'Vote Buying' Scandal." *BBC Online*, Dec. 12, 1998. http://news.bbc.co.uk/1/hi/world/europe/233742.stm.

Young, David C. *The Modern Olympics: A Struggle for Revival*. Baltimore: Johns Hopkins Univ. Press, 1996.

# Index

Page numbers in italics signify photographs.

International Olympic Committee (IOC):
age limit of members, 11, 118, 157,
191n15; Athletes Commission, 159;
and BMA, 95, 212n72; Code of Ethics,
101, 109; crisis management by, xx,
16–18, 22–25, 26, 40, 52, 80, 103, 167;
D'Alessandro on, xxiv, 28–31, 47–51,
54, 56–57, 80, 85, 87, 105, 195n78;
double standard of, 53, 73–75, 87,
105; establishment of, 117, 225n68;
European dominance in, 145–46,
169–70, 233nn8–10, 238n52; expulsions and censures, xx, 32, 35, 37, 57,
60–61, 71, 72, 75, 82, 122; financial
autonomy and diversification of, 8, 11,
165, 186n36; financial records of, 81,
209n10; global expansion of, 12, 21–22,
166; Hodler Rules for, 20, 166; Hodler
whistleblowing on, 18–22, 108, 166,
191n19, 192n29; image problem of,
56–57, 59, 81, 101, 143, 165; International Relations Commission, 156;
and ISFs and NOCs, 1, 8, 147, 154,
169; Juridical Commission, 16, 17;
Marketing Commission, 24, 156; and
media, xv–xvi, 22–23, 36–37, 39–40,
41–42, 57, 80; membership size and
selection, xxi, 118–19, 157; mission of,
168; Nominations Committee, 157,
239n59; and Olympic Movement unity,
11, 188n49; public relations effort of,
xx, 26, 36–37, 62, 226n77; and recession of 2008, 167, 241–41n92; reform
measures of, xxi, 102, 104–9, 122, 143,
156–58; relationship with sponsors, xxv,
23–24, 46–47, 52–53, 56–57, 61, 75, 81,
202n3, 208n6; representation and voting blocs within, 57, 77–78, 157, 203n8;
Samaranch elections in, 1–2, 6, 11, 141;
siege mentality in, 58, 203n10; staff of,
225–26n73; term limits, xxi, 87, 93, 118,
157; transformation under Samaranch,
xvi, xviii, xxvi–xxvii, 7–14, 17, 21, 141,
147, 167, 217n97; transparency and
accountability in, 47, 60, 68, 87, 93,
94, 118, 156–57; US Congress and,
80–81, 97–100, 110–13, 119–24; USOC
relations with, 95–97, 151–52, 153–56,
169–70, 214n85, 224n64, 234n21,
238n56; voting procedures in, 61, 71,
204n23; women's representation in,
148; and World Conference on Doping
in Sport, xix–xx, 22, 43–45, 58, 167,
193n42; and world political leaders, 10,
11. *See also* Olympic bidding process;
Salt Lake City bid scandal; Samaranch,
Juan Antonio
International Olympic Committee Reform
Act of 1999, 98, 214n84
International Sport Federations (ISFs), xix,
xxvi, 1, 8, 119, 147, 157
IOC Ad Hoc Commission, 25, 33–34,
35–36, 53–54; dissolution of, 74; establishment of, xx, 17, 18; expulsion and
censure recommendations, 59, 60–61,
65–66, 82
IOC Ethics Commission, 36, 37, 54, 101,
109, 243n97; Ad Hoc Commission's
responsibilities transferred to, 74; composition and structure, 81, 88, 101, 157,
207n92, 208–9n8; establishment of,
xx–xxi, 76–77, 80, 100–101, 103; list of
people investigated by, 101, 214–16n96;
and Olympic brand recovery, 143, 167;
Samaranch and, xx–xxi, 37, 63
IOC sessions: 108th Session, xx, xxi,
54–55, 56, 62–79, 167; 109th Session,
100, 103, 108; 110th Session, 104,
117–19, 158; 112th Session, 159–60;
121st Session, 146

World Anti-Doping Agency (WADA), xix–
  xx, 58, 144, 146, 148
World Conference on Doping in Sport
  (WCDS), xix–xx, 22, 43–45, 58, 167,
  193n42
Wyden, Ron, 222n42

Xerox, 54, 93, 202n3

Yang Yang, 133

Young, Brigham, 129
Youth Olympics, 168–69
Yugoslavia, 12

Zang, Frank, 15
Zátopek, Emil, 3
Zerguini, Mohamed, 53
Zimmer, Markus, 127, 228n5
Zoeggeler, Armin, 133
Zuckerman Spaeder, 126
Zuckoff, Mitchell, 68